CRACKING THE

CODING
INTERVIEW
5th Edition

ALSO BY GAYLE LAAKMANN MCDOWELL

THE GOOGLE RESUME

How to Prepare for a Career and Land a Job at
Apple, Microsoft, Google, or any Top Tech Company

CRACKING THE

CODING

INTERVIEW
5th Edition

150 Programming
Questions and Solutions

GAYLE LAAKMANN MCDOWELL
Founder and CEO, CareerCup.com

CareerCup, LLC
Palo Alto, CA

CRACKING THE CODING INTERVIEW, FIFTH EDITION

Published by CareerCup, LLC, Palo Alto, CA. Version 5.01290713101100.

For more information, contact support@careercup.com.

978-0984782802 (ISBN 13)

To Pauline "Oma" Venti
for her eternal support

Table of Contents

Table of Contents

Table of Contents

*Join us at **www.CrackingTheCodingInterview.com** to download full, compilable Java / Eclipse solutions, discuss problems from this book with other readers, report issues, view this book's errata, post your resume, and seek additional advice.*

Dear Reader,

Let's get the introductions out of the way.

I am not a recruiter. I am a software engineer. And as such, I know what it's like to be asked to whip up brilliant algorithms on the spot, and then write flawless code on a whiteboard. I know because I've been asked to do the same thing—in interviews at Google, Microsoft, Apple, and Amazon, among other companies.

I also know because I've been on the other side of the table, asking candidates to do this. I've combed through stacks of resumes to find the engineers who I thought might be able to actually pass these interviews. And I've debated in Google's Hiring Committee whether or not a candidate did well enough to merit an offer. I understand and have experienced the full hiring circle.

And you, reader, are probably preparing for an interview, perhaps tomorrow, next week, or next year. You likely have or are working towards a Computer Science or related degree. I am not here to re-teach you the basics of what a binary search tree is, or how to traverse a linked list. You already know such things, and if not, there are plenty of other resources to learn them.

I am here to help you take your understanding of Computer Science fundamentals to the next level, to learn how to apply those fundamentals to crack the coding interview.

The 5th edition of *Cracking the Coding Interview* updates the 4th edition with over 200 pages of additional questions, revised solutions, new chapter introductions, and other content. Be sure to check out our website, www.careercup.com, to connect with other candidates and discover new resources.

I'm excited for you and for the skills you are going to develop. Thorough preparation will give you a wide range of technical and communication skills. It will be well-worth it no matter where the effort takes you!

I encourage you to read these introductory chapters carefully. They contain important insight that just might make the difference between a "hire" and a "no hire."

And remember—interviews are hard! In my years of interviewing at Google, I saw some interviewers ask "easy" questions while others ask harder questions. But you know what? Getting the easy questions doesn't make it any easier to get the offer. Receiving an offer is not about solving questions flawlessly (very few candidates do!), but rather, it is about answering questions *better than other candidates*. So don't stress out when you get a tricky question—everyone else probably thought it was hard too.

Study hard, practice, and good luck!

Gayle L. McDowell

Founder / CEO, CareerCup.com
Author of *The Google Resume* and *Cracking the Coding Interview*

Introduction

Something's Wrong

We walked out of the hiring meeting frustrated, again. Of the ten "passable" candidates we reviewed that day, none would receive offers. Were we being too harsh, we wondered?

I, in particular, was disappointed. We had rejected one of *my* candidates. A former student. One who I had referred. He had a 3.73 GPA from the University of Washington, one of the best computer science schools in the world, and had done extensive work on open source projects. He was energetic. He was creative. He worked hard. He was sharp. He was a true geek in all the best ways.

But, I had to agree with the rest of the committee: the data wasn't there. Even if my emphatic recommendation would sway them to reconsider, he would surely get rejected in the later stages of the hiring process. There were just too many red flags.

Though the interviewers generally believed that he was quite intelligent, he had struggled to solve the interview problems. Most successful candidates could fly through the first question, which was a twist on a well-known problem, but he had trouble developing an algorithm. When he came up with one, he failed to consider solutions that optimized for other scenarios. Finally, when he began coding, he flew through the code with an initial solution, but it was riddled with mistakes that he then failed to catch. Though he wasn't the worst candidate we'd seen by any measure, he was far from meeting "the bar." Rejected.

When he asked for feedback over the phone a couple of weeks later, I struggled with what to tell him. Be smarter? No, I knew he was brilliant. Be a better coder? No, his skills were on-par with some of the best I'd seen.

Like many motivated candidates, he had prepared extensively. He had read K&R's classic C book and he'd reviewed CLRS' famous algorithms textbook. He could describe in detail the myriad of ways of balancing a tree, and he could do things in C that no sane programmer should ever want to do.

I had to tell him the unfortunate truth: those books aren't enough. Academic books prepare you for fancy research, but they're not going to help you much in an interview. Why? I'll give you a hint: your interviewers haven't seen Red-Black Trees since *they* were in school either.

To crack the coding interview, you need to prepare with *real* interview questions. You must practice on *real* problems and learn their patterns.

Cracking the Coding Interview is the result of my first-hand experience interviewing at top companies. It is the result of hundreds of conversations with candidates. It is the result of the thousands of questions contributed by candidates and interviewers. And it's the result of seeing so many interview questions from so many firms. Enclosed in this book are 150 of the best interview questions, selected from thousands of potential problems.

My Approach

The focus of **Cracking the Coding Interview** is algorithm, coding and design questions. Why? Because while you can and will be asked behavioral questions, the answers will be as varied as your resume. Likewise, while many firms will ask so-called "trivia" questions (e.g., "What is a virtual function?"), the skills developed through practicing these questions are limited to very specific bits of knowledge. The book will briefly touch on some of these questions to show you what they're like, but I have chosen to allocate space where there's more to learn.

My Passion

Teaching is my passion. I love helping people understand new concepts and giving them tools so that they can excel in their passions.

My first "official" experience teaching was in college at the University of Pennsylvania when I became a teaching assistant for an undergraduate Computer Science course during my second year. I went on to TA for several other courses, and I eventually launched my own CS course at the university focused on "hands-on" skills.

As an engineer at Google, training and mentoring "Nooglers" (yes, that's really what they call new Google employees!) were some of the things I enjoyed most. I went on to use my "20% time" to teach two Computer Science courses at the University of Washington.

Cracking the Coding Interview, **The Google Resume**, and **CareerCup.com** reflect my passion for teaching. Even now, you can often find me "hanging out" at CareerCup.com, helping users who stop by for assistance.

Join us.

Gayle L. McDowell

The Interview Process

I

Most companies conduct their interviews in very similar ways. We will offer an overview of how companies interview and what they're looking for. This information should guide your interview preparation and your reactions during and after the interview.

Once you are selected for an interview, you usually go through a screening interview. This is typically conducted over the phone. College candidates who attend top schools may have these interviews in-person.

Don't let the name fool you; the "screening" interview often involves coding and algorithms questions, and the bar can be just as high as it is for in-person interviews. If you're unsure whether or not the interview will be technical, ask your recruiting coordinator what position your interviewer holds. An engineer will usually perform a technical interview.

Many companies have taken advantage of online synchronized document editors, but others will expect you to write code on paper and read it back over the phone. Some interviewers may even give you "homework" to solve after you hang up the phone or just ask you to email them the code you wrote.

You typically do one or two screening interviewers before being brought on-site.

In an on-site interview round, you usually have 4 to 6 in-person interviews. One of these will be over lunch. The lunch interview is usually not technical, and the interviewer may not even submit feedback. This is a good person to discuss your interests with and to ask about the company culture. Your other interviews will be mostly technical and will involve a combination of coding and algorithm questions. You should also expect some questions about your resume.

Afterwards, the interviewers meet to discuss your performance and/or submit written feedback. At most companies, your recruiter should respond to you within a week with an update on your status.

If you have waited more than a week, you should follow up with your recruiter. If your recruiter does not respond, this does *not* mean that you are rejected (at least not at any major tech company, and almost any other company). Let me repeat that again: not responding indicates nothing about your status. The intention is that all recruiters should tell candidates once a final decision is made.

Delays can and do happen. Follow up with your recruiter if you expect a delay, but be respectful when you do. Recruiters are just like you. They get busy and forgetful too.

Candidates frequently ask me what the "recent" interview questions are at a specific company, assuming that the questions change over time. The reality is that the company itself has typically little to do with selecting the questions. It's all up to the interviewer. Allow me to explain.

At a large company, interviewers typically go through an interviewer training course. My "training" course at Google was outsourced to another company. Half of the one-day training course focused on the legal aspects of interviewing: don't ask a candidate if they're married, don't ask about their ethnicity, and so on. The other half discussed "troublesome" candidates: the ones who get angry or rude when asked a coding question or other questions they think are "beneath" them. After the training course, I "shadowed" two real interviews to show me what happened in an interview—as though I didn't already know! After that, I was sent off to interview candidates on my own.

That's it. That's all the training we got—and that's very typical of companies.

There was no list of "official Google interview questions." No one ever told me that I should ask a particular question, and no one told me to avoid certain topics.

So where did my questions come from? From the same places as everyone else's.

Interviewers borrow questions that they were asked as candidates. Some swap questions amongst each other. Others look on the internet for questions, including—yes—on CareerCup.com. And some interviewers take questions from the earlier mentioned resources and tweak them in minor or major ways.

It's unusual for a company to ever give interviewers a list of questions. Interviewers pick their own questions and tend to each have a pool of five or so questions that they prefer.

So next time you want to know what the "recent" Google interview questions are, stop and think. Google interview questions are really no different from Amazon interview questions since the questions aren't decided at a company-wide level. The "recent" questions are also irrelevant. Questions don't change much over time since no one's telling anyone what to do.

There are some differences in broad terms across companies. Web-based companies are more likely to ask system design questions, and a company using databases heavily is more likely to ask you database questions. Most questions, however, fall into the broad "data structures and algorithms" category and could be asked by any company.

Acing an interview starts well before the interview itself—years before, in fact. You need to get the right technical experience, apply to companies, and begin preparing to actually solve questions. The following timeline outlines what you should be thinking about when.

If you're starting late into this process, don't worry. Do as much "catching up" as you can, and then focus on preparation. Good luck!

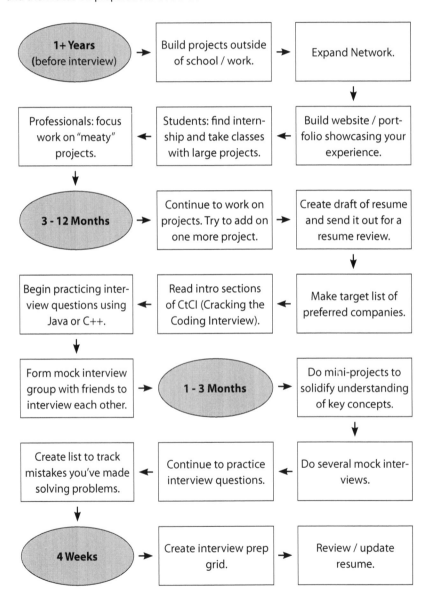

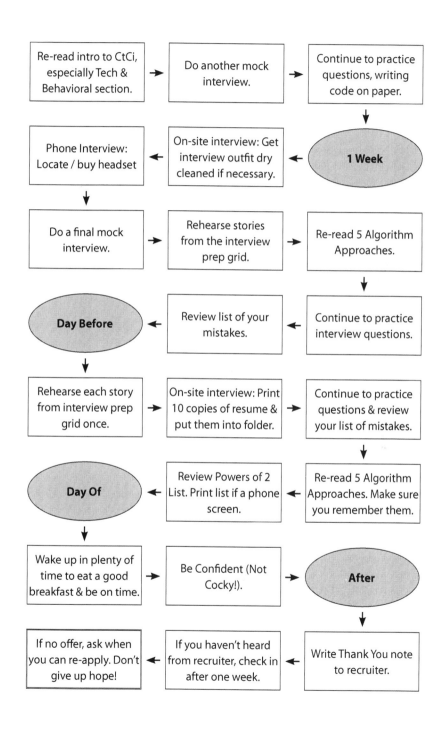

Most recruiters will probably tell you that candidates are evaluated on four aspects: prior experience, culture fit, coding skills, and analytical ability. These four components are certainly all in play, but typically, the decision comes down to your coding skills and your analytical ability (or intelligence). This is why most of this book is devoted to improving your coding and algorithm skills.

However, just because the decision usually comes down to coding and algorithm skills doesn't mean you should overlook the other two as factors.

At bigger tech companies, your prior experience tends not to be a direct deciding factor once you're actually interviewing, but it may bias an interviewer's perception of the rest of your interview. For example, if you demonstrate brilliance when you discuss some tricky program you wrote, your interviewer is more likely to think, "Wow, she's brilliant!" And once he's decided that you're smart, he's more likely to subconsciously overlook your little mistakes. Interviewing, after all, is not an exact science. Preparing for "softer" questions is well worth your time.

Culture fit (or your personality, particularly with relation to the company) tends to matter more at smaller companies than at big companies. One way it might come up is if the company's culture is to let employees make decisions independently, and you need direction.

It's not unusual for a candidate to get rejected because they appear too arrogant, argumentative, or defensive. I once had a candidate blame his struggling with a question on my wording of the problem, and later, on the way that I'd coached him through it. I recorded this defensiveness as a potential red flag—and, as it turns out, so did the other interviewers. He was rejected. Who wants to work with a teammate like that?

What this means for you is the following:

- If people often perceive you as arrogant or argumentative, or with any other nasty adjectives, keep an eye on this behavior in an interview. Even an otherwise superstar candidate may get rejected if people don't want to work with them.

- Spend some time preparing for questions about your resume. It's not the most important factor, but it matters. Even a little bit of time here can help you improve in major ways. It's a great "bang for your buck."

- Focus mainly on coding and algorithm questions.

Finally, it's worth noting that interviewing is not a perfect science. There is some randomness not only in your performance, but also in the decision of the hiring committee (or whoever decides on your offer). Like any group, the hiring committee is easily swayed by the most outspoken individuals. It may not be fair, but that's the way it is.

And remember—a rejection is not a life sentence. You can almost always reapply within a year, and many candidates get offers from companies that previously rejected them.

Don't get discouraged. Keep at it.

One of the most pervasive—and dangerous—rumors is that candidates need to get every question right. That's not even close to true.

First, responses to interview questions shouldn't be thought of as "correct" or "incorrect." When I evaluate how someone performed in an interview, I never ask myself, how many questions did they get right? Rather, it's about how optimal your final solution was, how long it took you to get there, and how clean your code was. It's not a binary right vs. wrong; there are a range of factors.

Second, your performance is evaluated *in comparison to other candidates*. For example, if you solve a question optimally in 15 minutes, and someone else solves an easier question in five minutes, did that person do better than you? Maybe, but maybe not. If you are asked really easy questions, then you might be expected to get optimal solutions really quickly. But if the questions are hard, then a number of mistakes are expected.

In evaluating thousands of hiring packets at Google, I have only once seen a candidate have a "flawless" set of interviews. Everyone else, including the hundreds who got offers, made mistakes.

Software engineers and those in similar positions typically dress less formally. This is reflected in the appropriate interview attire. A good rule of thumb for any interview is to dress one small notch better than the employees in your position.

More specifically, I would recommend the following attire for software engineering (and testing) interviews. These rules are designed to put you in the "safe zone": not too dressy, and not too casual. Many people interview at start-ups and big companies in jeans and a t-shirt and don't face any problems. After all, your coding skills matter far more than your sense of style.

	Start-Ups	Microsoft, Google, Amazon, Facebook, e.t.c.	Non-Tech Companies (including banks)
Men	Khakis, slacks, or nice jeans. Polo shirt or dress shirt.	Khakis, slacks, or nice jeans. Polo shirt or dress shirt.	Suit, no tie. (Consider bringing a tie just in case.)
Women	Khakis, slacks, or nice jeans. Nice top or sweater.	Khakis, slacks, or nice jeans. Nice top or sweater.	Suit, or nice slacks with a nice top.

These are just good advisements, and you should consider the culture of the company with which you're interviewing. If you are interviewing for a Program Manager, Dev Lead, or any role closer to management or the business side, you should lean towards the more dressy side.

#1 | Practicing on a Computer

If you were training for an ocean swim race, would you practice only by swimming in a pool? Probably not. You'd want to get a feel for the waves and other "terrain" differences. I bet you'd want to practice in the ocean, too.

Using a compiler to practice interview questions is like doing all your training in the pool. Put away the compiler and get out the old pen and paper. Use a compiler only to verify your solutions *after* you've written and hand-tested your code.

#2 | Not Rehearsing Behavioral Questions

Many candidates spend all their time prepping for technical questions and overlook the behavioral questions. Guess what? Your interviewer is judging those too!

And, not only that—your performance on behavioral questions might bias your interviewer's perception of your technical performance. Behavioral prep is relatively easy and well-worth your time. Look over your projects and positions and rehearse your key stories.

#3 | Not Doing a Mock Interview

Imagine you're preparing for a big speech. Your whole school, company, or whatever will be there. Your future depends on this. You'd be crazy to only practice the speech silently in your head.

Not doing a mock interview to prepare for your real one is just like this. If you're an engineer, you must know other engineers. Grab a buddy and ask him/her to do a mock interview with you. You can even return the favor!

#4 | Trying to Memorize Solutions

Memorizing the solution to a specific problem will help you solve that one if it comes up in an interview, but it won't help you to solve new problems. It's very unlikely that all, or even most, of your interview questions will come from this book.

It's much more effective to try to struggle through the problems in this book yourself, without flipping to the solutions. This will help you develop strategies to approach new problems. Even if you review fewer problems in the end, this kind of preparation will go much further. Quality beats quantity.

#5 |Not Solving Problems Out Loud

Psst—let me tell you a secret: I don't know what's going on in your head. So if you aren't talking, I don't know what you're thinking. If you don't talk for a long time, I'll assume that you aren't making any progress. Speak up often, and try to talk your way through a solution. This shows your interviewer that you're tackling the problem and aren't stuck.

And it lets them guide you when you get off-track, helping you get to the answer faster. Best of all, it demonstrates your awesome communication skills. What's not to love?

#6 | Rushing

Coding is not a race, and neither is interviewing. Take your time when working on a coding problem. Rushing leads to mistakes and suggests that you are careless. Go slowly and methodically, testing often and thinking through the problem thoroughly. In the end, you'll finish the problem in less time and with fewer mistakes.

#7 | Sloppy Coding

Did you know that you can write bug-free code but still perform horribly on a coding question? It's true! Duplicated code, messy data structures (i.e., lack of object-oriented design), and so on. Bad, bad, bad! When you write code, imagine you're writing for real-world maintainability. Break code into sub-routines, and design data structures to link appropriate data.

#8 | Not Testing

You probably wouldn't write code in the real world without testing it, so why do that in an interview? When you finish writing code in an interview, "run" (or walk through) the code to test it. Or, on more complicated problems, test the code while writing it.

#9 | Fixing Mistakes Carelessly

Bugs will happen; they're just a matter of life, or of coding. If you're testing your code carefully, then you will probably discover bugs. That's okay.

The important thing is that when you find a bug, you think through why it occurred before fixing it. Some candidates, when they find that their function returns `false` for particular parameters, will just flip the return value and check if that fixes the issue. Of course, it rarely does; in fact, it tends to create even more bugs and demonstrates that you're careless.

Bugs are acceptable, but changing your code randomly to fix the bugs is not.

#10 | Giving Up

I know interview questions can be overwhelming, but that's part of what the interviewer is testing. Do you rise to a challenge, or do you shrink back in fear? It's important that you step up and eagerly meet a tricky problem head-on. After all, remember that interviews are supposed to be hard. It shouldn't be a surprise when you get a really tough problem.

Should I tell my interviewer if I know a question?

Yes! You should definitely tell your interviewer if you've previously heard the question. This seems silly to some people—if you already know the question (and answer), you could ace the question, right? Not quite.

Here's why we strongly recommend that you tell your interviewer that you've heard the problem before:

1. Big honesty points. This shows a lot of integrity—that's huge! Remember that the interviewer is evaluating you as a potential teammate. I don't know about you, but I personally prefer to work with honest people.

2. The question might have changed ever so slightly. You don't want to risk repeating the wrong answer.

3. If you easily belt out the right answer, it's obvious to the interviewer. They know how difficult a problem is supposed to be. If you instead try to pretend to struggle through a problem, you may very well wind up "struggling" *too* much and coming off unqualified.

What language should I use?

Many people will tell you to use whatever language you're most comfortable with, but ideally you want to use a language that your interviewer is comfortable with. I'd usually recommend coding in either C, C++ or Java, as the vast majority of interviewers will be comfortable in one of these languages. My personal preference for interviews is Java (unless it's a question requiring C / C++), because it's quick to write and almost everyone can read and understand Java, even if they code mostly in C++. For this reason, almost all the solutions in this book are written in Java.

I didn't hear back immediately after my interview. Am I rejected?

No. Almost every company intends to tell candidates when they're rejected. Not hearing back quickly could mean almost anything. You might have done very well, but the recruiter is on vacation and can't process your offer yet. The company might be going through a re-org and be unclear what their head count is. Or, it might be that you did poorly, but you got stuck with a lazy or overworked recruiter who hasn't gotten a chance to notify you. It would be a strange company that actually decides, "Hey, we're rejecting this person, so we just won't respond." It's in the company's best interest to notify you of your ultimate decision. Always follow up.

Can I re-apply to a company after getting rejected?

Almost always, but you typically have to wait a bit (6 months – 1 year). Your first bad interview usually won't affect you too much when you re-interview. Lots of people get rejected from Google or Microsoft and later get offers.

Behind the Scenes

II

II. Behind the Scenes

For many candidates, interviewing is a bit of a black box. You walk in, you get pounded with questions from a variety of interviewers, and then somehow, you return with an offer... or not.

Have you ever wondered:

- How do decisions get made?
- Do your interviewers talk to each other?
- What does the company really care about?

Well, wonder no more!

For this book, we sought out interviewing experts from five top companies–Microsoft, Amazon, Google, Apple, Facebook, and Yahoo!–to show you what really happens "behind the scenes."

These experts will guide us through a typical interview day, describing what takes place outside of the interviewing room and what transpires after you leave.

Our interviewing experts also told us what's different about their interview process. From bar raisers (Amazon) to Hiring Committees (Google), each company has its own quirks. Knowing these idiosyncrasies will help you to react better to a super-tough interviewer (Amazon), or to avoid being intimidated when two interviewers show up at the door (Apple).

In addition, our specialists offered insight as to what their company stresses in their interviews. While almost all software firms care about coding and algorithms, some companies focus more than others on specific aspects of the interview. Whether this is because of the company's technology or its history, now you'll know what and how to prepare.

So, join us as we take you behind the scenes at Microsoft, Facebook, Google, Amazon, Yahoo! and Apple.

Microsoft wants smart people. Geeks. People who are passionate about technology. You probably won't be tested on the ins and outs of C++ APIs, but you will be expected to write code on the board.

In a typical interview, you'll show up at Microsoft at some time in the morning and fill out initial paper work. You'll have a short interview with a recruiter who will give you a sample question. Your recruiter is usually there to prep you, not to grill you on technical questions. If you get asked some basic technical questions, it may be because your recruiter wants to ease you into the interview so that you're less nervous when the "real" interview starts.

Be nice to your recruiter. Your recruiter can be your biggest advocate, even pushing to re-interview you if you stumbled on your first interview. They can fight for you to be hired–or not!

During the day, you'll do four or five interviews, often with two different teams. Unlike many companies, where you meet your interviewers in a conference room, you'll meet with your Microsoft interviewers in their office. This is a great time to look around and get a feel for the team culture.

Depending on the team, interviewers may or may not share their feedback on you with the rest of the interview loop.

When you complete your interviews with a team, you might speak with a hiring manager. If so, that's a great sign! It likely means that you passed the interviews with a particular team. It's now down to the hiring manager's decision.

You might get a decision that day, or it might be a week. After one week of no word from HR, send a friendly email asking for a status update.

If your recruiter isn't very responsive, it's because she's busy, not because you're being silently rejected.

Definitely Prepare:

"Why do you want to work for Microsoft?"

In this question, Microsoft wants to see that you're passionate about technology. A great answer might be, "I've been using Microsoft software as long as I can remember, and I'm really impressed at how Microsoft manages to create a product that is universally excellent. For example, I've been using Visual Studio recently to learn game programming, and its APIs are excellent." Note how this shows a passion for technology!

What's Unique:

You'll only reach the hiring manager if you've done well, so if you do, that's a great sign!

Amazon's recruiting process typically begins with two phone screens in which a candidate interviews with a specific team. A small portion of the time, a candidate may have three or more interviews, which can indicate either that one of their interviewers wasn't convinced or that they are being considered for a different team or profile. In more unusual cases, such as when a candidate is local or has recently interviewed for a different position, a candidate may only do one phone screen.

The engineer who interviews you will usually ask you to write simple code via a shared document editor, such as CollabEdit. They will also often ask a broad set of questions to explore what areas of technology you're familiar with.

Next, you fly to Seattle for four or five interviews with one or two teams that have selected you based on your resume and phone interviews. You will have to code on a whiteboard, and some interviewers will stress other skills. Interviewers are each assigned a specific area to probe and may seem very different from each other. They cannot see the other feedback until they have submitted their own, and they are discouraged from discussing it until the hiring meeting.

The "bar raiser" interviewer is charged with keeping the interview bar high. They attend special training and will interview candidates outside their group in order to balance out the group itself. If one interview seems significantly harder and different, that's most likely the bar raiser. This person has both significant experience with interviews and veto power in the hiring decision. Remember, though: just because you seem to be struggling more in this interview doesn't mean you're actually doing worse. Your performance is judged relative to other candidates; it's not evaluated on a simple "percent correct" basis.

Once your interviewers have entered their feedback, they will meet to discuss it. They will be the people making the hiring decision.

While Amazon's recruiters are usually excellent at following up with candidates, occasionally there are delays. If you haven't heard from Amazon within a week, we recommend a friendly email.

Definitely Prepare:

Amazon is a web-based company, and that means they care about scale. Make sure you prepare for scalability questions. You don't need a background in distributed systems to answer these questions. See our recommendations in the Scalability and Memory Limits chapter.

Additionally, Amazon tends to ask a lot of questions about object-oriented design. Check out the Object-Oriented Design chapter for sample questions and suggestions.

What's Unique:

The Bar Raiser is brought in from a different team to keep the bar high. You need to impress both this person and the hiring manager.

There are many scary rumors floating around about Google interviews, but they're mostly just that: rumors. The interview is not terribly different from Microsoft's or Amazon's.

A Google engineer performs the first phone screen, so expect tough technical questions. These questions may involve coding, sometimes via a shared document. Candidates are typically held to the same standard and are asked similar questions on phone screens as in on-site interviews.

On your on-site interview, you'll interview with four to six people, one of whom will be a lunch interviewer. Interviewer feedback is kept confidential from the other interviewers, so you can be assured that you enter each interview with blank slate. Your lunch interviewer doesn't submit feedback, so this is a great opportunity to ask honest questions.

Interviewers are not given specific focuses, and there is no "structure" or "system" as to what you're asked when. Each interviewer can conduct the interview however she would like.

Written feedback is submitted to a hiring committee (HC) of engineers and managers to make a hire / no-hire recommendation. Feedback is typically broken down into four categories (Analytical Ability, Coding, Experience, and Communication) and you are given an overall score from 1.0 to 4.0. The HC usually does not include any of your interviewers. If it does, it was purely by random chance.

To extend an offer, the HC wants to see at least one interviewer who is an "enthusiastic endorser." In other words, a packet with scores of 3.6, 3.1, 3.1 and 2.6 is better than all 3.1s.

You do not necessarily need to excel in every interview, and your phone screen performance is usually not a strong factor in the final decision.

If the hiring committee recommends an offer, your packet will go to a compensation committee and then to the executive management committee. Returning a decision can take several weeks because there are so many stages and committees.

Definitely Prepare:

As a web-based company, Google cares about how to design a scalable system. So, make sure you prepare for questions from "Scalability and Memory Limits." Additionally, many Google interviewers will ask questions involving Bit Manipulation, so you are advised to brush up on these topics as well.

What's Different:

Your interviewers do not make the hiring decision. Rather, they enter feedback which is passed to a hiring committee. The hiring committee recommends a decision which can be—though rarely is—rejected by Google executives.

Much like the company itself, Apple's interview process has minimal bureaucracy. The interviewers will be looking for excellent technical skills, but a passion for the position and the company is also very important. While it's not a prerequisite to be a Mac user, you should at least be familiar with the system.

The interview process usually begins with a recruiter phone screen to get a basic sense of your skills, followed up by a series of technical phone screens with team members.

Once you're invited on campus, you'll typically be greeted by the recruiter who provides an overview of the process. You will then have 6-8 interviews with members of the team with which you're interviewing, as well as key people with whom your team works.

You can expect a mix of 1-on-1 and 2-on-1 interviews. Be ready to code on a whiteboard and make sure all of your thoughts are clearly communicated. Lunch is with your potential future manager and appears more casual, but it is still an interview. Each interviewer usually focuses on a different area and is discouraged from sharing feedback with other interviewers unless there's something they want subsequent interviewers to drill into.

Towards the end of the day, your interviewers will compare notes. If everyone still feels you're a viable candidate, you will have an interview with the director and the VP of the organization to which you're applying. While this decision is rather informal, it's a very good sign if you make it. This decision also happens behind the scenes, and if you don't pass, you'll simply be escorted out of the building without ever having been the wiser (until now).

If you made it to the director and VP interviews, all of your interviewers will gather in a conference room to give an official thumbs up or thumbs down. The VP typically won't be present but can still veto the hire if they weren't impressed. Your recruiter will usually follow up a few days later, but feel free to ping him or her for updates.

Definitely Prepare:

If you know what team you're interviewing with, make sure you read up on that product. What do you like about it? What would you improve? Offering specific recommendations can show your passion for the job.

What's Unique:

Apple does 2-on-1 interviews often, but don't get stressed out about them—it's the same as a 1-on-1 interview!

Also, Apple employees are huge Apple fans. You should show this same passion in your interview.

Though Facebook's online engineering puzzles get a lot of hype, they're merely one more way to get noticed. You can still apply without solving these puzzles, through the traditional avenues like an online job application or your university career fair.

Once selected for an interview, candidates will generally do a minimum of two phone screens. Local candidates, however, will often do just one interview before being invited on-site. Phone screens will be technical and will involve coding, usually via Etherpad or another online document editor.

If you are in college and are interviewing on your campus, you will also do coding. This will be done either on a whiteboard (if one is available) or on a sheet of paper.

During your on-site interview, you will interview primarily with other software engineers, but hiring managers are also involved whenever they are available. All interviewers have gone through comprehensive interview training, and who you interview with has no bearing on your odds of getting an offer.

Each interviewer is given a "role" during the on-site interviews, which helps ensure that there are no repetitive questions and that they get a holistic picture of a candidate. Questions are broken down into algorithm / coding skills, architecture / design skills, and the ability to be successful in Facebook's fast-paced environment.

After your interview, interviewers submit written feedback, prior to discussing your performance with each other. This ensures that your performance in one interview will not bias another interviewer's feedback.

Once everyone's feedback is submitted, your interviewing team and a hiring manager get together to collaborate on a final decision. They come to a consensus decision and submit a final hire recommendation to the hiring committee.

Facebook looks for "ninja skills"–the ability to hack together an elegant and scalable solution using any language of choice. Knowing PHP is not especially important, particularly given that Facebook also does a lot of backend work in C++, Python, Erlang, and other languages.

Definitely Prepare:

The youngest of the "elite" tech companies, Facebook wants developers with an entrepreneurial spirit. In your interviews, you should show that you love to build stuff fast.

What's Unique:

Facebook interviews developers for the company "in general," not for a specific team. If you are hired, you will go through a six-week "bootcamp" which will help ramp you up in the massive code base. You'll get mentorship from senior devs, learn best practices, and, ultimately, get a greater flexibility in choosing a project than if you were assigned to a project in your interview.

While Yahoo! tends to only recruit from the top twenty schools, other candidates can still get interviewed through Yahoo's job board (or—better yet—through an internal referral). If you are selected for an interview, your interview process will start off with a phone screen. Your phone screen will be with a senior employee such as a tech lead or manager.

During your on-site interview, you will typically interview with 6 – 7 people on the same team for 45 minutes each. Each interviewer will have an area of focus. For example, one interviewer might focus on databases, while another interviewer might focus on your understanding of computer architecture. Interviews will often be composed as follows:

- *5 minutes:* General conversation. Tell me about yourself, your projects, etc.
- *20 minutes:* Coding question. For example, implement merge sort.
- *20 minutes:* System design. For example, design a large distributed cache. These questions will often focus on an area from your past experience or on something your interviewer is currently working on.

At the end of the day, you will likely meet with a Program Manager or someone else for a general conversation. This may include a product demos or a discussion about potential concerns about the company or your competing offers. This is usually not a factor in the decision.

Meanwhile, your interviewers will discuss your performance and attempt to come to a decision. The hiring manager has the ultimate say and will weigh the positive feedback against the negative.

If you have done well, you will often get a decision that day, but this is not always the case. There can be many reasons that you might not be told for several days—for example, the team may feel it needs to interview several other people.

Definitely Prepare:

Yahoo!, almost as a rule, asks questions about system design, so make sure you prepare for that. They want to know that you can not only write code, but can also design software. Don't worry if you don't have a background in this–you can still reason your way through it!

What's Unique:

Your phone interview will likely be performed by someone with more influence, such as a hiring manager.

Yahoo! is also unusual in that it often gives a decision (if you're hired) on the same day. Your interviewers will discuss your performance while you meet with a final interviewer.

Special Situations

If you read the prior section carefully, the following shouldn't surprise you: experienced candidates are asked very similar questions as inexperienced candidates, and the standards don't vary significantly.

Most questions, as you may know, are general questions covering data structures and algorithms. The major companies feel that this is a good test of one's abilities, so they hold everyone to that test.

Some interviewers may hold experienced candidates to a slightly higher standard on those questions. After all, an experienced candidate has many more years of experience and *should* perform better, right?

It turns out that other interviewers see things in exactly the opposite way. Experienced candidates are years out of school and may not have touched some of these concepts since then. It's expected that they would forget some details, so we *should* hold them to a lower standard.

On average, it balances out. If you're an experienced candidate, you'll be asked roughly the same types of questions and held to roughly the same standard.

The exception to this rule is system design and architecture questions, as well as questions on your resume.

Typically, students don't study much system architecture, so experience with such challenges would only come professionally. Your performance in such interview questions would be evaluated with respect to your experience level. However, students and recent graduates are still asked these questions and should be prepared to solve them as well as they can.

Additionally, experienced candidates will be expected to give a more in-depth, impressive response to questions like, "What was the hardest bug you've faced?" You have more experience, and your response to these questions should show it.

S DETs are in a tough spot. Not only do they have to be great coders, but they must also be great testers.

We recommend the following preparation process:

- *Prepare the Core Testing Problems:* For example, how would you test a light bulb? A pen? A cash register? Microsoft Word? The Testing chapter will give you more background on these problems.

- *Practice the Coding Questions:* The number one thing that SDETs get rejected for is coding skills. Although coding standards are typically lower for an SDET than for an SDE, SDETs are still expected to be very strong in coding and algorithms. Make sure that you practice solving all the same coding and algorithm questions that a regular developer would get.

- *Practice Testing the Coding Questions:* A very popular format for SDET questions is "Write code to do X," followed up by, "OK, now test it." Even when the question doesn't specifically require this, you should ask yourself, "How would I test this?" Remember: any problem can be an SDET problem!

Strong communication skills can also be very important for testers, since your job requires you to work with so many different people. Do not neglect the Behavioral Questions section.

Career Advice

Finally, a word of career advice: if, like many candidates, you are hoping to apply to an SDET position as the "easy" way into a company, be aware that many candidates find it very difficult to move from an SDET position to a dev position. Make sure to keep your coding and algorithms skills very sharp if you hope to make this move, and try to switch within one to two years. Otherwise, you might find it very difficult to be taken seriously in a dev interview.

Never let your coding skills atrophy.

These "PM" roles vary wildly across companies and even within a company. At Microsoft, for instance, some PMs may be essentially customer evangelists, working in a customer-facing role that borders on marketing. Across campus though, other PMs may spend much of their day coding. The latter type of PMs would likely be tested on coding, since this is an important part of their job function.

Generally speaking, interviewers for PM positions are looking for candidates to demonstrate skills in the following areas:

- *Handling Ambiguity:* This is typically not the most critical area for an interview, but you should be aware that interviewers do look for skill here. Interviewers want to see that, when faced with an ambiguous situation, you don't get overwhelmed and stall. They want to see you tackle the problem head on: seeking new information, prioritizing the most important parts, and solving the problem in a structured way. This will typically not be tested directly (though it can be), but it may be one of many things the interviewer is looking for in a problem.

- *Customer Focus (Attitude):* Interviewers want to see that your attitude is customer focused. Do you assume that everyone will use the product just like you? Or are you the type of person who puts himself in the customer's shoes and tries to understand how they want to use the product? Questions like "Design an alarm clock for the blind" are ripe for examining this aspect. When you hear a question like this, be sure to ask a lot of questions to understand *who* the customer is and *how* they are using the product. The skills covered in the Testing section are closely related to this.

- *Customer Focus (Technical Skills):* Some teams with more complex products need to ensure that their PMs walk in with a strong understanding of the product, as it would be difficult to acquire this knowledge on the job. An intimate knowledge of instant messengers is probably not necessary to work on the MSN Messenger team, whereas an understanding of security might be necessary to work on Windows Security. Hopefully, you wouldn't interview with a team that required specific technical skills unless you at least claim to possess the requisite skills.

- *Multi-Level Communication:* PMs need to be able to communicate with people at all levels in the company, across many positions and ranges of technical skills. Your interviewer will want to see that you possess this flexibility in your communication. This is often examined directly, through a question such as, "Explain TCP/IP to your grandmother." Your communication skills may also be assessed by how you discuss your prior projects.

- *Passion for Technology:* Happy employees are productive employees, so a company wants to make sure that you'll enjoy the job and be excited about your work. A passion for technology—and, ideally, the company or team—should come across in your answers. You may be asked a question directly like, "Why are you interested in Microsoft?" Additionally, your interviewers will look for enthusiasm in how you discuss your prior experience and how you discuss the team's challenges. They want to see that you will be eager to face the challenges of the job.

- *Teamwork / Leadership:* This may be the most important aspect of the interview, and—not surprisingly—the job itself. All interviewers will be looking for your ability to work well with other people. Most commonly, this is assessed with questions like, "Tell me about a time when a teammate wasn't pulling his / her own weight." Your interviewer is looking to see that you handle conflicts well, that you take initiative, that you understand people, and that people like working with you. Your work preparing for behavioral questions will be extremely important here.

All of the above areas are important skills for PMs to master and are therefore key focus areas of the interview. The weighting of each of these areas will roughly match the importance that the area holds in the actual job.

S trong coding skills are almost always required for dev lead positions and often for management positions as well. If you'll be coding on the job, make sure to be very strong with coding and algorithms—just like a dev would be. Google, in particular, holds managers to high standards when it comes to coding.

In addition, prepare to be examined for skills in the following areas:

- *Teamwork / Leadership:* Anyone in a management-like role needs to be able to both lead and work with people. You will be examined implicitly and explicitly in these areas. Explicit evaluation will come in the form of asking you how you handled prior situations, such as when you disagreed with a manager. The implicit evaluation comes in the form of your interviewers watching how you interact with them. If you come off as too arrogant or too passive, your interviewer may feel you aren't great as a manager.

- *Prioritization:* Managers are often faced with tricky issues, such as how to make sure a team meets a tough deadline. Your interviewers will want to see that you can prioritize a project appropriately, cutting the less important aspects. Prioritization means asking the right questions to understand what is critical and what you can reasonably expect to accomplish.

- *Communication:* Managers need to communicate with people both above and below them and potentially with customers and other much less technical people. Interviewers will look to see that you can communicate at many levels and that you can do so in a way that is friendly and engaging. This is, in some ways, an evaluation of your personality.

- *"Getting Things Done":* Perhaps the most important thing that a manager can do is be a person who "gets things done." This means striking the right balance between preparing for a project and actually implementing it. You need to understand how to structure a project and how to motivate people so you can accomplish the team's goals.

Ultimately, most of these areas come back to your prior experience and your personality. Be sure to prepare very, very thoroughly using the interview preparation grid.

The application and interview process for start-ups is highly variable. We can't go through every start-up, but we can offer some general pointers. Understand, however, that the process at a specific start-up might deviate from this.

The Application Process

Many start-ups might post job listings, but for the hottest start-ups, often the best way in is through a personal referral. This referrer doesn't necessarily need to be a close friend or a coworker. Often just by reaching out and expressing your interest, you can get someone to pick up your resume to see if you're a good fit.

Visas and Work Authorization

Unfortunately, most smaller start-ups in the U.S. are not able to sponsor work visas. They hate the system as much you do, but you won't be able to convince them to hire you anyway. If you require a visa and wish to work at a start-up, your best bet is to reach out to a professional recruiter who works with many start-ups or to focus your search on bigger start-ups.

Resume Selection Factors

Start-ups are engineers who are not only smart and who can code, but also people who would work well in an entrepreneurial environment. Your resume should ideally show initiative.

Being able to "hit the ground running" is also very important; they want people who already know the language of the company.

The Interview Process

In contrast to big companies, which tend to look mostly at your general aptitude with respect to software development, start-ups often look closely at your personality fit, skill set, and prior experience.

- *Personality Fit:* Personality fit is typically assessed by how you interact with your interviewer. Establishing a friendly, engaging conversation with your interviewers is your ticket to many job offers.

- *Skill Set:* Because start-ups need people who can hit the ground running, they are likely to assess your skills with specific programming languages. If you know a language that the start-up works with, make sure to brush up on the details.

- *Prior Experience:* Start-ups are likely to ask you a lot of questions about your prior experience. Pay special attention to the Behavioral Questions section.

In addition to the above areas, the coding and algorithms questions that you see in this book are also very common.

Before the Interview

IV

Although offer decisions are typically based more on the interview than anything else, it's your resume—and therefore your prior experience—that gets you the interview. You should think actively about how to enhance your technical (and non-technical) experience. Both students and professionals will benefit greatly by adding additional coding experience.

For current students, this may mean the following:

- *Take the Big Project Classes:* If you're in school, don't shy away from the classes with big, "meaty" projects. These projects belong on your resume and will greatly improve your chances at getting an interview with the top companies. The more relevant the project is to the real world, the better.

- *Get an Internship:* Even at a relatively early stage in school, students can get relevant professional experience. Freshmen and sophomores can get early experience through programs like Microsoft Explorer and Google Summer of Code. If you can't score one of these internships, start-ups are also a great option.

- *Start Something:* Trying your hand at something more entrepreneurial will impress almost any company. It develops your technical experience and shows that you have initiative and can "get things done." Use your weekends and breaks to build some software on your own. If you get to know a professor, you might even get her to agree to "sponsor" your work as an independent study.

Professionals, on the other hand, may already have the right experience to switch to their dream company. For instance, a Google dev probably already has sufficient experience to switch to Facebook. However, if you're trying to move from a lesser known company to one of the "biggies," or from testing / IT into a dev role, the following advice will be useful:

- *Shift Work Responsibilities More Towards Coding:* Without revealing to your manager that you are thinking of leaving, you can discuss your eagerness to take on bigger coding challenges. As much as possible, try to ensure that these projects are "meaty," use relevant technologies, and lend themselves well to a resume bullet or two. It is these coding projects that will, ideally, form the bulk of your resume.

- *Use Your Nights and Weekends:* If you have some free time, use it to build a mobile app, a web app, or a piece of desktop software. Doing such projects is also a great way to get experience with new technologies, making you more relevant to today's companies. This project work should definitely be listed on your resume; few things are as impressive to an interviewer as a candidate who built something "just for fun."

All of these boil down to the two big things that companies want to see: that you're smart and that you can code. If you can prove that, you can land your interview.

In addition, you should think in advance about where you want your career to go. If you want to move into management down the road, even though you're currently looking for a dev position, you should find ways now of developing leadership experience.

You probably already know that many people get jobs from their friends. But what you may not know is that, in fact, even more people get jobs from their *friends of friends*. And this really makes perfect sense. To drop into geek-speak for a second, you may have N friends, but you have N^2 friends of friends.

So what does this all mean for your job-finding possibilities? It means that both your immediate and your extended network is critical to finding a job.

What Makes a Network a "Good Network"

A good network is one that is both broad and close. If it seems contradictory, that's because it is (somewhat).

- *Broad:* A network should be somewhat focused on your own industry (technology), but it should also be broad and cover many industries. An accountant, for example, can be valuable to you career-wise simply because he or she probably has lots of friends outside of accounting. Some of those friends—who are *your* friends or friends—will probably be looking for someone just like you at some point. Be open to connecting with anyone you meet.

- *Close:* It's much easier to access a friend of a friend via a close friend of yours than it is through a more distant acquaintance. Moreover, people who are seen as "professional networkers" or "card collectors" are often written off by others as being too fake. Make your connections deep and meaningful.

The trick to finding a balance here is to meet whoever you can, but to be open and genuine to everyone. When you just try to "collect cards," you often wind up with nothing at all.

How to Build a Strong Network

Some people argue that you "just" need to get out and meet people, and that's mostly true. But where? And how do you go from an introduction to a real connection?

The following basic steps will help:

1. Use websites like Meetup.com or your alumni network to discover events that are relevant to your interests and goals. Bring business cards. If you don't have them because you're unemployed or a student, make some.

2. Walk up and say, "Hello," to people. It may seem scary to you, but honestly, no one will hold it against you. Most people will even appreciate your assertiveness. What's the worst that can happen? They don't like you, don't establish a connection with you, and you never see them again?

3. Be open about your interests, and talk to people about theirs. If they're running a start-up or something else you might have some interest in, ask to grab coffee to chat more.

4. Follow-up after the events by adding the person on LinkedIn and by emailing them. Or, even better, ask to meet them for coffee to discuss their start-up, or whatever they're working on that could be mutually interesting.

5. And, most importantly, *be helpful*. By lending a hand in some way to people, you will be seen as generous and friendly. People will want to help you if you have helped them.

And remember, your network is more than just your face-to-face network. In this day and age, your network can extend to strictly online interactions through blogs, Twitter, Facebook, and email.

However, when your interaction has been strictly online, you must work much harder to actually establish a bond.

Resume screeners look for the same things that interviewers do. They want to know that you're smart and that you can code.

That means you should prepare your resume to highlight those two things. Your love of tennis, traveling, or magic cards won't do much to show that. Think twice before cutting more technical lines in order to allow space for your non-technical hobbies.

Appropriate Resume Length

In the US, it is strongly advised to keep a resume to one page if you have less than ten years of experience, and no more than two pages otherwise. Why is this? Here are two great reasons to do this:

- Recruiters only spend a fixed amount of time (about 20 seconds) looking at your resume. If you limit the content to the most impressive items, the recruiter is sure to see them. Adding additional items just distracts the recruiter from what you'd really like them to see.

- Some people just flat-out refuse to read long resumes. Do you really want to risk having your resume tossed for this reason?

If you are thinking right now that you have too much experience and can't fit it all on one page, trust me, *you can*. Everyone says this at first. Long resumes are not a reflection of having tons of experience; they're a reflection of not understanding how to prioritize content.

Employment History

Your resume does not—and should not—include a full history of every role you've ever had. Your job serving ice cream, for example, will not show that you're smart or that you can code. You should include only the relevant positions.

Writing Strong Bullets

For each role, try to discuss your accomplishments with the following approach: "Accomplished X by implementing Y which led to Z." Here's an example:

- "Reduced object rendering time by 75% by implementing distributed caching, leading to a 10% reduction in log-in time."

Here's another example with an alternate wording:

- "Increased average match accuracy from 1.2 to 1.5 by implementing a new comparison algorithm based on windiff."

Not everything you did will fit into this approach, but the principle is the same: show what you did, how you did it, and what the results were. Ideally, you should try to make the results "measurable" somehow.

Projects

Developing the projects section on your resume is often the best way to present yourself as more experienced. This is especially true for college students or recent grads.

The projects should include your 2 - 4 most significant projects. State what the project was and which languages or technologies it employed. You may also want to consider including details such as whether the project was an individual or a team project, and whether it was completed for a course or independently. These details are not required, so only include them if they make you look better.

Do not add too many projects. Many candidates make the mistake of adding all 13 of their prior projects, cluttering their resume with small, non-impressive projects.

Programming Languages and Software

Software

Generally speaking, I do not recommend listing that you're familiar with Microsoft Office. Everyone is, and it just dilutes the "real" information. Familiarity with highly technical software (e.g., Visual Studio, Linux) *can* be useful, but, frankly, it usually doesn't make much of a difference.

Languages

Knowing which languages to include on your resume is always a tricky thing. Do you list everything you've ever worked with, or do you shorten the list to just the ones that you're most comfortable with? I recommend the following compromise: list most of the languages you've used, but add your experience level. This approach is shown below:

- Languages: Java (expert), C++ (proficient), JavaScript (prior experience).

Advice for Non-Native English Speakers and Internationals

Some companies will throw out your resume just because of a typo. Please get at least one native English speaker to proofread your resume.

Additionally, for US positions, do *not* include age, marital status, or nationality. This sort of personal information is not appreciated by companies, as it creates a legal liability for them.

Behavioral Questions V

Behavioral questions are asked for a variety of reasons. They can be asked to get to know your personality, to understand your resume more deeply, or just to ease you into an interview. Either way, these questions are important and can be prepared for.

How to Prepare

Behavioral questions are usually of the form "Tell me about a time when you...," and may require an example from a specific project or position. I recommend filling in the following "preparation grid" as shown below:

Common Questions	Project 1	Project 2	Project 3	Project 4
Most Challenging				
What You Learned				
Most Interesting				
Hardest Bug				
Enjoyed Most				
Conflicts with Teammates				

Along the top, as columns, you should list all the major aspects of your resume, including each project, job, or activity. Along the side, as rows, you should list the common questions: what you enjoyed most, what you enjoyed least, what you considered most challenging, what you learned, what the hardest bug was, and so on. In each cell, put the corresponding story.

In your interview, when you're asked about a project, you'll be able to come up with an appropriate story effortlessly. Study this grid before your interview.

I recommend reducing each story to just a couple of keywords that you can write in each cell. This will make the grid easier to study and remember.

If you're doing a phone interview, you should have this grid out in front of you. When each story has just a couple of keywords to trigger your memory, it will be much easier to give a fluid response than if you're trying to re-read a paragraph.

It may also be useful to extend this grid to "softer" questions, such as conflicts on a team, failures, or times you had to persuade someone. Questions like these are very common outside of strictly software engineer roles, such as dev lead, PM or even testing role. If you are applying for one of these positions, I would recommend making a second grid covering these softer areas.

When answering these questions, you're not just trying to find a story that matches their question. You're telling them about yourself. Think deeply about what each story communicates about you.

What are your weaknesses?

When asked about your weaknesses, give a real weakness! Answers like "My greatest weakness is that I work too hard" tell your interviewer that you're arrogant and/or won't admit to your faults. No one wants to work with someone like that. A better answer conveys a real, legitimate weakness but emphasizes how you work to overcome it. For example: "Sometimes, I don't have a very good attention to detail. While that's good because it lets me execute quickly, it also means that I sometimes make careless mistakes. Because of that, I make sure to always have someone else double check my work."

What was the most challenging part of that project?

When asked what the most challenging part was, don't say "I had to learn a lot of new languages and technologies." This is the "cop out" answer when you don't know what else to say. It tells the interviewer that nothing was really very hard.

What questions should you ask the interviewer?

Most interviewers will give you a chance to ask them questions. The quality of your questions will be a factor, whether subconsciously or consciously, in their decisions.

Some questions may come to you during the interview, but you can—and should—prepare questions in advance. Doing research on the company or team may help you with preparing questions.

Questions can be divided into three different categories.

Genuine Questions

These are the questions you actually want to know the answers to. Here are a few ideas of questions that are valuable to many candidates:

1. "How much of your day do you spend coding?"

2. "How many meetings do you have every week?"

3. "What is the ratio of testers to developers to program managers? What is the interaction like? How does project planning happen on the team?"

These questions will give you a good feel for what the day-to-day life is like at the company.

Insightful Questions

These questions are designed to demonstrate your deep knowledge of programming or technologies, and they also demonstrate your passion for the company or product.

1. "I noticed that you use technology X. How do you handle problem Y?"

2. "Why did the product choose to use the X protocol over the Y protocol? I know it has

benefits like A, B, C, but many companies choose not to use it because of issue D."

Asking such questions will typically require advance research about the company.

Passion Questions

These questions are designed to demonstrate your passion for technology. They show that you're interested in learning and will be a strong contributor to the company.

1. "I'm very interested in scalability. Did you come in with a background in this, or what opportunities are there to learn about it?"

2. "I'm not familiar with technology X, but it sounds like a very interesting solution. Could you tell me a bit more about how it works?"

As stated earlier, interviews usually start and end with "chit chat" or "soft skills." This is a time for your interviewer to ask questions about your resume or general questions, and it's also a time for you ask your interviewer questions about the company. This part of the interview is targeted at getting to know you, as well as relaxing you.

Remember the following advice when responding to questions.

Be Specific, Not Arrogant

Arrogance is a red flag, but you still want to make yourself sound impressive. So how do you make yourself sound good without being arrogant? By being specific!

Specificity means giving just the facts and letting the interviewer derive an interpretation. Consider an example:

- Candidate #1: "I basically did all the hard work for the team."

- Candidate #2: "I implemented the file system, which was considered one of the most challenging components because ..."

Candidate #2 not only sounds more impressive, but she also appears less arrogant.

Limit Details

When a candidate blabbers on about a problem, it's hard for an interviewer who isn't well versed in the subject or project to understand it. Stay light on details and just state the key points. That is, consider something like this: "By examining the most common user behavior and applying the Rabin-Karp algorithm, I designed a new algorithm to reduce search from $O(n)$ to $O(\log n)$ in 90% of cases. I can go into more details if you'd like." This demonstrates the key points while letting your interviewer ask for more details if he wants to.

Give Structured Answers

There are two common ways to think about structuring responses to a behavioral question: nugget first and S.A.R.. These techniques can be used separately or in together.

Nugget First

Nugget First means starting your response with a "nugget" that succinctly describes what your response will be about.

For example:

- Interviewer: "Tell me about a time you had to persuade a group of people to make a big change."

- Candidate: "Sure, let me tell you about the time when I convinced my school to let undergraduates teach their own courses. Initially, my school had a rule where..."

This technique grabs your interviewer's attention and makes it very clear what your story will be about. If you have a tendency to ramble, it also helps you be more focused in your communication, since you've made it very clear to yourself what the gist of your response is.

S.A.R. (Situation, Action, Result)

The S.A.R. approach means that you start off outlining the situation, then explaining the actions you took, and lastly, describing the result.

Example: "Tell me about a challenging interaction with a teammate."

- **Situation:** On my operating systems project, I was assigned to work with three other people. While two were great, the third team member didn't contribute much. He stayed quiet during meetings, rarely chipped in during email discussions, and struggled to complete his components.

- **Action:** One day after class, I pulled him aside to speak about the course and then moved the discussion into talking about the project. I asked him open-ended questions about how he felt it was going and which components he was most excited about tackling. He suggested all the easiest components, and yet offered to do the write-up. I realized then that he wasn't lazy—he was actually just really confused about the project and lacked confidence. I worked with him after that to break down the components into smaller pieces, and I made sure to compliment him a lot on his work to boost his confidence.

- **Result:** He was still the weakest member of the team, but he got a lot better. He was able to finish all his work on time, and he contributed more in discussions. We were happy to work with him on a future project.

The situation and the result should be very succinct. Your interviewer generally does not need many details to understand what happened and, in fact, may be confused by them..

By using the S.A.R. model with clear situations, actions and results, the interviewer will be able to easily identify how you made an impact and why it mattered.

Technical Questions

VI

You've purchased this book, so you've already gone a long way towards good technical preparation. Nice work!

That said, there are better and worse ways to prepare. Many candidates just read through problems and solutions. That's like trying to learn calculus by reading a problem and its solution. You need to practice solving problems. Memorizing solutions won't help you.

How to Practice a Question

For each problem in this book (and any other problem you might encounter), do the following:

1. *Try to solve the problem on your own.* I mean, *really* try to solve it. Many questions are designed to be tough—that's ok! When you're solving a problem, make sure to think about the space and time efficiency. Ask yourself if you could improve the time efficiency by reducing the space efficiency, or vice versa.

2. *Write the code for the algorithm on paper.* You've been coding all your life on a computer, and you've gotten used to the many nice things about it. But, in your interview, you won't have the luxury of syntax highlighting, code completion, or compiling. Mimic this situation by coding on paper.

3. *Test your code—on paper.* This means testing the general cases, base cases, error cases, and so on. You'll need to do this during your interview, so it's best to practice this in advance.

4. *Type your paper code as-is into a computer.* You will probably make a bunch of mistakes. Start a list of all the errors you make so that you can keep these in mind in the real interview.

In addition, mock interviews are extremely useful. CareerCup.com offers mock interviews with actual Microsoft, Google and Amazon employees, but you can also practice with friends. You and your friend can trade giving each other mock interviews. Though your friend may not be an expert interviewer, he or she may still be able to walk you through a coding or algorithm problem.

What You Need To Know

Most interviewers won't ask about specific algorithms for binary tree balancing or other complex algorithms. Frankly, being several years out of school, they probably don't remember these algorithms either.

You're usually only expected to know the basics. Here's a list of the absolute, must-have knowledge:

Data Structures	Algorithms	Concepts
Linked Lists	Breadth First Search	Bit Manipulation
Binary Trees	Depth First Search	Singleton Design Pattern
Tries	Binary Search	Factory Design Pattern
Stacks	Merge Sort	Memory (Stack vs. Heap)
Queues	Quick Sort	Recursion
Vectors / ArrayLists	Tree Insert / Find / e.t.c.	Big-O Time
Hash Tables		

For each of the topics above, make sure you understand how to use and implement them and, where applicable, what the space and time complexity is.

For the data structures and algorithms, be sure to practice implementing them from scratch. You might be asked to implement one directly, or you might be asked to implement a modification of one. Either way, the more comfortable you are with implementations, the better.

In particular, hash tables are an extremely important topic. You will find that you use them frequently in solving interview questions.

Powers of 2 Table

Some people have already committed this to memory, but if you haven't, you should before your interview. The table comes in handy often in scalability questions in computing how much space a set of data will take up.

Power of 2	Exact Value (X)	Approx. Value	X Bytes into MB, GB, e.t.c.
7	128		
8	256		
10	1024	1 thousand	1 K
16	65,536		64 K
20	1,048,576	1 million	1 MB
30	1,073,741,824	1 billion	1 GB
32	4,294,967,296		4 GB
40	1,099,511,627,776	1 trillion	1 TB

Using this table, you could easily compute, for example, that a hash table mapping every 32-bit integer to a boolean value could fit in memory on a single machine.

If you are doing a phone screen with a web-based company, it may be useful to have this table in front of you.

Do you need to know details of C++, Java, or other programming languages?

While I personally never liked asking these sorts of questions (e.g., "what is a vtable?"), many interviewers do ask them.

For big companies like Microsoft, Google, and Amazon, I wouldn't stress too much about these questions. You should understand the main concepts of any language you claim to know, but you should focus more on data structures and algorithms preparation.

At smaller companies and non-software companies, these questions can be more important. Look up your company on CareerCup.com to decide for yourself. If your company isn't listed, find a similar company as a reference. In general, start-ups tend to look for skills in "their" programming language.

Interviews are supposed to be difficult. If you don't get every—or any—diately, that's ok! In fact, in my experience, maybe only 10 people out of the I've interviewed have gotten my favorite questions right instantly.

So when you get a hard question, don't panic. Just start talking aloud about how you would solve it. Show your interviewer how you're tackling the problem so that he doesn't think you're stuck.

And, one more thing: you're not done until the interviewer says you're done! What I mean here is that when you come up with an algorithm, start thinking about the problems accompanying it. When you write code, start trying to find bugs. If you're anything like the other 110 candidates that I've interviewed, you probably made some mistakes.

Five Steps to a Technical Question

A technical interview question can be solved utilizing a five step approach:

1. Ask your interviewer questions to resolve ambiguity.

2. Design an Algorithm.

3. Write pseudocode first, but make sure to tell your interviewer that you'll eventually write "real" code.

4. Write your code at a moderate pace.

5. Test your code and *carefully* fix any mistakes.

We will go through each of these steps in more detail below.

Step 1: Ask Questions

Technical problems are more ambiguous than they might appear, so make sure to ask questions to resolve anything that might be unclear. You may eventually wind up with a very different—or much easier—problem than you had initially thought. In fact, many interviewers (especially at Microsoft) will specifically test to see if you ask good questions.

Good questions might be ones like: What are the data types? How much data is there? What assumptions do you need to solve the problem? Who is the user?

Example: "Design an algorithm to sort a list."

- Question: What sort of list? An array? A linked list?

  Answer: An array.

- Question: What does the array hold? Numbers? Characters? Strings?

  Answer: Numbers.

- Question: And are the numbers integers?

Answer: Yes.

- Question: Where did the numbers come from? Are they IDs? Values of something?

  Answer: They are the ages of customers.

- Question: And how many customers are there?

  Answer: About a million.

We now have a pretty different problem: sort an array containing a million integers between 0 and 130 (a reasonable maximum age). How do we solve this? Just create an array with 130 elements and count the number of ages at each value.

Step 2: Design an Algorithm

Designing an algorithm can be tough, but our Five Approaches to Algorithms (see next section) can help you out. While you're designing your algorithm, don't forget to ask yourself the following:

- What are its space and time complexity?

- What happens if there is a lot of data?

- Does your design cause other issues? For example, if you're creating a modified version of a binary search tree, did your design impact the time for insert, find, or delete?

- If there are other issues or limitations, did you make the right trade-offs? For which scenarios might the trade-off be less optimal?

- If they gave you specific data (e.g., mentioned that the data is ages, or in sorted order), have you leveraged that information? Usually there's a reason that an interviewer gave you specific information.

It's perfectly acceptable, and even recommended, to first mention the brute force solution. You can then continue to optimize from there. You can assume that you're always expected to create the most optimal solution possible, but that doesn't mean that the first solution you give must be perfect.

Step 3: Pseudocode

Writing pseudocode first can help you outline your thoughts clearly and reduce the number of mistakes you commit. But, make sure to tell your interviewer that you're writing pseudocode first and that you'll follow it up with "real" code. Many candidates will write pseudocode in order to "escape" writing real code, and you certainly don't want to be confused with those candidates.

Step 4: Code

You don't need to rush through your code; in fact, this will most likely hurt you. Just go at a nice, slow, methodical pace. Also, remember this advice:

- *Use Data Structures Generously:* Where relevant, use a good data structure or define your own. For example, if you're asked a problem involving finding the minimum age for a group of people, consider defining a data structure to represent a Person. This shows your interviewer that you care about good object-oriented design.

- *Don't Crowd Your Coding:* This is a minor thing, but it can really help. When you're writing code on a whiteboard, start in the upper left hand corner rather than in the middle. This will give you plenty of space to write your answer.

Step 5: Test

Yes, you need to test your code! Consider testing for:

- Extreme cases: 0, negative, null, maximums, minimums.
- User error: What happens if the user passes in null or a negative value?
- General cases: Test the normal case.

If the algorithm is complicated or highly numerical (bit shifting, arithmetic, etc.), consider testing while you're writing the code rather than just at the end.

When you find mistakes (which you will), carefully think through *why* the bug is occurring before fixing the mistake. You do not want to be seen as a "random fixer" candidate: one who, for example, finds that their function returns `true` instead of `false` for a particular value, and so just flips the return value and tests to see if the function works. This might fix the issue for that particular case, but it inevitably creates several new issues.

When you notice problems in your code, really think deeply about why your code failed before fixing the mistake. You'll create beautiful, clean code much, much faster.

There's no surefire approach to solving a tricky algorithm problem, but the approaches below can be useful. Keep in mind that the more problems you practice, the easier it will be to identify which approach to use.

The five approaches below can be "mixed and matched." That is, after you've applied "Simplify & Generalize," you may want to try "Pattern Matching" next.

Approach I: Examplify

We'll start with an approach you are probably familiar with, even if you've never seen it labeled. Under Examplify, you write out specific examples of the problem and see if you can derive a general rule from there.

Example: Given a time, calculate the angle between the hour and minute hands.

Let's start with an example like 3:27. We can draw a picture of a clock by selecting where the 3 hour hand is and where the 27 minute hand is.

For the below solution, we'll assume that h is the hour and m is the minute. We'll also assume that the hour is specified as an integer between 0 and 23, inclusive.

By playing around with these examples, we can develop a rule:

- Angle between the minute hand and 12 o'clock: `360 * m / 60`
- Angle between the hour hand and 12 o'clock: `360 * (h % 12) / 12 + 360 * (m / 60) * (1 / 12)`
- Angle between hour and minute: `(hour angle - minute angle) % 360`

By simple arithmetic, this reduces to `30h - 5.5m`.

Approach II: Pattern Matching

Under the Pattern Matching approach, we consider what problems the algorithm is similar to and try to modify the solution to the related problem to develop an algorithm for this problem.

Example: A sorted array has been rotated so that the elements might appear in the order 3 4 5 6 7 1 2. How would you find the minimum element? You may assume that the array has all unique elements.

There are two problems that jump to mind as similar:

- Find the minimum element in an array.
- Find a particular element in a sorted array (i.e., binary search).

The Approach

Finding the minimum element in an array isn't a particularly interesting algorithm (you

---

could just iterate through all the elements), nor does it use the inform; (that the array is sorted). It's unlikely to be useful here.

However, binary search is very applicable. You know that the array is sorted, but rotated. So, it must proceed in an increasing order, then reset, and increase again. The minimum element is the "reset" point.

If you compare the middle and last element (6 and 2), you will know the reset point must be between those values, since `MID > RIGHT`. This wouldn't be possible unless the array "reset" between those values.

If `MID` were less than `RIGHT`, then either the reset point is on the left half, or there is no reset point (the array is truly sorted). Either way, the minimum element could be found there.

We can continue to apply this approach, dividing the array in half in a manner much like binary search. We will eventually find the minimum element (or the reset point).

Approach III: Simplify and Generalize

With Simplify and Generalize, we implement a multi-step approach. First, we change a constraint such as the data type or amount of data. Doing this helps us simplify the problem. Then, we solve this new simplified version of the problem. Finally, once we have an algorithm for the simplified problem, we generalize the problem and try to adapt the earlier solution for the more complex version.

Example: A ransom note can be formed by cutting words out of a magazine to form a new sentence. How would you figure out if a ransom note (represented as a string) can be formed from a given magazine (string)?

To simplify the problem, we can modify it so that we are cutting *characters* out of a magazine instead of whole words.

We can solve the simplified ransom note problem with characters by simply creating an array and counting the characters. Each spot in the array corresponds to one letter. First, we count the number of times each character in the ransom note appears and then we go through the magazine to see if we have all of those characters.

When we generalize the algorithm, we do a very similar thing. This time, rather than creating an array with character counts, we create a hash table that maps from a word to its frequency.

Approach IV: Base Case and Build

Base Case and Build is a great approach for certain types of problems. With Base Case and Build, we solve the problem first for a base case (e.g., n = 1). This usually means just recording the correct result. Then, we try to solve the problem for n = 2, assuming that you have the answer for n = 1. Next, we try to solve it for n = 3, assuming that you have the answer for n = 1 and n = 2,

Eventually, we can build a solution that can always compute the result for N if we know the correct result for N-1. It may not be until N equals 3 or 4 that we get an instance that's interesting enough to try to build the solution based on the previous result.

Example: Design an algorithm to print all permutations of a string. For simplicity, assume all characters are unique.

Consider a test string abcdefg.

```
Case "a" --> {"a"}
Case "ab" --> {"ab", "ba"}
Case "abc" --> ?
```

This is the first "interesting" case. If we had the answer to P("ab"), how could we generate P("abc")? Well, the additional letter is "c," so we can just stick c in at every possible point. That is:

```
P("abc") = insert "c" into all locations of all strings in P("ab")
P("abc") = insert "c" into all locations of all strings in
{"ab","ba"}
P("abc") = merge({"cab", "acb", "abc"}, {"cba", "bca", bac"})
P("abc") = {"cab", "acb", "abc", "cba", "bca", bac"}
```

Now that we understand the pattern, we can develop a general recursive algorithm. We generate all permutations of a string $s_1 \ldots s_n$ by "chopping off" the last character and generating all permutations of $s_1 \ldots s_{n-1}$. Once we have the list of all permutations of $s_1 \ldots s_{n-1}$, we iterate through this list, and for each string in it, we insert s_n into every location of the string.

Base Case and Build algorithms often lead to natural recursive algorithms.

Approach V: Data Structure Brainstorm

This approach is certainly hacky, but it often works. We can simply run through a list of data structures and try to apply each one. This approach is useful because solving a problem may be trivial once it occurs to us to use, say, a tree.

Example: Numbers are randomly generated and stored into an (expanding) array. How would you keep track of the median?

Our data structure brainstorm might look like the following:

- Linked list? Probably not. Linked lists tend not to do very well with accessing and sorting numbers.

- Array? Maybe, but you already have an array. Could you somehow keep the elements sorted? That's probably expensive. Let's hold off on this and return to it if it's needed.

- Binary tree? This is possible, since binary trees do fairly well with ordering. In fact, if the binary search tree is perfectly balanced, the top might be the median. But, be careful—if there's an even number of elements, the median is actually the average of the middle two elements. The middle two elements can't both be at the top. This is probably a workable algorithm, but let's come back to it.

- Heap? A heap is really good at basic ordering and keeping track of max and mins. This is actually interesting—if you had two heaps, you could keep track of the bigger half and the smaller half of the elements. The bigger half is kept in a min heap, such that the smallest element in the bigger half is at the root. The smaller half is kept in a max heap, such that the biggest element of the smaller half is at the root. Now, with these data structures, you have the potential median elements at the roots. If the heaps are no longer the same size, you can quickly "rebalance" the heaps by popping an element off the one heap and pushing it onto the other.

Note that the more problems you do, the more developed your instinct on which data structure to apply will be. You will also develop a more finely tuned instinct as to which of these approaches is the most useful.

You probably know by now that employers want to see that you write "good, clean" code. But what does this really mean, and how is this demonstrated in an interview?

Broadly speaking, good code has the following properties:

- **Correct:** The code should operate correctly on all expected and unexpected inputs.

- **Efficient:** The code should operate as efficiently as possible in terms of both time and space. This "efficiency" includes both the asymptotic (big-O) efficiency and the practical, real-life efficiency. That is, a constant factor might get dropped when you compute the big-O time, but in real life, it can very much matter.

- **Simple:** If you can do something in 10 lines instead of 100, you should. Code should be as quick as possible for a developer to write.

- **Readable:** A different developer should be able to read your code and understand what it does and how it does it. Readable code has comments where necessary, but it implements things in an easily understandable way. That means that your fancy code that does a bunch of complex bit shifting is not necessarily *good* code.

- **Maintainable:** Code should be reasonably adaptable to changes during the life cycle of a product and should be easy to maintain by other developers as well as the initial developer.

Striving for these aspects requires a balancing act. For example, it's often advisable to sacrafice some degree of efficiency to make code more maintainable, and vice versa.

You should think about these elements as you code during an interview. The following aspects of code are more specific ways to demonstrate the earlier list.

Use Data Structures Generously

Suppose you were asked to write a function to add two simple mathematical expressions which are of the form $Ax^a + Bx^b + ...$ (where the coefficients and exponents can be any positive or negative real number). That is, the expression is a sequence of terms, where each term is simply a constant times an exponent. The interviewer also adds that she doesn't want you to have to do string parsing, so you can use whatever data structure you'd like to hold the expressions.

There are a number of different ways you can implement this.

Bad Implementation

A bad implementation would be to store the expression as a single array of doubles, where the kth element corresponds to the coefficient of the x^k term in the expression. This structure is problematic because it could not support expressions with negative or non-integer exponents. It would also require an array of 1000 elements to store just the expression x^{1000}.

```
1   int[] sum(double[] expr1, double[] expr2) {
2       ...
```

```
3   }
```

Less Bad Implementation

A slightly less bad implementation would be to store the expression as a set of two arrays, coefficients and exponents. Under this approach, the terms of the expression are stored in any order, but "matched" such that the ith term of the expression is represented by coefficients[i] * $x^{exponents[i]}$.

Under this implementation, if coefficients[p] = k and exponents[p] = m, then the pth term is kx^m. Although this doesn't have the same limitations as the earlier solution, it's still very messy. You need to keep track of two arrays for just one expression. Expressions could have "undefined" values if the arrays were of different lengths. And returning an expression is annoying, since you need to return two arrays.

```
1   ??? sum(double[] coeffs1, double[] expon1,
2           double[] coeffs2, double[] expon2) {
3       ...
4   }
```

Good Implementation

A good implementation for this problem is to design your own data structure for the expression.

```
1   class ExprTerm {
2       double coefficient;
3       double exponent;
4   }
5
6   ExprTerm[] sum(ExprTerm[] expr1, ExprTerm[] expr2) {
7       ...
8   }
```

Some might (and have) argued that this is "over-optimizing." Perhaps so, perhaps not. Regardless of whether you think it's over-optimizing, the above code demonstrates that you think about how to design your code and don't just slop something together in the fastest way possible.

Appropriate Code Reuse

Suppose you were asked to write a function to check if the value of a binary number (passed as a string) equals the hexadecimal representation of a string.

An elegant implementation of this problem leverages code reuse.

```
1   public boolean compareBinToHex(String binary, String hex) {
2       int n1 = convertToBase(binary, 2);
3       int n2 = convertToBase(hex, 16);
4       if (n1 < 0 || n2 < 0) {
5           return false;
```

```
7        } else {
8            return n1 == n2;
9        }
   }

11  public int digitToValue(char c) {
12      if (c >= '0' && c <= '9') return c - '0';
13      else if (c >= 'A' && c <= 'F') return 10 + c - 'A';
14      else if (c >= 'a' && c <= 'f') return 10 + c - 'a';
15      return -1;
16  }

18  public int convertToBase(String number, int base) {
19      if (base < 2 || (base > 10 && base != 16)) return -1;
20      int value = 0;
21      for (int i = number.length() - 1; i >= 0; i--) {
22          int digit = digitToValue(number.charAt(i));
23          if (digit < 0 || digit >= base) {
24              return -1;
25          }
26          int exp = number.length() - 1 - i;
27          value += digit * Math.pow(base, exp);
28      }
29      return value;
30  }
```

We could have implemented separate code to convert a binary number and a hexadecimal code, but this just makes our code harder to write and harder to maintain. Instead,
we reuse code by writing one convertToBase method and one digitToValue
method.

Modular

Writing modular code means separating isolated chunks of code out into their own
methods. This helps keep the code more maintainable, readable, and testable.

Imagine you are writing code to swap the minimum and maximum element in an
integer array. You could implement it all in one method like this:

```
1   public void swapMinMax(int[] array) {
2       int minIndex = 0;
3       for (int i = 1; i < array.length; i++) {
4           if (array[i] < array[minIndex]) {
5               minIndex = i;
6           }
7       }
8
9       int maxIndex = 0;
10      for (int i = 1; i < array.length; i++) {
11          if (array[i] > array[maxIndex]) {
```

```
12            maxIndex = i;
13        }
14    }
15
16    int temp = array[minIndex];
17    array[minIndex] = array[maxIndex];
18    array[maxIndex] = temp;
19 }
```

Or, you could implement in a more modular way by separating the relatively isolated chunks of code into their own methods.

```
1  public static int getMinIndex(int[] array) {
2      int minIndex = 0;
3      for (int i = 1; i < array.length; i++) {
4          if (array[i] < array[minIndex]) {
5              minIndex = i;
6          }
7      }
8      return minIndex;
9  }
10
11 public static int getMaxIndex(int[] array) {
12     int maxIndex = 0;
13     for (int i = 1; i < array.length; i++) {
14         if (array[i] > array[maxIndex]) {
15             maxIndex = i;
16         }
17     }
18     return maxIndex;
19 }
20
21 public static void swap(int[] array, int m, int n) {
22     int temp = array[m];
23     array[m] = array[n];
24     array[n] = temp;
25 }
26
27 public static void swapMinMaxBetter(int[] array) {
28     int minIndex = getMinIndex(array);
29     int maxIndex = getMaxIndex(array);
30     swap(array, minIndex, maxIndex);
31 }
```

While the non-modular isn't particularly awful, the nice thing about the modular code is that it's easily testable since each component can be verified separately. As code gets more complex, it becomes increasingly important to write it in a modular way. This will make it easier to read and maintain. Your interviewer wants to see you demonstrate these skills in your interview.

Flexible and Robust

Just because your interviewer only asks you to write code to check if a normal tic-tac-toe board has a winner doesn't mean you *must* assume that it's a 3x3 board. Why not write the code in a more general way that implements it for an NxN board?

Writing flexible, general-purpose code may also mean using constants instead of variables or using templates / generics to solve a problem. If we can write our code to solve a more general problem, we should.

Of course, there is a limit to this. If the solution is much more complex for the general case, and it seems unnecessary at this point in time, it may be better just to implement the simple, expected case.

Error Checking

One sign of a careful coder is that she doesn't make assumptions about the input. Instead, she validates that the input is what it should be, either through ASSERT statements or if-statements.

For example, recall the earlier code to convert a number from its base i (e.g., base 2 or base 16) representation to an int.

```
1   public int convertToBase(String number, int base) {
2      if (base < 2 || (base > 10 && base != 16)) return -1;
3      int value = 0;
4      for (int i = number.length() - 1; i >= 0; i--) {
5         int digit = digitToValue(number.charAt(i));
6         if (digit < 0 || digit >= base) {
7            return -1;
8         }
9         int exp = number.length() - 1 - i;
10        value += digit * Math.pow(base, exp);
11     }
12     return value;
13  }
```

In line 2, we check to see that base is valid (we assume that bases greater than 10, other than base 16, have no standard representation in string form). In line 6, we do another error check: making sure that each digit falls within the allowable range.

Checks like these are critical in production code and, therefore, in interview code as well.

Of course, writing these error checks can be tedious and can waste precious time in an interview. The important thing is to point out that you *would* write the checks. If the error checks are much more than a quick if-statement, it may be best to leave some space where the error checks would go and indicate to your interviewer that you'll fill them in when you're finished with the rest of the code.

The Offer and Beyond

VII

Just when you thought you could sit back and relax after your interviews, now you're faced with the post-interview stress: Should you accept the offer? Is it the right one? How do you decline an offer? What about deadlines? We'll handle a few of these issues here and go into more details about how to evaluate an offer, and how to negotiate it.

Offer Deadlines and Extensions

When companies extend an offer, there's almost always a deadline attached to it. Usually these deadlines are one to four weeks out. If you're still waiting to hear back from other companies, you can ask for an extension. Companies will usually try to accommodate this, if possible.

Declining an Offer

How you decline an offer matters. Even if you aren't interested in working for this company right now, you might be interested in working for it in a few years. (Or, your contacts might move to another more exciting company.) It's in your best interest to decline the offer on good terms and keep a line of communication open.

When you decline an offer, offer a reason that is non-offensive and inarguable. For example, if you were declining a big company for a start-up, you could explain that you feel a start-up is the right choice for you at this time. The big company can't suddenly "become" a start-up, so they can't argue about your reasoning.

Handling Rejection

The big tech companies reject around 80% of their interview candidates and recognize that interviews are not a perfect test of skills. For this reason, companies are often eager to re-interview previously rejected candidate. Some companies will even reach out to old candidates or expedite their application *because* of their prior performance.

When you do get the unfortunate call, you should see this as a setback but not a life sentence. Thank your recruiter for his time, explain that you're disappointed but that you understand their position, and ask when you can reapply to the company.

Finding out why you were rejected is incredibly difficult. Recruiters are unlikely to reveal the reason, though you might have slightly better luck if you instead ask where you should focus your preparation. You can try to reflect on your performance yourself, but in my experience, candidates can rarely properly analyze their performance. You may think that you struggled on a question, but it's all relative; did you struggle more or less than other candidates on the same question? Instead, just remember that candidates are typically rejected because of their coding and algorithm skills, and so you should focus your preparation there.

Congratulations! You got an offer! And—if you're lucky—you may have even gotten multiple offers. Your recruiter's job is now to do everything he can to encourage you to accept it. How do you know if the company is the right fit for you? We'll go through a few things you should consider in evaluating an offer.

The Financial Package

Perhaps the biggest mistake that candidates make in evaluating an offer is looking too much at their salary. Candidates often look so much at this one number that they wind up accepting the offer that is *worse* financially. Salary is just one part of your financial compensation. You should also look at:

- *Signing Bonus, Relocation, and Other One Time Perks:* Many companies offer a signing bonus and/or relocation. When comparing offers, it's wise to amortize this cash over three years (or however long you expect to stay).

- *Cost of Living Difference:* If you've received offers in multiple locations, do not over-look the impact of cost of living differences. Silicon Valley, for example, is about 20 to 30% more expensive than Seattle (in part due to a 10% California state income tax). A variety of online sources can estimate the cost of living difference.

- *Annual Bonus:* Annual bonuses at tech companies can range from anywhere from 3% to 30%. Your recruiter might reveal the average annual bonus, but if not, check with friends at the company.

- *Stock Options and Grants:* Equity compensation can form another big part of your annual compensation. Like signing bonuses, stock compensation between companies can be compared by amortizing it over three years and then lumping that value into salary.

Remember, though, that what you learn and how a company advances your career often makes far more of a difference to your long term finances than the salary. Think very carefully about how much emphasis you really want to put on money right now.

Career Development

As thrilled as you may be to receive this offer, odds are, in a few years, you'll start thinking about interviewing again. Therefore, it's important that you think right now about how this offer would impact your career path. This means considering the following questions:

- How good does the company's name look on my resume?

- How much will I learn? Will I learn relevant things?

- What is the promotion plan? How do the careers of developers progress?

- If I want to move into management, does this company offer a realistic plan?

- Is the company or team growing?

- If I do want to leave the company, is it situated near other companies I'm interested in, or will I need to move?

The final point is extremely important and usually overlooked. If you're working for Microsoft in Silicon Valley and wish to leave, you'll get your choice of almost any other company. In Microsoft-Seattle, however, you're limited to Amazon, Google and a handful of other smaller tech companies. If you go to AOL in Dulles, Virginia, your options are even more limited. You may find yourself forced to stay at a company simply because there's nowhere else to go without uprooting your whole life.

Company Stability

Everyone's situation is a little bit different, but I typically encourage candidates to not focus too much on the stability of a company. If they do let you go, you can usually find an offer from an equivalent company. The question for you to answer is: what will happen if you get laid off? Do you feel reasonably comfortable in your ability to find a new job?

The Happiness Factor

Last but not least, you should of course consider how happy you will be. Any of the following factors may impact that:

- *The Product:* Many people look heavily at what product they are building, and of course this matters a bit. However, for most engineers, there are more important factor, such as who you work with.

- *Manager and Teammates:* When people say that they love, or hate, their job, it's often because of their teammates and their manager. Have you met them? Did you enjoy talking with them?

- *Company Culture:* Culture is tied to everything from how decisions get made, to the social atmosphere, to how the company is organized. Ask your future teammates how they would describe the culture.

- *Hours:* Ask future teammates about how long they typically work, and figure out if that meshes with your lifestyle. Remember, though, that hours before major deadlines are typically much longer.

Additionally, note that if you are given the opportunity to switch teams easily (like you are at Google), you'll have an opportunity to find a team and product that matches you well.

In late 2010, I signed up for a negotiations class. On the first day, the instructor asked us to imagine a scenario where we wanted to buy a car. Dealership A sells the car for a fixed $20,000—no negotiating. Dealership B allows us to negotiate. How much would the car have to be (after negotiating) for us to go to Dealership B? (Quick! Answer this for yourself!)

On average, the class said that the car would have to be $750 cheaper. In other words, students were willing to pay $750 just to avoid having to negotiate for an hour or so. Not surprisingly, in a class poll, most of these students also said they didn't negotiate their job offer. They just accepted whatever the company gave them.

Do yourself a favor. Negotiate. Here are some tips to get you started.

1. *Just Do It*. Yes, I know it's scary; (almost) no one likes negotiating. But it's so, so worth it. Recruiters will not revoke an offer because you negotiated, so you have nothing to lose.

2. *Have a Viable Alternative*. Fundamentally, recruiters negotiate with you because they're concerned you may not join the company otherwise. If you have alternative options, that will make their concern that you'll decline their offer much more real.

3. *Have a Specific "Ask"*: It's much for effective to ask for an additional $7000 in salary than to just ask for "more." After all, if you just ask for more, the recruiter could throw in another $1000 and technically have satisfied your wishes.

4. *Overshoot:* In negotiations, people usually don't agree to whatever you demand. It's a back and forth conversation. Ask for a bit more than you're really hoping to get, since the company will probably meet you in the middle.

5. *Think Beyond Salary:* Companies are often more willing to negotiate on non-salary components, since boosting your salary too much could mean that they're paying you more than your peers. Consider asking for more equity or a bigger signing bonus. Alternatively, you may be able to ask for your relocation benefits in cash, instead of having the company pay directly for the moving fees. This is a great avenue for many college students, whose actual moving expenses are fairly cheap.

6. *Use Your Best Medium:* Many people will advise you to only negotiate over the phone. To a certain extent, they're right; it is better to negotiate over the phone. However, if you don't feel comfortable on a phone negotiation, do it via email. It's more important that you attempt to negotiate than that you do it via a specific medium.

Additionally, if you're negotiating with a big company, you should know that they often have "levels" for employees, where all employees at a particular level are paid around the same amount. Microsoft has a particularly well-defined system for this. You can negotiate within the salary range for your level, but going beyond that requires bumping up a level. If you're looking for a big bump, you'll need to convince the recruiter and your future team that your experience matches this higher level—a difficult, but feasible, thing to do.

Navigating your career path doesn't end at the interview. In fact, it's just getting started. Once you actually join a company, you need to start thinking about your career path. Where will you go from here, and how will you get there?

Set a Timeline

It's a common story: you join a company, and you're psyched. Everything is great. Five years later, you're still there. And it's then that you realize that these last three years didn't add much to your skill set or to your resume. Why didn't you just leave after two years?

When you're enjoying your job, it's very easy to get wrapped up in it and not realize that your career is not advancing. This is why you should outline your career path before starting a new job. Where do you want to be in ten years? And what are the steps necessary to get there? In addition, each year, think about what the next year of experience will bring you and how your career or your skill set advanced in the last year.

By outlining your path in advance and checking in on it regularly, you can avoid falling into this complacency trap.

Build Strong Relationships

When you move on to something new, your network will be critical. After all, applying online is tricky; a personal referral is much better, and your ability to do so hinges on your network.

At work, establish strong relationships with your manager and teammates. When employees leave, keep in touch with them. Just a friendly note a few weeks after their departure will help to bridge that connection from a work acquaintance to a personal acquaintance.

This same approach applies to your personal life. Your friends, and your friends of friends, are valuable connections. Be open to helping others, and they'll be more likely to help you.

Ask for What You Want

While some managers may really try to grow your career, others will take a more hands-off approach. It's up to you to pursue the challenges that are right for your career.

Be (reasonably) frank about your goals with your manager. If you want to take on more back-end coding projects, say so. If you'd like to explore more leadership opportunities, discuss how you might be able to do so.

You need to be your best advocate, so that you can achieve goals according to your timeline.

Interview Questions

VIII

Join us at **www.CrackingTheCodingInterview.com** to download full, compilable Java / Eclipse solutions, discuss problems from this book with other readers, report issues, view this book's errata, post your resume, and seek additional advice.

Data Structures

Interview Questions and Advice

1

Arrays and Strings

Hopefully, all readers of this book are familiar with what arrays and strings are, so we won't bore you with such details. Instead, we'll focus on some of the more common techniques and issues with these data structures.

Please note that array questions and string questions are often interchangeable. That is, a question that this book states using an array may be asked instead as a string question, and vice versa.

Hash Tables

A hash table is a data structure that maps keys to values for highly efficient lookup. In a very simple implementation of a hash table, the hash table has an underlying array and a *hash function*. When you want to insert an object and its key, the hash function maps the key to an integer, which indicates the index in the array. The object is then stored at that index.

Typically, though, this won't quite work right. In the above implementation, the hash value of all possible keys must be unique, or we might accidentally overwrite data. The array would have to be extremely large—the size of all possible keys—to prevent such "collisions."

Instead of making an extremely large array and storing objects at index hash(key), we can make the array much smaller and store objects in a linked list at index hash(key) % array_length. To get the object with a particular key, we must search the linked list for this key.

Alternatively, we can implement the hash table with a binary search tree. We can then guarantee an O(log n) lookup time, since we can keep the tree balanced. Additionally, we may use less space, since a large array no longer needs to be allocated in the very beginning.

Prior to your interview, we recommend you practice both implementing and using hash tables. They are one of the most common data structures for interviews, and it's almost a sure bet that you will encounter them in your interview process.

Below is a simple Java example of working with a hash table.

```java
1   public HashMap<Integer, Student> buildMap(Student[] students) {
2       HashMap<Integer, Student> map = new HashMap<Integer, Student>();
3       for (Student s : students) map.put(s.getId(), s);
4       return map;
5   }
```

Note that while the use of a hash table is sometimes explicitly required, more often than not, it's up to you to figure out that you need to use a hash table to solve the problem.

ArrayList (Dynamically Resizing Array)

An ArrayList, or a dynamically resizing array, is an array that resizes itself as needed while still providing O(1) access. A typical implementation is that when the array is full, the array doubles in size. Each doubling takes O(n) time, but happens so rarely that its amortized time is still O(1).

```java
1   public ArrayList<String> merge(String[] words, String[] more) {
2       ArrayList<String> sentence = new ArrayList<String>();
3       for (String w : words) sentence.add(w);
4       for (String w : more) sentence.add(w);
5       return sentence;
6   }
```

StringBuffer

Imagine you were concatenating a list of strings, as shown below. What would the running time of this code be? For simplicity, assume that the strings are all the same length (call this x) and that there are n strings.

```java
1   public String joinWords(String[] words) {
2       String sentence = "";
3       for (String w : words) {
4           sentence = sentence + w;
5       }
6       return sentence;
7   }
```

On each concatenation, a new copy of the string is created, and the two strings are copied over, character by character. The first iteration requires us to copy x characters. The second iteration requires copying 2x characters. The third iteration requires 3x, and so on. The total time therefore is $O(x + 2x + ... + nx)$. This reduces to $O(xn^2)$. (Why isn't it $O(xn^n)$? Because $1 + 2 + ... + n$ equals $n(n+1)/2$, or $O(n^2)$.)

StringBuffer can help you avoid this problem. StringBuffer simply creates an array of all the strings, copying them back to a string only when necessary.

```java
1   public String joinWords(String[] words) {
2       StringBuffer sentence = new StringBuffer();
3       for (String w : words) {
```

```
4        sentence.append(w);
5    }
6    return sentence.toString();
7 }
```

A good exercise to practice strings, arrays, and general data structures is to implement your own version of StringBuffer.

Interview Questions

1.1 Implement an algorithm to determine if a string has all unique characters. What if you cannot use additional data structures?

pg 172

1.2 Implement a function void reverse(char* str) in C or C++ which reverses a null-terminated string.

pg 173

1.3 Given two strings, write a method to decide if one is a permutation of the other.

pg 174

1.4 Write a method to replace all spaces in a string with '%20'. You may assume that the string has sufficient space at the end of the string to hold the additional characters, and that you are given the "true" length of the string. (Note: if implementing in Java, please use a character array so that you can perform this operation in place.)

EXAMPLE

Input: "Mr John Smith   "

Output: "Mr%20John%20Smith"

pg 175

1.5 Implement a method to perform basic string compression using the counts of repeated characters. For example, the string aabcccccaaa would become a2b1c5a3. If the "compressed" string would not become smaller than the original string, your method should return the original string.

pg 176

1.6 Given an image represented by an NxN matrix, where each pixel in the image is 4 bytes, write a method to rotate the image by 90 degrees. Can you do this in place?

pg 179

1.7 Write an algorithm such that if an element in an MxN matrix is 0, its entire row and column are set to 0.

pg 180

1.8 Assume you have a method isSubstring which checks if one word is a substring of another. Given two strings, s1 and s2, write code to check if s2 is a rotation of s1 using only one call to isSubstring (e.g., "waterbottle" is a rotation of "erbottlewat").

pg 181

Additional Questions: Bit Manipulation (#5.7), Object-Oriented Design (#8.10), Recursion (#9.3), Sorting and Searching (#11.6), C++ (#13.10), Moderate (#17.7, #17.8, #17.14)

2

Linked Lists

Because of the lack of constant time access and the frequency of recursion, linked list questions can stump many candidates. The good news is that there is comparatively little variety in linked list questions, and many problems are merely variants of well-known questions.

Linked list problems rely so much on the fundamental concepts, so it is essential that you can implement a linked list from scratch. We have provided the code below.

Creating a Linked List

The code below implements a very basic singly linked list.

```
1   class Node {
2      Node next = null;
3      int data;
4
5      public Node(int d) {
6         data = d;
7      }
8
9      void appendToTail(int d) {
10        Node end = new Node(d);
11        Node n = this;
12        while (n.next != null) {
13           n = n.next;
14        }
15        n.next = end;
16     }
17  }
```

Remember that when you're discussing a linked list in an interview, you must understand whether it is a singly linked list or a doubly linked list.

Deleting a Node from a Singly Linked List

Deleting a node from a linked list is fairly straightforward. Given a node n, we find the previous node prev and set prev.next equal to n.next. If the list is doubly linked, we must also update n.next to set n.next.prev equal to n.prev. The important things to remember are (1) to check for the null pointer and (2) to update the head or tail pointer as necessary.

Additionally, if you are implementing this code in C, C++ or another language that requires the developer to do memory management, you should consider if the removed node should be deallocated.

```
1   Node deleteNode(Node head, int d) {
2       Node n = head;
3
4       if (n.data == d) {
5           return head.next; /* moved head */
6       }
7
8       while (n.next != null) {
9           if (n.next.data == d) {
10              n.next = n.next.next;
11              return head; /* head didn't change */
12          }
13          n = n.next;
14      }
15      return head;
16  }
```

The "Runner" Technique

The "runner" (or second pointer) technique is used in many linked list problems. The runner technique means that you iterate through the linked list with two pointers simultaneously, with one ahead of the other. The "fast" node might be ahead by a fixed amount, or it might be hopping multiple nodes for each one node that the "slow" node iterates through.

For example, suppose you had a linked list $a_1 -> a_2 -> \ldots -> a_n -> b_1 -> b_2 -> \ldots -> b_n$ and you wanted to rearrange it into $a_1 -> b_1 -> a_2 -> b_2 -> \ldots -> a_n -> b_n$. You do not know the length of the linked list (but you do know that the length is an even number).

You could have one pointer p1 (the fast pointer) move every two elements for every one move that p2 makes. When p1 hits the end of the linked list, p2 will be at the midpoint. Then, move p1 back to the front and begin "weaving" the elements. On each iteration, p2 selects an element and inserts it after p1.

Recursive Problems

A number of linked list problems rely on recursion. If you're having trouble solving a

---

linked problem, you should explore if a recursive approach will work. We won't go into depth on recursion here, since a later chapter is devoted to it.

However, you should remember that recursive algorithms take at least O(n) space, where n is the depth of the recursive call. All recursive algorithms *can* be implemented iteratively, although they may be much more complex.

Interview Questions

2.1   Write code to remove duplicates from an unsorted linked list.

FOLLOW UP

How would you solve this problem if a temporary buffer is not allowed?

pg 184

2.2   Implement an algorithm to find the kth to last element of a singly linked list.

pg 185

2.3   Implement an algorithm to delete a node in the middle of a singly linked list, given only access to that node.

EXAMPLE

Input: the node c from the linked list a->b->c->d->e

Result: nothing is returned, but the new linked list looks like a->b->d->e

pg 187

2.4   Write code to partition a linked list around a value x, such that all nodes less than x come before all nodes greater than or equal to x.

pg 188

2.5   You have two numbers represented by a linked list, where each node contains a single digit. The digits are stored in *reverse* order, such that the 1's digit is at the head of the list. Write a function that adds the two numbers and returns the sum as a linked list.

EXAMPLE

Input: (7-> 1 -> 6) + (5 -> 9 -> 2). That is, 617 + 295.

Output: 2 -> 1 -> 9. That is, 912.

FOLLOW UP

Suppose the digits are stored in forward order. Repeat the above problem.

EXAMPLE

Input: (6 -> 1 -> 7) + (2 -> 9 -> 5). That is, 617 + 295.

Output: 9 -> 1 -> 2. That is, 912.

pg 188

2.6   Given a circular linked list, implement an algorithm which returns the node at the beginning of the loop.

DEFINITION

Circular linked list: A (corrupt) linked list in which a node's next pointer points to an earlier node, so as to make a loop in the linked list.

EXAMPLE

Input: A -> B -> C -> D -> E -> C [the same C as earlier]

Output: C

pg 193

2.7   Implement a function to check if a linked list is a palindrome.

pg 196

Additional Questions: Trees and Graphs (#4.4), Object-Oriented Design (#8.10), Scalability and Memory Limits (#10.7), Moderate (#17.13)

3

Stacks and Queues

Like linked list questions, questions on stacks and queues will be much easier to handle if you are comfortable with the ins and outs of the data structure. The problems can be quite tricky though. While some problems may be slight modifications on the original data structure, others have much more complex challenges.

Implementing a Stack

Recall that a stack uses the LIFO (last-in first-out) ordering. That is, like a stack of dinner plates, the most recent item added to the stack is the first item to be removed.

We have provided simple sample code to implement a stack. Note that a stack can also be implemented using a linked list. In fact, they are essentially the same thing, except that a stack usually prevents the user from "peeking" at items below the top node.

```
1   class Stack {
2      Node top;
3
4      Object pop() {
5         if (top != null) {
6            Object item = top.data;
7            top = top.next;
8            return item;
9         }
10        return null;
11     }
12
13     void push(Object item) {
14        Node t = new Node(item);
15        t.next = top;
16        top = t;
17     }
18
19     Object peek() {
20        return top.data;
21     }
22  }
```

Implementing a Queue

A queue implements FIFO (first-In first-out) ordering. Like a line or queue at a ticket stand, items are removed from the data structure in the same order that they are added.

A queue can also be implemented with a linked list, with new items added to the tail of the linked list.

```
1   class Queue {
2      Node first, last;
3
4      void enqueue(Object item) {
5         if (first == null) {
6            last = new Node(item);
7            first = last;
8         } else {
9            last.next = new Node(item);
10           last = last.next;
11        }
12     }
13
14     Node dequeue() {
15        if (first != null) {
16           Object item = first.data;
17           first = first.next;
18           return item;
19        }
20        return null;
21     }
22  }
```

Interview Questions

3.1 Describe how you could use a single array to implement three stacks.

pg 202

3.2 How would you design a stack which, in addition to push and pop, also has a function min which returns the minimum element? Push, pop and min should all operate in O(1) time.

pg 206

3.3 Imagine a (literal) stack of plates. If the stack gets too high, it might topple. Therefore, in real life, we would likely start a new stack when the previous stack exceeds some threshold. Implement a data structure SetOfStacks that mimics this. SetOfStacks should be composed of several stacks and should create a new stack once the previous one exceeds capacity. SetOfStacks.push() and SetOfStacks.pop() should behave identically to a single stack (that is, pop() should return the same values as it would if there were just a single stack).

FOLLOW UP

Implement a function popAt(int index) which performs a pop operation on a specific sub-stack.

_pg 208

3.4 In the classic problem of the Towers of Hanoi, you have 3 towers and N disks of different sizes which can slide onto any tower. The puzzle starts with disks sorted in ascending order of size from top to bottom (i.e., each disk sits on top of an even larger one). You have the following constraints:

(1) Only one disk can be moved at a time.

(2) A disk is slid off the top of one tower onto the next tower.

(3) A disk can only be placed on top of a larger disk.

Write a program to move the disks from the first tower to the last using stacks.

_pg 211

3.5 Implement a MyQueue class which implements a queue using two stacks.

_pg 213

3.6 Write a program to sort a stack in ascending order (with biggest items on top). You may use additional stacks to hold items, but you may not copy the elements into any other data structure (such as an array). The stack supports the following operations: push, pop, peek, and isEmpty.

_pg 215

3.7 An animal shelter holds only dogs and cats, and operates on a strictly "first in, first out" basis. People must adopt either the "oldest" (based on arrival time) of all animals at the shelter, or they can select whether they would prefer a dog or a cat (and will receive the oldest animal of that type). They cannot select which specific animal they would like. Create the data structures to maintain this system and implement operations such as enqueue, dequeueAny, dequeueDog and dequeueCat. You may use the built-in LinkedList data structure.

_pg 216

Additional Questions: Linked Lists (#2.7), Mathematics and Probability (#7.7)

4

Trees and Graphs

Many interviewees find trees and graphs problems to be some of the trickiest. Searching the data structure is more complicated than in a linearly organized data structure like an array or linked list. Additionally, the worst case and average case time may vary wildly, and we must evaluate both aspects of any algorithm. Fluency in implementing a tree or graph from scratch will prove essential.

Potential Issues to Watch Out For

Trees and graphs questions are ripe for ambiguous details and incorrect assumptions. Be sure to watch out for the following issues and seek clarification when necessary.

Binary Tree vs. Binary Search Tree

When given a binary tree question, many candidates assume that the interviewer means binary *search* tree. Be sure to ask whether or not the tree is a binary search tree. A binary search tree imposes the condition that, for all nodes, the left children are less than or equal to the current node, which is less than all the right nodes.

Balanced vs. Unbalanced

While many trees are balanced, not all are. Ask your interviewer for clarification on this issue. If the tree is unbalanced, you should describe your algorithm in terms of both the average and the worst case time. Note that there are multiple ways to balance a tree, and balancing a tree implies only that the depth of subtrees will not vary by more than a certain amount. It does not mean that the left and right subtrees are exactly the same size.

Full and Complete

Full and complete trees are trees in which all leaves are at the bottom of the tree, and all non-leaf nodes have exactly two children. Note that full and complete trees are *extremely* rare, as a tree must have exactly $2^n - 1$ nodes to meet this condition.

Binary Tree Traversal

Prior to your interview, you should be comfortable implementing in-order, post-order, and pre-order traversal. The most common of these, in-order traversal, works by visiting the left side, then the current node, then the right.

Tree Balancing: Red-Black Trees and AVL Trees

Though learning how to implement a balanced tree may make you a better software engineer, it's very rarely asked during an interview. You should be familiar with the runtime of operations on balanced trees, and vaguely familiar with how you might balance a tree. The details, however, are probably unnecessary for the purposes of an interview.

Tries

A trie is a variant of an n-ary tree in which characters are stored at each node. Each path down the tree may represent a word. A simple trie might look something like:

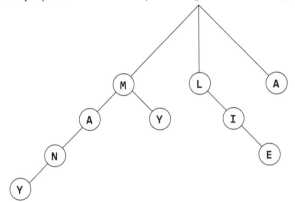

Graph Traversal

While most candidates are reasonably comfortable with binary tree traversal, graph traversal can prove more challenging. Breadth First Search is especially difficult.

Note that Breadth First Search (BFS) and Depth First Search (DFS) are usually used in different scenarios. DFS is typically the easiest if we want to visit every node in the graph, or at least visit every node until we find whatever we're looking for. However, if we have a very large tree and want to be prepared to quit when we get too far from the original node, DFS can be problematic; we might search thousands of ancestors of the node, but never even search all of the node's children. In these cases, BFS is typically preferred.

Depth First Search (DFS)

In DFS, we visit a node r and then iterate through each of r's adjacent nodes. When visiting a node n that is adjacent to r, we visit all of n's adjacent nodes before going on to r's other adjacent nodes. That is, n is exhaustively searched before r moves on to searching its other children.

Note that pre-order and other forms of tree traversal are a form of DFS. The key difference is that when implementing this algorithm for a graph, we must check if the node has been visited. If we don't, we risk getting stuck in infinite loop.

The pseudocode below implements DFS.

```
1   void search(Node root) {
2       if (root == null) return;
3       visit(root);
4       root.visited = true;
5       foreach (Node n in root.adjacent) {
6           if (n.visited == false)
7               search(n);
8       }
9   }
10  }
```

Breadth First Search (BFS)

BFS is considerably less intuitive, and most interviewees struggle with it unless they are already familiar with the implementation.

In BFS, we visit each of a node r's adjacent nodes before searching any of r's "grandchildren." An iterative solution involving a queue usually works best.

```
1   void search(Node root) {
2       Queue queue = new Queue();
3       root.visited = true;
4       visit(root);
5       queue.enqueue(root); // Add to end of queue
6
7       while (!queue.isEmpty()) {
8           Node r = queue.dequeue(); // Remove from front of queue
9           foreach (Node n in r.adjacent) {
10              if (n.visited == false) {
11                  visit(n);
12                  n.visited = true;
13                  queue.enqueue(n);
14              }
15          }
16      }
17  }
```

If you are asked to implement BFS, the key thing to remember is the use of the queue. The rest of the algorithm flows from this fact.

Interview Questions

4.1   Implement a function to check if a binary tree is balanced. For the purposes of this question, a balanced tree is defined to be a tree such that the heights of the two subtrees of any node never differ by more than one.

_____pg 220

4.2   Given a directed graph, design an algorithm to find out whether there is a route between two nodes.

_____pg 221

4.3   Given a sorted (increasing order) array, write an algorithm to create a binary search tree with minimal height.

_____pg 222

4.4   Given a binary tree, design an algorithm which creates a linked list of all the nodes at each depth (e.g., if you have a tree with depth D, you'll have D linked lists).

_____pg 224

4.5   Implement a function to check if a binary tree is a binary search tree.

_____pg 225

4.6   Write an algorithm to find the 'next' node (i.e., in-order successor) of a given node in a binary search tree. You may assume that each node has a link to its parent.

_____pg 228

4.7   Design an algorithm and write code to find the first common ancestor of two nodes in a binary tree. Avoid storing additional nodes in a data structure. NOTE: This is not necessarily a binary search tree.

_____pg 230

4.8   You have two very large binary trees: T1, with millions of nodes, and T2, with hundreds of nodes. Create an algorithm to decide if T2 is a subtree of T1.

A tree T2 is a subtree of T1 if there exists a node n in T1 such that the subtree of n is identical to T2. That is, if you cut off the tree at node n, the two trees would be identical.

_____pg 234

4.9   You are given a binary tree in which each node contains a value. Design an algorithm to print all paths which sum to a given value. Note that a path can start or end anywhere in the tree.

_____pg 237

Additional Questions: Scalability and Memory Limits (#10.2, #10.5), Sorting and Searching (#11.8), Moderate (#17.13, #17.14), Hard (#18.6, #18.8, #18.9, #18.10, #18.13)

Concepts and Algorithms

Interview Questions and Advice

5

Bit Manipulation

Bit manipulation is used in a variety of problems. Sometimes, the question explicitly calls for bit manipulation, while at other times, it's simply a useful technique to optimize your code. You should be comfortable with bit manipulation by hand, as well as with code. But be very careful; it's easy to make little mistakes on bit manipulation problems. Make sure to test your code thoroughly after you're done writing it, or even while writing it.

Bit Manipulation By Hand

The practice exercises below will be useful if you have the oh-so-common fear of bit manipulation. When you get stuck or confused, try to work these operations through as a base 10 number. You can then apply the same process to a binary number.

Remember that ^ indicates an XOR operation, and ~ is a not (negation) operation. For simplicity, assume that these are four-bit numbers. The third column can be solved manually, or with "tricks" (described below).

0110 + 0010	0011 * 0101	0110 + 0110
0011 + 0010	0011 * 0011	0100 * 0011
0110 - 0011	1101 >> 2	1101 ^ (~1101)
1000 - 0110	1101 ^ 0101	1011 & (~0 << 2)

Solutions: line 1 (1000, 1111, 1100); line 2 (0101, 1001, 1100); line 3 (0011, 0011, 1111); line 4 (0010, 1000, 1000).

The tricks in Column 3 are as follows:

1. 0110 + 0110 is equivalent to 0110 * 2, which is equivalent to shifting 0110 left by 1.

2. Since 0100 equals 4, we are just multiplying 0011 by 4. Multiplying by 2^n just shifts a number by n. We shift 0011 left by 2 to get 1100.

3. Think about this operation bit by bit. If you XOR a bit with its own negated value, you will always get 1. Therefore, the solution to a^(~a) will be a sequence of 1s.

4. An operation like x & (~0 << n) clears the n rightmost bits of x. The value ~0 is simply a sequence of 1s, so by shifting it left by n, we have a bunch of ones followed by n zeros. By doing an AND with x, we clear the rightmost n bits of x.

For more problems, open the Windows calculator and go to View > Programmer. From this application, you can perform many binary operations, including AND, XOR, and shifting.

Bit Facts and Tricks

In solving bit manipulation problems, it's useful to understand the following facts. Don't just memorize them though; think deeply about why each of these is true. We use "1s" and "0s" to indicate a sequence of 1s or 0s, respectively.

x ^ 0s = x	x & 0s = 0	x | 0s = x
x ^ 1s = ~x	x & 1s = x	x | 1s = 1s
x ^ x = 0	x & x = x	x | x = x

To understand these expressions, recall that these operations occur bit-by-bit, with what's happening on one bit never impacting the other bits. This means that if one of the above statements is true for a single bit, then it's true for a sequence of bits.

Common Bit Tasks: Get, Set, Clear, and Update Bit

The following operations are very important to know, but do not simply memorize them. Memorizing leads to mistakes that are impossible to recover from. Rather, understand *how* to implement these methods, so that you can implement these, and other, bit problems.

Get Bit

This method shifts 1 over by i bits, creating a value that looks like 00010000. By performing an AND with num, we clear all bits other than the bit at bit i. Finally, we compare that to 0. If that new value is not zero, then bit i must have a 1. Otherwise, bit i is a 0.

```
1   boolean getBit(int num, int i) {
2      return ((num & (1 << i)) != 0);
3   }
```

Set Bit

SetBit shifts 1 over by i bits, creating a value like 00010000. By performing an OR with num, only the value at bit i will change. All other bits of the mask are zero and will not affect num.

```
1   int setBit(int num, int i) {
2      return num | (1 << i);
3   }
```

Clear Bit

This method operates in almost the reverse of setBit. First, we create a number like 11101111 by creating the reverse of it (00010000) and negating it. Then, we perform an AND with num. This will clear the ith bit and leave the remainder unchanged.

```
1   int clearBit(int num, int i) {
2       int mask = ~(1 << i);
3       return num & mask;
4   }
```

To clear all bits from the most significant bit through i (inclusive), we do:

```
1   int clearBitsMSBthroughI(int num, int i) {
2       int mask = (1 << i) - 1;
3       return num & mask;
4   }
```

To clear all bits from i through 0 (inclusive), we do:

```
1   int clearBitsIthrough0(int num, int i) {
2       int mask = ~((1 << (i+1)) - 1);
3       return num & mask;
4   }
```

Update Bit

This method merges the approaches of setBit and clearBit. First, we clear the bit at position i by using a mask that looks like 11101111. Then, we shift the intended value, v, left by i bits. This will create a number with bit i equal to v and all other bits equal to 0. Finally, we OR these two numbers, updating the ith bit if v is 1 and leaving it as 0 otherwise.

```
1   int updateBit(int num, int i, int v) {
2       int mask = ~(1 << i);
3       return (num & mask) | (v << i);
4   }
```

Interview Questions

5.1   You are given two 32-bit numbers, N and M, and two bit positions, i and j. Write a method to insert M into N such that M starts at bit j and ends at bit i. You can assume that the bits j through i have enough space to fit all of M. That is, if M = 10011, you can assume that there are at least 5 bits between j and i. You would not, for example, have j = 3 and i = 2, because M could not fully fit between bit 3 and bit 2.

EXAMPLE

Input: N = 10000000000, M = 10011, i = 2, j = 6

Output: N = 10001001100

pg 242

5.2 Given a real number between 0 and 1 (e.g., 0.72) that is passed in as a double, print the binary representation. If the number cannot be represented accurately in binary with at most 32 characters, print "ERROR."

pg 243

5.3 Given a positive integer, print the next smallest and the next largest number that have the same number of 1 bits in their binary representation.

pg 244

5.4 Explain what the following code does: `((n & (n-1)) == 0)`.

pg 250

5.5 Write a function to determine the number of bits required to convert integer A to integer B.

EXAMPLE

Input: 31, 14

Output: 2

pg 250

5.6 Write a program to swap odd and even bits in an integer with as few instructions as possible (e.g., bit 0 and bit 1 are swapped, bit 2 and bit 3 are swapped, and so on).

pg 251

5.7 An array A contains all the integers from 0 to n, except for one number which is missing. In this problem, we cannot access an entire integer in A with a single operation. The elements of A are represented in binary, and the only operation we can use to access them is "fetch the jth bit of A[i]," which takes constant time. Write code to find the missing integer. Can you do it in O(n) time?

pg 252

5.8 A monochrome screen is stored as a *single* array of bytes, allowing eight consecutive pixels to be stored in one byte. The screen has width w, where w is divisible by 8 (that is, no byte will be split across rows). The height of the screen, of course, can be derived from the length of the array and the width. Implement a function `drawHorizontalLine(byte[] screen, int width, int x1, int x2, int y)` which draws a horizontal line from `(x1, y)` to `(x2, y)`.

pg 255

Additional Questions: Arrays and Strings (#1.1, #1.7), Recursion (#9.4, #9.11), Scalability and Memory Limits (#10.3, #10.4), C++ (#13.9), Moderate (#17.1, #17.4), Hard (#18.1)

6

Brain Teasers

Brain teasers are some of the most hotly debated questions, and many companies have policies banning them. Unfortunately, even when these questions are banned, you still may find yourself being asked a brain teaser. Why? Because no one can agree on a definition of what a brain teaser is.

The good news is that if you are asked a brain teaser, it's likely to be a reasonably fair one. It probably won't rely on a trick of wording, and it can almost always be logically deduced. Many brain teasers even have their foundations in mathematics or computer science.

We'll go through some common approaches for tackling brain teasers.

Start Talking

Don't panic when you get a brain teaser. Like algorithm questions, interviewers want to see how you tackle a problem; they don't expect you to immediately know the answer. Start talking, and show the interviewer how you approach a problem.

Develop Rules and Patterns

In many cases, you will find it useful to write down "rules" or patterns that you discover while solving the problem. And yes, you really should write these down—it will help you remember them as you solve the problem. Let's demonstrate this approach with an example.

You have two ropes, and each takes exactly one hour to burn. How would you use them to time exactly 15 minutes? Note that the ropes are of uneven densities, so half the rope length-wise does not necessarily take half an hour to burn.

Tip: Stop here and spend some time trying to solve this problem on your own. If you absolutely must, read through this section for hints—but do so slowly. Every paragraph will get you a bit closer to the solution.

From the statement of the problem, we immediately know that we can time one hour.

We can also time two hours, by lighting one rope, waiting until it is burnt, and then lighting the second. We can generalize this into a rule.

Rule 1: Given a rope that takes x minutes to burn and another that takes y minutes, we can time x+y minutes.

What else can we do with the rope? We can probably assume that lighting a rope in the middle (or anywhere other than the ends) won't do us much good. The flames would expand in both directions, and we have no idea how long it would take to burn.

However, we can light a rope at both ends. The two flames would meet after 30 minutes.

Rule 2: Given a rope that takes x minutes to burn, we can time x/2 minutes.

We now know that we can time 30 minutes using a single rope. This also means that we can remove 30 minutes of burning time from the second rope, by lighting rope 1 on both ends and rope 2 on just one end.

Rule 3: If rope 1 takes x minutes to burn and rope 2 takes y minutes, we can turn rope 2 into a rope that takes (y-x) minutes or (y-x/2) minutes.

Now, let's piece all of these together. We can turn rope 2 into a rope with 30 minutes of burn time. If we then light rope 2 on the other end (see rule 2), rope 2 will be done after 15 minutes.

From start to end, our approach is as follows:

1. Light rope 1 at both ends and rope 2 at one end.

2. When the two flames on Rope 1 meet, 30 minutes will have passed. Rope 2 has 30 minutes left of burn-time.

3. At that point, light Rope 2 at the other end.

4. In exactly fifteen minutes, Rope 2 will be completely burnt.

Note how solving this problem is made easier by listing out what you've learned and what "rules" you've discovered.

Worst Case Shifting

Many brain teasers are worst-case minimization problems, worded either in terms of *minimizing* an action or in doing something at most a specific number of times. A useful technique is to try to "balance" the worst case. That is, if an early decision results in a skewing of the worst case, we can sometimes change the decision to balance out the worst case. This will be clearest when explained with an example.

The "nine balls" question is a classic interview question. You have nine balls. Eight are of the same weight, and one is heavier. You are given a balance which tells you only whether the left side or the right side is heavier. Find the heavy ball in just two uses of the scale.

A first approach is to divide the balls in sets of four, with the ninth ball sitting off to the side. The heavy ball is in the heavier set. If they are the same weight, then we know that the ninth ball is the heavy one. Replicating this approach for the remaining sets would result in a worst case of three weighings—one too many!

This is an imbalance in the worst case: the ninth ball takes just one weighing to discover if it's heavy, whereas others take three. If we *penalize* the ninth ball by putting more balls off to the side, we can lighten the load on the others. This is an example of "worst case balancing."

If we divide the balls into sets of three items each, we will know after just one weighing which set has the heavy one. We can even formalize this into a *rule*: given N balls, where N is divisible by 3, one use of the scale will point us to a set of N/3 balls with the heavy ball.

For the final set of three balls, we simply repeat this: put one ball off to the side and weigh two. Pick the heavier of the two. Or, if the balls are the same weight, pick the third one.

Algorithm Approaches

If you're stuck, consider applying one of the five approaches for solving algorithm questions. Brain teasers are often nothing more than algorithm questions with the technical aspects removed. Examplify, Simplify and Generalize, Pattern Matching, and Base Case and Build can be especially useful.

Interview Questions

6.1 You have 20 bottles of pills. 19 bottles have 1.0 gram pills, but one has pills of weight 1.1 grams. Given a scale that provides an exact measurement, how would you find the heavy bottle? You can only use the scale once.

pg 258

6.2 There is an 8x8 chess board in which two diagonally opposite corners have been cut off. You are given 31 dominos, and a single domino can cover exactly two squares. Can you use the 31 dominos to cover the entire board? Prove your answer (by providing an example or showing why it's impossible).

pg 258

6.3 You have a five-quart jug, a three-quart jug, and an unlimited supply of water (but no measuring cups). How would you come up with exactly four quarts of water? Note that the jugs are oddly shaped, such that filling up exactly "half" of the jug would be impossible.

pg 259

6.4 A bunch of people are living on an island, when a visitor comes with a strange order: all blue-eyed people must leave the island as soon as possible. There will be a flight out at 8:00pm every evening. Each person can see everyone else's eye color, but they do not know their own (nor is anyone allowed to tell them). Additionally, they do not know how many people have blue eyes, although they do know that at least one person does. How many days will it take the blue-eyed people to leave?

pg 260

6.5 There is a building of 100 floors. If an egg drops from the Nth floor or above, it will break. If it's dropped from any floor below, it will not break. You're given two eggs. Find N, while minimizing the number of drops for the worst case.

pg 261

6.6 There are 100 closed lockers in a hallway. A man begins by opening all 100 lockers. Next, he closes every second locker. Then, on his third pass, he toggles every third locker (closes it if it is open or opens it if it is closed). This process continues for 100 passes, such that on each pass i, the man toggles every ith locker. After his 100th pass in the hallway, in which he toggles only locker #100, how many lockers are open?

pg 262

7

Mathematics and Probability

Although many mathematical problems given during an interview read as brain teasers, most can be tackled with a logical, methodical approach. They are typically rooted in the rules of mathematics or computer science, and this knowledge can facilitate either solving the problem or validating your solution. We'll cover the most relevant mathematical concepts in this section.

Prime Numbers

As you probably know, every positive integer can be decomposed into a product of primes. For example:

$$84 = 2^2 * 3^1 * 5^0 * 7^1 * 11^0 * 13^0 * 17^0 * \ldots$$

Note that many of these primes have an exponent of zero.

Divisibility

The prime number law stated above means that, in order for a number x to divide a number y (written $x \backslash y$, or $mod(y, x) = 0$), all primes in x's prime factorization must be in y's prime factorization. Or, more specifically:

Let $x = 2^{j0} * 3^{j1} * 5^{j2} * 7^{j3} * 11^{j4} * \ldots$

Let $y = 2^{k0} * 3^{k1} * 5^{k2} * 7^{k3} * 11^{k4} * \ldots$

If $x \backslash y$, then for all i, $ji <= ki$.

In fact, the greatest common divisor of x and y will be:

$$gcd(x, y) = 2^{min(j0, k0)} * 3^{min(j1, k1)} * 5^{min(j2, k2)} * \ldots$$

The least common multiple of x and y will be:

$$lcm(x, y) = 2^{max(j0, k0)} * 3^{max(j1, k1)} * 5^{max(j2, k2)} * \ldots$$

As a fun exercise, stop for a moment and think what would happen if you did gcd * lcm:

$$gcd * lcm = 2^{min(j0, k0)} * 2^{max(j0, k0)} * 3^{min(j1, k1)} * 3^{max(j1, k1)} * \ldots$$

$$= 2^{min(j0,\ k0)\ +\ max(j0,\ k0)}\ *\ 3^{min(j1,\ k1)\ +\ max(j1,\ k1)}\ *\ \ldots$$

$$= 2^{j0\ +\ k0}\ *\ 3^{j1\ +\ k1}\ *\ \ldots$$

$$= 2^{j0}\ *\ 2^{k0}\ *\ 3^{j1}\ *\ 3^{k1}\ *\ \ldots$$

$$= xy$$

Checking for Primality

This question is so common that we feel the need to specifically cover it. The naive way is to simply iterate from 2 through n-1, checking for divisibility on each iteration.

```
1    boolean primeNaive(int n) {
2        if (n < 2) {
3            return false;
4        }
5        for (int i = 2; i < n; i++) {
6            if (n % i == 0) {
7                return false;
8            }
9        }
10       return true;
11   }
```

A small but important improvement is to iterate only up through the square root of n.

```
1    boolean primeSlightlyBetter(int n) {
2        if (n < 2) {
3            return false;
4        }
5        int sqrt = (int) Math.sqrt(n);
6        for (int i = 2; i <= sqrt; i++) {
7            if (n % i == 0) return false;
8        }
9        return true;
10   }
```

The sqrt is sufficient because, for every number a which divides n evenly, there is a complement b, where a * b = n. If a > sqrt, then b < sqrt (since sqrt * sqrt = n). We therefore don't need a to check n's primality, since we would have already checked with b.

Of course, in reality, all we *really* need to do is to check if n is divisible by a prime number. This is where the Sieve of Eratosthenes comes in.

Generating a List of Primes: The Sieve of Eratosthenes

The Sieve of Eratosthenes is a highly efficient way to generate a list of primes. It works by recognizing that all non-prime numbers are divisible by a prime number.

We start with a list of all the numbers up through some value max. First, we cross off all numbers divisible by 2. Then, we look for the next prime (the next non-crossed off number) and cross off all numbers divisible by it. By crossing off all numbers divisible by 2, 3, 5, 7, 11, and so on, we wind up with a list of prime numbers from 2 through max.

The code below implements the Sieve of Eratosthenes.

```
1   boolean[] sieveOfEratosthenes(int max) {
2       boolean[] flags = new boolean[max + 1];
3       int count = 0;
4
5       init(flags); // Set all flags to true other than 0 and 1
6       int prime = 2;
7
8       while (prime <= max) {
9           /* Cross off remaining multiples of prime */
10          crossOff(flags, prime);
11
12          /* Find next value which is true */
13          prime = getNextPrime(flags, prime);
14
15          if (prime >= flags.length) {
16              break;
17          }
18      }
19
20      return flags;
21  }
22
23  void crossOff(boolean[] flags, int prime) {
24      /* Cross off remaining multiples of prime. We can start with
25       * (prime*prime), because if we have a k * prime, where
26       * k < prime, this value would have already been crossed off in
27       * a prior iteration. */
28      for (int i = prime * prime; i < flags.length; i += prime) {
29          flags[i] = false;
30      }
31  }
32
33  int getNextPrime(boolean[] flags, int prime) {
34      int next = prime + 1;
35      while (next < flags.length && !flags[next]) {
36          next++;
37      }
38      return next;
39  }
```

Of course, there are a number of optimizations that can be made to this. One simple one is to only use odd numbers in the array, which would allow us to reduce our space usage by half.

Probability

Probability can be a complex topic, but it's based in a few basic laws that can be logically derived.

Let's look at a Venn diagram to visualize two events A and B. The areas of the two circles represent their relative probability, and the overlapping area is the event {A and B}.

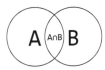

Probability of A and B

Imagine you were throwing a dart at this Venn diagram. What is the probability that you would land in the intersection between A and B? If you knew the odds of landing in A, and you also knew the percent of A that's also in B (that is, the odds of being in B given that you were in A), then you could express the probability as:

```
P(A and B) = P(B given A) P(A)
```

For example, imagine we were picking a number between 1 and 10 (inclusive). What's the probability of picking an even number *and* a number between 1 and 5? The odds of picking a number between 1 and 5 is 50%, and the odds of a number between 1 and 5 being even is 40%. So, the odds of doing both are:

```
P(x is even and x <= 5)
    = P(x is even given x <= 5) P(x <= 5)
    = (2/5) * (1/2)
    = 1/5
```

Probability of A or B

Now, imagine you wanted to know what the probability of landing in A or B is. If you knew the odds of landing in each individually, and you also knew the odds of landing in their intersection, then you could express the probability as:

```
P(A or B) = P(A) + P(B) - P(A and B)
```

Logically, this makes sense. If we simply added their sizes, we would have double-counted their intersection. We need to subtract this out. We can again visualize this through a Venn diagram:

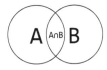

For example, imagine we were picking a number between 1 and 10 (inclusive). What's the probability of picking an even number *or* a number between 1 and 5? We have a 50% probability of picking an even number and a 50% probability of picking a number between 1 and 5. The odds of doing both are 20%. So the odds are:

```
P(x is even or x <=5)
    = P(x is even) + P(x <= 5) - P(x is even and x <= 5)
    = (1/2) + (1/2) - (1/5)
    = 4/5
```

From here, getting the special case rules for independent events and for mutually exclusive events is easy.

Independence

If A and B are independent (that is, one happening tells you nothing about the other happening), then `P(A and B) = P(A) P(B)`. This rule simply comes from recognizing that `P(B given A) = P(B)`, since A indicates nothing about B.

Mutual Exclusivity

If A and B are mutually exclusive (that is, if one happens, then the other cannot happen), then `P(A or B) = P(A) + P(B)`. This is because `P(A and B) = 0`, so this term is removed from the earlier `P(A or B)` equation.

Many people, strangely, mix up the concepts of independence and mutual exclusivity. They are *entirely* different. In fact, two events cannot be both independent and mutually exclusive (provided both have probabilities greater than 0). Why? Because mutual exclusivity means that if one happens then the other cannot. Independence, however, says that one event happening means absolutely *nothing* about the other event. Thus, as long as two events have non-zero probabilities, they will never be both mutually exclusive and independent.

If one or both events have a probability of zero (that is, it is impossible), then the events are both independent and mutually exclusive. This is provable through a simple application of the definitions (that is, the formulas) of independence and mutual exclusivity.

Things to Watch Out For

1. Be careful with the difference in precision between floats and doubles.

2. Don't assume that a value (such as the slope of a line) is an `int` unless you've been told so.

3. Unless otherwise specified, do not assume that events are independent (or mutually exclusive). You should be careful, therefore, of blindly multiplying or adding probabilities.

Interview Questions

7.1 You have a basketball hoop and someone says that you can play one of two games.

Game 1: You get one shot to make the hoop.

Game 2: You get three shots and you have to make two of three shots.

If p is the probability of making a particular shot, for which values of p should you pick one game or the other?

pg 264

7.2 There are three ants on different vertices of a triangle. What is the probability of collision (between any two or all of them) if they start walking on the sides of the triangle? Assume that each ant randomly picks a direction, with either direction being equally likely to be chosen, and that they walk at the same speed.

Similarly, find the probability of collision with n ants on an n-vertex polygon.

pg 265

7.3 Given two lines on a Cartesian plane, determine whether the two lines would intersect.

pg 266

7.4 Write methods to implement the multiply, subtract, and divide operations for integers. Use only the add operator.

pg 267

7.5 Given two squares on a two-dimensional plane, find a line that would cut these two squares in half. Assume that the top and the bottom sides of the square run parallel to the x-axis.

pg 269

7.6 Given a two-dimensional graph with points on it, find a line which passes the most number of points.

pg 271

7.7 Design an algorithm to find the kth number such that the only prime factors are 3, 5, and 7.

pg 273

Additional Questions: Moderate (#17.11), Hard (#18.2)

8

Object-Oriented Design

Object-oriented design questions require a candidate to sketch out the classes and methods to implement technical problems or real-life objects. These problems give—or at least are believed to give—an interviewer insight into your coding style.

These questions are not so much about regurgitating design patterns as they are about demonstrating that you understand how to create elegant, maintainable object-oriented code. Poor performance on this type of question may raise serious red flags.

How to Approach Object-Oriented Design Questions

Regardless of whether the object is a physical item or a technical task, object-oriented design questions can be tackled in similar ways. The following approach will work well for many problems.

Step 1: Handle Ambiguity

Object-oriented design (OOD) questions are often intentionally vague in order to test whether you'll make assumptions or if you'll ask clarifying questions. After all, a developer who just codes something without understanding what she is expected to create wastes the company's time and money, and may create much more serious issues.

When being asked an object-oriented design question, you should inquire *who* is going to use it and *how* they are going to use it. Depending on the question, you may even want to go through the "six Ws": who, what, where, when, how, why.

For example, suppose you were asked to describe the object-oriented design for a coffee maker. This seems straightforward enough, right? Not quite.

Your coffee maker might be an industrial machine designed to be used in a massive restaurant servicing hundreds of customers per hour and making ten different kinds of coffee products. Or it might be a very simple machine, designed to be used by the elderly for just simple black coffee. These use cases will significantly impact your design.

Step 2: Define the Core Objects

Now that we understand what we're designing, we should consider what the "core objects" in a system are. For example, suppose we are asked to do the object-oriented design for a restaurant. Our core objects might be things like Table, Guest, Party, Order, Meal, Employee, Server, and Host.

Step 3: Analyze Relationships

Having more or less decided on our core objects, we now want to analyze the relationships between the objects. Which objects are members of which other objects? Do any objects inherit from any others? Are relationships many-to-many or one-to-many?

For example, in the restaurant question, we may come up with the following design:

- Party should have an array of Guests.

- Server and Host inherit from Employee.

- Each Table has one Party, but each Party may have multiple Tables.

- There is one Host for the Restaurant.

Be very careful here—you can often make incorrect assumptions. For example, a single Table may have multiple Parties (as is common in the trendy "communal tables" at some restaurants). You should talk to your interviewer about how general purpose your design should be.

Step 4: Investigate Actions

At this point, you should have the basic outline of your object-oriented design. What remains is to consider the key actions that the objects will take and how they relate to each other. You may find that you have forgotten some objects, and you will need to update your design.

For example, a Party walks into the Restaurant, and a Guest requests a Table from the Host. The Host looks up the Reservation and, if it exists, assigns the Party to a Table. Otherwise, the Party is added to the end of the list. When a Party leaves, the Table is freed and assigned to a new Party in the list.

Design Patterns

Because interviewers are trying to test your capabilities and not your knowledge, design patterns are mostly beyond the scope of an interview. However, the Singleton and Factory Method design patterns are especially useful for interviews, so we will cover them here.

There are far more design patterns than this book could possibly discuss. A fantastic way to improve your software engineering skills is to pick up a book that focuses on this area specifically.

Singleton Class

The Singleton pattern ensures that a class has only one instance and ensures access to the instance through the application. It can be useful in cases where you have a "global" object with exactly one instance. For example, we may want to implement Restaurant such that it has exactly one instance of Restaurant.

```
1   public class Restaurant {
2       private static Restaurant _instance = null;
3       public static Restaurant getInstance() {
4           if (_instance == null) {
5               _instance = new Restaurant();
6           }
7           return _instance;
8       }
9   }
```

Factory Method

The Factory Method offers an interface for creating an instance of a class, with its subclasses deciding which class to instantiate. You might want to implement this with the creator class being abstract and not providing an implementation for the Factory method. Or, you could have the Creator class be a concrete class that provides an implementation for the Factory method. In this case, the Factory method would take a parameter representing which class to instantiate.

```
1   public class CardGame {
2       public static CardGame createCardGame(GameType type) {
3           if (type == GameType.Poker) {
4               return new PokerGame();
5           } else if (type == GameType.BlackJack) {
6               return new BlackJackGame();
7           }
8           return null;
9       }
10  }
```

Interview Questions

8.1   Design the data structures for a generic deck of cards. Explain how you would subclass the data structures to implement blackjack.

pg 280

8.2 Imagine you have a call center with three levels of employees: respondent, manager, and director. An incoming telephone call must be first allocated to a respondent who is free. If the respondent can't handle the call, he or she must escalate the call to a manager. If the manager is not free or not able to handle it, then the call should be escalated to a director. Design the classes and data structures for this problem. Implement a method dispatchCall() which assigns a call to the first available employee.

8.3 Design a musical jukebox using object-oriented principles.

8.4 Design a parking lot using object-oriented principles.

8.5 Design the data structures for an online book reader system.

8.6 Implement a jigsaw puzzle. Design the data structures and explain an algorithm to solve the puzzle. You can assume that you have a fitsWith method which, when passed two puzzle pieces, returns true if the two pieces belong together.

8.7 Explain how you would design a chat server. In particular, provide details about the various backend components, classes, and methods. What would be the hardest problems to solve?

8.8 Othello is played as follows: Each Othello piece is white on one side and black on the other. When a piece is surrounded by its opponents on both the left and right sides, or both the top and bottom, it is said to be captured and its color is flipped. On your turn, you must capture at least one of your opponent's pieces. The game ends when either user has no more valid moves. The win is assigned to the person with the most pieces. Implement the object-oriented design for Othello.

8.9 Explain the data structures and algorithms that you would use to design an in-memory file system. Illustrate with an example in code where possible.

8.10 Design and implement a hash table which uses chaining (linked lists) to handle collisions.

Additional Questions: Threads and Locks (#16.3)

9

Recursion and Dynamic Programming

While there is a wide variety of recursive problems, many follow similar patterns. A good hint that a problem is recursive is that it can be built off sub-problems.

When you hear a problem beginning with the following statements, it's often (though not always) a good candidate for recursion: "Design an algorithm to compute the nth ..."; "Write code to list the first n..."; "Implement a method to compute all..."; etc..

Practice makes perfect! The more problems you do, the easier it will be to recognize recursive problems.

How to Approach

Recursive solutions, by definition, are built off solutions to sub-problems. Many times, this will mean simply to compute f(n) by adding something, removing something, or otherwise changing the solution for f(n-1). In other cases, you might have to do something more complicated.

You should consider both bottom-up and top-down recursive solutions. The Base Case and Build approach works quite well for recursive problems.

Bottom-Up Recursion

Bottom-up recursion is often the most intuitive. We start with knowing how to solve the problem for a simple case, like a list with only one element, and figure out how to solve the problem for two elements, then for three elements, and so on. The key here is to think about how you can *build* the solution for one case off of the previous case.

Top-Down Recursion

Top-Down Recursion can be more complex, but it's sometimes necessary for problems. In these problems, we think about how we can divide the problem for case N into sub-problems. Be careful of overlap between the cases.

Dynamic Programming

Dynamic programming (DP) problems are rarely asked because, quite simply, they're too difficult for a 45-minute interview. Even good candidates would generally do so poorly on these problems that it's not a good evaluation technique.

If you're unlucky enough to get a DP problem, you can approach it much the same way as a recursion problem. The difference is that intermediate results are "cached" for future calls.

Simple Example of Dynamic Programming: Fibonacci Numbers

As a very simple example of dynamic programming, imagine you're asked to implement a program to generate the nth Fibonacci number. Sounds simple, right?

```
1   int fibonacci(int i) {
2       if (i == 0) return 0;
3       if (i == 1) return 1;
4       return fibonacci(i - 1) + fibonacci(i - 2);
5   }
```

What is the runtime of this function? Computing the nth Fibonacci number depends on the previous n-1 numbers. But *each* call does two recursive calls. This means that the runtime is $O(2^n)$. The below graph shows this exponential increase, as computed on a standard desktop computer.

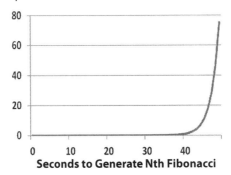

Seconds to Generate Nth Fibonacci

With just a small modification, we can tweak this function to run in $O(N)$ time. We simply "cache" the results of fibonacci(i) between calls.

```
1   int[] fib = new int[max];
2   int fibonacci(int i) {
3       if (i == 0) return 0;
4       if (i == 1) return 1;
5       if (fib[i] != 0) return fib[i]; // Return cached result.
6       fib[i] = fibonacci(i - 1) + fibonacci(i - 2); // Cache result
7       return fib[i];
8   }
```

While the first recursive one may take over a minute to generate the 50th Fibonacci number on a standard computer, the dynamic programming method can generate the

10,000th Fibonacci number in just fractions of a millisecond. (Of course, with this exact code, the int would have overflowed very early on.)

Dynamic programming, as you can see, is nothing to be scared of. It's little more than recursion where you cache the results. A good way to approach such a problem is often to implement it as a normal recursive solution, and then to add the caching part.

Recursive vs. Iterative Solutions

Recursive algorithms can be very space inefficient. Each recursive call adds a new layer to the stack, which means that if your algorithm has O(n) recursive calls, then it uses O(n) memory. Ouch!

All recursive code can be implemented iteratively, although sometimes the code to do so is much more complex. Before diving into recursive code, ask yourself how hard it would be to implement it iteratively, and discuss the trade-offs with your interviewer.

Interview Questions

9.1   A child is running up a staircase with n steps, and can hop either 1 step, 2 steps, or 3 steps at a time. Implement a method to count how many possible ways the child can run up the stairs.

pg 316

9.2   Imagine a robot sitting on the upper left corner of an X by Y grid. The robot can only move in two directions: right and down. How many possible paths are there for the robot to go from (0,0) to (X,Y)?

FOLLOW UP

Imagine certain spots are "off limits," such that the robot cannot step on them. Design an algorithm to find a path for the robot from the top left to the bottom right.

pg 317

9.3   A magic index in an array A[0...n-1] is defined to be an index such that A[i] = i. Given a sorted array, write a method to find a magic index, if one exists, in array A.

FOLLOW UP

What if the values are not distinct?

pg 319

9.4   Write a method to return all subsets of a set.

pg 321

9.5   Write a method to compute all permutations of a string.

pg 324

9.6 Implement an algorithm to print all valid (e.g., properly opened and closed) combinations of n-pairs of parentheses.

EXAMPLE

Input: 3

Output: $((()))$, $(()())$, $(())()$, $()(())$, $()()()$

pg 325

9.7 Implement the "paint fill" function that one might see on many image editing programs. That is, given a screen (represented by a two-dimensional array of colors), a point, and a new color, fill in the surrounding area until the color changes from the original color.

pg 328

9.8 Given an infinite number of quarters (25 cents), dimes (10 cents), nickels (5 cents) and pennies (1 cent), write code to calculate the number of ways of representing n cents.

pg 329

9.9 Write an algorithm to print all ways of arranging eight queens on an 8x8 chess board so that none of them share the same row, column or diagonal. In this case, "diagonal" means all diagonals, not just the two that bisect the board.

pg 331

9.10 You have a stack of n boxes, with widths w_i, heights h_i, and depths d_i. The boxes cannot be rotated and can only be stacked on top of one another if each box in the stack is strictly larger than the box above it in width, height, and depth. Implement a method to build the tallest stack possible, where the height of a stack is the sum of the heights of each box.

pg 333

9.11 Given a boolean expression consisting of the symbols 0, 1, &, |, and ^, and a desired boolean result value `result`, implement a function to count the number of ways of parenthesizing the expression such that it evaluates to `result`.

EXAMPLE

Expression: `1^0|0|1`

Desired result: `false (0)`

Output: 2 ways. `1^((0|0)|1)` and `1^(0|(0|1))`.

pg 335

Additional Questions: Linked Lists (#2.2, #2.5, #2.7), Stacks and Queues (#3.3), Trees and Graphs (#4.1, #4.3, #4.4, #4.5, #4.7, #4.8, #4.9), Bit Manipulation (#5.7), Brain Teasers (#6.4), Sorting and Searching (#11.5, #11.6, #11.7, #11.8), C++ (#13.7), Moderate (#17.13, #17.14), Hard (#18.4, #18.7, #18.12, #18.13)

10

Scalability and Memory Limits

Despite how intimidating they seem, scalability questions can be among the easiest questions. There are no "gotchas," no tricks, and no fancy algorithms—at least not usually. You don't need any courses in distributed systems, nor do you need any experience in system design. With a bit of practice, any thorough and intelligent software engineer can handle these questions with ease.

The Step-By-Step Approach

Interviewers are not trying to test your knowledge of system design; in fact, interviewers rarely try to test knowledge of anything but the most basic Computer Science concepts. Instead, they are evaluating your ability to break down a tricky problem and to solve problems using what you do know. The following approach works well for many system design problems.

Step 1: Make Believe

Pretend that the data can all fit on one machine and there are no memory limitations. How would you solve the problem? This answer to this question will provide the general outline for your solution.

Step 2: Get Real

Now, go back to the original problem. How much data can you fit on one machine, and what problems will occur when you split the data up? Common problems include figuring out how to logically divide the data up, and how one machine would identify where to look up a different piece of data.

Step 3: Solve Problems

Finally, think about how to solve the issues you identified in Step 2. Remember that the solution for each issue might be to actually remove the issue entirely, or it might be to simply mitigate the issue. Usually, you can continue to use (with modifications) the approach you outlined in Step 1, but occasionally you will need to fundamentally alter the approach.

Note that an iterative approach is typically useful. That is, once you have solved the problems from Step 2, new problems may have emerged, and you must tackle those as well.

Your goal is not to re-architect a complex system that companies have spent millions of dollars building, but rather, to demonstrate that you can analyze and solve problems. Poking holes in your own solution is a fantastic way to demonstrate this.

What You Need to Know: Information, Strategies and Issues

A Typical System

Though super-computers are still in use, most web-based companies use large systems of interconnected machines. You can almost always assume that you will be working in such a system.

Prior to your interview, you should fill in the following chart. This chart will help you to ballpark how much data a computer can store.

Component	Typical Capacity / Value
Hard Drive Space	
Memory	
Internet Transfer Latency	

Dividing Up Lots of Data

Though we can sometimes increase hard drive space in a computer, there comes a point where data simply must be divided up across machines. The question, then, is what data belongs on which machine? There are a few strategies for this.

- *By Order of Appearance:*

  We could simply divide up data by order of appearance. That is, as new data comes in, we wait for our current machine to fill up before adding an additional machine. This has the advantage of never using more machines than are necessary. However, depending on the problem and our data set, our lookup table may be more complex and potentially very large.

- *By Hash Value:*

  An alternative approach is to store the data on the machine corresponding to the hash value of the data. More specifically, we do the following: (1) pick some sort of *key* relating to the data, (2) hash the key, (3) mod the hash value by the number of machines, and (4) store the data on the machine with that value. That is, the data is stored on machine #[mod(hash(key), N)].

  The nice thing about this is that there's no need for a lookup table. Every machine will automatically know where a piece of data is. The problem, however, is that a machine may get more data and eventually exceed its capacity. In this case, we may need to either shift data around the other machines for better load balancing (which is very expensive), or split this machine's data into two machines (causing a tree-like structure of machines).

- *By Actual Value:*

  Dividing up data by hash value is essentially arbitrary; there is no relationship between what the data represents and which machine stores the data. In some cases, we may be able to reduce system latency by using information about what the data represents.

  For example, suppose you're designing a social network. While people do have friends around the world, the reality is that someone living in Mexico will probably have a lot more friends from Mexico than an average Russian citizen. We could, perhaps, store "similar" data on the same machine so that looking up the Mexican person's friends requires fewer machine hops.

- *Arbitrarily:*

  Frequently, data just gets arbitrarily broken up and we implement a lookup table to identify which machine holds a piece of data. While this does necessitate a potentially large lookup table, it simplifies some aspects of system design and can enable us to do better load balancing.

Example: Find all documents that contain a list of words

Given a list of millions of documents, how would you find all documents that contain a list of words? The words do not need to appear in any particular order, but they must be complete words. That is, "book" does not match "bookkeeper."

Before we start solving the problem, we need to understand whether this is a one time only operation, or if this findWords procedure will be called repeatedly. Let's assume that we will be calling findWords many times for the same set of documents, and we can therefore accept the burden of pre-processing.

Step 1

The first step is to forget about the millions of documents and pretend we just had a few dozen documents. How would we implement findWords in this case? (Tip: stop here and try to solve this yourself, before reading on.)

One way to do this is to pre-process each document and create a hash table index. This hash table would map from a word to a list of the documents that contain that word.

```
"books" -> {doc2, doc3, doc6, doc8}
"many"  -> {doc1, doc3, doc7, doc8, doc9}
```

To search for "many books," we would simply do an intersection on the values for "books" and "many", and return {doc3, doc8} as the result.

Step 2

Now, go back to the original problem. What problems are introduced with millions of documents? For starters, we probably need to divide up the documents across many machines. Also, depending on a variety of factors, such as the number of possible words and the repetition of words in a document, we may not be able to fit the full hash table on one machine. Let's assume that this is the case.

This division introduces the following key concerns:

1. How will we divide up our hash table? We could divide it up by keyword, such that a given machine contains the full document list for a given word. Or, we could divide by document, such that a machine contains the keyword mapping for only a subset of the documents.

2. Once we decide how to divide up the data, we may need to process a document on one machine and push the results off to other machines. What does this process look like? (Note: if we divide the hash table by document, this step may not be necessary.)

3. We will need a way to knowing which machine holds a piece of data. What does this lookup table look like, and where is it stored?

These are just three concerns. There may be many others.

Step 3

In step 3, we find solutions to each of these issues. One solution is to divide up the words alphabetically by keyword, such that each machine controls a range of words (e.g., "after" through "apple").

We can implement a simple algorithm in which we iterate through the keywords alphabetically, storing as much data as possible on one machine. When that machine is full, we will move to the next machine.

The advantage of this approach is that the lookup table is small and simple (since it must only specify a range of values), and each machine can store a copy of the lookup table. The disadvantage, however, is that if new documents or words are added, we may need to perform an expensive shift of keywords.

To find all the documents that match a list of strings, we would first sort the list and then send each machine a lookup request for the strings that the machine owns. For example, if our string is "after builds boat amaze banana", machine 1 would get a lookup request for {"after", "amaze"}.

Machine 1 would look up the documents containing "after" and "amaze," and perform an intersection on these document lists. Machine 3 would do the same for {"banana", "boat", "builds"}, and intersect their lists.

In the final step, the initial machine would do an intersection on the results from Machine 1 and Machine 3.

The following diagram explains this process.

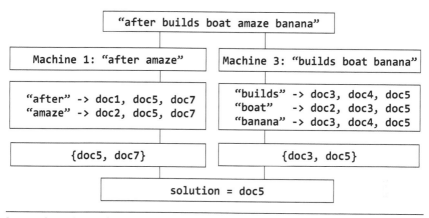

Interview Questions

10.1 Imagine you are building some sort of service that will be called by up to 1000 client applications to get simple end-of-day stock price information (open, close, high, low). You may assume that you already have the data, and you can store it in any format you wish. How would you design the client-facing service which provides the information to client applications? You are responsible for the development, rollout, and ongoing monitoring and maintenance of the feed. Describe the different methods you considered and why you would recommend your approach. Your service can use any technologies you wish, and can distribute the information to the client applications in any mechanism you choose.

pg 342

10.2 How would you design the data structures for a very large social network like Facebook or LinkedIn? Describe how you would design an algorithm to show the connection, or path, between two people (e.g., Me -> Bob -> Susan -> Jason -> You).

pg 344

10.3 Given an input file with four billion non-negative integers, provide an algorithm to generate an integer which is not contained in the file. Assume you have 1 GB of memory available for this task.

FOLLOW UP

What if you have only 10 MB of memory? Assume that all the values are distinct.

pg 347

10.4 You have an array with all the numbers from 1 to N, where N is at most 32,000. The array may have duplicate entries and you do not know what N is. With only 4 kilobytes of memory available, how would you print all duplicate elements in the array?

pg 350

10.5 If you were designing a web crawler, how would you avoid getting into infinite loops?

pg 351

10.6 You have 10 billion URLs. How do you detect the duplicate documents? In this case, assume that "duplicate" means that the URLs are identical.

pg 353

10.7 Imagine a web server for a simplified search engine. This system has 100 machines to respond to search queries, which may then call out using processSearch(string query) to another cluster of machines to actu-ally get the result. The machine which responds to a given query is chosen at random, so you can not guarantee that the same machine will always respond to the same request. The method processSearch is very expensive. Design a caching mechanism for the most recent queries. Be sure to explain how you would update the cache when data changes.

pg 354

Additional Questions: Object-Oriented Design (#8.7)

11

Sorting and Searching

Understanding the common sorting and searching algorithms is incredibly valuable, as many of sorting and searching problems are tweaks of the well-known algorithms. A good approach is therefore to run through the different sorting algorithms and see if one applies particularly well.

For example, suppose you are asked the following question: Given a very large array of Person objects, sort the people in increasing order of age.

We're given two interesting bits of knowledge here:

1. It's a large array, so efficiency is very important.

2. We are sorting based on ages, so we know the values are in a small range.

By scanning through the various sorting algorithms, we might notice that bucket sort (or radix sort) would be a perfect candidate for this algorithm. In fact, we can make the buckets small (just 1 year each) and get $O(n)$ running time.

Common Sorting Algorithms

Learning (or re-learning) the common sorting algorithms is a great way to boost your performance. Of the five algorithms explained below, Merge Sort, Quick Sort and Bucket Sort are the most commonly used in interviews.

Bubble Sort | Runtime: $O(n^2)$ average and worst case. Memory: $O(1)$.

In bubble sort, we start at the beginning of the array and swap the first two elements if the first is greater than the second. Then, we go to the next pair, and so on, continuously making sweeps of the array until it is sorted.

Selection Sort | Runtime: $O(n^2)$ average and worst case. Memory: $O(1)$.

Selection sort is the child's algorithm: simple, but inefficient. Find the smallest element using a linear scan and move it to the front (swapping it with the front element). Then, find the second smallest and move it, again doing a linear scan. Continue doing this until all the elements are in place.

Merge Sort | Runtime: O(n Log(n)) average and worst case. Memory: Depends.

Merge sort divides the array in half, sorts each of those halves, and then merges them back together. Each of those halves has the same sorting algorithm applied to it. Eventually, you are merging just two single-element arrays. It is the "merge" part that does all the heavy lifting.

The merge method operates by copying all the elements from the target array segment into a helper array, keeping track of where the start of the left and right halves should be (`helperLeft` and `helperRight`). We then iterate through `helper`, copying the smaller element from each half into the array. At the end, we copy any remaining elements into the target array.

```
1   void mergesort(int[] array, int low, int high) {
2       if (low < high) {
3           int middle = (low + high) / 2;
4           mergesort(array, low, middle); // Sort left half
5           mergesort(array, middle + 1, high); // Sort right half
6           merge(array, low, middle, high); // Merge them
7       }
8   }
9
10  void merge(int[] array, int low, int middle, int high) {
11      int[] helper = new int[array.length];
12
13      /* Copy both halves into a helper array */
14      for (int i = low; i <= high; i++) {
15          helper[i] = array[i];
16      }
17
18      int helperLeft = low;
19      int helperRight = middle + 1;
20      int current = low;
21
22      /* Iterate through helper array. Compare the left and right
23       * half, copying back the smaller element from the two halves
24       * into the original array. */
25      while (helperLeft <= middle && helperRight <= high) {
26          if (helper[helperLeft] <= helper[helperRight]) {
27              array[current] = helper[helperLeft];
28              helperLeft++;
29          } else { // If right element is smaller than left element
30              array[current] = helper[helperRight];
31              helperRight++;
32          }
33          current++;
34      }
35
```

```
36    /* Copy the rest of the left side of the array into the
37     * target array */
38    int remaining = middle - helperLeft;
39    for (int i = 0; i <= remaining; i++) {
40        array[current + i] = helper[helperLeft + i];
41    }
42 }
```

You may notice that only the remaining elements from the left half of the helper array are copied into the target array. Why not the right half? The right half doesn't need to be copied because it's *already* there.

Consider, for example, an array like [1, 4, 5 || 2, 8, 9] (the "||" indicates the partition point). Prior to merging the two halves, both the helper array and the target array segment will end with [8, 9]. Once we copy over four elements (1, 4, 5, and 2) into the target array, the [8, 9] will still be in place in both arrays. There's no need to copy them over.

Quick Sort | Runtime: O(n Log(n)) average, O(n²) worst case. Memory: O(Log(n)).

In quick sort, we pick a random element and partition the array, such that all numbers that are less than the partitioning element come before all elements that are greater than it. The partitioning can be performed efficiently through a series of swaps (see below).

If we repeatedly partition the array (and its sub-arrays) around an element, the array will eventually become sorted. However, as the partitioned element is not guaranteed to be the median (or anywhere near the median), our sorting could be very slow. This is the reason for the O(n²) worst case runtime.

```
1   void quickSort(int arr[], int left, int right) {
2       int index = partition(arr, left, right);
3       if (left < index - 1) { // Sort left half
4           quickSort(arr, left, index - 1);
5       }
6       if (index < right) { // Sort right half
7           quickSort(arr, index, right);
8       }
9   }
10
11  int partition(int arr[], int left, int right) {
12      int pivot = arr[(left + right) / 2]; // Pick pivot point
13      while (left <= right) {
14          // Find element on left that should be on right
15          while (arr[left] < pivot) left++;
16
17          // Find element on right that should be on left
18          while (arr[right] > pivot) right--;
19
20          // Swap elements, and move left and right indices
```

```
21        if (left <= right) {
22            swap(arr, left, right); // swaps elements
23            left++;
24            right--;
25        }
26    }
27    return left;
28 }
29
```

Radix Sort | Runtime: O(kn) (see below)

Radix sort is a sorting algorithm for integers (and some other data types) that takes advantage of the fact that integers have a finite number of bits. In radix sort, we iterate through each digit of the number, grouping numbers by each digit. For example, if we have an array of integers, we might first sort by the first digit, so that the 0s are grouped together. Then, we sort each of these groupings by the next digit. We repeat this process sorting by each subsequent digit, until finally the whole array is sorted.

Unlike comparison sorting algorithms, which cannot perform better than O(n log(n)) in the average case, radix sort has a runtime of O(kn), where n is the number of elements and k is the number of passes of the sorting algorithm.

Searching Algorithms

When we think of searching algorithms, we generally think of binary search. Indeed, this is a very useful algorithm to study. Note that although the concept is fairly simple, getting all the details right is far more difficult than you might think. As you study the code below, pay attention to the plus ones and minus ones.

```
1  int binarySearch(int[] a, int x) {
2      int low = 0;
3      int high = a.length - 1;
4      int mid;
5
6      while (low <= high) {
7          mid = (low + high) / 2;
8          if (a[mid] < x) {
9              low = mid + 1;
10         } else if (a[mid] > x) {
11             high = mid - 1;
12         } else {
13             return mid;
14         }
15     }
16     return -1; // Error
17 }
18
19 int binarySearchRecursive(int[] a, int x, int low, int high) {
```

```
20    if (low > high) return -1; // Error
21
22    int mid = (low + high) / 2;
23    if (a[mid] < x) {
24       return binarySearchRecursive(a, x, mid + 1, high);
25    } else if (a[mid] > x) {
26       return binarySearchRecursive(a, x, low, mid - 1);
27    } else {
28       return mid;
29    }
30 }
```

Potential ways to search a data structure extend beyond binary search, and you would do best not to limit yourself to just this option. You might, for example, search for a node by leveraging a binary tree, or by using a hash table. Think beyond binary search!

Interview Questions

11.1 You are given two sorted arrays, A and B, where A has a large enough buffer at the end to hold B. Write a method to merge B into A in sorted order.

pg 360

11.2 Write a method to sort an array of strings so that all the anagrams are next to each other.

pg 361

11.3 Given a sorted array of n integers that has been rotated an unknown number of times, write code to find an element in the array. You may assume that the array was originally sorted in increasing order.

EXAMPLE

Input: find 5 in {15, 16, 19, 20, 25, 1, 3, 4, 5, 7, 10, 14}

Output: 8 (the index of 5 in the array)

pg 362

11.4 Imagine you have a 20 GB file with one string per line. Explain how you would sort the file.

pg 364

11.5 Given a sorted array of strings which is interspersed with empty strings, write a method to find the location of a given string.

EXAMPLE

Input: find "ball" in {"at", "", "", "", "ball", "", "", "car", "", "", "dad", "", ""}

Output: 4

pg 364

11.6 Given an M x N matrix in which each row and each column is sorted in ascending order, write a method to find an element.

pg 365

11.7 A circus is designing a tower routine consisting of people standing atop one another's shoulders. For practical and aesthetic reasons, each person must be both shorter and lighter than the person below him or her. Given the heights and weights of each person in the circus, write a method to compute the largest possible number of people in such a tower.

EXAMPLE:

Input (ht, wt): `(65, 100) (70, 150) (56, 90) (75, 190) (60, 95)`
`        (68, 110)`

Output: The longest tower is length 6 and includes from top to bottom:

`(56, 90) (60,95) (65,100) (68,110) (70,150) (75,190)`

pg 371

11.8 Imagine you are reading in a stream of integers. Periodically, you wish to be able to look up the rank of a number x (the number of values less than or equal to x). Implement the data structures and algorithms to support these operations. That is, implement the method `track(int x)`, which is called when each number is generated, and the method `getRankOfNumber(int x)`, which returns the number of values less than or equal to x (not including x itself).

EXAMPLE

Stream (in order of appearance): `5, 1, 4, 4, 5, 9, 7, 13, 3`
`getRankOfNumber(1) = 0`
`getRankOfNumber(3) = 1`
`getRankOfNumber(4) = 3`

pg 374

Additional Questions: Arrays and Strings (#1.3), Recursion (#9.3), Moderate (#17.6, #17.12), Hard (#18.5)

12

Testing

Before you flip past this chapter saying, "but I'm not a tester," stop and think. Testing is an important task for a software engineer, and for this reason, testing questions may come up during your interview. Of course, if you are applying for Testing roles (or Software Engineer in Test), then that's all the more reason why you need to pay attention.

Testing problems usually fall under one of four categories: (1) Test a real world object (like a pen); (2) Test a piece of software; (3) Write test code for a function; (4) Troubleshoot an existing issue. We'll cover approaches for each of these four types.

Remember that all four types require you to not make an assumption that the input or the user will play nice. Expect abuse and plan for it.

What the Interviewer Is Looking For

At their surface, testing questions seem like they're just about coming up with an extensive list of test cases. And to some extent, that's right. You do need to come up with a reasonable list of test cases.

But in addition, interviewers want to test the following:

• *Big Picture Understanding:* Are you a person who understands what the software is really about? Can you prioritize test cases properly? For example, suppose you're asked to test an e-commerce system like Amazon. It's great to make sure that the product images appear in the right place, but it's even more important that payments work reliably, products are added to the shipment queue, and customers are never double charged.

• *Knowing How the Pieces Fit Together:* Do you understand how software works, and how it might fit into a greater ecosystem? Suppose you're asked to test Google Spreadsheets. It's important that you test opening, saving, and editing documents. But, Google Spreadsheets is part of a larger ecosystem. You need to test integration with Gmail, with plug-ins, and with other components.

- *Organization:* Do you approach the problem in a structured manner, or do you just spout off anything that comes to your head? Some candidates, when asked to come up with test cases for a camera, will just state anything and everything that comes to their head. A good candidate will break down the parts into categories like Taking Photos, Image Management, Settings, and so on. This structured approach will also help you to do a more thorough job creating the test cases.

- *Practicality:* Can you actually create reasonable testing plans? For example, if a user reports that the software crashes when they open a specific image, and you just tell them to reinstall the software, that's typically not very practical. Your testing plans need to be feasible and realistic for a company to implement.

Demonstrating these aspects will show that you will be a valuable member of the testing team.

Testing a Real World Object

Some candidates are surprised to be asked questions like how to test a pen. After all, you should be testing software, right? Maybe, but these "real world" questions are still very common. Let's walk through this with an example.

Question: How would you test a paperclip?

Step 1: Who will use it? And why?

You need to discuss with your interviewer who is using the product and for what purpose. The answer may not be what you think. The answer could be "by teachers, to hold papers together," or it could be "by artists, to bend into the shape of animal." Or, it could be both. The answer to this question will shape how you handle the remaining questions.

Step 2: What are the use cases?

It will be useful for you to make a list of the use cases. In this case, the use case might be simply fastening paper together in a non-damaging (to the paper) way.

For other questions, there might be multiple use cases. It might be, for example, that the product needs to be able to send and receive content, or write and erase, and so on.

Step 3: What are the bounds of use?

The bounds of use might mean holding up to thirty sheets of paper in a single usage without permanent damage (e.g., bending), and thirty to fifty sheets with minimal permanent bending.

The bounds also extend to environmental factors as well. For example, should the paperclip work during very warm temperatures (90 - 110 degrees Fahrenheit)? What about extreme cold?

Step 4: What are the stress / failure conditions?

No product is fail-proof, so analyzing failure conditions needs to be part of your testing. A good discussion to have with your interviewer is about when it's acceptable (or even necessary) for the product to fail, and what failure should mean.

For example, if you were testing a laundry machine, you might decide that the machine should be able to handle at least 30 shirts or pants. Loading 30 - 45 pieces of clothing may result in minor failure, such as the clothing being inadequately cleaned. At more than 45 pieces of clothing, extreme failure might be acceptable. However, extreme failure in this case should probably mean the machine never turning on the water. It should certainly *not* mean a flood or a fire.

Step 5: How would you perform the testing?

In some cases, it might also be relevant to discuss the details of performing the testing. For example, if you need to make sure a chair can withstand normal usage for five years, you probably can't actually place it in a home and wait five years. Instead, you'd need to define what "normal" usage is (How many "sits" per year on the seat? What about the armrest?). Then, in addition to doing some manual testing, you would likely want a machine to automate some of the usage.

Testing a Piece of Software

Testing a piece of software is actually very similar to testing a real world object. The major difference is that software testing generally places a greater emphasis on the details of performing testing.

Note that software testing has two core aspects to it:

- *Manual vs. Automated Testing:* In an ideal world, we might love to automate everything, but that's rarely feasible. Some things are simply much better with manual testing because some features are too qualitative for a computer to effectively examine (such as if content represents pornography). Additionally, whereas a computer can generally recognize only issues that it's been told to look for, human observation may reveal new issues that haven't been specifically examined. Both humans and computers form an essential part of the testing process.

- *Black Box Testing vs. White Box Testing:* This distinction refers to the degree of access we have into the software. In black box testing, we're just given the software as-is and need to test it. With white box testing, we have additional programmatic access to test individual functions. We can also automate some black box testing, although it's certainly much harder.

Let's walk through an approach from start to end.

Step 1: Are we doing Black Box Testing or White Box Testing?

Though this question can often be delayed to a later step, I like to get it out of the way early on. Check with your interviewer as to whether you're doing black box testing or white box testing—or both.

Step 2: Who will use it? And why?

Software typically has one or more target users, and the features are designed with this in mind. For example, if you're asked to test software for parental controls on a web browser, your target users include both parents (who are implementing the blocking) and children (who are the recipients of blocking). You may also have "guests" (people who should neither be implementing nor receiving blocking).

Step 3: What are the use cases?

In the software blocking scenario, the use cases of the parents include installing the software, updating controls, removing controls, and of course their own personal internet usage. For the children, the use cases include accessing legal content as well as "illegal" content.

Remember that it's not up to you to just magically decide the use cases. This is a conversation to have with your interviewer.

Step 4: What are the bounds of use?

Now that we have the vague use cases defined, we need to figure out what exactly this means. What does it mean for a website to be blocked? Should just the "illegal" page be blocked, or the entire website? Is the application supposed to "learn" what is bad content, or is it based on a white list or black list? If it's supposed to learn what inappropriate content is, what degree of false positives or false negatives is acceptable?

Step 5: What are the stress conditions / failure conditions?

When the software fails—which it inevitably will—what should the failure look like? Clearly, the software failure shouldn't crash the computer. Instead, it's likely that the software should just permit a blocked site, or ban an allowable site. In the latter case, you might want to discuss the possibility of a selective override with a password from the parents.

Step 6: What are the test cases? How would you perform the testing?

Here is where the distinctions between manual and automated testing, and between black box and white box testing, really come into play.

Steps 3 and 4 should have roughly defined the use cases. In step 6, we further define them and discuss how to perform the testing. What exact situations are you testing? Which of these steps can be automated? Which require human intervention?

Remember that while automation allows you to do some very powerful testing, it also has some significant drawbacks. Manual testing should usually be part of your test procedures.

When you go through this list, don't just rattle off every scenario you can think of. It's disorganized, and you're sure to miss major categories. Instead, approach this in a structured manner. Break down your testing into the main components, and go from there. Not only will you give a more complete list of test cases, but you'll also show that you're a structured, methodical person.

Testing a Function

In many ways, testing a function is the easiest type of testing. The conversation is typically briefer and less vague, as the testing is usually limited to validating input and output.

However, don't overlook the value of some conversation with your interviewer. You should discuss any assumptions with your interviewer, particularly with respect to how to handle specific situations.

Suppose you were asked to write code to test sort(int[] array), which sorts an array of integers. You might proceed as follows.

Step 1: Define the test cases

In general, you should think about the following types of test cases:

- *The normal case:* Does it generate the correct output for typical inputs? Remember to think about potential issues here. For example, because sorting often requires some sort of partitioning, it's reasonable to think that the algorithm might fail on arrays with an odd number of elements, since they can't be evenly partitioned. Your test case should list both examples.

- *The extremes:* What happens when you pass in an empty array? Or a very small (one element) array? What if you pass in a very large one?

- *Nulls and "illegal" input:* It is worthwhile to think about how the code should behave when given illegal input. For example, if you're testing a function to generate the nth Fibonacci number, your test cases should probably include the situation where n is negative.

- *Strange input:* A fourth kind of input sometimes comes up: strange input. What happens when you pass in an already sorted array? Or an array that's sorted in reverse order?

Generating these tests does require knowledge of the function you are writing. If you are unclear as to the constraints, you will need to ask your interviewer about this first.

Step 2: Define the expected result

Often, the expected result is obvious: the right output. However, in some cases, you might want to validate additional aspects. For instance, if the sort method returns a new sorted copy of the array, you should probably validate that the original array has not been touched.

Step 3: Write test code

Once you have the test cases and results defined, writing the code to implement the test cases should be fairly straightforward. Your code might look something like:

```
1   void testAddThreeSorted() {
2       MyList list = new MyList();
3       list.addThreeSorted(3, 1, 2); // Adds 3 items in sorted order
4       assertEquals(list.getElement(0), 1);
5       assertEquals(list.getElement(1), 2);
6       assertEquals(list.getElement(2), 3);
7   }
```

Troubleshooting Questions

A final type of question is explaining how you would debug or troubleshoot an existing issue. Many candidates balk at a question like this, given unrealistic answers like "reinstall the software." You can approach these questions in a structured manner, like anything else.

Let's walk through this problem with an example: You're working on the Google Chrome team when you receive a bug report: Chrome crashes on launch. What would you do?

Reinstalling the browser might solve this user's problem, but it wouldn't help the other users who might be experiencing the same issue. Your goal is to understand what's *really* happening, so that the developers can fix it.

Step 1: Understand the Scenario

The first thing you should do is ask questions to understand as much about the situation as possible.

- How long has the user been experiencing this issue?
- What version of the browser is it? What operating system?
- Does the issue happen consistently, or how often does it happen? When does it happen?
- Is there an error report that launches?

Step 2: Break Down the Problem

Now that you understand the details of the scenario, you want to break down the problem into testable units. In this case, you can imagine the flow of the situation as follows:

1. Go to Windows Start menu.
2. Click on Chrome icon.

3. Browser instance starts.

4. Browser loads settings.

5. Browser issues HTTP request for homepage.

6. Browser gets HTTP response.

7. Browser parses webpage.

8. Browser displays content.

At some point in this process, something fails and it causes the browser to crash. A strong tester would iterate through the elements of this scenario to diagnose the problem.

Step 3: Create Specific, Manageable Tests

Each of the above components should have realistic instructions—things that you can ask the user to do, or things that you can do yourself (such as replicating steps on your own machine). In the real world, you will be dealing with customers, and you can't give them instructions that they can't or won't do.

Interview Questions

12.1 Find the mistake(s) in the following code:

```
1  unsigned int i;
2  for (i = 100; i >= 0; --i)
3    printf("%d\n", i);
```

pg 378

12.2 You are given the source to an application which crashes when it is run. After running it ten times in a debugger, you find it never crashes in the same place. The application is single threaded, and uses only the C standard library. What programming errors could be causing this crash? How would you test each one?

pg 378

12.3 We have the following method used in a chess game: `boolean canMoveTo(int x, int y)`. This method is part of the `Piece` class and returns whether or not the piece can move to position (`x`, `y`). Explain how you would test this method.

pg 379

12.4 How would you load test a webpage without using any test tools?

pg 380

12.5 How would you test a pen?

pg 381

12.6 How would you test an ATM in a distributed banking system?

pg 382

Knowledge Based

Interview Questions and Advice

13

C and C++

A good interviewer won't demand that you code in a language you don't profess to know. Hopefully, if you're asked to code in C++, it's listed on your resume. If you don't remember all the APIs, don't worry—most interviewers (though not all) don't care that much. We do recommend, however, studying up on basic C++ syntax so that you can approach these questions with ease.

Classes and Inheritance

Though C++ classes have similar characteristics to those of other languages, we'll review some of the syntax below.

The code below demonstrates the implementation of a basic class with inheritance.

```
1   #include <iostream>
2   using namespace std;
3
4   #define NAME_SIZE 50 // Defines a macro
5
6   class Person {
7      int id; // all members are private by default
8      char name[NAME_SIZE];
9
10  public:
11     void aboutMe() {
12        cout << "I am a person.";
13     }
14  };
15
16  class Student : public Person {
17   public:
18     void aboutMe() {
19        cout << "I am a student.";
20     }
21  };
22
```

```
23  int main() {
24      Student * p = new Student();
25      p->aboutMe(); // prints "I am a student."
26      delete p; // Important! Make sure to delete allocated memory.
27      return 0;
28  }
```

All data members and methods are private by default in C++. One can modify this by introducing the keyword `public`.

Constructors and Destructors

The constructor of a class is automatically called upon an object's creation. If no constructor is defined, the compiler automatically generates one called the Default Constructor. Alternatively, we can define our own constructor.

```
1   Person(int a) {
2       id = a;
3   }
```

Fields within the class can also be initialized as follows:

```
1   Person(int a) : id(a) {
2       ...
3   }
```

The data member `id` is assigned before the actual object is created and before the remainder of the constructor code is called. It is particularly useful when we have constant fields that can only be assigned a value once.

The destructor cleans up upon object deletion and is automatically called when an object is destroyed. It cannot take an argument as we don't explicitly call a destructor.

```
1   ~Person() {
2       delete obj; // free any memory allocated within class
3   }
```

Virtual Functions

In an earlier example, we defined p to be of type `Student`:

```
1   Student * p = new Student();
2   p->aboutMe();
```

What would happen if we defined p to be a `Person*`, like so?

```
1   Person * p = new Student();
2   p->aboutMe();
```

In this case, "I am a person" would be printed instead. This is because the function aboutMe is resolved at compile-time, in a mechanism known as *static binding*.

If we want to ensure that the `Student`'s implementation of aboutMe is called, we can define aboutMe in the `Person` class to be `virtual`.

```
1   class Person {
```

```
2      ...
3      virtual void aboutMe() {
4          cout << "I am a person.";
5      }
6   };
7
8   class Student : public Person {
9    public:
10     void aboutMe() {
11         cout << "I am a student.";
12     }
13  };
```

Another usage for virtual functions is when we can't (or don't want to) implement a method for the parent class. Imagine, for example, that we want Student and Teacher to inherit from Person so that we can implement a common method such as addCourse(string s). Calling addCourse on Person, however, wouldn't make much sense since the implementation depends on whether the object is actually a Student or Teacher.

In this case, we might want addCourse to be a virtual function defined within Person, with the implementation being left to the subclass.

```
1   class Person {
2       int id; // all members are private by default
3       char name[NAME_SIZE];
4     public:
5       virtual void aboutMe() {
6           cout << "I am a person." << endl;
7       }
8       virtual bool addCourse(string s) = 0;
9   };
10
11  class Student : public Person {
12    public:
13      void aboutMe() {
14          cout << "I am a student." << endl;
15      }
16
17      bool addCourse(string s) {
18          cout << "Added course " << s << " to student." << endl;
19          return true;
20      }
21  };
22
23  int main() {
24      Person * p = new Student();
25      p->aboutMe(); // prints "I am a student."
26      p->addCourse("History");
27      delete p;
```

```
28  }
```

Note that by defining addCourse to be a "pure virtual function," Person is now an abstract class and we cannot instantiate it.

Virtual Destructor

The virtual function naturally introduces the concept of a "virtual destructor." Suppose we wanted to implement a destructor method for Person and Student. A naive solution might look like this:

```
1   class Person {
2     public:
3       ~Person() {
4         cout << "Deleting a person." << endl;
5       }
6   };
7
8   class Student : public Person {
9     public:
10      ~Student() {
11        cout << "Deleting a student." << endl;
12      }
13  };
14
15  int main() {
16    Person * p = new Student();
17    delete p; // prints "Deleting a person."
18  }
```

As in the earlier example, since p is a Person, the destructor for the Person class is called. This is problematic because the memory for Student may not be cleaned up.

To fix this, we simply define the destructor for Person to be virtual.

```
1   class Person {
2     public:
3       virtual ~Person() {
4         cout << "Deleting a person." << endl;
5       }
6   };
7
8   class Student : public Person {
9     public:
10      ~Student() {
11        cout << "Deleting a student." << endl;
12      }
13  };
14
15  int main() {
16    Person * p = new Student();
17    delete p;
```

```
18  }
```

This will output the following:

```
Deleting a student.
Deleting a person.
```

Default Values

Functions can specify default values, as shown below. Note that all default parameters must be on the right side of the function declaration, as there would be no other way to specify how the parameters line up.

```
1   int func(int a, int b = 3) {
2       x = a;
3       y = b;
4       return a + b;
5   }
6
7   w = func(4);
8   z = func(4, 5);
```

Operator Overloading

Operator overloading enables us to apply operators like + to objects that would otherwise not support these operations. For example, if we wanted to merge two Book-Shelves into one, we could overload the + operator as follows.

```
1   BookShelf BookShelf::operator+(BookShelf &other) { ... }
```

Pointers and References

A pointer holds the address of a variable and can be used to perform any operation that could be directly done on the variable, such as accessing and modifying it.

Two pointers can equal each other, such that changing one's value also changes the other's value (since they, in fact, point to the same address).

```
1   int * p = new int;
2   *p = 7;
3   int * q = p;
4   *p = 8;
5   cout << *q; // prints 8
```

Note that the size of a pointer varies depending on the architecture: 32 bits on a 32-bit machine and 64 bits on a 64-bit machine. Pay attention to this difference, as it's common for interviewers to ask exactly how much space a data structure takes up.

References

A reference is another name (an alias) for a pre-existing object and it does not have memory of its own. For example:

```
1   int a = 5;
```

```
2    int & b = a;
3    b = 7;
4    cout << a; // prints 7
```

In line 2 above, b is a reference to a; modifying b will also modify a.

You cannot create a reference without specifying where in memory it refers to. However, you can create a free-standing reference as shown below:

```
1    /* allocates memory to store 12 and makes b a reference to this
2     * piece of memory. */
3    int & b = 12;
```

Unlike pointers, references cannot be null and cannot be reassigned to another piece of memory.

Pointer Arithmetic

One will often see programmers perform addition on a pointer, such as what you see below:

```
1    int * p = new int[2];
2    p[0] = 0;
3    p[1] = 1;
4    p++;
5    cout << *p; // Outputs 1
```

Performing p++ will skip ahead by sizeof(int) bytes, such that the code outputs 1. Had p been of different type, it would skip ahead as many bytes as the size of the data structure.

Templates

Templates are a way of reusing code to apply the same class to different data types. For example, we might have a list-like data structure which we would like to use for lists of various types. The code below implements this with the ShiftedList class.

```
1    template <class T>
2    class ShiftedList {
3        T* array;
4        int offset, size;
5      public:
6        ShiftedList(int sz) : offset(0), size(sz) {
7           array = new T[size];
8        }
9
10       ~ShiftedList() {
11          delete [] array;
12       }
13
14       void shiftBy(int n) {
15          offset = (offset + n) % size;
16       }
```

```
17
18      T getAt(int i) {
19          return array[convertIndex(i)];
20      }
21
22      void setAt(T item, int i) {
23          array[convertIndex(i)] = item;
24      }
25
26   private:
27      int convertIndex(int i) {
28          int index = (i - offset) % size;
29          while (index < 0) index += size;
30          return index;
31      }
32   };
33
34   int main() {
35      int size = 4;
36      ShiftedList<int> * list = new ShiftedList<int>(size);
37      for (int i = 0; i < size; i++) {
38          list->setAt(i, i);
39      }
40      cout << list->getAt(0) << endl;
41      cout << list->getAt(1) << endl;
42      list->shiftBy(1);
43      cout << list->getAt(0) << endl;
44      cout << list->getAt(1) << endl;
45      delete list;
46   }
```

Interview Questions

13.1 Write a method to print the last K lines of an input file using C++.

pg 386

13.2 Compare and contrast a hash table and an STL map. How is a hash table implemented? If the number of inputs is small, which data structure options can be used instead of a hash table?

pg 387

13.3 How do virtual functions work in C++?

pg 388

13.4 What is the difference between deep copy and shallow copy? Explain how you would use each.

pg 389

13.5 What is the significance of the keyword "volatile" in C?

pg 389

13.6 Why does a destructor in base class need to be declared `virtual`?

pg 391

13.7 Write a method that takes a pointer to a Node structure as a parameter and returns a complete copy of the passed in data structure. The Node data structure contains two pointers to other Nodes.

pg 391

13.8 Write a smart pointer class. A smart pointer is a data type, usually implemented with templates, that simulates a pointer while also providing automatic garbage collection. It automatically counts the number of references to a `SmartPointer<T*>` object and frees the object of type T when the reference count hits zero.

pg 392

13.9 Write an aligned malloc and free function that supports allocating memory such that the memory address returned is divisible by a specific power of two.

EXAMPLE

`align_malloc(1000,128)` will return a memory address that is a multiple of 128 and that points to memory of size 1000 bytes.

`aligned_free()` will free memory allocated by `align_malloc`.

pg 395

13.10 Write a function in C called `my2DAlloc` which allocates a two-dimensional array. Minimize the number of calls to `malloc` and make sure that the memory is accessible by the notation `arr[i][j]`.

pg 396

Additional Questions: Arrays and Strings (#1.2), Linked Lists (#2.7), Testing (#12.1), Java (#14.4), Threads and Locks (#16.3)

14

Java

While Java-related questions are found throughout this book, this chapter deals with questions about the language and syntax. Such questions are more unusual at bigger companies, which believe more in testing a candidate's aptitude than a candidate's knowledge (and which have the time and resources to train a candidate in a particular language). However, at other companies, these pesky questions can be quite common.

How to Approach

As these questions focus so much on knowledge, it may seem silly to talk about an approach to these problems. After all, isn't it just about knowing the right answer?

Yes and no. Of course, the best thing you can do to master these questions is to learn Java inside and out. But, if you do get stumped, you can try to tackle it with the following approach:

1. Create an example of the scenario, and ask yourself how things should play out.

2. Ask yourself how other languages would handle this scenario.

3. Consider how you would design this situation if you were the language designer. What would the implications of each choice be?

Your interviewer may be equally—or more—impressed if you can derive the answer than if you automatically knew it. Don't try to bluff though. Tell the interviewer, "I'm not sure I can recall the answer, but let me see if I can figure it out. Suppose we have this code…"

final keyword

The final keyword in Java has a different meaning depending on whether it is applied to a variable, class or method.

- *Variable:* The value cannot be changed once initialized.
- *Method:* The method cannot be overridden by a subclass.
- *Class:* The class cannot be subclassed.

finally keyword

The `finally` keyword is used in association with a `try/catch` block and guarantees that a section of code will be executed, even if an exception is thrown. The `finally` block will be executed after the `try` and `catch` blocks, but before control transfers back to its origin.

Watch how this plays out in the example below.

```
1   public static String lem() {
2       System.out.println("lem");
3       return "return from lem";
4   }
5
6   public static String foo() {
7       int x = 0;
8       int y = 5;
9       try {
10        System.out.println("start try");
11        int b = y / x;
12        System.out.println("end try");
13        return "returned from try";
14      } catch (Exception ex) {
15        System.out.println("catch");
16        return lem() + " | returned from catch";
17      } finally {
18        System.out.println("finally");
19      }
20  }
21
22  public static void bar() {
23      System.out.println("start bar");
24      String v = foo();
25      System.out.println(v);
26      System.out.println("end bar");
27  }
28
29  public static void main(String[] args) {
30      bar();
31  }
```

The output for this code is the following:

```
1   start bar
2   start try
3   catch
```

```
4   lem
5   finally
6   return from lem | returned from catch
7   end bar
```

Look carefully at lines 3 to 5 in the output. The `catch` block is fully executed (including the function call in the `return` statement), then the `finally` block, and then the function actually returns.

finalize method

The automatic garbage collector calls the `finalize()` method just before actually destroying the object. A class can therefore override the `finalize()` method from the `Object` class in order to define custom behavior during garbage collection.

```
1   protected void finalize() throws Throwable {
2       /* Close open files, release resources, etc */
3   }
```

Overloading vs. Overriding

Overloading is a term used to describe when two methods have the same name but differ in the type or number of arguments.

```
1   public double computeArea(Circle c) { ... }
2   public double computeArea(Square s) { ... }
```

Overriding, however, occurs when a method shares the same name and function signature as another method in its super class.

```
1   public abstract class Shape {
2       public void printMe() {
3           System.out.println("I am a shape.");
4       }
5       public abstract double computeArea();
6   }
7
8   public class Circle extends Shape {
9       private double rad = 5;
10      public void printMe() {
11          System.out.println("I am a circle.");
12      }
13
14      public double computeArea() {
15          return rad * rad * 3.15;
16      }
17  }
18
19  public class Ambiguous extends Shape {
20      private double area = 10;
21      public double computeArea() {
22          return area;
```

```
23    }
24 }
25
26 public class IntroductionOverriding {
27    public static void main(String[] args) {
28        Shape[] shapes = new Shape[2];
29        Circle circle = new Circle();
30        Ambiguous ambiguous = new Ambiguous();
31
32        shapes[0] = circle;
33        shapes[1] = ambiguous;
34
35        for (Shape s : shapes) {
36            s.printMe();
37            System.out.println(s.computeArea());
38        }
39    }
40 }
```

The above code will print:

```
1    I am a circle.
2    78.75
3    I am a shape.
4    10.0
```

Observe that `Circle` overrode `printMe()`, whereas `Ambiguous` just left this method as-is.

Collection Framework

Java's collection framework is incredibly useful, and you will see it used throughout this book. Here are some of the most useful items:

`ArrayList`: An `ArrayList` is a dynamically resizing array, which grows as you insert elements.

```
1    ArrayList<String> myArr = new ArrayList<String>();
2    myArr.add("one");
3    myArr.add("two");
4    System.out.println(myArr.get(0)); /* prints <one> */
```

`Vector`: A vector is very similar to an `ArrayList`, except that it is synchronized. Its syntax is almost identical as well.

```
1    Vector<String> myVect = new Vector<String>();
2    myVect.add("one");
3    myVect.add("two");
4    System.out.println(myVect.get(0));
```

`LinkedList`: `LinkedList` is, of course, Java's built-in `LinkedList` class. Though it rarely comes up in an interview, it's useful to study because it demonstrates some of the syntax for an iterator.

```
1   LinkedList<String> myLinkedList = new LinkedList<String>();
2   myLinkedList.add("two");
3   myLinkedList.addFirst("one");
4   Iterator<String> iter = myLinkedList.iterator();
5   while (iter.hasNext()) {
6      System.out.println(iter.next());
7   }
```

HashMap: The HashMap collection is widely used, both in interviews and in the real world. We've provided a snippet of the syntax below.

```
1   HashMap<String, String> map = new HashMap<String, String>();
2   map.put("one", "uno");
3   map.put("two", "dos");
4   System.out.println(map.get("one"));
```

Before your interview, make sure you're very comfortable with the above syntax. You'll need it.

Interview Questions

Please note that because virtually all the solutions in this book are implemented with Java, we have selected only a small number of questions for this chapter. Moreover, most of these questions deal with the "trivia" of the languages, since the rest of the book is filled with Java programming questions.

14.1   In terms of inheritance, what is the effect of keeping a constructor private?

pg 400

14.2   In Java, does the finally block get executed if we insert a return statement inside the try block of a try-catch-finally?

pg 400

14.3   What is the difference between final, finally, and finalize?

pg 400

14.4   Explain the difference between templates in C++ and generics in Java.

pg 401

14.5   Explain what object reflection is in Java and why it is useful.

pg 403

14.6   Implement a CircularArray class that supports an array-like data structure which can be efficiently rotated. The class should use a generic type, and should support iteration via the standard for (Obj o : circularArray) notation.

pg 404

Additional Questions: Arrays and Strings (#1.4), Object-Oriented Design (#8.10), Threads and Locks (#16.3)

15

Databases

Candidates who profess experience with databases may be asked to demonstrate this knowledge by implementing SQL queries or designing a database for an application. We'll review some of the key concepts and offer an overview of how to approach these problems.

As you read these queries, don't be surprised by minor variations in syntax. There are a variety of flavors of SQL, and you might have worked with a slightly different one. The examples in this book have been tested against Microsoft SQL Server.

SQL Syntax and Variations

Developers commonly use both the implicit join and the explicit join in SQL queries. Both syntaxes are shown below.

```
1   /* Explicit Join */
2   SELECT CourseName, TeacherName
3   FROM    Courses INNER JOIN Teachers
4   ON      Courses.TeacherID = Teachers.TeacherID
5
6   /* Implicit Join */
7   SELECT CourseName, TeacherName
8   FROM    Courses, Teachers
9   WHERE     Courses.TeacherID = Teachers.TeacherID
```

The two statements above are equivalent, and it's a matter of personal preference which one you choose. For consistency, we will stick to the explicit join.

Denormalized vs. Normalized Databases

Normalized databases are designed to minimize redundancy, while denormalized databases are designed to optimize read time.

In a traditional normalized database with data like Courses and Teachers, Courses might contain a column called TeacherID, which is a foreign key to Teacher. One benefit of this is that information about the teacher (name, address, etc.) is only stored once in the database. The drawback is that many common queries will require expensive joins.

Instead, we can denormalize the database by storing redundant data. For example, if we knew that we would have to repeat this query often, we might store the teacher's name in the Courses table. Denormalization is commonly used to create highly scalable systems.

SQL Statements

Let's walk through a review of basic SQL syntax, using as an example the database that was mentioned earlier. This database has the following simple structure (* indicates a primary key):

```
Courses: CourseID*, CourseName, TeacherID
Teachers: TeacherID*, TeacherName
Students: StudentID*, StudentName
StudentCourses: CourseID*, StudentID*
```

Using the above table, implement the following queries.

Query 1: Student Enrollment

Implement a query to get a list of all students and how many courses each student is enrolled in.

At first, we might try something like this:

```
1   /* Incorrect Code */
2   SELECT Students.StudentName, count(*)
3   FROM Students INNER JOIN StudentCourses
4   ON Students.StudentID = StudentCourses.StudentID
5   GROUP BY Students.StudentID
```

This has three problems:

1. We have excluded students who are not enrolled in any courses, since StudentCourses only includes enrolled students. We need to change this to a LEFT JOIN.

2. Even if we changed it to a LEFT JOIN, the query is still not quite right. Doing count(*) would return how many items there are in a given group of StudentIDs. Students enrolled in zero courses would still have one item in their group. We need to change this to count the number of CourseIDs in each group: count(StudentCourses.CourseID).

3. We've grouped by Students.StudentID, but there are still multiple StudentNames in each group. How will the database know which StudentName to return? Sure, they may all have the same value, but the database doesn't understand that. We need to apply an *aggregate* function to this, such as first(Students.StudentName).

Fixing these issues gets us to this query:

```
1   /* Solution 1: Wrap with another query */
2   SELECT StudentName, Students.StudentID, Cnt
3   FROM (
4       SELECT  Students.StudentID,
5               count(StudentCourses.CourseID) as [Cnt]
6       FROM Students LEFT JOIN StudentCourses
7       ON Students.StudentID = StudentCourses.StudentID
8       GROUP BY Students.StudentID
9   ) T INNER JOIN Students on T.studentID = Students.StudentID
```

Looking at this code, one might ask why we don't just select the student name on line 3 to avoid having to wrap lines 3 through 6 with another query. This (incorrect) solution is shown below.

```
1   /* Incorrect Code */
1   SELECT StudentName, Students.StudentID,
2           count(StudentCourses.CourseID) as [Cnt]
3   FROM Students LEFT JOIN StudentCourses
4   ON Students.StudentID = StudentCourses.StudentID
5   GROUP BY Students.StudentID
```

The answer is that we *can't* do that - at least not exactly as shown. We can only select values that are in an aggregate function or in the GROUP BY clause.

Alternatively, we could resolve the above issues with either of the following statements:

```
1   /* Solution 2: Add StudentName to GROUP BY clause. */
2   SELECT StudentName, Students.StudentID,
3           count(StudentCourses.CourseID) as [Cnt]
4   FROM Students LEFT JOIN StudentCourses
5   ON Students.StudentID = StudentCourses.StudentID
6   GROUP BY Students.StudentID, Students.StudentName
```

OR

```
1   /* Solution 3: Wrap with aggregate function. */
2   SELECT  max(StudentName) as [StudentName], Students.StudentID,
3           count(StudentCourses.CourseID) as [Count]
4   FROM Students LEFT JOIN StudentCourses
5   ON Students.StudentID = StudentCourses.StudentID
6   GROUP BY Students.StudentID
```

Query 2: Teacher Class Size

Implement a query to get a list of all teachers and how many students they each teach. If a teacher teaches the same student in two courses, you should double count the student. Sort the list in descending order of the number of students a teacher teaches.

We can construct this query step by step. First, let's get a list of TeacherIDs and how many students are associated with each TeacherID. This is very similar to the earlier query.

```
1   SELECT TeacherID, count(StudentCourses.CourseID) AS [Number]
```

```
2   FROM Courses INNER JOIN StudentCourses
3   ON Courses.CourseID = StudentCourses.CourseID
4   GROUP BY Courses.TeacherID
```

Note that this INNER JOIN will not select teachers who aren't teaching classes. We'll handle that in the below query when we join it with the list of all teachers.

```
1   SELECT TeacherName, isnull(StudentSize.Number, 0)
2   FROM Teachers LEFT JOIN
3       (SELECT TeacherID, count(StudentCourses.CourseID) AS [Number]
4        FROM Courses INNER JOIN StudentCourses
5        ON Courses.CourseID = StudentCourses.CourseID
6        GROUP BY Courses.TeacherID) StudentSize
7   ON Teachers.TeacherID = StudentSize.TeacherID
8   ORDER BY StudentSize.Number DESC
```

Note how we handled the NULL values in the SELECT statement to convert the NULL values to zeros.

Small Database Design

Additionally, you might be asked to design your own database. We'll walk you through an approach for this. You might notice the similarities between this approach and the approach for object-oriented design.

Step 1: Handle Ambiguity

Database questions often have some ambiguity, intentionally or unintentionally. Before you proceed with your design, you must understand exactly what you need to design.

Imagine you are asked to design a system to represent an apartment rental agency. You will need to know whether this agency has multiple locations or just one. You should also discuss with your interviewer how general you should be. For example, it would be extremely rare for a person to rent two apartments in the same building. But does that mean you shouldn't be able to handle that? Maybe, maybe not. Some very rare conditions might be best handled through a work around (like duplicating the person's contact information in the database).

Step 2: Define the Core Objects

Next, we should look at the core objects of our system. Each of these core objects typically translates into a table. In this case, our core objects might be Property, Building, Apartment, Tenant and Manager.

Step 3: Analyze Relationships

Outlining the core objects should give us a good sense of what the tables should be. How do these tables relate to each other? Are they many-to-many? One-to-many?

If Buildings has a one-to-many relationship with Apartments (one Building has many Apartments), then we might represent this as follows:

Buildings		
BuildingID	BuildingName	BuildingAddress

Apartments		
ApartmentID	ApartmentAddress	BuildingID

Note that the Apartments table links back to Buildings with a BuildingID column.

If we want to allow for the possibility that one person rents more than one apartment, we might want to implement a many-to-many relationship as follows:

Tenants		
TenantID	TenantName	TenantAddress

Apartments		
ApartmentID	ApartmentAddress	BuildingID

TenantApartments	
TenantID	ApartmentID

The TenantApartments table stores a relationship between Tenants and Apartments.

Step 4: Investigate Actions

Finally, we fill in the details. Walk through the common actions that will be taken and understand how to store and retrieve the relevant data. We'll need to handle lease terms, moving out, rent payments, etc. Each of these actions requires new tables and columns.

Large Database Design

When designing a large, scalable database, joins (which are required in the above examples) are generally very slow. Thus, you must *denormalize* your data. Think carefully about how data will be used—you'll probably need to duplicate the data in multiple tables.

Interview Questions

Questions 1 through 3 refer to the below database schema:

Apartments		Buildings		Tenants	
AptID	int	BuildingID	int	TenantID	int
UnitNumber	varchar	ComplexID	int	TenantName	varchar

Apartments		Buildings		Tenants	
BuildingID	int	BuildingName	varchar		
		Address	varchar		

Complexes		AptTenants		Requests	
ComplexID	int	TenantID	int	RequestID	int
ComplexName	varchar	AptID	int	Status	varchar
				AptID	int
				Description	varchar

Note that each apartment can have multiple tenants, and each tenant can have multiple apartments. Each apartment belongs to one building, and each building belongs to one complex.

15.1 Write a SQL query to get a list of tenants who are renting more than one apartment.

pg 408

15.2 Write a SQL query to get a list of all buildings and the number of open requests (Requests in which status equals 'Open').

pg 408

15.3 Building #11 is undergoing a major renovation. Implement a query to close all requests from apartments in this building.

pg 409

15.4 What are the different types of joins? Please explain how they differ and why certain types are better in certain situations.

pg 409

15.5 What is denormalization? Explain the pros and cons.

pg 411

15.6 Draw an entity-relationship diagram for a database with companies, people, and professionals (people who work for companies).

pg 412

15.7 Imagine a simple database storing information for students' grades. Design what this database might look like and provide a SQL query to return a list of the honor roll students (top 10%), sorted by their grade point average.

pg 412

Additional Questions: Object-Oriented Design (#8.6)

16

Threads and Locks

In a Microsoft, Google or Amazon interview, it's not terribly common to be asked to implement an algorithm with threads (unless you're working in a team for which this is a particularly important skill). It is, however, relatively common for interviewers at any company to assess your general understanding of threads, particularly your understanding of deadlocks.

This chapter will provide an introduction to this topic.

Threads in Java

Every thread in Java is created and controlled by a unique object of the `java.lang.Thread` class. When a standalone application is run, a user thread is automatically created to execute the `main()` method. This thread is called the main thread.

In Java, we can implement threads in one of two ways:

- By implementing the `java.lang.Runnable` interface
- By extending the `java.lang.Thread` class

We will cover both of these below.

Implementing the Runnable Interface

The Runnable interface has the following very simple structure.

```
1   public interface Runnable {
2      void run();
3   }
```

To create and use a thread using this interface, we do the following:

1. Create a class which implements the Runnable interface. An object of this class is a Runnable object.

2. Create an object of type Thread by passing a Runnable object as argument to the Thread constructor. The Thread object now has a Runnable object that implements the run() method.

---

3. The `start()` method is invoked on the Thread object created in the previous step.

For example:

```
1   public class RunnableThreadExample implements Runnable {
2       public int count = 0;
3
4       public void run() {
5           System.out.println("RunnableThread starting.");
6           try {
7               while (count < 5) {
8                   Thread.sleep(500);
9                   count++;
10              }
11          } catch (InterruptedException exc) {
12              System.out.println("RunnableThread interrupted.");
13          }
14          System.out.println("RunnableThread terminating.");
15      }
16  }
17
18  public static void main(String[] args) {
19      RunnableThreadExample instance = new RunnableThreadExample();
20      Thread thread = new Thread(instance);
21      thread.start();
22
23      /* waits until above thread counts to 5 (slowly) */
24      while (instance.count != 5) {
25          try {
26              Thread.sleep(250);
27          } catch (InterruptedException exc) {
28              exc.printStackTrace();
29          }
30      }
31  }
```

In the above code, observe that all we really needed to do is have our class implement the `run()` method (line 4). Another method can then pass an instance of the class to new `Thread(obj)` (lines 19 - 20) and call `start()` on the thread (line 21).

Extending the Thread Class

Alternatively, we can create a thread by extending the Thread class. This will almost always mean that we override the `run()` method, and the subclass may also call the thread constructor explicitly in its constructor.

The below code provides an example of this.

```
1   public class ThreadExample extends Thread {
2       int count = 0;
3
4       public void run() {
```

```
5          System.out.println("Thread starting.");
6          try {
7            while (count < 5) {
8              Thread.sleep(500);
9              System.out.println("In Thread, count is " + count);
10             count++;
11           }
12         } catch (InterruptedException exc) {
13           System.out.println("Thread interrupted.");
14         }
15         System.out.println("Thread terminating.");
16     }
17 }
18
19 public class ExampleB {
20     public static void main(String args[]) {
21         ThreadExample instance = new ThreadExample();
22         instance.start();
23
24         while (instance.count != 5) {
25           try {
26             Thread.sleep(250);
27           } catch (InterruptedException exc) {
28             exc.printStackTrace();
29           }
30         }
31     }
32 }
```

This code is very similar to the first approach. The difference is that since we are extending the Thread class, rather than just implementing an interface, we can call start() on the instance of the class itself.

Extending the Thread Class vs. Implementing the Runnable Interface

When creating threads, there are two reasons why implementing the Runnable interface may be preferable to extending the Thread class:

- Java does not support multiple inheritance. Therefore, extending the Thread class means that the subclass cannot extend any other class. A class implementing the Runnable interface will be able to extend another class.

- A class might only be interested in being runnable, and therefore, inheriting the full overhead of the Thread class would be excessive.

Synchronization and Locks

Threads within a given process share the same memory space, which is both a positive and a negative. It enables threads to share data, which can be valuable. However, it also creates the opportunity for issues when two threads modify a resource at the same time. Java provides synchronization in order to control access to shared resources.

The keyword synchronized and the lock form the basis for implementing synchronized execution of code.

Synchronized Methods

Most commonly, we restrict access to shared resources through the use of the synchronized keyword. It can be applied to methods and code blocks, and restricts multiple threads from executing the code simultaneously *on the same object.*

To clarify the last point, consider the following code:

```
1   public class MyClass extends Thread  {
2       private String name;
3       private MyObject myObj;
4
5       public MyClass(MyObject obj, String n) {
6           name = n;
7           myObj = obj;
8       }
9
10      public void run() {
11          myObj.foo(name);
12      }
13  }
14
15  public class MyObject {
16      public synchronized void foo(String name) {
17          try {
18              System.out.println("Thread " + name + ".foo(): starting");
19              Thread.sleep(3000);
20              System.out.println("Thread " + name + ".foo(): ending");
21          } catch (InterruptedException exc) {
22              System.out.println("Thread " + name + ": interrupted.");
23          }
24      }
25  }
```

Can two instances of MyClass call foo at the same time? It depends. If they have the same instance of MyObject, then no. But, if they hold different references, then the answer is yes.

```
1   /* Difference references - both threads can call MyObject.foo() */
2   MyObject obj1 = new MyObject();
3   MyObject obj2 = new MyObject();
4   MyClass thread1 = new MyClass(obj1, "1");
5   MyClass thread2 = new MyClass(obj2, "2");
6   thread1.start();
7   thread2.start()
8
9   /* Same reference to obj. Only one will be allowed to call foo,
```

```
10   * and the other will be forced to wait. */
11  MyObject obj = new MyObject();
12  MyClass thread1 = new MyClass(obj, "1");
13  MyClass thread2 = new MyClass(obj, "2");
14  thread1.start()
15  thread2.start()
```

Static methods synchronize on the *class lock*. The two threads above could not simultaneously execute synchronized static methods on the same class, even if one is calling
foo and the other is calling bar.

```
1   public class MyClass extends Thread  {
2      ...
3      public void run() {
4          if (name.equals("1")) MyObject.foo(name);
5          else if (name.equals("2")) MyObject.bar(name);
6      }
7   }
8
9   public class MyObject {
10      public static synchronized void foo(String name) {
11          /* same as before */
12      }
13
14      public static synchronized void bar(String name) {
15          /* same as foo */
16      }
17  }
```

If you run this code, you will see the following printed:

```
Thread 1.foo(): starting
Thread 1.foo(): ending
Thread 2.bar(): starting
Thread 2.bar(): ending
```

Synchronized Blocks

Similarly, a block of code can be synchronized. This operates very similarly to synchronizing a method.

```
1   public class MyClass extends Thread  {
2      ...
3      public void run() {
4          myObj.foo(name);
5      }
6   }
7   public class MyObject {
8      public void foo(String name) {
9          synchronized(this) {
10             ...
11         }
12      }
```

```
13  }
```

Like synchronizing a method, only one thread per instance of MyObject can execute the code within the synchronized block. That means that, if thread1 and thread2 have the same instance of MyObject, only one will be allowed to execute the code block at a time.

Locks

For more granular control, we can utilize a lock. A lock (or monitor) is used to synchronize access to a shared resource by associating the resource with the lock. A thread gets access to a shared resource by first acquiring the lock associated with the resource. At any given time, at most one thread can hold the lock and, therefore, only one thread can access the shared resource.

A common use case for locks is when a resource is accessed from multiple places, but should be only accessed by one thread *at a time*. This case is demonstrated in the code below.

```
1   public class LockedATM {
2       private Lock lock;
3       private int balance = 100;
4
5       public LockedATM() {
6           lock = new ReentrantLock();
7       }
8
9       public int withdraw(int value) {
10          lock.lock();
11          int temp = balance;
12          try {
13              Thread.sleep(100);
14              temp = temp - value;
15              Thread.sleep(100);
16              balance = temp;
17          } catch (InterruptedException e) {     }
18          lock.unlock();
19          return temp;
20      }
21
22      public int deposit(int value) {
23          lock.lock();
24          int temp = balance;
25          try {
26              Thread.sleep(100);
27              temp = temp + value;
28              Thread.sleep(300);
29              balance = temp;
30          } catch (InterruptedException e) {     }
31          lock.unlock();
```

```
32        return temp;
33    }
34 }
```

Of course, we've added code to intentionally slow down the execution of `withdraw` and `deposit`, as it helps to illustrate the potential problems that can occur. You may not write code exactly like this, but the situation it mirrors is very, very real. Using a lock will help protect a shared resource from being modified in unexpected ways.

Deadlocks and Deadlock Prevention

A deadlock is a situation where a thread is waiting for an object lock that another thread holds, and this second thread is waiting for an object lock that the first thread holds (or an equivalent situation with several threads). Since each thread is waiting for the other thread to relinquish a lock, they both remain waiting forever. The threads are said to be deadlocked.

In order for a deadlock to occur, you must have all four of the following conditions met:

1. *Mutual Exclusion:* Only one process can access a resource at a given time. (Or, more accurately, there is limited access to a resource. A deadlock could also occur if a resource has limited quantity.)

2. *Hold and Wait:* Processes already holding a resource can request additional resources, without relinquishing their current resources.

3. *No Preemption:* One process cannot forcibly remove another process' resource.

4. *Circular Wait:* Two or more processes form a circular chain where each process is waiting on another resource in the chain.

Deadlock prevention entails removing any of the above conditions, but it gets tricky because many of these conditions are difficult to satisfy. For instance, removing #1 is difficult because many resources can only be used by one process at a time (e.g., printers). Most deadlock prevention algorithms focus on avoiding condition #4: circular wait.

Interview Questions

16.1   What's the difference between a thread and a process?

pg 416

16.2   How would you measure the time spent in a context switch?

pg 416

16.3 In the famous dining philosophers problem, a bunch of philosophers are sitting around a circular table with one chopstick between each of them. A philosopher needs both chopsticks to eat, and always picks up the left chopstick before the right one. A deadlock could potentially occur if all the philosophers reached for the left chopstick at the same time. Using threads and locks, implement a simulation of the dining philosophers problem that prevents deadlocks.

pg 418

16.4 Design a class which provides a lock only if there are no possible deadlocks.

pg 420

16.5 Suppose we have the following code:

```
public class Foo {
    public Foo() { ... }
    public void first() { ... }
    public void second() { ... }
    public void third() { ... }
}
```

The same instance of Foo will be passed to three different threads. ThreadA will call first, threadB will call second, and threadC will call third. Design a mechanism to ensure that first is called before second and second is called before third.

pg 425

16.6 You are given a class with synchronized method A and a normal method C. If you have two threads in one instance of a program, can they both execute A at the same time? Can they execute A and C at the same time?

pg 427

Additional Review Problems

Interview Questions and Advice

17

Moderate

17.1   Write a function to swap a number in place (that is, without temporary variables).

pg 430

17.2   Design an algorithm to figure out if someone has won a game of tic-tac-toe.

pg 431

17.3   Write an algorithm which computes the number of trailing zeros in n factorial.

pg 434

17.4   Write a method which finds the maximum of two numbers. You should not use if-else or any other comparison operator.

pg 436

17.5   The Game of Master Mind is played as follows:

The computer has four slots, and each slot will contain a ball that is red (R), yellow (Y), green (G) or blue (B). For example, the computer might have RGGB (Slot #1 is red, Slots #2 and #3 are green, Slot #4 is blue).

You, the user, are trying to guess the solution. You might, for example, guess YRGB.

When you guess the correct color for the correct slot, you get a "hit." If you guess a color that exists but is in the wrong slot, you get a "pseudo-hit." Note that a slot that is a hit can never count as a pseudo-hit.

For example, if the actual solution is RGBY and you guess GGRR, you have one hit and one pseudo-hit.

Write a method that, given a guess and a solution, returns the number of hits and pseudo-hits.

pg 438

17.6 Given an array of integers, write a method to find indices m and n such that if you sorted elements m through n, the entire array would be sorted. Minimize n - m (that is, find the smallest such sequence).

EXAMPLE

Input: `1, 2, 4, 7, 10, 11, 7, 12, 6, 7, 16, 18, 19`

Output: `(3, 9)`

pg 439

17.7 Given any integer, print an English phrase that describes the integer (e.g., "One Thousand, Two Hundred Thirty Four").

pg 442

17.8 You are given an array of integers (both positive and negative). Find the contiguous sequence with the largest sum. Return the sum.

EXAMPLE

Input: `2, -8, 3, -2, 4, -10`

Output: `5 (i.e., {3, -2, 4})`

pg 443

17.9 Design a method to find the frequency of occurrences of any given word in a book.

pg 445

17.10 Since XML is very verbose, you are given a way of encoding it where each tag gets mapped to a pre-defined integer value. The language/grammar is as follows:

```
Element    --> Tag Attributes END Children END
Attribute  --> Tag Value
END        --> 0
Tag        --> some predefined mapping to int
Value      --> string value END
```

For example, the following XML might be converted into the compressed string below (assuming a mapping of `family -> 1`, `person ->2`, `firstName -> 3`, `lastName -> 4`, `state -> 5`).

```
<family lastName="McDowell" state="CA">
  <person firstName="Gayle">Some Message</person>
</family>
```

Becomes:

`1 4 McDowell 5 CA 0 2 3 Gayle 0 Some Message 0 0.`

Write code to print the encoded version of an XML element (passed in `Element` and `Attribute` objects).

pg 446

17.11 Implement a method rand7() given rand5(). That is, given a method that generates a random number between 0 and 4 (inclusive), write a method that generates a random number between 0 and 6 (inclusive).

pg 447

17.12 Design an algorithm to find all pairs of integers within an array which sum to a specified value.

pg 450

17.13 Consider a simple node-like data structure called BiNode, which has pointers to two other nodes.

```
1  public class BiNode {
2      public BiNode node1, node2;
3      public int data;
4  }
```

The data structure BiNode could be used to represent both a binary tree (where node1 is the left node and node2 is the right node) or a doubly linked list (where node1 is the previous node and node2 is the next node). Implement a method to convert a binary search tree (implemented with BiNode) into a doubly linked list. The values should be kept in order and the operation should be performed in place (that is, on the original data structure).

pg 451

17.14 Oh, no! You have just completed a lengthy document when you have an unfortunate Find/Replace mishap. You have accidentally removed all spaces, punctuation, and capitalization in the document. A sentence like "I reset the computer. It still didn't boot!" would become "iresetthecomputeritstilldidntboot". You figure that you can add back in the punctation and capitalization later, once you get the individual words properly separated. Most of the words will be in a dictionary, but some strings, like proper names, will not.

Given a dictionary (a list of words), design an algorithm to find the optimal way of "unconcatenating" a sequence of words. In this case, "optimal" is defined to be the parsing which minimizes the number of unrecognized sequences of characters.

For example, the string "jesslookedjustliketimherbrother" would be optimally parsed as "JESS looked just like TIM her brother". This parsing has seven unrecognized characters, which we have capitalized for clarity.

pg 455

18

Hard

18.1 Write a function that adds two numbers. You should not use + or any arithmetic operators.

pg 462

18.2 Write a method to shuffle a deck of cards. It must be a perfect shuffle—in other words, each of the 52! permutations of the deck has to be equally likely. Assume that you are given a random number generator which is perfect.

pg 463

18.3 Write a method to randomly generate a set of m integers from an array of size n. Each element must have equal probability of being chosen.

pg 464

18.4 Write a method to count the number of 2s that appear in all the numbers between 0 and n (inclusive).

EXAMPLE

Input: 25

Output: 9 (2, 12, 20, 21, 22, 23, 24 and 25. Note that 22 counts for two 2s.)

pg 465

18.5 You have a large text file containing words. Given any two words, find the shortest distance (in terms of number of words) between them in the file. Can you make the searching operation in O(1) time? What about the space complexity for your solution?

pg 468

18.6 Describe an algorithm to find the smallest one million numbers in one billion numbers. Assume that the computer memory can hold all one billion numbers.

pg 469

18.7 Given a list of words, write a program to find the longest word made of other words in the list.

EXAMPLE

Input: `cat, banana, dog, nana, walk, walker, dogwalker`

Output: `dogwalker`

18.8 Given a string s and an array of smaller strings T, design a method to search s for each small string in T.

18.9 Numbers are randomly generated and passed to a method. Write a program to find and maintain the median value as new values are generated.

18.10 Given two words of equal length that are in a dictionary, write a method to transform one word into another word by changing only one letter at a time. The new word you get in each step must be in the dictionary.

EXAMPLE

Input: DAMP, LIKE

Output: DAMP -> LAMP -> LIMP -> LIME -> LIKE

18.11 Imagine you have a square matrix, where each cell (pixel) is either black or white Design an algorithm to find the maximum subsquare such that all four borders are filled with black pixels.

18.12 Given an NxN matrix of positive and negative integers, write code to find the submatrix with the largest possible sum.

18.13 Given a list of millions of words, design an algorithm to create the largest possible rectangle of letters such that every row forms a word (reading left to right) and every column forms a word (reading top to bottom). The words need not be chosen consecutively from the list, but all rows must be the same length and all columns must be the same height.

Solutions

IX

*Join us at **www.CrackingTheCodingInterview.com** to download full, compilable Java / Eclipse solutions, discuss problems from this book with other readers, report issues, view this book's errata, post your resume, and seek additional advice.*

Arrays and Strings

Data Structures: Solutions

Chapter 1

1.1   *Implement an algorithm to determine if a string has all unique characters. What if you cannot use additional data structures?*

pg 73

SOLUTION

You may want to start off with asking your interviewer if the string is an ASCII string or a Unicode string. This is an important question, and asking it will show an eye for detail and a deep understanding of Computer Science.

We'll assume for simplicity that the character set is ASCII. If not, we would need to increase the storage size, but the rest of the logic would be the same.

Given this, one simple optimization we can make to this problem is to automatically return false if the length of the string is greater than the number of unique characters in the alphabet. After all, you can't have a string with 280 unique characters if there are only 256 possible unique characters.

Our first solution is to create an array of boolean values, where the flag at index i indicates whether character i in the alphabet is contained in the string. If you run across this character a second time, you can immediately return false.

The code below implements this algorithm.

```
1   public boolean isUniqueChars2(String str) {
2       if (str.length() > 256) return false;
3
4       boolean[] char_set = new boolean[256];
5       for (int i = 0; i < str.length(); i++) {
6           int val = str.charAt(i);
7           if (char_set[val]) { // Already found this char in string
8               return false;
9           }
10          char_set[val] = true;
11      }
12      return true;
13  }
```

The time complexity for this code is O(n), where n is the length of the string. The space complexity is O(1).

We can reduce our space usage by a factor of eight by using a bit vector. We will assume, in the below code, that the string only uses the lower case letters a through z. This will allow us to use just a single int.

```
1   public boolean isUniqueChars(String str) {
2       if (str.length() > 256) return false;
3
4       int checker = 0;
5       for (int i = 0; i < str.length(); i++) {
6           int val = str.charAt(i) - 'a';
```

```
7          if ((checker & (1 << val)) > 0) {
8              return false;
9          }
10         checker |= (1 << val);
11     }
12     return true;
13 }
```

Alternatively, we could do the following:

1. Compare every character of the string to every other character of the string. This will take O(n²) time and O(1) space.

2. If we are allowed to modify the input string, we could sort the string in O(n log(n)) time and then linearly check the string for neighboring characters that are identical. Careful, though: many sorting algorithms take up extra space.

These solutions are not as optimal in some respects, but might be better depending on the constraints of the problem.

1.2 *Implement a function void reverse(char* str) in C or C++ which reverses a null-terminated string.*

pg 73

SOLUTION

This is a classic interview question. The only "gotcha" is to try to do it in place, and to be careful for the null character.

We will implement this in C.

```
1  void reverse(char *str) {
2      char* end = str;
3      char tmp;
4      if (str) {
5        while (*end) { /* find end of the string */
6            ++end;
7        }
8        --end; /* set one char back, since last char is null */
9
10       /* swap characters from start of string with the end of the
11        * string, until the pointers meet in middle. */
12       while (str < end) {
13         tmp = *str;
14         *str++ = *end;
15         *end-- = tmp;
16       }
17     }
18 }
```

This is just one of many ways to implement this solution. We could even implement this code recursively (but we wouldn't recommend it).

1.3   *Given two strings, write a method to decide if one is a permutation of the other.*

pg 73

SOLUTION

Like in many questions, we should confirm some details with our interviewer. We should understand if the anagram comparison is case sensitive. That is, is God an anagram of dog? Additionally, we should ask if whitespace is significant.

We will assume for this problem that the comparison is case sensitive and whitespace is significant. So, "god   " is different from "dog".

Whenever we compare two strings, we know that if they are different lengths then they cannot be anagrams.

There are two easy ways to solve this problem, both of which use this optimization.

Solution #1: Sort the strings.

If two strings are anagrams, then we know they have the same characters, but in different orders. Therefore, sorting the strings will put the characters from two anagrams in the same order. We just need to compare the sorted versions of the strings.

```
1   public String sort(String s) {
2       char[] content = s.toCharArray();
3       java.util.Arrays.sort(content);
4       return new String(content);
5   }
6
7   public boolean permutation(String s, String t) {
8       if (s.length() != t.length()) {
9           return false;
10      }
11      return sort(s).equals(sort(t));
12  }
```

Though this algorithm is not as optimal in some senses, it may be preferable in one sense: it's clean, simple and easy to understand. In a practical sense, this may very well be a superior way to implement the problem.

However, if efficiency is very important, we can implement it a different way.

Solution #2: Check if the two strings have identical character counts.

We can also use the definition of an anagram—two words with the same character counts—to implement this algorithm. We simply iterate through this code, counting how many times each character appears. Then, afterwards, we compare the two arrays.

```
1    public boolean permutation(String s, String t) {
2        if (s.length() != t.length()) {
3            return false;
4        }
5
6        int[] letters = new int[256]; // Assumption
7
8        char[] s_array = s.toCharArray();
9        for (char c : s_array) { // count number of each char in s.
10           letters[c]++;
11       }
12
13       for (int i = 0; i < t.length(); i++) {
14           int c = (int) t.charAt(i);
15           if (--letters[c] < 0) {
16               return false;
17           }
18       }
19
20       return true;
21   }
```

Note the assumption on line 6. In your interview, you should always check with your interviewer about the size of the character set. We assumed that the character set was ASCII.

1.4 *Write a method to replace all spaces in a string with '%20'. You may assume that the string has sufficient space at the end of the string to hold the additional characters, and that you are given the "true" length of the string. (Note: if implementing in Java, please use a character array so that you can perform this operation in place.)*

pg 73

SOLUTION

A common approach in string manipulation problems is to edit the string starting from the end and work backwards. This is useful because we have extra buffer at the end, which allows us to change characters without worrying about what we're overwriting.

We will use this approach in this problem. The algorithm works through a two scan approach. In the first scan, we count how many spaces there are in the string. This is used to compute how long the final string should be. In the second pass, which is done in reverse order, we actually edit the string. When we see a space, we copy %20 into the next spots. If there is no space, then we copy the original character.

The code below implements this algorithm.

```
1    public void replaceSpaces(char[] str, int length) {
2        int spaceCount = 0, newLength, i = 0;
3        for (i = 0; i < length; i++) {
```

```
4        if (str[i] == ' ') {
5          spaceCount++;
6        }
7      }
8      newLength = length + spaceCount * 2;
9      str[newLength] = '\0';
10     for (i = length - 1; i >= 0; i--) {
11       if (str[i] == ' ') {
12         str[newLength - 1] = '0';
13         str[newLength - 2] = '2';
14         str[newLength - 3] = '%';
15         newLength = newLength - 3;
16       } else {
17         str[newLength - 1] = str[i];
18         newLength = newLength - 1;
19       }
20     }
21   }
```

We have implemented this problem using character arrays, since Java strings are immutable. If we used strings directly, this would require returning a new copy of the string, but it would allow us to implement this in just one pass.

1.5 *Implement a method to perform basic string compression using the counts of repeated characters. For example, the string* aabcccccaaa *would become* a2b1c5a3. *If the "compressed" string would not become smaller than the original string, your method should return the original string.*

pg 73

SOLUTION

At first glance, implementing this method seems fairly straightforward, but perhaps a bit tedious. We iterate through the string, copying characters to a new string and counting the repeats. How hard could it be?

```
1    public String compressBad(String str) {
2      String mystr = "";
3      char last = str.charAt(0);
4      int count = 1;
5      for (int i = 1; i < str.length(); i++) {
6        if (str.charAt(i) == last) { // Found repeat char
7          count++;
8        } else { // Insert char count, and update last char
9          mystr += last + "" + count;
10         last = str.charAt(i);
11         count = 1;
12       }
13     }
14     return mystr + last + count;
```

```
15  }
```

This code doesn't handle the case when the compressed string is longer than the original string, but it otherwise works. Is it efficient though? Take a look at the runtime of this code.

The runtime is $O(p + k^2)$, where p is the size of the original string and k is the number of character sequences. For example, if the string is aabccdeeaa, then there are six character sequences. It's slow because string concatenation operates in $O(n^2)$ time (see **StringBuffer** in Chapter 1).

We can make this somewhat better by using a StringBuffer.

```
1   String compressBetter(String str) {
2       /* Check if compression would create a longer string */
3       int size = countCompression(str);
4       if (size >= str.length()) {
5           return str;
6       }
7
8       StringBuffer mystr = new StringBuffer();
9       char last = str.charAt(0);
10      int count = 1;
11      for (int i = 1; i < str.length(); i++) {
12          if (str.charAt(i) == last) { // Found repeated char
13              count++;
14          } else { // Insert char count, and update last char
15              mystr.append(last); // Insert char
16              mystr.append(count); // Insert count
17              last = str.charAt(i);
18              count = 1;
19          }
20      }
21
22      /* In lines 15 - 16 above, characters are inserted when the
23       * repeated character changes. We need to update the string at
24       * the end of the method as well, since the very last set of
25       * repeated characters wouldn't be set in the compressed string
26       * yet. */
27      mystr.append(last);
28      mystr.append(count);
29      return mystr.toString();
30  }
31
32  int countCompression(String str) {
33      char last = str.charAt(0);
34      int size = 0;
35      int count = 1;
36      for (int i = 1; i < str.length(); i++) {
37          if (str.charAt(i) == last) {
38              count++;
```

```
39        } else {
40            last = str.charAt(i);
41            size += 1 + String.valueOf(count).length();
42            count = 1;
43        }
44    }
45    size += 1 + String.valueOf(count).length();
46    return size;
47 }
```

This algorithm is much better. Note that we have added the size check in lines 2 through 5.

If we don't want to (or aren't allowed to) use a StringBuffer, we can still solve this problem efficiently. In line 2, we compute the end size of the string. This allows us to create a char array of the correct size, so we can implement the code as follows:

```
1  String compressAlternate(String str) {
2      /* Check if compression would create a longer string */
3      int size = countCompression(str);
4      if (size >= str.length()) {
5          return str;
6      }
7
8      char[] array = new char[size];
9      int index = 0;
10     char last = str.charAt(0);
11     int count = 1;
12     for (int i = 1; i < str.length(); i++) {
13         if (str.charAt(i) == last) { // Found repeated character
14             count++;
15         } else {
16             /* Update the repeated character count */
17             index = setChar(array, last, index, count);
18             last = str.charAt(i);
19             count = 1;
20         }
21     }
22
23     /* Update string with the last set of repeated characters. */
24     index = setChar(array, last, index, count);
25     return String.valueOf(array);
26 }
27
28 int setChar(char[] array, char c, int index, int count) {
29     array[index] = c;
30     index++;
31
32     /* Convert the count to a string, then to an array of chars */
33     char[] cnt = String.valueOf(count).toCharArray();
34
```

```
35    /* Copy characters from biggest digit to smallest */
36    for (char x : cnt) {
37        array[index] = x;
38        index++;
39    }
40    return index;
41 }
42
43 int countCompression(String str) {
44    /* same as earlier */
45 }
```

Like the second solution, the above code runs in O(N) time and O(N) space.

1.6   *Given an image represented by an NxN matrix, where each pixel in the image is 4 bytes, write a method to rotate the image by 90 degrees. Can you do this in place?*

pg 73

SOLUTION

Because we're rotating the matrix by 90 degrees, the easiest way to do this is to imple-ment the rotation in layers. We perform a circular rotation on each layer, moving the top edge to the right edge, the right edge to the bottom edge, the bottom edge to the left edge, and the left edge to the top edge.

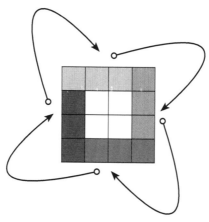

How do we perform this four-way edge swap? One option is to copy the top edge to an array, and then move the left to the top, the bottom to the left, and so on. This requires O(N) memory, which is actually unnecessary.

A better way to do this is to implement the swap index by index. In this case, we do the following:

```
1  for i = 0 to n
2      temp = top[i];
```

```
3      top[i] = left[i]
4      left[i] = bottom[i]
5      bottom[i] = right[i]
6      right[i] = temp
```

We perform such a swap on each layer, starting from the outermost layer and working our way inwards. (Alternatively, we could start from the inner layer and work outwards.)

The code for this algorithm is below.

```
1   public void rotate(int[][] matrix, int n) {
2      for (int layer = 0; layer < n / 2; ++layer) {
3         int first = layer;
4         int last = n - 1 - layer;
5         for(int i = first; i < last; ++i) {
6            int offset = i - first;
7            // save top
8            int top = matrix[first][i];
9
10           // left -> top
11           matrix[first][i] = matrix[last-offset][first];
12
13           // bottom -> left
14           matrix[last-offset][first] = matrix[last][last - offset];
15
16           // right -> bottom
17           matrix[last][last - offset] = matrix[i][last];
18
19           // top -> right
20           matrix[i][last] = top;
21        }
22     }
23  }
```

This algorithm is $O(N^2)$, which is the best we can do since any algorithm must touch all N^2 elements.

1.7 *Write an algorithm such that if an element in an MxN matrix is 0, its entire row and column are set to 0.*

pg 73

SOLUTION

At first glance, this problem seems easy: just iterate through the matrix and every time we see a cell with value zero, set its row and column to 0. There's one problem with that solution though: when we come across other cells in that row or column, we'll see the zeros and change their row and column to zero. Pretty soon, our entire matrix will be set to zeros.

One way around this is to keep a second matrix which flags the zero locations. We would then do a second pass through the matrix to set the zeros. This would take O(MN) space.

Do we really need O(MN) space? No. Since we're going to set the entire row and column to zero, we don't need to track that it was exactly cell[2][4] (row 2, column 4). We only need to know that row 2 has a zero somewhere, and column 4 has a zero somewhere. We'll set the entire row and column to zero anyway, so why would we care to keep track of the exact location of the zero?

The code below implements this algorithm. We use two arrays to keep track of all the rows with zeros and all the columns with zeros. We then make a second pass of the matrix and set a cell to zero if its row or column is zero.

```
1   public void setZeros(int[][] matrix) {
2       boolean[] row = new boolean[matrix.length];
3       boolean[] column = new boolean[matrix[0].length];
4
5       // Store the row and column index with value 0
6       for (int i = 0; i < matrix.length; i++) {
7           for (int j = 0; j < matrix[0].length;j++) {
8               if (matrix[i][j] == 0) {
9                   row[i] = true;
10                  column[j] = true;
11              }
12          }
13      }
14
15      // Set arr[i][j] to 0 if either row i or column j has a 0
16      for (int i = 0; i < matrix.length; i++) {
17          for (int j = 0; j < matrix[0].length; j++) {
18              if (row[i] || column[j]) {
19                  matrix[i][j] = 0;
20              }
21          }
22      }
23  }
```

To make this somewhat more space efficient, we could use a bit vector instead of a boolean array.

1.8 *Assume you have a method isSubstring which checks if one word is a substring of another. Given two strings, s1 and s2, write code to check if s2 is a rotation of s1 using only one call to isSubstring (e.g., "waterbottle" is a rotation of "erbottlewat").*

pg 74

SOLUTION

If we imagine that s2 is a rotation of s1, then we can ask what the rotation point is. For example, if you rotate waterbottle after wat, you get erbottlewat. In a rotation, we cut s1 into two parts, x and y, and rearrange them to get s2.

```
s1 = xy = waterbottle
x = wat
y = erbottle
s2 = yx = erbottlewat
```

So, we need to check if there's a way to split s1 into x and y such that xy = s1 and yx = s2. Regardless of where the division between x and y is, we can see that yx will always be a substring of xyxy. That is, s2 will always be a substring of s1s1.

And this is precisely how we solve the problem: simply do isSubstring(s1s1, s2).

The code below implements this algorithm.

```
1   public boolean isRotation(String s1, String s2) {
2       int len = s1.length();
3       /* check that s1 and s2 are equal length and not empty */
4       if (len == s2.length() && len > 0) {
5           /* concatenate s1 and s1 within new buffer */
6           String s1s1 = s1 + s1;
7           return isSubstring(s1s1, s2);
8       }
9       return false;
10  }
```

Linked Lists

Data Structures: Solutions

Chapter 2

2.1   *Write code to remove duplicates from an unsorted linked list.*

FOLLOW UP

How would you solve this problem if a temporary buffer is not allowed?

pg 77

SOLUTION

In order to remove duplicates from a linked list, we need to be able to track duplicates. A simple hash table will work well here.

In the below solution, we simply iterate through the linked list, adding each element to a hash table. When we discover a duplicate element, we remove the element and continue iterating. We can do this all in one pass since we are using a linked list.

```
1   public static void deleteDups(LinkedListNode n) {
2       Hashtable table = new Hashtable();
3       LinkedListNode previous = null;
4       while (n != null) {
5           if (table.containsKey(n.data)) {
6               previous.next = n.next;
7           } else {
8               table.put(n.data, true);
9               previous = n;
10          }
11          n = n.next;
12      }
13  }
```

The above solution takes O(N) time, where N is the number of elements in the linked list.

Follow Up: No Buffer Allowed

If we don't have a buffer, we can iterate with two pointers: `current` which iterates through the linked list, and `runner` which checks all subsequent nodes for duplicates.

```
1   public static void deleteDups(LinkedListNode head) {
2       if (head == null) return;
3
4       LinkedListNode current = head;
5       while (current != null) {
6           /* Remove all future nodes that have the same value */
7           LinkedListNode runner = current;
8           while (runner.next != null) {
9               if (runner.next.data == current.data) {
10                  runner.next = runner.next.next;
11              } else {
12                  runner = runner.next;
13              }
14          }
```

```
15        current = current.next;
16    }
17  }
```

This code runs in O(1) space, but O(N²) time.

2.2   *Implement an algorithm to find the kth to last element of a singly linked list.*

pg 77

SOLUTION

We will approach this problem both recursively and non-recursively. Remember that recursive solutions are often cleaner but less optimal. For example, in this problem, the recursive implementation is about half the length of the iterative solution but also takes O(n) space, where n is the number of elements in the linked list.

Note that for this solution, we have defined k such that passing in k = 1 would return the last element, k = 2 would return to the second to last element, and so on. It is equally acceptable to define k such that k = 0 would return the last element.

Solution #1: If linked list size is known

If the size of the linked list is known, then the kth to last element is the (length - k) th element. We can just iterate through the linked list to find this element. Because this solution is so trivial, we can almost be sure that this is not what the interviewer intended.

Solution #2: Recursive

This algorithm recurses through the linked list. When it hits the end, the method passes back a counter set to 0. Each parent call adds 1 to this counter. When the counter equals k, we know we have reached the kth to last element of the linked list.

Implementing this is short and sweet—provided we have a way of "passing back" an integer value through the stack. Unfortunately, we can't pass back a node and a counter using normal return statements. So how do we handle this?

Approach A: Don't Return the Element.

One way to do this is to change the problem to simply printing the kth to last element. Then, we can pass back the value of the counter simply through return values.

```
1   public static int nthToLast(LinkedListNode head, int k) {
2       if (head == null) {
3           return 0;
4       }
5       int i = nthToLast(head.next, k) + 1;
6       if (i == k) {
7           System.out.println(head.data);
8       }
```

```
9      return i;
10 }
```

Of course, this is only a valid solution if the interviewer says it is valid.

Approach B: Use C++.

A second way to solve this is to use C++ and to pass values by reference. This allows us to return the node value, but also update the counter by passing a pointer to it.

```
1   node* nthToLast(node* head, int k, int& i) {
2      if (head == NULL) {
3         return NULL;
4      }
5      node * nd = nthToLast(head->next, k, i);
6      i = i + 1;
7      if (i == k) {
8         return head;
9      }
10     return nd;
11 }
```

Approach C: Create a Wrapper Class.

We described earlier that the issue was that we couldn't simultaneously return a counter and an index. If we wrap the counter value with simple class (or even a single element array), we can mimic passing by reference.

```
1   public class IntWrapper {
2      public int value = 0;
3   }
4
5   LinkedListNode nthToLastR2(LinkedListNode head, int k,
6                              IntWrapper i) {
7      if (head == null) {
8         return null;
9      }
10     LinkedListNode node = nthToLastR2(head.next, k, i);
11     i.value = i.value + 1;
12     if (i.value == k) { // We've found the kth element
13        return head;
14     }
15     return node;
16 }
17
```

Each of these recursive solutions takes O(n) space due to the recursive calls.

There are a number of other solutions that we haven't addressed. We could store the counter in a static variable. Or, we could create a class that stores both the node and the counter, and return an instance of that class. Regardless of which solution we pick, we need a way to update both the node and the counter in a way that all levels of the recursive stack will see.

Solution #3: Iterative

A more optimal, but less straightforward, solution is to implement this iteratively. We can use two pointers, p1 and p2. We place them k nodes apart in the linked list by putting p1 at the beginning and moving p2 k nodes into the list. Then, when we move them at the same pace, p2 will hit the end of the linked list after LENGTH - k steps. At that point, p1 will be LENGTH - k nodes into the list, or k nodes from the end.

The code below implements this algorithm.

```
1   LinkedListNode nthToLast(LinkedListNode head, int k) {
2      if (k <= 0) return null;
3
4      LinkedListNode p1 = head;
5      LinkedListNode p2 = head;
6
7      // Move p2 forward k nodes into the list.
8      for (int i = 0; i < k - 1; i++) {
9         if (p2 == null) return null; // Error check
10        p2 = p2.next;
11     }
12     if (p2 == null) return null;
13
14     /* Now, move p1 and p2 at the same speed. When p2 hits the end,
15      * p1 will be at the right element. */
16     while (p2.next != null) {
17        p1 = p1.next;
18        p2 = p2.next;
19     }
20     return p1;
21  }
```

This algorithm takes O(n) time and O(1) space.

2.3   *Implement an algorithm to delete a node in the middle of a singly linked list, given only access to that node.*

pg 77

SOLUTION

In this problem, you are not given access to the head of the linked list. You only have access to that node. The solution is simply to copy the data from the next node over to the current node, and then to delete the next node.

The code below implements this algorithm.

```
1   public static boolean deleteNode(LinkedListNode n) {
2      if (n == null || n.next == null) {
3         return false; // Failure
4      }
```

```
5       LinkedListNode next = n.next;
6       n.data = next.data;
7       n.next = next.next;
8       return true;
9   }
```

Note that this problem cannot be solved if the node to be deleted is the last node in the linked list. That's ok—your interviewer wants you to point that out, and to discuss how to handle this case. You could, for example, consider marking the node as dummy.

2.4   *Write code to partition a linked list around a value x, such that all nodes less than x come before all nodes greater than or equal to x.*

pg 77

SOLUTION

If this were an array, we would need to be careful about how we shifted elements. Array shifts are very expensive.

However, in a linked list, the situation is much easier. Rather than shifting and swapping elements, we can actually create two different linked lists: one for elements less than x, and one for elements greater than or equal to x.

We iterate through the linked list, inserting elements into our `before` list or our `after` list. Once we reach the end of the linked list and have completed this splitting, we merge the two lists.

The code below implements this approach.

```
1   /* Pass in the head of the linked list and the value to partition
2    * around */
3   public LinkedListNode partition(LinkedListNode node, int x) {
4       LinkedListNode beforeStart = null;
5       LinkedListNode beforeEnd = null;
6       LinkedListNode afterStart = null;
7       LinkedListNode afterEnd = null;
8
9       /* Partition list */
10      while (node != null) {
11          LinkedListNode next = node.next;
12          node.next = null;
13          if (node.data < x) {
14              /* Insert node into end of before list */
15              if (beforeStart == null) {
16                  beforeStart = node;
17                  beforeEnd = beforeStart;
18              } else {
19                  beforeEnd.next = node;
20                  beforeEnd = node;
```

```
21              }
22          } else {
23              /* Insert node into end of after list */
24              if (afterStart == null) {
25                  afterStart = node;
26                  afterEnd = afterStart;
27              } else {
28                  afterEnd.next = node;
29                  afterEnd = node;
30              }
31          }
32          node = next;
33      }
34
35      if (beforeStart == null) {
36          return afterStart;
37      }
38
39      /* Merge before list and after list */
40      beforeEnd.next = afterStart;
41      return beforeStart;
42  }
```

If it bugs you to keep around four different variables for tracking two linked lists, you're not alone. We can get rid of some of these, with just a minor hit to the efficiency. This drop in efficiency comes because we have to traverse the linked list an extra time. The big-O time will remain the same though, and we get shorter, cleaner code.

The second solution operates in a slightly different way. Instead of inserting nodes into the end of the before list and the after list, it inserts nodes into the front of them.

```
1   public LinkedListNode partition(LinkedListNode node, int x) {
2       LinkedListNode beforeStart = null;
3       LinkedListNode afterStart = null;
4
5       /* Partition list */
6       while (node != null) {
7           LinkedListNode next = node.next;
8           if (node.data < x) {
9               /* Insert node into start of before list */
10              node.next = beforeStart;
11              beforeStart = node;
12          } else {
13              /* Insert node into front of after list */
14              node.next = afterStart;
15              afterStart = node;
16          }
17          node = next;
18      }
19
20      /* Merge before list and after list */
```

```
21    if (beforeStart == null) {
22       return afterStart;
23    }
24
25    /* Find end of before list, and merge the lists */
26    LinkedListNode head = beforeStart;
27    while (beforeStart.next != null) {
28       beforeStart = beforeStart.next;
29    }
30    beforeStart.next = afterStart;
31
32    return head;
33 }
```

Note that in this problem, we need to be very careful about null values. Check out line 7 in the above solution. The line is here because we are modifying the linked list as we're looping through it. We need to store the next node in a temporary variable so that we remember which node should be next in our iteration.

2.5   *You have two numbers represented by a linked list, where each node contains a single digit. The digits are stored in reverse order, such that the 1's digit is at the head of the list. Write a function that adds the two numbers and returns the sum as a linked list.*

FOLLOW UP

Suppose the digits are stored in forward order. Repeat the above problem.

pg 77

SOLUTION

It's useful to remember in this problem how exactly addition works. Imagine the problem:

```
  6 1 7
+ 2 9 5
```

First, we add 7 and 5 to get 12. The digit 2 becomes the last digit of the number, and 1 gets carried over to the next step. Second, we add 1, 1, and 9 to get 11. The 1 becomes the second digit, and the other 1 gets carried over the final step. Third and finally, we add 1, 6 and 2 to get 9. So, our value becomes 912.

We can mimic this process recursively by adding node by node, carrying over any "excess" data to the next node. Let's walk through this for the below linked list:

```
    7 -> 1 -> 6
  + 5 -> 9 -> 2
```

We do the following:

1. We add 7 and 5 first, getting a result of 12. 2 becomes the first node in our linked list,

and we "carry" the 1 to the next sum.

List: 2 -> ?

2. We then add 1 and 9, as well as the "carry," getting a result of 11. 1 becomes the second element of our linked list, and we carry the 1 to the next sum.

List: 2 -> 1 -> ?

3. Finally, we add 6, 2 and our "carry," to get 9. This become the final element of our linked list.

List: 2 -> 1 -> 9.

The code below implements this algorithm.

```
1   LinkedListNode addLists(LinkedListNode l1, LinkedListNode l2,
2                         int carry) {
3     /* We're done if both lists are null AND the carry value is 0 */
4     if (l1 == null && l2 == null && carry == 0) {
5       return null;
6     }
7
8     LinkedListNode result = new LinkedListNode(carry, null, null);
9
10    /* Add value, and the data from l1 and l2 */
11    int value = carry;
12    if (l1 != null) {
13      value += l1.data;
14    }
15    if (l2 != null) {
16      value += l2.data;
17    }
18
19    result.data = value % 10; /* Second digit of number */
20
21    /* Recurse */
22    if (l1 != null || l2 != null || value >= 10) {
23      LinkedListNode more = addLists(l1 == null ? null : l1.next,
24                                     l2 == null ? null : l2.next,
25                                     value >= 10 ? 1 : 0);
26      result.setNext(more);
27    }
28    return result;
29  }
```

In implementing this code, we must be careful to handle the condition when one linked list is shorter than another. We don't want to get a null pointer exception.

Follow Up

Part B is conceptually the same (recurse, carry the excess), but has some additional complications when it comes to implementation:

1. One list may be shorter than the other, and we cannot handle this "on the fly." For example, suppose we were adding (1 -> 2 -> 3 -> 4) and (5 -> 6 -> 7). We need to know that the 5 should be "matched" with the 2, not the 1. We can accomplish this by comparing the lengths of the lists in the beginning and padding the shorter list with zeros.

2. In the first part, successive results were added to the tail (i.e., passed forward). This meant that the recursive call would be *passed* the carry, and would return the result (which is then appended to the tail). In this case, however, results are added to the head (i.e., passed backward). The recursive call must return the result, as before, as well as the carry. This is not terribly challenging to implement, but it is more cumbersome. We can solve this issue by creating a wrapper class called Partial Sum.

The code below implements this algorithm.

```
1   public class PartialSum {
2       public LinkedListNode sum = null;
3       public int carry = 0;
4   }
5
6   LinkedListNode addLists(LinkedListNode l1, LinkedListNode l2) {
7       int len1 = length(l1);
8       int len2 = length(l2);
9
10      /* Pad the shorter list with zeros - see note (1) */
11      if (len1 < len2) {
12          l1 = padList(l1, len2 - len1);
13      } else {
14          l2 = padList(l2, len1 - len2);
15      }
16
17      /* Add lists */
18      PartialSum sum = addListsHelper(l1, l2);
19      ⸳
20      /* If there was a carry value left over, insert this at the
21       * front of the list. Otherwise, just return the linked list. */
22      if (sum.carry == 0) {
23          return sum.sum;
24      } else {
25          LinkedListNode result = insertBefore(sum.sum, sum.carry);
26          return result;
27      }
28  }
29
30  PartialSum addListsHelper(LinkedListNode l1, LinkedListNode l2) {
31      if (l1 == null && l2 == null) {
32          PartialSum sum = new PartialSum();
33          return sum;
34      }
35      /* Add smaller digits recursively */
```

```
36        PartialSum sum = addListsHelper(l1.next, l2.next);
37
38        /* Add carry to current data */
39        int val = sum.carry + l1.data + l2.data;
40
41        /* Insert sum of current digits */
42        LinkedListNode full_result = insertBefore(sum.sum, val % 10);
43
44        /* Return sum so far, and the carry value */
45        sum.sum = full_result;
46        sum.carry = val / 10;
47        return sum;
48    }
49
50    /* Pad the list with zeros */
51    LinkedListNode padList(LinkedListNode l, int padding) {
52        LinkedListNode head = l;
53        for (int i = 0; i < padding; i++) {
54            LinkedListNode n = new LinkedListNode(0, null, null);
55            head.prev = n;
56            n.next = head;
57            head = n;
58        }
59        return head;
60    }
61
62    /* Helper function to insert node in the front of a linked list */
63    LinkedListNode insertBefore(LinkedListNode list, int data) {
64        LinkedListNode node = new LinkedListNode(data, null, null);
65        if (list != null) {
66            list.prev = node;
67            node.next = list;
68        }
69        return node;
70    }
```

Note how we have pulled insertBefore(), padList(), and length() (not listed) into their own methods. This makes the code cleaner and easier to read—a wise thing to do in your interviews!

2.6   *Given a circular linked list, implement an algorithm which returns the node at the beginning of the loop.*

pg 78

SOLUTION

This is a modification of a classic interview problem: detect if a linked list has a loop. Let's apply the Pattern Matching approach.

Solutions to Chapter 2 | Linked Lists

Part 1: Detect If Linked List Has A Loop

An easy way to detect if a linked list has a loop is through the FastRunner / Slow-Runner approach. FastRunner moves two steps at a time, while SlowRunner moves one step. Much like two cars racing around a track at different steps, they must eventually meet.

An astute reader may wonder if FastRunner might "hop over" SlowRunner completely, without ever colliding. That's not possible. Suppose that FastRunner *did* hop over SlowRunner, such that SlowRunner is at spot i and FastRunner is at spot i + 1. In the previous step, SlowRunner would be at spot i - 1 and FastRunner would at spot ((i + 1) - 2), or spot i - 1. That is, they would have collided.

Part 2: When Do They Collide?

Let's assume that the linked list has a "non-looped" part of size k.

If we apply our algorithm from part 1, when will FastRunner and SlowRunner collide?

We know that for every p steps that SlowRunner takes, FastRunner has taken 2p steps. Therefore, when SlowRunner enters the looped portion after k steps, FastRunner has taken 2k steps total and must be 2k - k steps, or k steps, into the looped portion. Since k might be much larger than the loop length, we should actually write this as mod(k, LOOP_SIZE) steps, which we will denote as K.

At each subsequent step, FastRunner and SlowRunner get either one step farther away or one step closer, depending on your perspective. That is, because we are in a circle, when A moves q steps away from B, it is also moving q steps closer to B.

So now we know the following facts:

1. SlowRunner is 0 steps into the loop.

2. FastRunner is K steps into the loop.

3. SlowRunner is K steps behind FastRunner.

4. FastRunner is LOOP_SIZE - K steps behind SlowRunner.

5. FastRunner catches up to SlowRunner at a rate of 1 step per unit of time.

So, when do they meet? Well, if FastRunner is LOOP_SIZE - K steps behind Slow-Runner, and FastRunner catches up at a rate of 1 step per unit of time, then they meet after LOOP_SIZE - K steps. At this point, they will be K steps before the head of the loop. Let's call this point CollisionSpot.

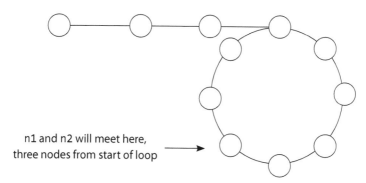

n1 and n2 will meet here,
three nodes from start of loop

Part 3: How Do You Find The Start of the Loop?

We now know that CollisionSpot is K nodes before the start of the loop. Because K = mod(k, LOOP_SIZE) (or, in other words, k = K + M * LOOP_SIZE, for any integer M), it is also correct to say that it is k nodes from the loop start. For example, if node N is 2 nodes into a 5 node loop, it is also correct to say that it is 7, 12, or even 397 nodes into the loop.

Therefore, both CollisionSpot and LinkedListHead are k nodes from the start of the loop.

Now, if we keep one pointer at CollisionSpot and move the other one to LinkedLis-tHead, they will each be k nodes from LoopStart. Moving the two pointers at the same speed will cause them to collide again—this time after k steps, at which point they will both be at LoopStart. All we have to do is return this node.

Part 4: Putting It All Together

To summarize, we move FastPointer twice as fast as SlowPointer. When Slow-Pointer enters the loop, after k nodes, FastPointer is k nodes into the linked list. This means that FastPointer and SlowPointer are LOOP_SIZE - k nodes away from each other.

Next, if FastPointer moves two nodes for each node that SlowPointer moves, they move one node closer to each other on each turn. Therefore, they will meet after LOOP_SIZE - k turns. Both will be k nodes from the front of the loop.

The head of the linked list is also k nodes from the front of the loop. So, if we keep one pointer where it is, and move the other pointer to the head of the linked list, then they will meet at the front of the loop.

Our algorithm is derived directly from parts 1, 2 and 3.

1. Create two pointers, FastPointer and SlowPointer.

2. Move FastPointer at a rate of 2 steps and SlowPointer at a rate of 1 step.

3. When they collide, move SlowPointer to LinkedListHead. Keep FastPointer

where it is.

4. Move SlowPointer and FastPointer at a rate of one step. Return the new collision point.

The code below implements this algorithm.

```
1   LinkedListNode FindBeginning(LinkedListNode head) {
2       LinkedListNode slow = head;
3       LinkedListNode fast = head;
4
5       /* Find meeting point. This will be LOOP_SIZE - k steps into the
6        * linked list. */
7       while (fast != null && fast.next != null) {
8           slow = slow.next;
9           fast = fast.next.next;
10          if (slow == fast) { // Collision
11              break;
12          }
13      }
14
15      /* Error check - no meeting point, and therefore no loop */
16      if (fast == null || fast.next == null) {
17          return null;
18      }
19
20      /* Move slow to Head. Keep fast at Meeting Point. Each are k
21       * steps from the Loop Start. If they move at the same pace,
22       * they must meet at Loop Start. */
23      slow = head;
24      while (slow != fast) {
25          slow = slow.next;
26          fast = fast.next;
27      }
28
29      /* Both now point to the start of the loop. */
30      return fast;
31  }
```

2.7   *Implement a function to check if a linked list is a palindrome.*

pg 78

SOLUTION

To approach this problem, we can picture a palindrome like 0 -> 1 -> 2 -> 1
-> 0. We know that, since it's a palindrome, the list must be the same backwards and
forwards. This leads us to our first solution.

Solution #1: Reverse and Compare

Our first solution is to reverse the linked list and compare the reversed list to the original list. If they're the same, the lists are identical.

Note that when we compare the linked list to the reversed list, we only actually need to compare the first half of the list. If the first half of the normal list matches the first half of the reversed list, then the second half of the normal list must match the second half of the reversed list.

Solution #2: Iterative Approach

We want to detect linked lists where the front half of the list is the reverse of the second half. How would we do that? By reversing the front half of the list. A stack can accomplish this.

We need to push the first half of the elements onto a stack. We can do this in two different ways, depending on whether or not we know the size of the linked list.

If we know the size of the linked list, we can iterate through the first half of the elements in a standard for loop, pushing each element onto a stack. We must be careful, of course, to handle the case where the length of the linked list is odd.

If we don't know the size of the linked list, we can iterate through the linked list, using the fast runner / slow runner technique described in the beginning of the chapter. At each step in the loop, we push the data from the slow runner onto a stack. When the fast runner hits the end of the list, the slow runner will have reached the middle of the linked list. By this point, the stack will have all the elements from the front of the linked list, but in reverse order.

Now, we simply iterate through the rest of the linked list. At each iteration, we compare the node to the top of the stack. If we complete the iteration without finding a difference, then the linked list is a palindrome.

```
1   boolean isPalindrome(LinkedListNode head) {
2       LinkedListNode fast = head;
3       LinkedListNode slow = head;
4
5       Stack<Integer> stack = new Stack<Integer>();
6
7       /* Push elements from first half of linked list onto stack. When
8        * fast runner (which is moving at 2x speed) reaches the end of
9        * the linked list, then we know we're at the middle */
10      while (fast != null && fast.next != null) {
11          stack.push(slow.data);
12          slow = slow.next;
13          fast = fast.next.next;
14      }
15
16      /* Has odd number of elements, so skip the middle element */
17      if (fast != null) {
```

```
18        slow = slow.next;
19    }
20
21    while (slow != null) {
22        int top = stack.pop().intValue();
23
24        /* If values are different, then it's not a palindrome */
25        if (top != slow.data) {
26            return false;
27        }
28        slow = slow.next;
29    }
30    return true;
31 }
```

Solution #3: Recursive Approach

First, a word on notation: in the below solution, when we use the notation node Kx, the variable K indicates the value of the node data, and x (which is either f or b) indicates whether we are referring to the front node with that value or the back node. For example, in the below linked list, node 3b would refer to the second (back) node with value 3.

Now, like many linked list problems, you can approach this problem recursively. We may have some intuitive idea that we want to compare element 0 and element n, element 1 and element n-1, element 2 and element n-2, and so on, until the middle element(s). For example:

$$0 \ (\ 1 \ (\ 2 \ (\ 3 \ ) \ 2 \ ) \ 1 \ ) \ 0$$

In order to apply this approach, we first need to know when we've reached the middle element, as this will form our base case. We can do this by passing in length - 2 for the length each time. When the length equals 0 or 1, we're at the center of the linked list.

```
1    recurse(Node n, int length) {
2        if (length == 0 || length == 1) {
3            return [something]; // At middle
4        }
5        recurse(n.next, length - 2);
6        ...
7    }
```

This method will form the outline of the isPalindrome method. The "meat" of the algorithm though is comparing node i to node n - i to check if the linked list is a palindrome. How do we do that?

Let's examine what the call stack looks like:

```
1    v1 = isPalindrome: list = 0 ( 1 ( 2 ( 3 ) 2 ) 1 ) 0. length = 7
2      v2 = isPalindrome: list = 1 ( 2 ( 3 ) 2 ) 1 ) 0. length = 5
3        v3 = isPalindrome: list = 2 ( 3 ) 2 ) 1 ) 0. length = 3
```

```
4            v4 = isPalindrome: list = 3 ) 2 ) 1 ) 0. length = 1
5              returns v3
6          returns v2
7      returns v1
8   returns ?
```

In the above call stack, each call wants to check if the list is a palindrome by comparing its head node with the corresponding node from the back of the list. That is:

- Line 1 needs to compare node 0f with node 0b

- Line 2 needs to compare node 1f with node 1b

- Line 3 needs to compare node 2f with node 2b

- Line 4 needs to compare node 3f with node 3b.

If we rewind the stack, passing nodes back as described below, we can do just that:

- Line 4 sees that it is the middle node (since length = 1), and passes back head. next. The value head equals node 3, so head.next is node 2b.

- Line 3 compares its head, node 2f, to returned_node (the value from the previous recursive call), which is node 2b. If the values match, it passes a reference to node 1b (returned_node.next) up to line 2.

- Line 2 compares its head (node 1f) to returned_node (node 1b). If the values match, it passes a reference to node 0b (or, returned_node.next) up to line 1.

- Line 1 compares its head, node 0f, to returned_node, which is node 0b. If the values match, it returns true.

To generalize, each call compares its head to returned_node, and then passes returned_node.next up the stack. In this way, every node i gets compared to node n - i. If at any point the values do not match, we return false, and every call up the stack checks for that value.

But wait, you might ask, sometimes we said we'll return a boolean value, and sometimes we're returning a node. Which is it?

It's both. We create a simple class with two members, a boolean and a node, and return an instance of that class.

```
1   class Result {
2       public LinkedListNode node;
3       public boolean result;
4   }
```

The example below illustrates the parameters and return values from this sample list.

```
1   isPalindrome: list = 0 ( 1 ( 2 ( 3 ( 4 ) 3 ) 2 ) 1 ) 0. len = 9
2     isPalindrome: list = 1 ( 2 ( 3 ( 4 ) 3 ) 2 ) 1 ) 0. len = 7
3       isPalindrome: list = 2 ( 3 ( 4 ) 3 ) 2 ) 1 ) 0. len = 5
4         isPalindrome: list = 3 ( 4 ) 3 ) 2 ) 1 ) 0. len = 3
```

```
5              isPalindrome: list = 4 ) 3 ) 2 ) 1 ) 0. len = 1
6                  returns node 3b, true
7               returns node 2b, true
8            returns node 1b, true
9      returns node 0b, true
10  returns nobe 0b, true
```

Implementing this code is now just a matter of filling in the details.

```
1   Result isPalindromeRecurse(LinkedListNode head, int length) {
2       if (head == null || length == 0) {
3           return new Result(null, true);
4       } else if (length == 1) {
5           return new Result(head.next, true);
6       } else if (length == 2) {
7           return new Result(head.next.next,
8                             head.data == head.next.data);
9       }
10      Result res = isPalindromeRecurse(head.next, length - 2);
11      if (!res.result || res.node == null) {
12          return res;
13      } else {
14          res.result = head.data == res.node.data;
15          res.node = res.node.next;
16          return res;
17      }
18  }
19
20  boolean isPalindrome(LinkedListNode head) {
21      Result p = isPalindromeRecurse(head, listSize(head));
22      return p.result;
23  }
```

Some of you might be wondering why we went through all this effort to create a special Result class. Isn't there a better way? Not really—at least not in Java.

However, if we were implementing this in C or C++, we could have passed in a double pointer.

```
1   bool isPalindromeRecurse(Node head, int length, Node** next) {
2       ...
3   }
```

It's ugly, but it works.

Stacks and Queues

Data Structures: Solutions

Chapter 3

Solutions to Chapter 3 | Stacks and Queues

3.1 *Describe how you could use a single array to implement three stacks.*

pg 80

SOLUTION

Like many problems, this one somewhat depends on how well we'd like to support these stacks. If we're ok with simply allocating a fixed amount of space for each stack, we can do that. This may mean though that one stack runs out of space, while the others are nearly empty.

Alternatively, we can be flexible in our space allocation, but this significantly increases the complexity of the problem.

Approach 1: Fixed Division

We can divide the array in three equal parts and allow the individual stack to grow in that limited space. Note: we will use the notation "[" to mean inclusive of an end point and "(" to mean exclusive of an end point.

- For stack 1, we will use $[0, n/3)$.
- For stack 2, we will use $[n/3, 2n/3)$.
- For stack 3, we will use $[2n/3, n)$.

The code for this solution is below.

```
1   int stackSize = 100;
2   int[] buffer = new int [stackSize * 3];
3   int[] stackPointer = {-1, -1, -1}; // pointers to track top element
4
5   void push(int stackNum, int value) throws Exception {
6       /* Check if we have space */
7       if (stackPointer[stackNum] + 1 >= stackSize) { // Last element
8           throw new Exception("Out of space.");
9       }
10      /* Increment stack pointer and then update top value */
11      stackPointer[stackNum]++;
12      buffer[absTopOfStack(stackNum)] = value;
13  }
14
15  int pop(int stackNum) throws Exception {
16      if (stackPointer[stackNum] == -1) {
17          throw new Exception("Trying to pop an empty stack.");
18      }
19      int value = buffer[absTopOfStack(stackNum)]; // Get top
20      buffer[absTopOfStack(stackNum)] = 0; // Clear index
21      stackPointer[stackNum]--; // Decrement pointer
22      return value;
23  }
24
```

```
25  int peek(int stackNum) {
26      int index = absTopOfStack(stackNum);
27      return buffer[index];
28  }
29
30  boolean isEmpty(int stackNum) {
31      return stackPointer[stackNum] == -1;
32  }
33
34  /* returns index of top of stack "stackNum", in absolute terms */
35  int absTopOfStack(int stackNum) {
36      return stackNum * stackSize + stackPointer[stackNum];
37  }
```

If we had additional information about the expected usages of the stacks, then we could modify this algorithm accordingly. For example, if we expected Stack 1 to have many more elements than Stack 2, we could allocate more space to Stack 1 and less space to Stack 2.

Approach 2: Flexible Divisions

A second approach is to allow the stack blocks to be flexible in size. When one stack exceeds its initial capacity, we grow the allowable capacity and shift elements as necessary.

We will also design our array to be circular, such that the final stack may start at the end of the array and wrap around to the beginning.

Please note that the code for this solution is far more complex than would be appropriate for an interview. You could be responsible for pseudocode, or perhaps the code of individual components, but the entire implementation would be far too challenging.

```
1   /* StackData is a simple class that holds a set of data about each
2    * stack. It does not hold the actual items in the stack. */
3   public class StackData {
4       public int start;
5       public int pointer;
6       public int size = 0;
7       public int capacity;
8       public StackData(int _start, int _capacity) {
9           start = _start;
10          pointer = _start - 1;
11          capacity = _capacity;
12      }
13
14      public boolean isWithinStack(int index, int total_size) {
15          /* Note: if stack wraps, the head (right side) wraps around
16           * to the left. */
17          if (start <= index && index < start + capacity) {
18              // non-wrapping, or "head" (right side) of wrapping case
```

```
19          return true;
20       } else if (start + capacity > total_size &&
21                   index < (start + capacity) % total_size) {
22          // tail (left side) of wrapping case
23          return true;
24       }
25       return false;
26    }
27 }
28
29 public class QuestionB {
30    static int number_of_stacks = 3;
31    static int default_size = 4;
32    static int total_size = default_size * number_of_stacks;
33    static StackData [] stacks = {new StackData(0, default_size),
34       new StackData(default_size, default_size),
35       new StackData(default_size * 2, default_size)};
36    static int [] buffer = new int [total_size];
37
38    public static void main(String [] args) throws Exception  {
39       push(0, 10);
40       push(1, 20);
41       push(2, 30);
42       int v = pop(0);
43       ...
44    }
45
46    public static int numberOfElements() {
47       return stacks[0].size + stacks[1].size + stacks[2].size;
48    }
49
50    public static int nextElement(int index) {
51       if (index + 1 == total_size) return 0;
52       else return index + 1;
53    }
54
55    public static int previousElement(int index) {
56       if (index == 0) return total_size - 1;
57       else return index - 1;
58    }
59
60    public static void shift(int stackNum) {
61       StackData stack = stacks[stackNum];
62       if (stack.size >= stack.capacity) {
63          int nextStack = (stackNum + 1) % number_of_stacks;
64          shift(nextStack); // make some room
65          stack.capacity++;
66       }
67
68       // Shift elements in reverse order
```

```
69      for (int i = (stack.start + stack.capacity - 1) % total_size;
70          stack.isWithinStack(i, total_size);
71          i = previousElement(i)) {
72        buffer[i] = buffer[previousElement(i)];
73      }
74
75      buffer[stack.start] = 0;
76      stack.start = nextElement(stack.start); // move stack start
77      stack.pointer = nextElement(stack.pointer); // move pointer
78      stack.capacity--; // return capacity to original
79    }
80
81    /* Expand stack by shifting over other stacks */
82    public static void expand(int stackNum) {
83      shift((stackNum + 1) % number_of_stacks);
84      stacks[stackNum].capacity++;
85    }
86
87    public static void push(int stackNum, int value)
88          throws Exception {
89      StackData stack = stacks[stackNum];
90      /* Check that we have space */
91      if (stack.size >= stack.capacity) {
92        if (numberOfElements() >= total_size) { // Totally full
93          throw new Exception("Out of space.");
94        } else { // just need to shift things around
95          expand(stackNum);
96        }
97      }
98      /* Find the index of the top element in the array + 1,
99       * and increment the stack pointer */
100     stack.size++;
101     stack.pointer = nextElement(stack.pointer);
102     buffer[stack.pointer] = value;
103   }
104
105   public static int pop(int stackNum) throws Exception {
106     StackData stack = stacks[stackNum];
107     if (stack.size == 0) {
108       throw new Exception("Trying to pop an empty stack.");
109     }
110     int value = buffer[stack.pointer];
111     buffer[stack.pointer] = 0;
112     stack.pointer = previousElement(stack.pointer);
113     stack.size--;
114     return value;
115   }
116
117   public static int peek(int stackNum) {
118     StackData stack = stacks[stackNum];
```

```
119        return buffer[stack.pointer];
120    }
121
122    public static boolean isEmpty(int stackNum) {
123        StackData stack = stacks[stackNum];
124        return stack.size == 0;
125    }
126 }
```

In problems like this, it's important to focus on writing clean, maintainable code. You should use additional classes, as we did with StackData, and pull chunks of code into separate methods. Of course, this advice applies to the "real world" as well.

3.2   *How would you design a stack which, in addition to push and pop, also has a function min which returns the minimum element? Push, pop and min should all operate in O(1) time.*

pg 80

SOLUTION

The thing with minimums is that they don't change very often. They only change when a smaller element is added.

One solution is to have just a single int value, minValue, that's a member of the Stack class. When minValue is popped from the stack, we search through the stack to find the new minimum. Unfortunately, this would break the constraint that push and pop operate in O(1) time.

To further understand this question, let's walk through it with a short example:

```
push(5); // stack is {5}, min is 5
push(6); // stack is {6, 5}, min is 5
push(3); // stack is {3, 6, 5}, min is 3
push(7); // stack is {7, 3, 6, 5}, min is 3
pop(); // pops 7. stack is {3, 6, 5}, min is 3
pop(); // pops 3. stack is {6, 5}. min is 5.
```

Observe how once the stack goes back to a prior state ({6, 5}), the minimum also goes back to its prior state (5). This leads us to our second solution.

If we kept track of the minimum at each state, we would be able to easily know the minimum. We can do this by having each node record what the minimum beneath itself is. Then, to find the min, you just look at what the top element thinks is the min.

When you push an element onto the stack, the element is given the current minimum. It sets its "local min" to be the min.

```
1   public class StackWithMin extends Stack<NodeWithMin> {
2       public void push(int value) {
3           int newMin = Math.min(value, min());
```

```
4        super.push(new NodeWithMin(value, newMin));
5    }
6
7    public int min() {
8        if (this.isEmpty()) {
9            return Integer.MAX_VALUE; // Error value
10       } else {
11           return peek().min;
12       }
13   }
14 }
15
16 class NodeWithMin {
17   public int value;
18   public int min;
19   public NodeWithMin(int v, int min){
20       value = v;
21       this.min = min;
22   }
23 }
```

There's just one issue with this: if we have a large stack, we waste a lot of space by keeping track of the min for every single element. Can we do better?

We can (maybe) do a bit better than this by using an additional stack which keeps track of the mins.

```
1    public class StackWithMin2 extends Stack<Integer> {
2        Stack<Integer> s2;
3        public StackWithMin2() {
4            s2 = new Stack<Integer>();
5        }
6
7        public void push(int value){
8            if (value <= min()) {
9                s2.push(value);
10           }
11           super.push(value);
12       }
13
14       public Integer pop() {
15           int value = super.pop();
16           if (value == min()) {
17               s2.pop();
18           }
19           return value;
20       }
21
22       public int min() {
23           if (s2.isEmpty()) {
24               return Integer.MAX_VALUE;
```

```
25          } else {
26              return s2.peek();
27          }
28      }
29  }
```

Why might this be more space efficient? Suppose we had a very large stack and the first element inserted happened to be the minimum. In the first solution, we would be keeping n ints, where n is the size of the stack. In the second solution though, we store just a few pieces of data: a second stack with one element and the members within this stack.

3.3 *Imagine a (literal) stack of plates. If the stack gets too high, it might topple. Therefore, in real life, we would likely start a new stack when the previous stack exceeds some threshold. Implement a data structure SetOfStacks that mimics this. SetOf-Stacks should be composed of several stacks and should create a new stack once the previous one exceeds capacity. SetOfStacks.push() and SetOfStacks. pop() should behave identically to a single stack (that is, pop() should return the same values as it would if there were just a single stack).*

FOLLOW UP

Implement a function popAt(int index) which performs a pop operation on a specific sub-stack.

pg 80

SOLUTION

In this problem, we've been told what our data structure should look like:

```
1   class SetOfStacks {
2       ArrayList<Stack> stacks = new ArrayList<Stack>();
3       public void push(int v) { ... }
4       public int pop() { ... }
5   }
```

We know that push() should behave identically to a single stack, which means that we need push() to call push() on the last stack in the array of stacks. We have to be a bit careful here though: if the last stack is at capacity, we need to create a new stack. Our code should look something like this:

```
1   public void push(int v) {
2       Stack last = getLastStack();
3       if (last != null && !last.isFull()) { // add to last stack
4           last.push(v);
5       } else { // must create new stack
6           Stack stack = new Stack(capacity);
7           stack.push(v);
8           stacks.add(stack);
9       }
```

```
10 }
```

What should pop() do? It should behave similarly to push() in that it should operate on the last stack. If the last stack is empty (after popping), then we should remove the stack from the list of stacks.

```
1   public int pop() {
2       Stack last = getLastStack();
3       int v = last.pop();
4       if (last.size == 0) stacks.remove(stacks.size() - 1);
5       return v;
6   }
```

Follow Up: Implement popAt(int index)

This is a bit trickier to implement, but we can imagine a "rollover" system. If we pop an element from stack 1, we need to remove the *bottom* of stack 2 and push it onto stack 1. We then need to rollover from stack 3 to stack 2, stack 4 to stack 3, etc.

You could make an argument that, rather than "rolling over," we should be OK with some stacks not being at full capacity. This would improve the time complexity (by a fair amount, with a large number of elements), but it might get us into tricky situations later on if someone assumes that all stacks (other than the last) operate at full capacity. There's no "right answer" here; you should discuss this trade-off with your interviewer.

```
1   public class SetOfStacks {
2       ArrayList<Stack> stacks = new ArrayList<Stack>();
3       public int capacity;
4       public SetOfStacks(int capacity) {
5           this.capacity = capacity;
6       }
7
8       public Stack getLastStack() {
9           if (stacks.size() == 0) return null;
10          return stacks.get(stacks.size() - 1);
11      }
12
13      public void push(int v) { /* see earlier code */ }
14      public int pop() { /* see earlier code */ }
15      public boolean isEmpty() {
16          Stack last = getLastStack();
17          return last == null || last.isEmpty();
18      }
19
20      public int popAt(int index) {
21          return leftShift(index, true);
22      }
23
24      public int leftShift(int index, boolean removeTop) {
25          Stack stack = stacks.get(index);
26          int removed_item;
```

```
27          if (removeTop) removed_item = stack.pop();
28          else removed_item = stack.removeBottom();
29          if (stack.isEmpty()) {
30             stacks.remove(index);
31          } else if (stacks.size() > index + 1) {
32             int v = leftShift(index + 1, false);
33             stack.push(v);
34          }
35          return removed_item;
36       }
37    }
38
39    public class Stack {
40       private int capacity;
41       public Node top, bottom;
42       public int size = 0;
43
44       public Stack(int capacity) { this.capacity = capacity; }
45       public boolean isFull() { return capacity == size; }
46
47       public void join(Node above, Node below) {
48          if (below != null) below.above = above;
49          if (above != null) above.below = below;
50       }
51
52       public boolean push(int v) {
53          if (size >= capacity) return false;
54          size++;
55          Node n = new Node(v);
56          if (size == 1) bottom = n;
57          join(n, top);
58          top = n;
59          return true;
60       }
61
62       public int pop() {
63          Node t = top;
64          top = top.below;
65          size--;
66          return t.value;
67       }
68
69       public boolean isEmpty() {
70          return size == 0;
71       }
72
73       public int removeBottom() {
74          Node b = bottom;
75          bottom = bottom.above;
76          if (bottom != null) bottom.below = null;
```

```
77        size--;
78        return b.value;
79    }
80 }
```

This problem is not conceptually that tough, but it requires a lot of code to implement it fully. Your interviewer would not ask you to implement the entire code.

A good strategy on problems like this is to separate code into other methods, like a leftShift method that popAt can call. This will make your code cleaner and give you the opportunity to lay down the skeleton of the code before dealing with some of the details.

3.4   *In the classic problem of the Towers of Hanoi, you have 3 towers and N disks of different sizes which can slide onto any tower. The puzzle starts with disks sorted in ascending order of size from top to bottom (i.e., each disk sits on top of an even larger one). You have the following constraints:*

(1) Only one disk can be moved at a time.

(2) A disk is slid off the top of one tower onto the next rod.

(3) A disk can only be placed on top of a larger disk.

Write a program to move the disks from the first tower to the last using Stacks.

pg 81

SOLUTION

This problem sounds like a good candidate for the Base Case and Build approach.

Let's start with the smallest possible example: n = 1.

Case n = 1. Can we move Disk 1 from Tower 1 to Tower 3? Yes.

1. We simply move Disk 1 from Tower 1 to Tower 3.

Case n = 2. Can we move Disk 1 and Disk 2 from Tower 1 to Tower 3? Yes.

1. Move Disk 1 from Tower 1 to Tower 2

2. Move Disk 2 from Tower 1 to Tower 3

3. Move Disk 1 from Tower 2 to Tower 3

Note how in the above steps, Tower 2 acts as a buffer, holding a disk while we move other disks to Tower 3.

Case n = 3. Can we move Disk 1, 2, and 3 from Tower 1 to Tower 3? Yes.

1. We know we can move the top two disks from one tower to another (as shown earlier), so let's assume we've already done that. But instead, let's move them to Tower 2.

2. Move Disk 3 to Tower 3.

3. Move Disk 1 and Disk 2 to Tower 3. We already know how to do this—we just repeat what we did in Step 1.

Case n = 4. Can we move Disk 1, 2, 3 and 4 from Tower 1 to Tower 3? Yes.

1. Move Disks 1, 2, and 3 to Tower 2. We know how to do that from the earlier examples.

2. Move Disk 4 to Tower 3.

3. Move Disks 1, 2 and 3 back to Tower 3.

Remember that the labels of Tower 2 and Tower 3 aren't important. They're equivalent towers. So, moving disks to Tower 3 with Tower 2 serving as a buffer is equivalent to moving disks to Tower 2 with Tower 3 serving as a buffer.

This approach leads to a natural recursive algorithm. In each part, we are doing the following steps, outlined below with pseudocode:

```
1   moveDisks(int n, Tower origin, Tower destination, Tower buffer) {
2       /* Base case */
3       if (n <= 0) return;
4
5       /* move top n - 1 disks from Tower 1 to Tower 2, using Tower 3
6        * as a buffer. */
7       moveDisks (n - 1, Tower 1, Tower 2, Tower 3);
8
9       /* move top from Tower 1 to Tower 3 */
10      moveTop(Tower 1, Tower 3);
11
12      /* move top n - 1 disks from Tower 2 to Tower 3, using
13       * Tower 1 as a buffer. */
14      moveDisks(n - 1, Tower 2, Tower 3, Tower 1);
15  }
```

The following code provides a more detailed implementation of this algorithm, using concepts of object-oriented design.

```
1   public static void main(String[] args) {
2       int n = 3;
3       Tower[] towers = new Tower[n];
4       for (int i = 0; i < 3; i++) {
5           towers[i] = new Tower(i);
6       }
7
```

```
8      for (int i = n - 1; i >= 0; i--) {
9          towers[0].add(i);
10     }
11     towers[0].moveDisks(n, towers[2], towers[1]);
12  }
13
14  public class Tower {
15      private Stack<Integer> disks;
16      private int index;
17      public Tower(int i) {
18          disks = new Stack<Integer>();
19          index = i;
20      }
21
22      public int index() {
23          return index;
24      }
25
26      public void add(int d) {
27          if (!disks.isEmpty() && disks.peek() <= d) {
28              System.out.println("Error placing disk " + d);
29          } else {
30              disks.push(d);
31          }
32      }
33
34      public void moveTopTo(Tower t) {
35          int top = disks.pop();
36          t.add(top);
37          System.out.println("Move disk " + top + " from " + index() +
38                              " to " + t.index());
39      }
40
41      public void moveDisks(int n, Tower destination, Tower buffer) {
42          if (n > 0) {
43              moveDisks(n - 1, buffer, destination);
44              moveTopTo(destination);
45              buffer.moveDisks(n - 1, destination, this);
46          }
47      }
48  }
```

Implementing the towers as their own object is not strictly necessary, but it does help to make the code cleaner in some respects.

3.5   *Implement a MyQueue class which implements a queue using two stacks.*

pg 81

SOLUTION

Since the major difference between a queue and a stack is the order (first-in first-out vs. last-in first-out), we know that we need to modify peek() and pop() to go in reverse order. We can use our second stack to reverse the order of the elements (by popping s1 and pushing the elements on to s2). In such an implementation, on each peek() and pop() operation, we would pop everything from s1 onto s2, perform the peek / pop operation, and then push everything back.

This will work, but if two pop / peeks are performed back-to-back, we're needlessly moving elements. We can implement a "lazy" approach where we let the elements sit in s2 until we absolutely must reverse the elements.

In this approach, stackNewest has the newest elements on top and stackOldest has the oldest elements on top. When we dequeue an element, we want to remove the oldest element first, and so we dequeue from stackOldest. If stackOldest is empty, then we want to transfer all elements from stackNewest into this stack in reverse order. To insert an element, we push onto stackNewest, since it has the newest elements on top.

The code below implements this algorithm.

```
1   public class MyQueue<T> {
2      Stack<T> stackNewest, stackOldest;
3
4      public MyQueue() {
5         stackNewest = new Stack<T>();
6         stackOldest = new Stack<T>();
7      }
8
9      public int size() {
10        return stackNewest.size() + stackOldest.size();
11     }
12
13     public void add(T value) {
14        /* Push onto stackNewest, which always has the newest
15         * elements on top */
16        stackNewest.push(value);
17     }
18
19     /* Move elements from stackNewest into stackOldest. This is
20      * usually done so that we can do operations on stackOldest. */
21     private void shiftStacks() {
22        if (stackOldest.isEmpty()) {
23           while (!stackNewest.isEmpty()) {
24              stackOldest.push(stackNewest.pop());
25           }
26        }
27     }
```

```
28
29    public T peek() {
30        shiftStacks(); // Ensure stackOldest has the current elements
31        return stackOldest.peek(); // retrieve the oldest item.
32    }
33
34    public T remove() {
35        shiftStacks(); // Ensure stackOldest has the current elements
36        return stackOldest.pop(); // pop the oldest item.
37    }
38 }
```

During your actual interview, you may find that you forget the exact API calls. Don't stress too much if that happens to you. Most interviewers are okay with your asking for them to refresh your memory on little details. They're much more concerned with your big picture understanding.

3.6 *Write a program to sort a stack in ascending order (with biggest items on top). You may use additional stacks to hold items, but you may not copy the elements into any other data structure (such as an array). The stack supports the following operations: push, pop, peek, and isEmpty.*

pg 81

SOLUTION

One approach is to implement a rudimentary sorting algorithm. We search through the entire stack to find the minimum element and then push that onto a new stack. Then, we find the new minimum element and push that. This will actually require a total of three stacks: s1 is the original stack, s2 is the final sorted stack, and s3 acts as a buffer during our searching of s1. To search s1 for each minimum, we need to pop elements from s1 and push them onto the buffer, s3.

Unfortunately, this requires three stacks. Can we do better? Yes.

Rather than searching for the minimum repeatedly, we can sort s1 by inserting each element from s1 in order into s2. How would this work?

Imagine we have the following stacks, where s2 is "sorted" and s1 is not:

s1	s2
	12
5	8
10	3
7	1

When we pop 5 from s1, we need to find the right place in s2 to insert this number. In this case, the correct place is on s2 just above 3. How do we get it there? We can do this by popping 5 from s1 and holding it in a temporary variable. Then, we move 12 and 8 over to s1 (by popping them from s2 and pushing them onto s1) and then push 5 onto s2.

Step 1		Step 2		Step 3	
s1	**s2**	**s1**	**s2**	**s1**	**s2**
	12	8		8	
	8	12		12	5
10	3	10	3	10	3
7	1	7	1	7	1
tmp = 5		tmp = 5		tmp = --	

Note that 8 and 12 are still in s1 -- and that's okay! We just repeat the same steps for those two numbers as we did for 5, each time popping off the top of s1 and putting it into the "right place" on s2. (Of course, since 8 and 12 were moved from s2 to s1 precisely *because* they were larger than 5, the "right place" for these elements will be right on top of 5. We won't need to muck around with s2's other elements, and the inside of the below while loop will not be run when tmp is 8 or 12.)

```
1   public static Stack<Integer> sort(Stack<Integer> s) {
2       Stack<Integer> r = new Stack<Integer>();
3       while (!s.isEmpty()) {
4           int tmp = s.pop(); // Step 1
5           while (!r.isEmpty() && r.peek() > tmp) { // Step 2
6               s.push(r.pop());
7           }
8           r.push(tmp); // Step 3
9       }
10      return r;
11  }
```

This algorithm is O(N²) time and O(N) space.

3.7 An animal shelter holds only dogs and cats, and operates on a strictly "first in, first out" basis. People must adopt either the "oldest" (based on arrival time) of all animals at the shelter, or they can select whether they would prefer a dog or a cat (and will receive the oldest animal of that type). They cannot select which specific animal they would like. Create the data structures to maintain this system and implement operations such as enqueue, dequeueAny, dequeueDog and dequeueCat. You may use the built-in LinkedList data structure.

pg 81

SOLUTION

We could explore a variety of solutions to this problem. For instance, we could maintain a single queue. This would make dequeueAny easy, but dequeueDog and dequeueCat would require iteration through the queue to find the first dog or cat. This would increase the complexity of the solution and decrease the efficiency.

An alternative approach that is simple, clean and efficient is to simply use separate queues for dogs and cats, and to place them within a wrapper class called Animal-Queue. We then store some sort of timestamp to mark when each animal was enqueued. When we call dequeueAny, we peek at the heads of both the dog and cat queue and return the oldest.

```
1    public abstract class Animal {
2        private int order;
3        protected String name;
4        public Animal(String n) {
5            name = n;
6        }
7
8        public void setOrder(int ord) {
9            order = ord;
10       }
11
12       public int getOrder() {
13           return order;
14       }
15
16       public boolean isOlderThan(Animal a) {
17           return this.order < a.getOrder();
18       }
19   }
20
21   public class AnimalQueue {
22       LinkedList<Dog> dogs = new LinkedList<Dog>();
23       LinkedList<Cat> cats = new LinkedList<Cat>();
24       private int order = 0; // acts as timestamp
25
26       public void enqueue(Animal a) {
27           /* Order is used as a sort of timestamp, so that we can
28            * compare the insertion order of a dog to a cat. */
29           a.setOrder(order);
30           order++;
31
32           if (a instanceof Dog) dogs.addLast((Dog) a);
33           else if (a instanceof Cat) cats.addLast((Cat)a);
34       }
35
36       public Animal dequeueAny() {
37           /* Look at tops of dog and cat queues, and pop the stack
38            * with the oldest value. */
39           if (dogs.size() == 0) {
40               return dequeueCats();
```

```
41        } else if (cats.size() == 0) {
42            return dequeueDogs();
43        }
44
45        Dog dog = dogs.peek();
46      , Cat cat = cats.peek();
47     if (dog.isOlderThan(cat)) {
48      , return dequeueDogs();
49     } else {
50        return dequeueCats();
51     }
52
53     public Dog dequeueDogs() {
54        return dogs.poll();
55     }
56
57     public Cat dequeueCats() {
58        return cats.poll();
59     }
60 }
61
62 public class Dog extends Animal {
63    public Dog(String n) {
64        super(n);
65    }
66 }
67
68 public class Cat extends Animal {
69    public Cat(String n) {
70        super(n);
71    }
72 }
```

Trees and Graphs

Data Structures: Solutions

Chapter 4

4.1 *Implement a function to check if a binary tree is balanced. For the purposes of this question, a balanced tree is defined to be a tree such that the heights of the two subtrees of any node never differ by more than one.*

pg 86

SOLUTION

In this question, we've been fortunate enough to be told exactly what balanced means: that for each node, the two subtrees differ in height by no more than one. We can implement a solution based on this definition. We can simply recurse through the entire tree, and for each node, compute the heights of each subtree.

```
1   public static int getHeight(TreeNode root) {
2       if (root == null) return 0; // Base case
3       return Math.max(getHeight(root.left),
4                       getHeight(root.right)) + 1;
5   }
6
7   public static boolean isBalanced(TreeNode root) {
8       if (root == null) return true; // Base case
9
10      int heightDiff = getHeight(root.left) - getHeight(root.right);
11      if (Math.abs(heightDiff) > 1) {
12          return false;
13      } else { // Recurse
14          return isBalanced(root.left) && isBalanced(root.right);
15      }
16  }
```

Although this works, it's not very efficient. On each node, we recurse through its entire subtree. This means that getHeight is called repeatedly on the same nodes. The algorithm is therefore O(N^2).

We need to cut out some of the calls to getHeight.

If we inspect this method, we may notice that getHeight could actually check if the tree is balanced as the same time as it's checking heights. What do we do when we discover that the subtree isn't balanced? Just return -1.

This improved algorithm works by checking the height of each subtree as we recurse down from the root. On each node, we recursively get the heights of the left and right subtrees through the checkHeight method. If the subtree is balanced, then check-Height will return the actual height of the subtree. If the subtree is not balanced, then checkHeight will return -1. We will immediately break and return -1 from the current call.

The code below implements this algorithm.

```
1   public static int checkHeight(TreeNode root) {
2       if (root == null) {
```

```
3        return 0; // Height of 0
4     }
5
6     /* Check if left is balanced. */
7     int leftHeight = checkHeight(root.left);
8     if (leftHeight == -1) {
9        return -1; // Not balanced
10    }
11    /* Check if right is balanced. */
12    int rightHeight = checkHeight(root.right);
13    if (rightHeight == -1) {
14       return -1; // Not balanced
15    }
16
17    /* Check if current node is balanced. */
18    int heightDiff = leftHeight - rightHeight;
19    if (Math.abs(heightDiff) > 1) {
20       return -1; // Not balanced
21    } else {
22       /* Return height */
23       return Math.max(leftHeight, rightHeight) + 1;
24    }
25 }
26
27 public static boolean isBalanced(TreeNode root) {
28    if (checkHeight(root) == -1) {
29       return false;
30    } else {
31       return true;
32    }
33 }
```

This code runs in O(N) time and O(log N) space.

4.2 *Given a directed graph, design an algorithm to find out whether there is a route between two nodes.*

pg 86

SOLUTION

This problem can be solved by just simple graph traversal, such as depth first search or breadth first search. We start with one of the two nodes and, during traversal, check if the other node is found. We should mark any node found in the course of the algorithm as "already visited" to avoid cycles and repetition of the nodes.

The code below provides an iterative implementation of breadth first search.

```
1   public enum State {
2      Unvisited, Visited, Visiting;
```

```
3    }
4
5    public static boolean search(Graph g, Node start, Node end) {
6        // operates as Queue
7        LinkedList<Node> q = new LinkedList<Node>();
8
9        for (Node u : g.getNodes()) {
10           u.state = State.Unvisited;
11       }
12       start.state = State.Visiting;
13       q.add(start);
14       Node u;
15       while (!q.isEmpty()) {
16           u = q.removeFirst(); // i.e., dequeue()
17           if (u != null) {
18               for (Node v : u.getAdjacent()) {
19                   if (v.state == State.Unvisited) {
20                       if (v == end) {
21                           return true;
22                       } else {
23                           v.state = State.Visiting;
24                           q.add(v);
25                       }
26                   }
27               }
28               u.state = State.Visited;
29           }
30       }
31       return false;
32   }
```

It may be worth discussing with your interviewer the trade-offs between breadth first search and depth first search for this and other problems. For example, depth first search is a bit simpler to implement since it can be done with simple recursion. Breadth first search can also be useful to find the shortest path, whereas depth first search may traverse one adjacent node very deeply before ever going onto the immediate neighbors.

4.3   *Given a sorted (increasing order) array, write an algorithm to create a binary search tree with minimal height.*

pg 86

SOLUTION

To create a tree of minimal height, we need to match the number of nodes in the left subtree to the number of nodes in the right subtree as much as possible. This means that we want the root to be the middle of the array, since this would mean that half the elements would be less than the root and half would be greater than it.

We proceed with constructing our tree in a similar fashion. The middle of each subsection of the array becomes the root of the node. The left half of the array will become our left subtree, and the right half of the array will become the right subtree.

One way to implement this is to use a simple `root.insertNode(int v)` method which inserts the value v through a recursive process that starts with the root node. This will indeed construct a tree with minimal height but it will not do so very efficiently. Each insertion will require traversing the tree, giving a total cost of `O(N log N)` to the tree.

Alternatively, we can cut out the extra traversals by recursively using the `createMinimalBST` method. This method is passed just a subsection of the array and returns the root of a minimal tree for that array.

The algorithm is as follows:

1. Insert into the tree the middle element of the array.

2. Insert (into the left subtree) the left subarray elements.

3. Insert (into the right subtree) the right subarray elements.

4. Recurse.

The code below implements this algorithm.

```
1   TreeNode createMinimalBST(int arr[], int start, int end) {
2       if (end < start) {
3           return null;
4       }
5       int mid = (start + end) / 2;
6       TreeNode n = new TreeNode(arr[mid]);
7       n.left = createMinimalBST(arr, start, mid - 1);
8       n.right = createMinimalBST(arr, mid + 1, end);
9       return n;
10  }
11
12  TreeNode createMinimalBST(int array[]) {
13      return createMinimalBST(array, 0, array.length - 1);
14  }
```

Although this code does not seem especially complex, it can be very easy to make little off-by-one errors. Be sure to test these parts of the code very thoroughly.

4.4 *Given a binary tree, design an algorithm which creates a linked list of all the nodes at each depth (e.g., if you have a tree with depth D, you'll have D linked lists).*

pg 86

SOLUTION

Though we might think at first glance that this problem requires a level-by-level traversal, this isn't actually necessary. We can traverse the graph any way that we'd like, provided we know which level we're on as we do so.

We can implement a simple modification of the pre-order traversal algorithm, where we pass in `level + 1` to the next recursive call. The code below provides an implementation using depth first search.

```
1   void createLevelLinkedList(TreeNode root,
2        ArrayList<LinkedList<TreeNode>> lists, int level) {
3     if (root == null) return; // base case
4
5     LinkedList<TreeNode> list = null;
6     if (lists.size() == level) { // Level not contained in list
7       list = new LinkedList<TreeNode>();
8       /* Levels are always traversed in order. So, if this is the
9        * first time we've visited level i, we must have seen levels
10       * 0 through i - 1. We can therefore safely add the level at
11       * the end. */
12      lists.add(list);
13    } else {
14      list = lists.get(level);
15    }
16    list.add(root);
17    createLevelLinkedList(root.left, lists, level + 1);
18    createLevelLinkedList(root.right, lists, level + 1);
19  }
20
21  ArrayList<LinkedList<TreeNode>> createLevelLinkedList(
22       TreeNode root) {
23    ArrayList<LinkedList<TreeNode>> lists =
24       new ArrayList<LinkedList<TreeNode>>();
25    createLevelLinkedList(root, lists, 0);
26    return lists;
27  }
```

Alternatively, we can also implement a modification of breadth first search. With this implementation, we want to iterate through the root first, then level 2, then level 3, and so on.

With each level i, we will have already fully visited all nodes on level i - 1. This means that to get which nodes are on level i, we can simply look at all children of the nodes of level i - 1.

The code below implements this algorithm.

```
1   ArrayList<LinkedList<TreeNode>> createLevelLinkedList(
2       TreeNode root) {
3     ArrayList<LinkedList<TreeNode>> result =
4       new ArrayList<LinkedList<TreeNode>>();
5     /* "Visit" the root */
6     LinkedList<TreeNode> current = new LinkedList<TreeNode>();
7     if (root != null) {
8       current.add(root);
9     }
10
11    while (current.size() > 0) {
12      result.add(current); // Add previous level
13      LinkedList<TreeNode> parents = current; // Go to next level
14      current = new LinkedList<TreeNode>();
15      for (TreeNode parent : parents) {
16        /* Visit the children */
17        if (parent.left != null) {
18          current.add(parent.left);
19        }
20        if (parent.right != null) {
21          current.add(parent.right);
22        }
23      }
24    }
25    return result;
26  }
```

One might ask which of these solutions is more efficient. Both run in O(N) time, but what about the space efficiency? At first, we might want to claim that the second solution is more space efficient.

In a sense, that's correct. The first solution uses O(log N) recursive calls, each of which adds a new level to the stack. The second solution, which is iterative, does not require this extra space.

However, both solutions require returning O(N) data. The extra O(log N) space usage from the recursive implementation is dwarfed by the O(N) data that must be returned. So while the first solution may actually use more data, they are equally efficient when it comes to "big O."

4.5   *Implement a function to check if a binary tree is a binary search tree.*

pg 86

SOLUTION

We can implement this solution in two different ways. The first leverages the in-order traversal, and the second builds off the property that left <= current < right.

Solutions to Chapter 4 | Trees and Graphs

Solution #1: In-Order Traversal

Our first thought might be to do an in-order traversal, copy the elements to an array, and then check to see if the array is sorted. This solution takes up a bit of extra memory, but it works.

The pseudocode for this method looks something like:

```
1   public static int index = 0;
2   public static void copyBST(TreeNode root, int[] array) {
3       if (root == null) return;
4       copyBST(root.left, array);
5       array[index] = root.data;
6       index++;
7       copyBST(root.right, array);
8   }
9
10  public static boolean checkBST(TreeNode root) {
11      int[] array = new int[root.size];
12      copyBST(root, array);
13      for (int i = 1; i < array.length; i++) {
14          if (array[i] < array[i - 1]) return false;
15      }
16      return true;
17  }
```

Note that it is necessary to keep track of the logical "end" of the array, since it would be allocated to hold all the elements.

When we examine this solution, we find that the array is not actually necessary. We never use it other than to compare an element to the previous element. So why not just track the last element we saw and compare it as we go?

The code below implements this algorithm.

```
1   public static int last_printed = Integer.MIN_VALUE;
2   public static boolean checkBST(TreeNode n) {
3       if (n == null) return true;
4
5       // Check / recurse left
6       if (!checkBST(n.left)) return false;
7
8       // Check current
9       if (n.data < last_printed) return false;
10      last_printed = n.data;
11
12      // Check / recurse right
13      if (!checkBST(n.right)) return false;
14
15      return true; // All good!
16  }
```

If you don't like the use of static variables, then you can tweak this code to use a wrapper class for the integer, as shown below.

```
1   class WrapInt {
2       public int value;
3   }
```

Or, if you're implementing this in C++ or another language that supports passing integers by reference, then you can simply do that.

Solution #2: The Min / Max Solution

In the second solution, we leverage the definition of the binary search tree.

What does it mean for a tree to be a binary search tree? We know that it must, of course, satisfy the condition `left.data <= current.data < right.data` for each node, but this isn't quite sufficient. Consider the following small tree:

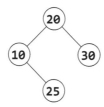

Although each node is bigger than its left node and smaller than its right node, this is clearly not a binary search tree since 25 is in the wrong place.

More precisely, the condition is that *all* left nodes must be less than or equal to the current node, which must be less than all the right nodes.

Using this thought, we can approach the problem by passing down the min and max values. As we iterate through the tree, we verify against progressively narrower ranges.

Consider the following sample tree:

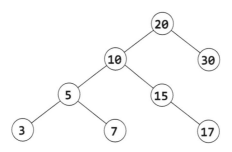

We start with a range of (`min = INT_MIN`, `max = INT_MAX`), which the root obviously meets. We then branch left, checking that these nodes are within the range (`min = INT_MIN`, `max = 20`). Then, we branch right, checking that the nodes are within the range (min = 10, max = 20).

We proceed through the tree with this approach. When we branch left, the max gets updated. When we branch right, the min gets updated. If anything fails these checks, we stop and return false.

The time complexity for this solution is O(N), where N is the number of nodes in the tree. We can prove that this is the best we can do, since any algorithm must touch all N nodes.

Due to the use of recursion, the space complexity is O(log N) on a balanced tree. There are up to O(log N) recursive calls on the stack since we may recurse up to the depth of the tree.

The recursive code for this is as follows:

```
1   boolean checkBST(TreeNode n) {
2       return checkBST(n, Integer.MIN_VALUE, Integer.MAX_VALUE);
3   }
4
5   boolean checkBST(TreeNode n, int min, int max) {
6       if (n == null) {
7           return true;
8       }
9       if (n.data <= min || n.data > max) {
10          return false;
11      }
12
13      if (!checkBST(n.left, min, n.data) ||
14              !checkBST(n.right, n.data, max)) {
15          return false;
16      }
17      return true;
18  }
```

Remember that in recursive algorithms, you should always make sure that your base cases, as well as your null cases, are well handled.

4.6   *Write an algorithm to find the 'next' node (i.e., in-order successor) of a given node in a binary search tree. You may assume that each node has a link to its parent.*

pg 86

SOLUTION

Recall that an in-order traversal traverses the left subtree, then the current node, then the right subtree. To approach this problem, we need to think very, very carefully about what happens.

Let's suppose we have a hypothetical node. We know that the order goes left subtree, then current side, then right subtree. So, the next node we visit should be on the right side.

But which node on the right subtree? It should be the first node we'd visit if we were doing an in-order traversal of that subtree. This means that it should be the leftmost node on the right subtree. Easy enough!

But what if the node doesn't have a right subtree? This is where it gets a bit trickier.

If a node n doesn't have a right subtree, then we are done traversing n's subtree. We need to pick up where we left off with n's parent, which we'll call q.

If n was to the left of q, then the next node we should traverse should be q (again, since left -> current -> right).

If n were to the right of q, then we have fully traversed q's subtree as well. We need to traverse upwards from q until we find a node x that we have *not* fully traversed. How do we know that we have not fully traversed a node x? We know we have hit this case when we move from a left node to its parent. The left node is fully traversed, but its parent is not.

The pseudocode looks like this:

```
1   Node inorderSucc(Node n) {
2       if (n has a right subtree) {
3           return leftmost child of right subtree
4       } else {
5           while (n is a right child of n.parent) {
6               n = n.parent; // Go up
7           }
8           return n.parent; // Parent has not been traversed
9       }
10  }
```

But wait—what if we traverse all the way up the tree before finding a left child? This will happen only when we've hit the very end of the in-order traversal. That is, if we're *already* on the far right of the tree, then there is no in-order successor. We should return null.

The code below implements this algorithm (and properly handles the null case).

```
1   public TreeNode inorderSucc(TreeNode n) {
2       if (n == null) return null;
3
4       /* Found right children -> return leftmost node of right
5        * subtree. */
6       if (n.parent == null || n.right != null) {
7           return leftMostChild(n.right);
8       } else {
9           TreeNode q = n;
10          TreeNode x = q.parent;
11          // Go up until we're on left instead of right
```

```
12        while (x != null && x.left != q) {
13            q = x;
14            x = x.parent;
15        }
16        return x;
17    }
18 }
19
20 public TreeNode leftMostChild(TreeNode n) {
21     if (n == null) {
22         return null;
23     }
24     while (n.left != null) {
25         n = n.left;
26     }
27     return n;
28 }
```

This is not the most algorithmically complex problem in the world, but it can be tricky to code perfectly. In a problem like this, it's useful to sketch out pseudocode to carefully outline the different cases.

4.7   *Design an algorithm and write code to find the first common ancestor of two nodes in a binary tree. Avoid storing additional nodes in a data structure. NOTE: This is not necessarily a binary search tree.*

pg 86

SOLUTION

If this were a binary search tree, we could modify the find operation for the two nodes and see where the paths diverge. Unfortunately, this is not a binary search tree, so we must try other approaches.

Let's assume we're looking for the common ancestor of nodes p and q. One question to ask here is if the nodes of our tree have links to its parents.

Solution #1: With Links to Parents

If each node has a link to its parent, we could trace p and q's paths up until they intersect. However, this may violate some assumptions of the problem as it would require either (a) being able to mark nodes as isVisited or (b) being able to store some data in an additional data structure, such as a hash table.

Solution #2: Without Links to Parents

Alternatively, you could follow a chain in which p and q are on the same side. That is, if p and q are both on the left of the node, branch left to look for the common ancestor. If they are both on the right, branch right to look for the common ancestor. When p and q are no longer on the same side, you must have found the first common ancestor.

The code below implements this approach.

```
1   /* Returns true if p is a descendent of root */
2   boolean covers(TreeNode root, TreeNode p) {
3       if (root == null) return false;
4       if (root == p) return true;
5       return covers(root.left, p) || covers(root.right, p);
6   }
7
8   TreeNode commonAncestorHelper(TreeNode root, TreeNode p,
9                                 TreeNode q) {
10      if (root == null) return null;
11      if (root == p || root == q) return root;
12
13      boolean is_p_on_left = covers(root.left, p);
14      boolean is_q_on_left = covers(root.left, q);
15
16      /* If p and q are on different sides, return root. */
17      if (is_p_on_left != is_q_on_left) return root;
18
19      /* Else, they are on the same side. Traverse this side. */
20      TreeNode child_side = is_p_on_left ? root.left : root.right;
21      return commonAncestorHelper(child_side, p, q);
22  }
23
24  TreeNode commonAncestor(TreeNode root, TreeNode p, TreeNode q) {
25      if (!covers(root, p) || !covers(root, q)) { // Error check
26          return null;
27      }
28      return commonAncestorHelper(root, p, q);
29  }
```

This algorithm runs in O(n) time on a balanced tree. This is because covers is called on 2n nodes in the first call (n nodes for the left side, and n nodes for the right side). After that, the algorithm branches left or right, at which point covers will be called on 2n/2 nodes, then 2n/4, and so on. This results in a runtime of O(n).

We know at this point that we cannot do better than that in terms of the asymptotic runtime since we need to potentially look at every node in the tree. However, we may be able to improve it by a constant multiple.

Solution #3: Optimized

Although the Solution #2 is optimal in its runtime, we may recognize that there is still some inefficiency in how it operates. Specifically, covers searches all nodes under root for p and q, including the nodes in each subtree (root.left and root.right). Then, it picks one of those subtrees and searches all of its nodes. Each subtree is searched over and over again.

We may recognize that we should only need to search the entire tree once to find p and q. We should then be able to "bubble up" the findings to earlier nodes in the stack. The basic logic is the same as the earlier solution.

We recurse through the entire tree with a function called commonAncestor(TreeNode root, TreeNode p, TreeNode q). This function returns values as follows:

- Returns p, if root's subtree includes p (and not q).

- Returns q, if root's subtree includes q (and not p).

- Returns null, if neither p nor q are in root's subtree.

- Else, returns the common ancestor of p and q.

Finding the common ancestor of p and q in the final case is easy. When commonAncestor(n.left, p, q) and commonAncestor(n.right, p, q) both return non-null values (indicating that p and q were found in different subtrees), then n will be the common ancestor.

The code below offers an initial solution, but it has a bug. Can you find it?

```
1   /* The below code has a bug. */
2   TreeNode commonAncestorBad(TreeNode root, TreeNode p, TreeNode q) {
3       if (root == null) {
4           return null;
5       }
6       if (root == p && root == q) {
7           return root;
8       }
9
10      TreeNode x = commonAncestorBad(root.left, p, q);
11      if (x != null && x != p && x != q) { // Already found ancestor
12          return x;
13      }
14
15      TreeNode y = commonAncestorBad(root.right, p, q);
16      if (y != null && y != p && y != q) { // Already found ancestor
17          return y;
18      }
19
20      if (x != null && y != null) { // p and q found in diff. subtrees
21          return root; // This is the common ancestor
22      } else if (root == p || root == q) {
23          return root;
24      } else {
25          /* If either x or y is non-null, return the non-null value */
26          return x == null ? y : x;
27      }
28  }
```

The problem with this code occurs in the case where a node is not contained in the tree.

For example, look at the tree below:

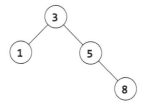

Suppose we call commonAncestor(node 3, node 5, node 7). Of course, node 7 does not exist—and that's where the issue will come in. The calling order looks like:

```
1   commonAncestor(node 3, node 5, node 7)          // --> 5
2     calls commonAncestor(node 1, node 5, node 7)  // --> null
3     calls commonAncestor(node 5, node 5, node 7)  // --> 5
4       calls commonAncestor(node 8, node 5, node 7) // --> null
```

In other words, when we call commonAncestor on the right subtree, the code will return node 5, just as it should. The problem is that, in finding the common ancestor of p and q, the calling function can't distinguish between the two cases:

- Case 1: p is a child of q (or, q is a child of p)

- Case 2: p is in the tree and q is not (or, q is in the tree and p is not)

In either of these cases, commonAncestor will return p. In the first case, this is the correct return value, but in the second case, the return value should be null.

We somehow need to distinguish between these two cases, and this is what the code below does. This code solves the problem by returning two values: the node itself and a flag indicating whether this node is actually the common ancestor.

```
1   public static class Result {
2     public TreeNode node;
3     public boolean isAncestor;
4     public Result(TreeNode n, boolean isAnc) {
5       node = n;
6       isAncestor = isAnc;
7     }
8   }
9
10  Result commonAncestorHelper(TreeNode root, TreeNode p, TreeNode q){
11    if (root == null) {
12      return new Result(null, false);
13    }
14    if (root == p && root == q) {
15      return new Result(root, true);
16    }
17
18    Result rx = commonAncestorHelper(root.left, p, q);
19    if (rx.isAncestor) { // Found common ancestor
```

```
20        return rx;
21    }
22
23    Result ry = commonAncestorHelper(root.right, p, q);
24    if (ry.isAncestor) { // Found common ancestor
25        return ry;
26    }
27
28    if (rx.node != null && ry.node != null) {
29        return new Result(root, true); // This is the common ancestor
30    } else if (root == p || root == q) {
31        /* If we're currently at p or q, and we also found one of
32         * those nodes in a subtree, then this is truly an ancestor
33         * and the flag should be true. */
34        boolean isAncestor = rx.node != null || ry.node != null ?
35                             true : false;
36        return new Result(root, isAncestor);
37    } else {
38        return new Result(rx.node!=null ? rx.node : ry.node, false);
39    }
40 }
41
42 TreeNode commonAncestor(TreeNode root, TreeNode p, TreeNode q) {
43    Result r = commonAncestorHelper(root, p, q);
44    if (r.isAncestor) {
45        return r.node;
46    }
47    return null;
48 }
```

Of course, as this issue only comes up in the case that p or q is not actually in the tree, an alternative solution would be to first search through the entire tree to make sure that both nodes exist.

4.8 *You have two very large binary trees: T1, with millions of nodes, and T2, with hundreds of nodes. Create an algorithm to decide if T2 is a subtree of T1.*

A tree T2 is a subtree of T1 if there exists a node n in T1 such that the subtree of n is identical to T2. That is, if you cut off the tree at node n, the two trees would be identical.

pg 86

SOLUTION

In problems like this, it's useful to attempt to solve the problem assuming that there is just a small amount of data. This will give us a basic idea of an approach that might work.

In this smaller, simpler problem, we could create a string representing the in-order and pre-order traversals. If T2's pre-order traversal is a substring of T1's pre-order traversal, and T2's in-order traversal is a substring of T1's in-order traversal, then T2 is a subtree of T1. Substrings can be checked with suffix trees in linear time, so this algorithm is relatively efficient in terms of the worst case time.

Note that we'll need to insert a special character into our strings to indicate when a left or right node is NULL. Otherwise, we would be unable to distinguish between the following cases:

These would have the same in-order and pre-order traversal, even though they are different trees.

```
T1, in-order:    3, 3
T1, pre-order:   3, 3
T2, in-order:    3, 3
T2, pre-order:   3, 3
```

However, if we mark the NULL values, we can distinguish between these two trees:

```
T1, in-order:    0, 3, 0, 3, 0
T1, pre-order:   3, 3, 0, 0, 0
T2, in-order:    0, 3, 0, 3, 0
T2, pre-order:   3, 0, 3, 0, 0
```

While this is a good solution for the simple case, our actual problem has much more data. Creating a copy of both trees may require too much memory given the constraints of the problem.

The Alternative Approach

An alternative approach is to search through the larger tree, T1. Each time a node in T1 matches the root of T2, call treeMatch. The treeMatch method will compare the two subtrees to see if they are identical.

Analyzing the runtime is somewhat complex. A naive answer would be to say that it is O(nm) time, where n is the number of nodes in T1 and m is the number of nodes in T2. While this is technically correct, a little more thought can produce a tighter bound.

We do not actually call treeMatch on every node in T2. Rather, we call it k times, where k is the number of occurrences of T2's root in T1. The runtime is closer to O(n + km).

In fact, even that overstates the runtime. Even if the root were identical, we exit treeMatch when we find a difference between T1 and T2. We therefore probably do not actually look at m nodes on each call of treeMatch.

The code below implements this algorithm.

```
1   boolean containsTree(TreeNode t1, TreeNode t2) {
2     if (t2 == null) { // The empty tree is always a subtree
3       return true;
4     }
5     return subTree(t1, t2);
6   }
7
8   boolean subTree(TreeNode r1, TreeNode r2) {
9     if (r1 == null) {
10      return false; // big tree empty & subtree still not found.
11    }
12    if (r1.data == r2.data) {
13      if (matchTree(r1,r2)) return true;
14    }
15    return (subTree(r1.left, r2) || subTree(r1.right, r2));
16  }
17
18  boolean matchTree(TreeNode r1, TreeNode r2) {
19    if (r2 == null && r1 == null) // if both are empty
20      return true; // nothing left in the subtree
21
22    // if one, but not both, are empty
23    if (r1 == null || r2 == null) {
24      return false;
25    }
26
27    if (r1.data != r2.data)
28      return false;  // data doesn't match
29    return (matchTree(r1.left, r2.left) &&
30        matchTree(r1.right, r2.right));
31  }
32  }
```

When might the simple solution be better, and when might the alternative approach be better? This is a great conversation to have with your interviewer. Here are a few thoughts on that matter though:

1. The simple solution takes $O(n + m)$ memory. The alternative solution takes $O(\log(n) + \log(m))$ memory. Remember: memory usage can be a very big deal when it comes to scalability.

2. The simple solution is $O(n + m)$ time and the alternative solution has a worst case time of $O(nm)$. However, the worst case time can be deceiving; we need to look deeper than that.

3. A slightly tighter bound on the runtime, as explained earlier, is $O(n + km)$, where k is the number of occurrences of T2's root in T1. Let's suppose the node data for T1 and T2 were random numbers picked between 0 and p. The value of k would be approximately n/p. Why? Because each of n nodes in T1 has a $1/p$ chance of

equaling the root, so approximately n/p nodes in T1 should equal T2.root. So, let's say p = `1000`, n = `1000000` and m = `100`. We would do somewhere around 1,100,000 node checks (`1100000` = `1000000` + `100*1000000/1000`).

4. More complex mathematics and assumptions could get us an even tighter bound. We assumed in #3 above that if we call `treeMatch`, we will end up traversing all m nodes of T2. It's far more likely though that we will find a difference very early on in the tree and will then exit early.

In summary, the alternative approach is certainly more optimal in terms of space and is likely more optimal in terms of time as well. It all depends on what assumptions you make and whether you prioritize reducing the average case runtime at the expense of the worst case runtime. This is an excellent point to make to your interviewer.

4.9 *You are given a binary tree in which each node contains a value. Design an algorithm to print all paths which sum to a given value. Note that a path can start or end anywhere in the tree.*

pg 86

SOLUTION

Let's approach this problem by using the Simplify and Generalize approach.

Part 1: Simplify—What if the path had to start at the root, but could end anywhere?

In this case, we would have a much easier problem.

We could start from the root and branch left and right, computing the sum thus far on each path. When we find the sum, we print the current path. Note that we don't stop traversing that path just because we found the sum. Why? Because the path could continue on to a +1 node and a -1 node (or any other sequence of nodes where the additional values sum to 0), and the full path would still sum to sum.

For example, if sum = 5, we could have following paths:

- p = {2, 3}
- q = {2, 3, -4, -2, 6}

If we stopped once we hit 2 + 3, we'd miss this second path and maybe some others. So, we keep going along every possible path.

Part 2: Generalize—The path can start anywhere.

Now, what if the path can start anywhere? In that case, we can make a small modification. On every node, we look "up" to see if we've found the sum. That is, rather than asking "Does this node start a path with the sum?," we ask, "Does this node complete a path with the sum?"

When we recurse through each node n, we pass the function the full path from root to n. This function then adds the nodes along the path in reverse order from n to root. When the sum of each subpath equals sum, then we print this path.

```
1   void findSum(TreeNode node, int sum, int[] path, int level) {
2       if (node == null) {
3           return;
4       }
5
6       /* Insert current node into path. */
7       path[level] = node.data;
8
9       /* Look for paths with a sum that ends at this node. */
10      int t = 0;
11      for (int i = level; i >= 0; i--){
12          t += path[i];
13          if (t == sum) {
14              print(path, i, level);
15          }
16      }
17
18      /* Search nodes beneath this one. */
19      findSum(node.left, sum, path, level + 1);
20      findSum(node.right, sum, path, level + 1);
21
22      /* Remove current node from path. Not strictly necessary, since
23       * we would ignore this value, but it's good practice. */
24      path[level] = Integer.MIN_VALUE;
25  }
26
27  public void findSum(TreeNode node, int sum) {
28      int depth = depth(node);
29      int[] path = new int[depth];
30      findSum(node, sum, path, 0);
31  }
32
33  public static void print(int[] path, int start, int end) {
34      for (int i = start; i <= end; i++) {
35          System.out.print(path[i] + " ");
36      }
37      System.out.println();
38  }
39
40  public int depth(TreeNode node) {
41      if (node == null) {
42          return 0;
43      } else {
44          return 1 + Math.max(depth(node.left), depth(node.right));
45      }
46  }
```

What is the time complexity of this algorithm (assuming a balanced binary tree)? Well, if a node is at level r, we do r amount of work (that's in the looking "up" step). We can take a guess at $O(n \log(n))$ since there are n nodes doing an average of $\log(n)$ amount of work on each step.

If that's too fuzzy for you, we can also be very mathematical about it. Note that there are 2^r nodes at level r.

```
1 * 2¹ + 2 * 2² + 3 * 2³ + 4 * 2⁴ + ... d * 2ᵈ
    = sum(r * 2ʳ, r from 0 to depth)
    = 2 * (d - 1) * 2ᵈ + 2
n = 2ᵈ
d = log(n)
```

Observe that $2^{\log(x)} = x$.

```
O(2 * (log(n) - 1) * 2^log(n) + 2)
    = O(2 (log n - 1) * n )
    = O(n log(n))
```

The space complexity is $O(\log n)$, since the algorithm will recurse $O(\log n)$ times and the path parameter is only allocated once (at $O(\log n)$ space) during this recursion.

Bit Manipulation

Concepts and Algorithms: Solutions | **Chapter 5**

5.1 You are given two 32-bit numbers, N and M, and two bit positions, i and j. Write a method to insert M into N such that M starts at bit j and ends at bit i. You can assume that the bits j through i have enough space to fit all of M. That is, if M = 10011, you can assume that there are at least 5 bits between j and i. You would not, for example, have j = 3 and i = 2, because M could not fully fit between bit 3 and bit 2.

EXAMPLE:

Input: N = 10000000000, M = 10011, i = 2, j = 6

Output: N = 10001001100

pg 91

SOLUTION

This problem can be approached in three key steps:

1. Clear the bits j through i in N

2. Shift M so that it lines up with bits j through i

3. Merge M and N.

The trickiest part is Step 1. How do we clear the bits in N? We can do this with a mask. This mask will have all 1s, except for 0s in the bits j through i. We create this mask by creating the left half of the mask first, and then the right half.

```
1   int updateBits(int n, int m, int i, int j) {
2       /* Create a mask to clear bits i through j in n
3        /* EXAMPLE: i = 2, j = 4. Result should be 11100011.
4        * For simplicity, we'll use just 8 bits for the example.
5        */
6       int allOnes = ~0; // will equal sequence of all 1s
7
8       // 1s before position j, then 0s. left = 11100000
9       int left = allOnes << (j + 1);
10
11      // 1's after position i. right = 00000011
12      int right = ((1 << i) - 1);
13
14      // All 1s, except for 0s between i and j. mask = 11100011
15      int mask = left | right;
16
17      /* Clear bits j through i then put m in there */
18      int n_cleared = n & mask; // Clear bits j through i.
19      int m_shifted = m << i; // Move m into correct position.
20
21      return n_cleared | m_shifted; // OR them, and we're done!
22  }
```

In a problem like this (and many bit manipulation problems), you should make sure to thoroughly test your code. It's extremely easy to wind up with off-by-one errors.

5.2 *Given a real number between 0 and 1 (e.g., 0.72) that is passed in as a double, print the binary representation. If the number cannot be represented accurately in binary with at most 32 characters, print "ERROR."*

pg 92

SOLUTION

NOTE: When otherwise ambiguous, we'll use the subscripts x_2 and x_{10} to indicate whether x is in base 2 or base 10.

First, let's start off by asking ourselves what a non-integer number in binary looks like. By analogy to a decimal number, the binary number 0.101_2 would look like:

$$0.101_2 = 1 * (1/2^1) + 0 * (1/2^2) + 1 * (1/2^3).$$

To print the decimal part, we can multiply by 2 and check if 2n is greater than or equal to 1. This is essentially "shifting" the fractional sum. That is:

$$r = 2_{10} * n$$
$$= 2_{10} * 0.101_2$$
$$= 1 * (1/2^0) + 0 * (1/2^1) + 1 * (1/2^2)$$
$$= 1.01_2$$

If $r >= 1$, then we know that n had a 1 right after the decimal point. By doing this continuously, we can check every digit.

```
1   public static String printBinary(double num) {
2       if (num >= 1 || num <= 0) {
3           return "ERROR";
4       }
5
6       StringBuilder binary = new StringBuilder();
7       binary.append(".");
8       while (num > 0) {
9           /* Setting a limit on length: 32 characters */
10          if (binary.length() >= 32) {
11              return "ERROR";
12          }
13
14          double r = num * 2;
15          if (r >= 1) {
16              binary.append(1);
17              num = r - 1;
18          } else {
19              binary.append(0);
20              num = r;
21          }
22      }
23      return binary.toString();
24  }
```

Alternatively, rather than multiplying the number by two and comparing it to 1, we can compare the number to .5, then .25, and so on. The code below demonstrates this approach.

```
1   public static String printBinary2(double num) {
2       if (num >= 1 || num <= 0) {
3           return "ERROR";
4       }
5
6       StringBuilder binary = new StringBuilder();
7       double frac = 0.5;
8       binary.append(".");
9       while (num > 0) {
10          /* Setting a limit on length: 32 characters */
11          if (binary.length() > 32) {
12              return "ERROR";
13          }
14          if (num >= frac) {
15              binary.append(1);
16              num -= frac;
17          } else {
18              binary.append(0);
19          }
20          frac /= 2;
21      }
22      return binary.toString();
23  }
```

Both approaches are equally good; it just depends on which approach you feel most comfortable with.

Either way, you should make sure to prepare thorough test cases for this problem—and to actually run through them in your interview.

5.3   *Given a positive integer, print the next smallest and the next largest number that have the same number of 1 bits in their binary representation.*

pg 92

SOLUTION

There are a number of ways to approach this problem, including using brute force, using bit manipulation, and using clever arithmetic. Note that the arithmetic approach builds on the bit manipulation approach. You'll want to understand the bit manipulation approach before going on to the arithmetic one.

The Brute Force Approach

An easy approach is simply brute force: count the number of 1s in n, and then increment (or decrement) until you find a number with the same number of 1s. Easy—but not terribly interesting. Can we do something a bit more optimal? Yes!

Let's start with the code for getNext, and then move on to getPrev.

Bit Manipulation Approach for Get Next Number

If we think about what the next number *should* be, we can observe the following. Given the number 13948, the binary representation looks like:

1	1	0	1	1	0	0	1	1	1	1	1	0	0
13	12	11	10	9	8	7	6	5	4	3	2	1	0

We want to make this number bigger (but not *too* big). We also need to keep the same number of ones.

Observation: Given a number n and two bit locations i and j, suppose we flip bit i from a 1 to a 0, and bit j from a 0 to a 1. If i > j, then n will have decreased. If i < j, then n will have increased.

We know the following:

1. If we flip a zero to a one, we must flip a one to a zero.

2. When we do that, the number will be bigger if and only if the zero-to-one bit was to the left of the one-to-zero bit.

3. We want to make the number bigger, but not unnecessarily bigger. Therefore, we need to flip the rightmost zero which has ones on the right of it.

To put this in a different way, we are flipping the rightmost non-trailing zero. That is, using the above example, the trailing zeros are in the 0th and 1st spot. The rightmost non-trailing zero is at bit 7. Let's call this position p.

Step 1: Flip rightmost non-trailing zero

1	1	0	1	1	0	1	1	1	1	1	1	0	0
13	12	11	10	9	8	7	6	5	4	3	2	1	0

With this change, we have increased the size of n. But, we also have one too many ones, and one too few zeros. We'll need to shrink the size of our number as much as possible while keeping that in mind.

We can shrink the number by rearranging all the bits to the right of bit p such that the 0s are on the left and the 1s are on the right. As we do this, we want to replace one of the 1s with a 0.

A relatively easy way of doing this is to count how many ones are to the right of p, clear all the bits from 0 until p, and then add back in $c_1 - 1$ ones. Let c_1 be the number of ones to the right of p and c_0 be the number of zeros to the right of p.

Let's walk through this with an example.

Step 2: Clear bits to the right of p. From before, $c_0 = 2$. $c_1 = 5$. $p = 7$.

1	1	0	1	1	0	1	0	0	0	0	0	0	0
13	12	11	10	9	8	7	6	5	4	3	2	1	0

To clear these bits, we need to create a mask that is a sequence of ones, followed by p zeros. We can do this as follows:

```
a = 1 << p; // all zeros except for a 1 at position p.
b = a - 1;     // all zeros, followed by p ones.
mask = ~b;    // all ones, followed by p zeros.
n = n & mask; // clears rightmost p bits.
```

Or, more concisely, we do:

```
n &= ~((1 << p) - 1).
```

Step 3: Add in c1 - 1 ones.

1	1	0	1	1	0	1	0	0	0	1	1	1	1
13	12	11	10	9	8	7	6	5	4	3	2	1	0

To insert c1 - 1 ones on the right, we do the following:

```
a = 1 << (c1 - 1); // 0s with a 1 at position c1 - 1
b = a - 1;             // 0s with 1s at positions 0 through c1 - 1
n = n | b;            // inserts 1s at positions 0 through c1 - 1
```

Or, more concisely:

```
n |= (1 << (c1 - 1)) - 1;
```

We have now arrived at the smallest number bigger than n with the same number of ones.

The code for getNext is below.

```
1   public int getNext(int n) {
2      /* Compute c0 and c1 */
3      int c = n;
4      int c0 = 0;
5      int c1 = 0;
6      while (((c & 1) == 0) && (c != 0)) {
7         c0++;
8         c >>= 1;
9      }
10
11     while ((c & 1) == 1) {
12        c1++;
13        c >>= 1;
14     }
15
16     /* Error: if n == 11..1100...00, then there is no bigger number
```

```
17      * with the same number of 1s. */
18     if (c0 + c1 == 31 || c0 + c1 == 0) {
19        return -1;
20     }
21
22     int p = c0 + c1; // position of rightmost non-trailing zero
23
24     n |= (1 << p); // Flip rightmost non-trailing zero
25     n &= ~((1 << p) - 1); // Clear all bits to the right of p
26     n |= (1 << (c1 - 1)) - 1; // Insert (c1-1) ones on the right.
27     return n;
28 }
```

Bit Manipulation Approach for Get Previous Number

To implement getPrev, we follow a very similar approach.

1. Compute c0 and c1. Note that c1 is the number of trailing ones, and c0 is the size of the block of zeros immediately to the left of the trailing ones.

2. Flip the rightmost non-trailing one to a zero. This will be at position p = c1 + c0.

3. Clear all bits to the right of bit p.

4. Insert c1 + 1 ones immediately to the right of position *p*.

Note that Step 2 sets bit p to a zero and Step 3 sets bits 0 through p-1 to a zero. We can merge these steps.

Let's walk through this with an example.

Step 1: Initial Number. p = 7. c1 = 2. c0 = 5.

1	0	0	1	1	1	1	0	0	0	0	0	1	1
13	12	11	10	9	8	7	6	5	4	3	2	1	0

Steps 2 & 3: Clear bits 0 through p.

1	0	0	1	1	1	0	0	0	0	0	0	0	0
13	12	11	10	9	8	7	6	5	4	3	2	1	0

We can do this as follows:

```
int a = ~0;           // Sequence of 1s
int b = a << (p + 1); // Sequence of 1s followed by p + 1 zeros.
n &= b;               // Clears bits 0 through p.
```

Steps 4: Insert c1 + 1 ones immediately to the right of position p.

1	0	0	1	1	1	0	1	1	1	0	0	0	0
13	12	11	10	9	8	7	6	5	4	3	2	1	0

Note that since $p = c_1 + c_0$, the $(c_1 + 1)$ ones will be followed by $(c_0 - 1)$ zeros.

We can do this as follows:

```
int a = 1 << (c1 + 1); // 0s with 1 at position (c1 + 1)
int b = a - 1;         // 0s followed by c1 + 1 ones
int c = b << (c0 - 1); // c1+1 ones followed by c0-1 zeros.
n |= c;
```

The code to implement this is below.

```
1   int getPrev(int n) {
2       int temp = n;
3       int c0 = 0;
4       int c1 = 0;
5       while (temp & 1 == 1) {
6           c1++;
7           temp >>= 1;
8       }
9
10      if (temp == 0)  return -1;
11
12      while (((temp & 1) == 0) && (temp != 0)) {
13          c0++;
14          temp >>= 1;
15      }
16
17      int p = c0 + c1; // position of rightmost non-trailing one
18      n &= ((~0) << (p + 1)); // clears from bit p onwards
19
20      int mask = (1 << (c1 + 1)) - 1; // Sequence of (c1+1) ones
21      n |= mask << (c0 - 1);
22
23      return n;
24  }
```

Arithmetic Approach to Get Next Number

If c_0 is the number of trailing zeros, c_1 is the size of the one block immediately following, and $p = c_0 + c_1$, we can word our solution from earlier as follows:

1. Set the pth bit to 1

2. Set all bits following p to 0

3. Set bits 0 through $c_1 - 1$ to 1.

A quick and dirty way to perform steps 1 and 2 is to set the trailing zeros to 1 (giving us p trailing ones), and then add 1. Adding one will flip all trailing ones, so we wind up with a 1 at bit p followed by p zeros. We can perform this arithmetically.

```
n += 2c0 - 1;      // Sets trailing 0s to 1, giving us p trailing 1s
n += 1;            // Flips first p 1s to 0s, and puts a 1 at bit p.
```

Now, to perform Step 3 arithmetically, we just do:

```
n += 2c1 - 1 - 1;  // Sets trailing c1 - 1 zeros to ones.
```

This math reduces to:

```
next = n + (2c0 - 1) + 1 + (2c1 - 1 - 1)
     = n + 2c0 + 2c1 - 1 - 1
```

The best part is that, using a little bit manipulation, it's simple to code.

```
1   int getNextArith(int n) {
2       /* ... same calculation for c0 and c1 as before ... */
3       return n + (1 << c0) + (1 << (c1 - 1)) - 1;
4   }
```

Arithmetic Approach to Get Previous Number

If c_1 is the number of trailing ones, c_0 is the size of the zero block immediately following, and $p = c_0 + c_1$, we can word the initial getPrev solution as follows:

1. Set the pth bit to 0

2. Set all bits following p to 1

3. Set bits 0 through $c_0 - 1$ to 0.

We can implement this arithmetically as follows. For clarity in the example, we will assume n = 10000011. This makes $c_1 = 2$ and $c_0 = 5$.

```
n -= 2c1 - 1;      // Removes trailing 1s. n is now 10000000.
n -= 1;            // Flips trailing 0s. n is now 01111111.
n -= 2c0 - 1 - 1;  // Flips last (c0-1) 0s. n is now 01110000.
```

This reduces mathematically to:

```
next  = n - (2c1 - 1) - 1 - (2c0 - 1 - 1).
      = n - 2c1 - 2c0 - 1 + 1
```

Again, this is very easy to implement.

```
1   int getPrevArith(int n) {
2       /* ... same calculation for c0 and c1 as before ... */
3       return n - (1 << c1) - (1 << (c0 - 1)) + 1;
4   }
```

Whew! Don't worry, you wouldn't be expected to get all this in an interview—at least not without a lot of help from an interviewer.

Solutions to Chapter 5 | Bit Manipulation

5.4   *Explain what the following code does: ((n & (n-1)) == 0).*

pg 92

SOLUTION

We can work backwards to solve this question.

What does it mean if A & B == 0?

It means that A and B never have a 1 bit in the same place. So if `n & (n-1) == 0`, then n and n-1 never share a 1.

What does n-1 look like (as compared with n)?

Try doing subtraction by hand (in base 2 or 10). What happens?

```
  1101011000 [base 2]              593100 [base 10]
-          1                     -      1
= 1101010111 [base 2]            = 593099 [base 10]
```

When you subtract 1 from a number, you look at the least significant bit. If it's a 1 you change it to 0, and you are done. If it's a zero, you must "borrow" from a larger bit. So, you go to increasingly larger bits, changing each bit from a 0 to a 1, until you find a 1. You flip that 1 to a 0 and you are done.

Thus, n-1 will look like n, except that n's initial 0s will be 1s in n-1, and n's least significant 1 will be a 0 in n-1. That is:

```
if    n = abcde1000
then n-1 = abcde0111
```

So what does n & (n-1) == 0 indicate?

n and n-1 must have no 1s in common. Given that they look like this:

```
if    n = abcde1000
then n-1 = abcde0111
```

abcde must be all 0s, which means that n must look like this: `00001000`. The value n is therefore a power of two.

So, we have our answer: `((n & (n-1)) == 0)` checks if n is a power of 2 (or if n is 0).

5.5   *Write a function to determine the number of bits required to convert integer A to integer B.*

pg 92

SOLUTION

This seemingly complex problem is actually rather straightforward. To approach this, ask yourself how you would figure out which bits in two numbers are different. Simple: with an XOR.

Each 1 in the XOR represents a bit that is different between A and B. Therefore, to check the number of bits that are different between A and B, we simply need to count the number of bits in A^B that are 1.

```
1   int bitSwapRequired(int a, int b) {
2       int count = 0;
3       for (int c = a ^ b; c != 0; c = c >> 1) {
4           count += c & 1;
5       }
6       return count;
7   }
```

This code is good, but we can make it a bit better. Rather than simply shifting c repeatedly while checking the least significant bit, we can continuously flip the least significant bit and count how long it takes c to reach 0. The operation c = c & (c - 1) will clear the least significant bit in c.

The code below utilizes this approach.

```
1   public static int bitSwapRequired(int a, int b) {
2       int count = 0;
3       for (int c = a ^ b; c != 0; c = c & (c-1)) {
4           count++;
5       }
6       return count;
7   }
```

The above code is one of those bit manipulation problems that comes up sometimes in interviews. Though it'd be hard to come up with it on the spot if you've never seen it before, it is useful to remember the trick for your interviews.

5.6   *Write a program to swap odd and even bits in an integer with as few instructions as possible (e.g., bit 0 and bit 1 are swapped, bit 2 and bit 3 are swapped, and so on).*

pg 92

SOLUTION

Like many of the previous problems, it's useful to think about this problem in a different way. Operating on individual pairs of bits would be difficult, and probably not that efficient either. So how else can we think about this problem?

We can approach this as operating on the odds bits first, and then the even bits. Can we take a number n and move the odd bits over by 1? Sure. We can mask all odd bits with 10101010 in binary (which is 0xAA), then shift them right by 1 to put them in the even spots. For the even bits, we do an equivalent operation. Finally, we merge these two values.

This takes a total of five instructions. The code below implements this approach.

```
1   public int swapOddEvenBits(int x) {
2       return ( ((x & 0xaaaaaaaa) >> 1) | ((x & 0x55555555) << 1) );
3   }
```

We've implemented the code above for 32-bit integers in Java. If you were working with 64-bit integers, you would need to change the mask. The logic, however, would remain the same.

5.7   An array A contains all the integers from 0 through n, except for one number which is missing. In this problem, we cannot access an entire integer in A with a single operation. The elements of A are represented in binary, and the only operation we can use to access them is "fetch the jth bit of A[i]," which takes constant time. Write code to find the missing integer. Can you do it in O(n) time?

pg 92

SOLUTION

You may have seen a very similar sounding problem: Given a list of numbers from 0 to n, with exactly one number removed, find the missing number. This problem can be solved by simply adding the list of numbers and comparing it to the actual sum of 0 through n, which is n * (n + 1) / 2. The difference will be the missing number.

We could solve this by computing the value of each number, based on its binary representation, and calculating the sum.

The runtime of this solution is n * length(n), when length is the number of bits in n. Note that length(n) = $\log_2(n)$. So, the runtime is actually O(n log(n)). Not quite good enough!

So how else can we approach it?

We can actually use a similar approach, but leverage the bit values more directly.

Picture a list of binary numbers (the - - - - - indicates the value that was removed):

00000	00100	01000	01100
00001	00101	01001	01101
00010	00110	01010	
- - - - -	00111	01011	

Removing the number above creates an imbalance of 1s and 0s in the least significant bit, which we'll call LSB_1. In a list of numbers from 0 to n, we would expect there to be the same number of 0s as 1s (if n is odd), or an additional 0 if n is even. That is:

```
if n % 2 == 1 then count(0s) = count(1s)
if n % 2 == 0 then count(0s) = 1 + count(1s)
```

Note that this means that count(0s) is always greater than or equal to count(1s).

When we remove a value v from the list, we'll know immediately if v is even or odd just by looking at the least significant bits of all the other values in the list.

	n % 2 == 0 count(0s) = 1 + count(1s)	n % 2 == 1 count(0s) = count(1s)
v % 2 == 0 $LSB_1(v)$ = 0	a 0 is removed. count(0s) = count(1s)	a 0 is removed. count(0s) < count(1s)
v % 2 == 1 $LSB_1(v)$ = 1	a 1 is removed. count(0s) > count(1s)	a 1 is removed. count(0s) > count(1s)

So, if count(0s) <= count(1s), then v is even. If count(0s) > count(1s), then v is odd.

Okay, but how do we figure out what the next bit in v is? If v were contained in our list, then we should expect to find the following (where $count_2$ indicates the number of 0s or 1s in the second least significant bit):

$$count_2(0s) = count_2(1s) \quad OR \quad count_2(0s) = 1 + count_2(1s)$$

As in the earlier example, we can deduce the value of the second least significant bit (LSB_2) of v.

	$count_2(0s) = 1 + count_2(1s)$	$count_2(0s) = count_2(1s)$
$LSB_2(v) == 0$	a 0 is removed. $count_2(0s) = count_2(1s)$	a 0 is removed. $count_2(0s) < count_2(1s)$
$LSB_2(v) == 1$	a 1 is removed. $count_2(0s) > count_2(1s)$	a 1 is removed. $count_2(0s) > count_2(1s)$

Again, we have the same conclusion:

- If $count_2(0s) <= count_2(1s)$, then $LSB_2(v) = 0$.
- If $count_2(0s) > count_2(1s)$, then $LSB_2(v) = 1$.

We can repeat this process for each bit. On each iteration, we count the number of 0s and 1s in bit i to check if $LSB_i(v)$ is 0 or 1. Then, we discard the numbers where $LSB_i(x)$!= $LSB_i(v)$. That is, if v is even, we discard the odd numbers, and so on.

By the end of this process, we will have computed all bits in v. In each successive iteration, we look at n, then n / 2, then n / 4, and so on, bits. This results in a runtime of O(N).

If it helps, we can also move through this more visually. In the first iteration, we start with all the numbers:

```
00000          00100          01000          01100
00001          00101          01001          01101
00010          00110          01010
-----          00111          01011
```

Since $count_1(0s) > count_1(1s)$, we know that $LSB_1(v) = 1$. Now, discard all numbers x where $LSB_1(x) != LSB_1(v)$.

```
00000          00100          01000          01100
00001          00101          01001          01101
00010          00110          01010
-----          00111          01011
```

Now, $count_2(0s) > count_2(1s)$, so we know that $LSB_2(v) = 1$. Now, discard all numbers x where $LSB_2(x) != LSB_2(v)$.

```
00000          00100          01000          01100
00001          00101          01001          01101
00010          00110          01010
-----          00111          01011
```

This time, $count_3(0s) <= count_3(1s)$, we know that $LSB_3(v) = 0$. Now, discard all numbers x where $LSB_3(x) != LSB_3(v)$.

```
00000          00100          01000          01100
00001          00101          01001          01101
00010          00110          01010
-----          00111          01011
```

We're down to just one number. In this case, $count_4(0s) <= count_4(1s)$, so $LSB_4(v) = 0$.

When we discard all numbers where $LSB_4(v) != 0$, we'll wind up with an empty list. Once the list is empty, then $count_i(0s) <= count_i(1s)$, so $LSB_i(v) = 0$. In other words, once we have an empty list, we can fill in the rest of the bits of v with 0.

This process will compute that, for the example above, $v = 00011$.

The code below implements this algorithm. We've implemented the discarding aspect by partitioning the array by bit value as we go.

```
1   public int findMissing(ArrayList<BitInteger> array) {
2      /* BitInteger.INTEGER_SIZE - 1 corresponds to the LSB. Start
3       * from there, and work our way through the bigger bits. */
4      return findMissing(array, BitInteger.INTEGER_SIZE - 1);
5   }
6
7   public int findMissing(ArrayList<BitInteger> input, int column) {
8      if (column < 0) { // Base case and error condition
9         return 0;
10     }
```

```
11    ArrayList<BitInteger> oneBits =
12       new ArrayList<BitInteger>(input.size()/2);
13    ArrayList<BitInteger> zeroBits =
14       new ArrayList<BitInteger>(input.size()/2);
15
16    for (BitInteger t : input) {
17       if (t.fetch(column) == 0) {
18          zeroBits.add(t);
19       } else {
20          oneBits.add(t);
21       }
22    }
23    if (zeroBits.size() <= oneBits.size()) {
24       int v = findMissing(zeroBits, column - 1);
25       return (v << 1) | 0;
26    } else {
27       int v = findMissing(oneBits, column - 1);
28       return (v << 1) | 1;
29    }
30 }
```

In lines 24 and 27, we recursively calculate the other bits of v. Then, we insert either a 0 or 1, depending on whether or not $count_1(0s) <= count_1(1s)$.

5.8 A monochrome screen is stored as a single array of bytes, allowing eight consecutive pixels to be stored in one byte. The screen has width w, where w is divisible by 8 (that is, no byte will be split across rows). The height of the screen, of course, can be derived from the length of the array and the width. Implement a function drawHorizontalLine(byte[] screen, int width, int x1, int x2, int y) which draws a horizontal line from (x1, y) to (x2, y).

pg 92

SOLUTION

A naive solution to the problem is straightforward: iterate in a for loop from x1 to x2, setting each pixel along the way. But that's hardly any fun, is it? (Nor is it very efficient.)

A better solution is to recognize that if x1 and x2 are far away from each other, several full bytes will be contained between them. These full bytes can be set one at a time by doing screen[byte_pos] = 0xFF. The residual start and end of the line can be set using masks.

```
1    void drawLine(byte[] screen, int width, int x1, int x2, int y) {
2       int start_offset = x1 % 8;
3       int first_full_byte = x1 / 8;
4       if (start_offset != 0) {
5          first_full_byte++;
6       }
7
```

```
8       int end_offset = x2 % 8;
9       int last_full_byte = x2 / 8;
10      if (end_offset != 7) {
11         last_full_byte--;
12      }
13
14      // Set full bytes
15      for (int b = first_full_byte; b <= last_full_byte; b++) {
16         screen[(width / 8) * y + b] = (byte) 0xFF;
17      }
18
19      // Create masks for start and end of line
20      byte start_mask = (byte) (0xFF >> start_offset);
21      byte end_mask = (byte) ~(0xFF >> (end_offset + 1));
22
23      // Set start and end of line
24      if ((x1 / 8) == (x2 / 8)) { // x1 and x2 are in the same byte
25         byte mask = (byte) (start_mask & end_mask);
26         screen[(width / 8) * y + (x1 / 8)] |= mask;
27      } else {
28         if (start_offset != 0) {
29            int byte_number = (width / 8) * y + first_full_byte - 1;
30            screen[byte_number] |= start_mask;
31         }
32         if (end_offset != 7) {
33            int byte_number = (width / 8) * y + last_full_byte + 1;
34            screen[byte_number] |= end_mask;
35         }
36      }
37   }
```

Be careful on this problem; there are a lot of "gotchas" and special cases. For example, you need to consider the case where x1 and x2 are in the same byte. Only the most careful candidates can implement this code bug-free.

Brain Teasers

| Concepts and Algorithms: Solutions | Chapter 6 |

Solutions to Chapter 6 | Brain Teasers

6.1 *You have 20 bottles of pills. 19 bottles have 1.0 gram pills, but one has pills of weight 1.1 grams. Given a scale that provides an exact measurement, how would you find the heavy bottle? You can only use the scale once.*

pg 95

SOLUTION

Sometimes, tricky constraints can be a clue. This is the case with the constraint that we can only use the scale once.

Because we can only use the scale once, we know something interesting: we must weigh multiple pills at the same time. In fact, we know we must weigh pills from at least 19 bottles at the same time. Otherwise, if we skipped two or more bottles entirely, how could we distinguish between those missed bottles? Remember that we only have *one* chance to use the scale.

So how can we weigh pills from more than one bottle and discover which bottle has the heavy pills? Let's suppose there were just two bottles, one of which had heavier pills. If we took one pill from each bottle, we would get a weight of 2.1 grams, but we wouldn't know which bottle contributed the extra 0.1 grams. We know we must treat the bottles differently somehow.

If we took one pill from Bottle #1 and two pills from Bottle #2, what would the scale show? It depends. If Bottle #1 were the heavy bottle, we would get 3.1 grams. If Bottle #2 were the heavy bottle, we would get 3.2 grams. And that is the trick to this problem.

We know the "expected" weight of a bunch of pills. The difference between the expected weight and the actual weight will indicate which bottle contributed the heavier pills, *provided* we select a different number of pills from each bottle.

We can generalize this to the full solution: take one pill from Bottle #1, two pills from Bottle #2, three pills from Bottle #3, and so on. Weigh this mix of pills. If all pills were one gram each, the scale would read 210 grams (1 + 2 + ... + 20 = 20 * 21 / 2 = 210). Any "overage" must come from the extra 0.1 gram pills.

This formula will tell you the bottle number: `(weight - 210 grams) / 0.1 grams`. So, if the set of pills weighed 211.3 grams, then Bottle #13 would have the heavy pills.

6.2 *There is an 8x8 chess board in which two diagonally opposite corners have been cut off. You are given 31 dominos, and a single domino can cover exactly two squares. Can you use the 31 dominos to cover the entire board? Prove your answer (by providing an example or showing why it's impossible).*

pg 95

SOLUTION

At first, it seems like this should be possible. It's an 8 x 8 board, which has 64 squares, but two have been cut off, so we're down to 62 squares. A set of 31 dominoes should be able to fit there, right?

When we try to lay down dominoes on row 1, which only has 7 squares, we may notice that one domino must stretch into the row 2. Then, when we try to lay down dominoes onto row 2, again we need to stretch a domino into row 3.

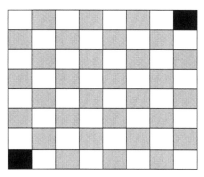

For each row we lay down, we'll always have one domino that needs to poke into the next row. No matter how many times and ways we try to solve this issue, we won't be able to successfully lay down all the dominoes.

There's a cleaner, more solid proof for why it won't work. The chess board initially has 32 black and 32 white squares. By removing opposite corners (which must be the same color), we're left with 30 of one color and 32 of the other color. Let's say, for the sake of argument, that we have 30 black and 32 white squares.

Each domino we set on the board will always take up one white and one black square. Therefore, 31 dominos will take up 31 white squares and 31 black squares exactly. On this board, however, we must have 30 black squares and 32 white squares. Hence, it is impossible.

6.3 *You have a five-quart jug, a three-quart jug, and an unlimited supply of water (but no measuring cups). How would you come up with exactly four quarts of water? Note that the jugs are oddly shaped, such that filling up exactly "half" of the jug would be impossible.*

pg 95

SOLUTION

If we just play around with the jugs, we'll find that we can pour water back and forth between them as follows:

5 Quart	3 Quart	Note
5	0	Filled 5 quart jug.
2	3	Filled 3 quart with 5 quart's contents.
0	2	Dumped 3 quart.
5	2	Filled 5 quart.
4	3	Fill remainder of 3 quart with 5 quart.
4		Done! We have four quarts.

Note that many brain teasers have a mathematical or computer science root to them, and this is one of them. As long as the two jug sizes are relatively prime (i.e., have no common prime factors), you can find a pour sequence for any value between one and the sum of the jug sizes.

6.4 *A bunch of people are living on an island, when a visitor comes with a strange order: all blue-eyed people must leave the island as soon as possible. There will be a flight out at 8:00pm every evening. Each person can see everyone else's eye color, but they do not know their own (nor is anyone allowed to tell them). Additionally, they do not know how many people have blue eyes, although they do know that at least one person does. How many days will it take the blue-eyed people to leave?*

pg 96

SOLUTION

Let's apply the Base Case and Build approach. Assume that there are n people on the island and c of them have blue eyes. We are explicitly told that $c > 0$.

Case c = 1: Exactly one person has blue eyes.

Assuming all the people are intelligent, the blue-eyed person should look around and realize that no one else has blue eyes. Since he knows that at least one person has blue eyes, he must conclude that it is him. Therefore, he would take the flight that evening.

Case c = 2: Exactly two people have blue eyes.

The two blue-eyed people see each other, but be unsure whether c is 1 or 2. They know, from the previous case, that if c = 1, the blue-eyed person would leave on the first night. Therefore, if the other blue-eyed person is still there, he must deduce that c = 2, which means that he himself has blue eyes. Both men would then leave on the second night.

Case c > 2: The General Case.

As we increase c, we can see that this logic continues to apply. If c = 3, then those three people will immediately know that there are either 2 or 3 people with blue eyes. If there were two people, then those two people would have left on the second night. So, when the others are still around after that night, each person would conclude that c = 3 and that they, therefore, have blue eyes too. They would leave that night.

This same pattern extends up through any value of c. Therefore, if c men have blue eyes, it will take c nights for the blue-eyed men to leave. All will leave on the same night.

6.5 *There is a building of 100 floors. If an egg drops from the Nth floor or above, it will break. If it's dropped from any floor below, it will not break. You're given two eggs. Find N, while minimizing the number of drops for the worst case.*

pg 96

SOLUTION

We may observe that, regardless of how we drop Egg 1, Egg 2 must do a linear search (from lowest to highest) between the "breaking floor" and the next highest non-breaking floor. For example, if Egg 1 is dropped from floors 5 and 10 without breaking, but it breaks when it's dropped from floor 15, then Egg 2 must be dropped, in the worst case, from floors 11, 12, 13, and 14.

The Approach

As a first try, suppose we drop an egg from the 10th floor, then the 20th, ...

- If Egg 1 breaks on the first drop (floor 10), then we have at most 10 drops total.

- If Egg 1 breaks on the last drop (floor 100), then we have at most 19 drops total (floors 10, 20, ...,90, 100, then 91 through 99).

That's pretty good, but all we've considered is the absolute worst case. We should do some "load balancing" to make those two cases more even.

Our goal is to create a system for dropping Egg 1 such that the number of drops is as consistent as possible, whether Egg 1 breaks on the first drop or the last drop.

1. A perfectly load-balanced system would be one in which Drops(Egg 1) + Drops(Egg 2) is always the same, regardless of where Egg 1 breaks.

2. For that to be the case, since each drop of Egg 1 takes one more step, Egg 2 is allowed one fewer step.

3. We must, therefore, reduce the number of steps potentially required by Egg 2 by one drop each time. For example, if Egg 1 is dropped on floor 20 and then floor 30, Egg 2 is potentially required to take 9 steps. When we drop Egg 1 again, we must reduce potential Egg 2 steps to only 8. That is, we must drop Egg 1 at floor 39.

4. We know, therefore, Egg 1 must start at floor X, then go up by X-1 floors, then X-2, ..., until it gets to 100.

5. Solve for X in: `X + (X-1) + (X-2) + ... + 1 = 100`.
   `X (X + 1) / 2 = 100 -> X = 14`.

We go to floor 14, then 27, then 39, ... This takes 14 steps in the worse case.

As in many other maximizing / minimizing problems, the key in this problem is "worst case balancing."

6.6 *There are 100 closed lockers in a hallway. A man begins by opening all 100 lockers. Next, he closes every second locker. Then, on his third pass, he toggles every third locker (closes it if it is open or opens it if it is closed). This process continues for 100 passes, such that on each pass i, the man toggles every ith locker. After his 100th pass in the hallway, in which he toggles only locker #100, how many lockers are open?*

pg 96

SOLUTION

We can tackle this problem by thinking through what it means for a door to be toggled. This will help us deduce which doors at the very end will be left opened.

Question: For which rounds is a door toggled (open or closed)?

A door n is toggled once for each factor of n, including itself and 1. That is, door 15 is toggled on rounds 1, 3, 5, and 15.

Question: When would a door be left open?

A door is left open if the number of factors (which we will call x) is odd. You can think about this by pairing factors off as an open and a close. If there's one remaining, the door will be open.

Question: When would x be odd?

The value x is odd if n is a perfect square. Here's why: pair n's factors by their complements. For example, if n is 36, the factors are (1, 36), (2, 18), (3, 12), (4, 9), (6, 6). Note that (6, 6) only contributes one factor, thus giving n an odd number of factors.

Question: How many perfect squares are there?

There are 10 perfect squares. You could count them (1, 4, 9, 16, 25, 36, 49, 64, 81, 100), or you could simply realize that you can take the numbers 1 through 10 and square them:

$$1*1, \quad 2*2, \quad 3*3, \quad ..., \quad 10*10$$

Therefore, there are 10 lockers open at the end of this process.

Mathematics and Probability

Concepts and Algorithms: Solutions

7.1 *You have a basketball hoop and someone says that you can play one of two games.*

Game 1: You get one shot to make the hoop.

Game 2: You get three shots and you have to make two of three shots.

If p is the probability of making a particular shot, for which values of p should you pick one game or the other?

pg 102

SOLUTION

To solve this problem, we can apply straightforward probability laws by comparing the probabilities of winning each game.

Probability of winning Game 1:

The probability of winning Game 1 is p, by definition.

Probability of winning Game 2:

Let `s(k,n)` be the probability of making exactly k shots out of n. The probability of winning Game 2 is the probability of making exactly two shots out of three OR making all three shots. In other words:

```
P(winning) = s(2,3) + s(3,3)
```

The probability of making all three shots is:

```
s(3,3) = p³
```

The probability of making exactly two shots is:

```
P(making 1 and 2, and missing 3)
      + P(making 1 and 3, and missing 2)
      + P(missing 1, and making 2 and 3)
    = p * p * (1 - p) + p * (1 - p) * p + (1 - p) * p * p
    = 3 (1 - p) p²
```

Adding these together, we get:

```
= p³ + 3 (1 - p) p²
= p³ + 3p² - 3p³
= 3p² - 2p³
```

Which game should you play?

You should play Game 1 if `P(Game 1) > P(Game 2)`:

```
p > 3p² - 2p³.
1 > 3p - 2p²
2p² - 3p + 1 > 0
(2p - 1)(p - 1) > 0
```

Both terms must be positive, or both must be negative. But we know p < 1, so p - 1

< 0. This means both terms must be negative.

```
2p - 1 < 0
2p < 1
p < .5
```

So, we should play Game1 if p < .5. If p = 0, 0.5, or 1, then P(Game 1) = P(Game 2), so it doesn't matter which game we play.

7.2 *There are three ants on different vertices of a triangle. What is the probability of collision (between any two or all of them) if they start walking on the sides of the triangle? Assume that each ant randomly picks a direction, with either direction being equally likely to be chosen, and that they walk at the same speed.*

Similarly, find the probability of collision with n ants on an n-vertex polygon.

pg 102

SOLUTION

The ants will collide if any of them are moving towards each other. So, the only way that they won't collide is if they are all moving in the same direction (clockwise or counter-clockwise). We can compute this probability and work backwards from there.

Since each ant can move in two directions, and there are three ants, the probability is:

$$P(\text{clockwise}) = (\tfrac{1}{2})^3$$
$$P(\text{counter clockwise}) = (\tfrac{1}{2})^3$$
$$P(\text{same direction}) = (\tfrac{1}{2})^3 + (\tfrac{1}{2})^3 = \tfrac{1}{4}$$

The probability of the ants colliding is therefore the probability of the ants *not* moving in the same direction:

$$P(\text{collision}) = 1 - P(\text{same direction}) = 1 - (\tfrac{1}{4}) = \tfrac{3}{4}$$

To generalize this to an n-vertex polygon: there are still only two ways in which the ants can move to avoid a collision, but there are 2^n ways they can move in total. Therefore, in general, probability of collision is:

$$P(\text{clockwise}) = (\tfrac{1}{2})^n$$

$$P(\text{counter}) = (\tfrac{1}{2})^n$$

$$P(\text{same direction}) = 2(\tfrac{1}{2})^n = (\tfrac{1}{2})^{n-1}$$

$$P(\text{collision}) = 1 - P(\text{same direction}) = 1 - (\tfrac{1}{2})^{n-1}$$

7.3 *Given two lines on a Cartesian plane, determine whether the two lines would inter-sect.*

pg 102

SOLUTION

There are a lot of unknowns in this problem: What format are the lines in? What if they are the same line? You should discuss these ambiguities with your interviewer.

We'll make the following assumptions:

- If two lines are the same (same slope and y-intercept), then they are considered to intersect.

- We get to decide the data structure for the line.

If two *different* lines are not parallel, then they intersect. Thus, to check if two lines intersect, we just need to check if the slopes are different (or if the lines are identical).

We can implement the code as follows:

```
1   public class Line {
2       static double epsilon = 0.000001;
3       public double slope;
4       public double yintercept;
5
6       public Line(double s, double y) {
7           slope = s;
8           yintercept = y;
9       }
10
11      public boolean intersect(Line line2) {
12          return Math.abs(slope - line2.slope) > epsilon ||
13                  Math.abs(yintercept - line2.yintercept) < epsilon;
14      }
15  }
```

In problems like these, be aware of the following:

- Ask questions. This question has a lot of unknowns—ask questions to clarify them. Many interviewers intentionally ask vague questions to see if you'll clarify your assumptions.

- When possible, design and use data structures. It shows that you understand and care about object-oriented design.

- Think through which data structures you design to represent a line. There are a lot of options, with lots of trade-offs. Pick one, and explain your choice.

- Don't assume that the slope and y-intercept are integers.

- Understand limitations of floating point representations. Never check for equality with ==. Instead, check if the difference is less than an epsilon value.

7.4 *Write methods to implement the multiply, subtract, and divide operations for inte-gers. Use only the add operator.*

pg 102

SOLUTION

The only operation we have to work with is the add operator. In each of these problems, it's useful to think in depth about what these operations really do or how to phrase them in terms of other operations (either add or operations we've already completed).

Subtraction

How can we phrase subtraction in terms of addition? This one is pretty straightforward. The operation a - b is the same thing as a + (-1) * b. However, because we are not allowed to use the * (multiply) operator, we must implement a negate function.

```
1   /* Flip a positive sign to negative or negative sign to positive */
2   public static int negate(int a) {
3       int neg = 0;
4       int d = a < 0 ? 1 : -1;
5       while (a != 0) {
6           neg += d;
7           a += d;
8       }
9       return neg;
10  }
11
12  /* Subtract two numbers by negating b and adding them */
13  public static int minus(int a, int b) {
14      return a + negate(b);
15  }
```

The negation of the value k is implemented by adding -1 k times.

Multiplication

The connection between addition and multiplication is equally straightforward. To multiply a by b, we just add a to itself b times.

```
1   /* Multiply a by b by adding a to itself b times */
2   public static int multiply(int a, int b) {
3       if (a < b) {
4           return multiply(b, a); // algorithm is faster if b < a
5       }
6       int sum = 0;
7       for (int i = abs(b); i > 0; i--) {
8           sum += a;
9       }
10      if (b < 0) {
11          sum = negate(sum);
```

```
12      }
13      return sum;
14  }
15
16  /* Return absolute value */
17  public static int abs(int a) {
18      if (a < 0) {
19          return negate(a);
20      } else {
21          return a;
22      }
23  }
```

The one thing we need to be careful of in the above code is to properly handle multiplication of negative numbers. If b is negative, we need to flip the value of sum. So, what this code really does is:

```
multiply(a, b) <-- abs(b) * a * (-1 if b < 0).
```

We also implemented a simple abs function to help.

Division

Of the three operations, division is certainly the hardest. The good thing is that we can use the multiply, subtract, and negate methods now to implement divide.

We are trying to compute x where x = a / b. Or, to put this another way, find x where a = bx. We've now changed the problem into one that can be stated with something we know how to do: multiplication.

We could implement this by multiplying b by progressively higher values, until we reach a. That would be fairly inefficient, particularly given that our implementation of multiply involves a lot of adding.

Alternatively, we can look at the equation a = xb to see that we can compute x by adding b to itself repeatedly until we reach a. The number of times we need to do that will equal x.

Of course, a might not be evenly divisible by b, and that's okay. Integer division, which is what we've been asked to implement, is supposed to floor the result.

The code below implements this algorithm.

```
1  public int divide(int a, int b)
2          throws java.lang.ArithmeticException {
3      if (b == 0) {
4          throw new java.lang.ArithmeticException("ERROR");
5      }
6      int absa = abs(a);
7      int absb = abs(b);
8
9      int product = 0;
```

```
10    int x = 0;
11    while (product + absb <= absa) { /* don't go past a */
12        product += absb;
13        x++;
14    }
15
16    if ((a < 0 && b < 0) || (a > 0 && b > 0)) {
17        return x;
18    } else {
19        return negate(x);
20    }
21 }
```

In tackling this problem, you should be aware of the following:

- A logical approach of going back to what exactly multiplication and division do comes in handy. Remember that. All (good) interview problems can be approached in a logical, methodical way!

- The interviewer is looking for this sort of logical work-your-way-through-it approach.

- This is a great problem to demonstrate your ability to write clean code—specifically, to show your ability to reuse code. For example, if you were writing this solution and didn't put negate in its own method, you should move it into its own method once you see that you'll use it multiple times.

- Be careful about making assumptions while coding. Don't assume that the numbers are all positive or that a is bigger than b.

7.5   *Given two squares on a two-dimensional plane, find a line that would cut these two squares in half. Assume that the top and the bottom sides of the square run parallel to the x-axis.*

pg 102

SOLUTION

Before we start, we should think about what exactly this problem means by a "line." Is a line defined by a slope and a y-intercept? Or by any two points on the line? Or, should the line be really a line segment, which starts and ends at the edges of the squares?

We will assume, since it makes the problem a bit more interesting, that we mean the third option: that the line should end at the edges of the squares. In an interview situation, you should discuss this with your interviewer.

This line that cuts two squares in half must connect the two middles. We can easily calculate the slope, knowing that $slope = \frac{y1-y2}{x1-x2}$. Once we calculate the slope using the two middles, we can use the same equation to calculate the start and end points of the line segment.

In the below code, we will assume the origin (0, 0) is in the upper left-hand corner.

```
1   public class Square {
2       ...
3       public Point middle() {
4           return new Point((this.left + this.right) / 2.0,
5                             (this.top + this.bottom) / 2.0);
6       }
7
8       /* Return the point where the line segment connecting mid1 and
9        * mid2 intercepts the edge of square 1. That is, draw a line
10       * from mid2 to mid1, and continue it out until the edge of
11       * the square.
12       */
13      public Point extend(Point mid1, Point mid2, double size) {
14          /* The line segment will hit on an edge of the square,
15           * which is (size / 2) units up, down, left, or right of the
16           * middle. If mid1 is to the left of mid2, then the line
17           * segment hits on the left of mid1. If mid1 is above mid2,
18           * then the line segment hits above mid1.
19           */
20          double xdir = mid1.x < mid2.x ? -1 : 1;
21          double ydir = mid1.y < mid2.y ? -1 : 1;
22
23          /* If mid1 and mid2 have the same x value, then the slope
24           * calculation will throw a divide by 0 exception. Instead,
25           * we do a special calculation, since we know the line
26           * segment will hit at the same x coordinate.
27           */
28          if (mid1.x == mid2.x) {
29              return new Point(mid1.x, mid1.y + ydir * size / 2.0);
30          }
31
32          double slope = (mid1.y - mid2.y) / (mid1.x - mid2.x);
33          double x1 = 0;
34          double y1 = 0;
35
36          /* Calculate x1 and y1 using the equation:
37           *    slope = (y1 - y2) / (x1 - x2).
38           * Note that if the slope is "steep," the end of the line
39           * segment will hit size / 2 units away from the middle on
40           * the y axis. If the slope is "shallow," the end of the
41           * line segment will hit size / 2 units away from the middle
42           * on the x axis.
43           */
44          if (Math.abs(slope) == 1) {
45              x1 = mid1.x + xdir * size / 2.0;
46              y1 = mid1.y + ydir * size / 2.0;
47          } else if (Math.abs(slope) < 1) { // shallow slope
48              x1 = mid1.x + xdir * size / 2.0;
```

```
49          y1 = slope * (x1 - mid1.x) + mid1.y;
50        } else { // steep slope
51          y1 = mid1.y + ydir * size / 2.0;
52          x1 = (y1 - mid1.y) / slope + mid1.x;
53        }
54        return new Point(x1, y1);
55      }
56
57      public Line cut(Square other) {
58        Point middle_s = this.middle();
59        Point middle_t = other.middle();
60        if (middle_s.isEqual(middle_t)) {
61          Square bigger = bottom - top > other.bottom - other.top ?
62                          this : other;
63          return new Line(new Point(bigger.left, bigger.top),
64                          new Point(bigger.right, bigger.bottom));
65        } else {
66          Point point_s = extend(middle_s, middle_t,
67                                 this.right - this.left);
68          Point point_t = extend(middle_t, middle_s,
69                                 other.right - other.left);
70          return new Line(point_s, point_t);      }
71      }
```

The main goal of this problem is to see how careful you are about coding. It's easy to glance over the special cases (e.g., the two squares having the same middle). You should make a list of these special cases before you start the problem and make sure to handle them appropriately. This is a question that requires careful and thorough testing.

7.6   *Given a two-dimensional graph with points on it, find a line which passes the most number of points.*

pg 102

SOLUTION

If we draw a line between every two points, we can check to see which line is the most common. A brute force approach would be to simply iterate through each line segment (with each line segment represented by a pair of points) and count how many points fall on it. This would take $O(N^3)$ time, since there are N^2 line segments and we need to iterate through $O(N)$ points for each line segment.

Before we discuss if we can do better, let's figure out how we will represent a line. A line can be represented in (at least) two different ways:

1. As a pair of points. This pair of points can be any two distinct points on the line, so the same line could be represented in an infinite number of ways.

2. As a slope and a y-intercept.

The second approach has an advantage in that every line segment on the same greater line will have identical slopes and y-intercepts.

Let's re-think our solution. We have a bunch of line segments, represented as a slope and y-intercept, and we want to find the most common slope and y-intercept pair. How can we find the most common one?

This is really no different than the classic "find the most common number in a list of numbers" problem. We just iterate through the lines segments and use a hash table to count the number of times we've seen each line.

```
1   public static Line findBestLine(GraphPoint[] points) {
2       Line bestLine = null;
3       HashMap<Line, Integer> line_count =
4           new HashMap<Line, Integer>();
5       for (int i = 0; i < points.length; i++) {
6           for (int j = i + 1; j < points.length; j++) {
7               Line line = new Line(points[i], points[j]);
8               if (!line_count.containsKey(line)) {
9                   line_count.put(line, 0);
10              }
11              line_count.put(line, line_count.get(line) + 1);
12              if (bestLine == null ||
13                  line_count.get(line) > line_count.get(bestLine)) {
14                  bestLine = line;
15              }
16          }
17      }
18      return bestLine;
19  }
20
21  public class Line {
22      private static double epsilon = .0001;
23      public double slope;
24      public double intercept;
25      private boolean infinite_slope = false;
26      public Line(GraphPoint p, GraphPoint q) {
27          if (Math.abs(p.x - q.x) > epsilon) { // if x's are diff.
28              slope = (p.y - q.y) / (p.x - q.x); // compute slope
29              intercept = p.y - slope * p.x; // y intercept from y=mx+b
30          } else {
31              infinite_slope = true;
32              intercept = p.x; // x-intercept, since slope is infinite
33          }
34      }
35
36      public boolean isEqual(double a, double b) {
37          return (Math.abs(a - b) < epsilon);
38      }
39
```

```
40      @Override
41      public int hashCode()  {
42          int sl = (int)(slope * 1000);
43          int in = (int)(intercept * 1000);
44          return sl | in;
45      }
46
47      @Override
48      public boolean equals(Object o) {
49          Line l = (Line) o;
50          if (isEqual(l.slope, slope) &&
51              isEqual(l.intercept, intercept) &&
52              infinite_slope == l.infinite_slope) {
53              return true;
54          }
55          return false;
56      }
57  }
```

We need to be careful about the calculation of the slope of a line. The line might be completely vertical. We can keep track of this in a separate flag (infinite_slope). We need to check this condition in the equals method.

Also, remember that when we perform division to calculate the slope, division is not exact. Therefore, rather than checking to see if two slopes are exactly equal, we need to check if their difference is greater than epsilon.

7.7   *Design an algorithm to find the kth number such that the only prime factors are 3, 5, and 7.*

pg 102

SOLUTION

We know that, by definition, any such number will look like $3^a * 5^b * 7^c$.

Let's picture a list of all numbers in that form. This problem asks us to find the kth such number.

1	-	$3^0 * 5^0 * 7^0$
3	3	$3^1 * 5^0 * 7^0$
5	5	$3^0 * 5^1 * 7^0$
7	7	$3^0 * 5^0 * 7^1$
9	3*3	$3^2 * 5^0 * 7^0$
15	3*5	$3^1 * 5^1 * 7^0$
21	3*7	$3^1 * 5^0 * 7^1$
25	5*5	$3^0 * 5^2 * 7^0$

1	-	$3^0 * 5^0 * 7^0$
27	3*9	$3^3 * 5^0 * 7^0$
35	5*7	$3^0 * 5^1 * 7^1$
45	5*9	$3^2 * 5^1 * 7^0$
49	7*7	$3^0 * 5^0 * 7^2$
63	3*21	$3^2 * 5^0 * 7^1$

We know that, since $3^{a-1} * 5^b * 7^c < 3^a * 5^b * 7^c$, $3^{a-1} * 5^b * 7^c$ must have already appeared in our list. In fact, all of the following values have already appeared in our list:

- $3^{a-1} * 5^b * 7^c$

- $3^a * 5^{b-1} * 7^c$

- $3^a * 5^b * 7^{c-1}$

Another way to think about this is that every number can be expressed as one of the following:

- 3 * (some previous number in list)

- 5 * (some previous number in list)

- 7 * (some previous number in list)

So, we know A_k can be expressed as $(3, 5$ or $7) *$ (some value in $\{A_1, \ldots, A_{k-1}\}$). We also know that A_k is, by definition, the next number in the list. Therefore, A_k will be the smallest "new" number (a number that it's already in $\{A_1, \ldots, A_{k-1}\}$) that can be formed by multiplying each value in the list by 3, 5 or 7.

How would we find A_k? Well, we could actually multiply each number in the list by 3, 5, and 7 and find the smallest element that has not yet been added to our list. This solution is $O(k^2)$. Not bad, but I think we can do better.

Rather than A_k trying to "pull" from a previous element in the list (by multiplying all of them by 3, 5 and 7), we can think about each previous value in the list as "pushing" out three subsequent values in the list. That is, each number A_i will eventually be used later in the list in the following forms:

- $3 * A_i$

- $5 * A_i$

- $7 * A_i$

We can use this thought to plan in advance. Each time we add a number A_i to the list, we hold on to the values $3A_i$, $5A_i$, and $7A_i$ in some sort of temporary list. To generate A_{i+1}, we search through this temporary list to find the smallest value.

Our code looks like this:

```
1   public static int removeMin(Queue<Integer> q) {
```

```
2        int min = q.peek();
3        for (Integer v : q) {
4            if (min > v) {
5                min = v;
6            }
7        }
8        while (q.contains(min)) {
9            q.remove(min);
10       }
11       return min;
12   }
13
14   public static void addProducts(Queue<Integer> q, int v) {
15       q.add(v * 3);
16       q.add(v * 5);
17       q.add(v * 7);
18   }
19
20   public static int getKthMagicNumber(int k) {
21       if (k < 0) return 0;
22
23       int val = 1;
24       Queue<Integer> q = new LinkedList<Integer>();
25       addProducts(q, 1);
26       for (int i = 0; i < k; i++) {
27           val = removeMin(q);
28           addProducts(q, val);
29       }
30       return val;
31   }
```

This algorithm is certainly much, much better than our first algorithm, but it's still not quite perfect.

To generate a new element A_i, we are searching through a linked list where each element looks like one of:

- 3 * previous element

- 5 * previous element

- 7 * previous element

Where is there unnecessary work that we might be able to optimize out?

Let's imagine our list looks like

$$q_6 = \{7A_1, \ 5A_2, \ 7A_2, \ 7A_3, \ 3A_4, \ 5A_4, \ 7A_4, \ 5A_5, \ 7A_5\}$$

When we search this list for the min, we check if $7A_1 <$ min, and then later we check if $7A_5 <$ min. That seems sort of silly, doesn't it? Since we know that $A_1 < A_5$, we should only need to check $7A_1$.

If we separated the list from the beginning by the constant factors, then we'd only need to check the first of the multiples of 3, 5 and 7. All subsequent elements would be bigger.

That is, our list above would look like:

Q36 = {3A$_4$}
Q56 = {5A$_2$, 5A$_4$, 5A$_5$}
Q76 = {7A$_1$, 7A$_2$, 7A$_3$, 7A$_4$, 7A$_5$}

To get the min, we only need to look at the fronts of each queue:

y = min(Q3.head(), Q5.head(), Q7.head())

Once we compute y, we need to insert 3y into Q3, 5y into Q3, and 7y into Q7. But, we only want to insert these elements if they aren't already in another list.

Why might, for example, 3y already be somewhere in the holding queues? Well, if y was pulled from Q7, then that means that y = 7x, for some smaller x. If 7x is the smallest value, we must have already seen 3x. And what did we do when we saw 3x? We inserted 7 * 3x into Q7. Note that 7 * 3x = 3 * 7x = 3y.

To put this another way, if we pull an element from Q7, it will look like 7 * suffix, and we know we have already handled 3 * suffix and 5 * suffix. In handling 3 * suffix, we inserted 7 * 3 * suffix into a Q7. And in handling 5 * suffix, we know we inserted 7 * 5 * suffix in Q7. The only value we haven't seen yet is 7 * 7 * suffix, so we just insert 7 * 7 * suffix into Q7.

Let's walk through this with an example to make it really clear.

```
initialize:
        Q3 = 3
        Q5 = 5
        Q7 = 7
remove min = 3. insert 3*3 in Q3, 5*3 into Q5, 7*3 into Q7.
        Q3 = 3*3
        Q5 = 5, 5*3
        Q7 = 7, 7*3
remove min = 5. 3*5 is a dup, since we already did 5*3. insert 5*5
into Q5, 7*5 into Q7.
        Q3 = 3*3
        Q5 = 5*3, 5*5
        Q7 = 7, 7*3, 7*5.
remove min = 7. 3*7 and 5*7 are dups, since we already did 7*3 and
7*5. insert 7*7 into Q7.
        Q3 = 3*3
        Q5 = 5*3, 5*5
        Q7 = 7*3, 7*5, 7*7
remove min = 3*3 = 9. insert 3*3*3 in Q3, 3*3*5 into Q5, 3*3*7
into Q7.
        Q3 = 3*3*3
        Q5 = 5*3, 5*5, 5*3*3
        Q7 = 7*3, 7*5, 7*7, 7*3*3
remove min = 5*3 = 15. 3*(5*3) is a dup, since we already did
```

5*(3*3). insert 5*5*3 in Q5, 7*5*3 into Q7.
```
Q3 = 3*3*3
Q5 = 5*5, 5*3*3, 5*5*3
Q7 = 7*3, 7*5, 7*7, 7*3*3, 7*5*3
```
remove min = 7*3 = 21. 3*(7*3) and 5*(7*3) are dups, since we already did 7*(3*3) and 7*(5*3). insert 7*7*3 into Q7.
```
Q3 = 3*3*3
Q5 = 5*5, 5*3*3, 5*5*3
Q7 = 7*5, 7*7, 7*3*3, 7*5*3, 7*7*3
```

Our pseudocode for this problem is as follows:

1. Initialize array and queues Q3, Q5, and Q7

2. Insert 1 into array.

3. Insert 1*3, 1*5 and 1*7 into Q3, Q5, and Q7 respectively.

4. Let x be the minimum element in Q3, Q5, and Q7. Append x to `magic`.

5. If x was found in:

    Q3 -> append x*3, x*5 and x*7 to Q3, Q5, and Q7. Remove x from Q3.

    Q5 -> append x*5 and x*7 to Q5 and Q7. Remove x from Q5.

    Q7 -> only append x*7 to Q7. Remove x from Q7.

6. Repeat steps 4 - 6 until we've found k elements.

The code below implements this algorithm.

```
1   public static int getKthMagicNumber(int k) {
2       if (k < 0) {
3           return 0;
4       }
5       int val = 0;
6       Queue<Integer> queue3 = new LinkedList<Integer>();
7       Queue<Integer> queue5 = new LinkedList<Integer>();
8       Queue<Integer> queue7 = new LinkedList<Integer>();
9       queue3.add(1);
10
11      /* Include 0th through kth iteration */
12      for (int i = 0; i <= k; i++) {
13          int v3 = queue3.size() > 0 ? queue3.peek() :
14                                       Integer.MAX_VALUE;
15          int v5 = queue5.size() > 0 ? queue5.peek() :
16                                       Integer.MAX_VALUE;
17          int v7 = queue7.size() > 0 ? queue7.peek() :
18                                       Integer.MAX_VALUE;
19          val = Math.min(v3, Math.min(v5, v7));
20          if (val == v3) { // enqueue into queue 3, 5 and 7
21              queue3.remove();
22              queue3.add(3 * val);
23              queue5.add(5 * val);
```

```
24       } else if (val == v5) { // enqueue into queue 5 and 7
25           queue5.remove();
26           queue5.add(5 * val);
27       } else if (val == v7) { // enqueue into Q7
28           queue7.remove();
29       }
30       queue7.add(7 * val); // Always enqueue into Q7
31   }
32   return val;
33 }
```

When you get this question, do your best to solve it—even though it's really difficult. You can start with a brute force approach (challenging, but not quite as tricky), and then you can start trying to optimize it. Or, try to find a pattern in the numbers.

Chances are that your interviewer will help you along when you get stuck. Whatever you do, don't give up! Think out loud, wonder out loud, and explain your thought process. Your interviewer will probably jump in to guide you.

Remember, perfection on this problem is not expected. Your performance is evaluated in comparison to other candidates. Everyone struggles on a tricky problem.

Object-Oriented Design

Concepts and Algorithms: Solutions

Chapter 8

8.1 *Design the data structures for a generic deck of cards. Explain how you would subclass the data structures to implement blackjack.*

pg 105

SOLUTION

First, we need to recognize that a "generic" deck of cards can mean many things. Generic could mean a standard deck of cards that can play a poker-like game, or it could even stretch to Uno or Baseball cards. It is important to ask your interviewer what she means by generic.

Let's assume that your interviewer clarifies that the deck is a standard 52-card set, like you might see used in a blackjack or poker game. If so, the design might look like this:

```
1   public enum Suit {
2       Club (0), Diamond (1), Heart (2), Spade (3);
3       private int value;
4       private Suit(int v) { value = v; }
5       public int getValue() { return value; }
6       public static Suit getSuitFromValue(int value) { ... }
7   }
8
9   public class Deck <T extends Card> {
10      private ArrayList<T> cards; // all cards, dealt or not
11      private int dealtIndex = 0; // marks first undealt card
12
13      public void setDeckOfCards(ArrayList<T> deckOfCards) { ... }
14
15      public void shuffle() { ... }
16      public int remainingCards() {
17          return cards.size() - dealtIndex;
18      }
19      public T[] dealHand(int number) { ... }
20      public T dealCard() { ... }
21  }
22
23  public abstract class Card {
24      private boolean available = true;
25
26      /* number or face that's on card - a number 2 through 10, or 11
27       * for Jack, 12 for Queen, 13 for King, or 1 for Ace */
28      protected int faceValue;
29      protected Suit suit;
30
31      public Card(int c, Suit s) {
32          faceValue = c;
33          suit = s;
34      }
35
```

```
36    public abstract int value();
37
38    public Suit suit() { return suit; }
39
40    /* Checks if the card is available to be given out to someone */
41    public boolean isAvailable() { return available; }
42    public void markUnavailable() { available = false; }
43
44    public void markAvailable() { available = true; }
45 }
46
47 public class Hand <T extends Card> {
48    protected ArrayList<T> cards = new ArrayList<T>();
49
50    public int score() {
51       int score = 0;
52       for (T card : cards) {
53          score += card.value();
54       }
55       return score;
56    }
57
58    public void addCard(T card) {
59       cards.add(card);
60    }
61 }
```

In the above code, we have implemented Deck with generics but restricted the type of T to Card. We have also implemented Card as an abstract class, since methods like value() don't make much sense without a specific game attached to them. (You could make a compelling argument that they should be implemented anyway, by defaulting to standard poker rules.)

Now, let's say we're building a blackjack game, so we need to know the value of the cards. Face cards are 10 and an ace is 11 (most of the time, but that's the job of the Hand class, not the following class).

```
1    public class BlackJackHand extends Hand<BlackJackCard> {
2       /* There are multiple possible scores for a blackjack hand,
3        * since aces have multiple values. Return the highest possible
4        * score that's under 21, or the lowest score that's over. */
5       public int score() {
6          ArrayList<Integer> scores = possibleScores();
7          int maxUnder = Integer.MIN_VALUE;
8          int minOver = Integer.MAX_VALUE;
9          for (int score : scores) {
10             if (score > 21 && score < minOver) {
11                minOver = score;
12             } else if (score <= 21 && score > maxUnder) {
13                maxUnder = score;
```

```
14          }
15        }
16        return maxUnder == Integer.MIN_VALUE ? minOver : maxUnder;
17      }
18
19      /* return a list of all possible scores this hand could have
20       * (evaluating each ace as both 1 and 11 */
21      private ArrayList<Integer> possibleScores() { ... }
22
23      public boolean busted() { return score() > 21; }
24      public boolean is21() { return score() == 21; }
25      public boolean isBlackJack() { ... }
26 }
27
28 public class BlackJackCard extends Card {
29      public BlackJackCard(int c, Suit s) { super(c, s); }
30      public int value() {
31        if (isAce()) return 1;
32        else if (faceValue >= 11 && faceValue <= 13) return 10;
33        else return faceValue;
34      }
35
36      public int minValue() {
37        if (isAce()) return 1;
38        else return value();
39      }
40
41      public int maxValue() {
42        if (isAce()) return 11;
43        else return value();
44      }
45
46      public boolean isAce() {
47        return faceValue == 1;
48      }
49
50      public boolean isFaceCard() {
51        return faceValue >= 11 && faceValue <= 13;
52      }
53 }
```

This is just one way of handling aces. We could, alternatively, create a class of type Ace that extends BlackJackCard.

An executable, fully automated version of blackjack is provided in the downloadable code attachment.

8.2 *Imagine you have a call center with three levels of employees: respondent, manager, and director. An incoming telephone call must be first allocated to a respondent who is free. If the respondent can't handle the call, he or she must escalate the call to a manager. If the manager is not free or not able to handle it, then the call should be escalated to a director. Design the classes and data structures for this problem. Implement a method* dispatchCall() *which assigns a call to the first available employee.*

pg 106

SOLUTION

All three ranks of employees have different work to be done, so those specific functions are profile specific. We should keep these things within their respective class.

There are a few things which are common to them, like address, name, job title, and age. These things can be kept in one class and can be extended or inherited by others.

Finally, there should be one CallHandler class which would route the calls to the correct person.

Note that on any object-oriented design question, there are many ways to design the objects. Discuss the trade-offs of different solutions with your interviewer. You should usually design for long-term code flexibility and maintenance.

We'll go through each of the classes below in detail.

CallHandler is implemented as a singleton class. It represents the body of the program, and all calls are funneled first through it.

```
1   public class CallHandler {
2       private static CallHandler instance;
3
4       /* 3 levels of employees: respondents, managers, directors. */
5       private final int LEVELS = 3;
6
7       /* Initialize 10 respondents, 4 managers, and 2 directors. */
8       private final int NUM_RESPONDENTS = 10;
9       private final int NUM_MANAGERS = 4;
10      private final int NUM_DIRECTORS = 2;
11
12      /* List of employees, by level.
13       * employeeLevels[0] = respondents
14       * employeeLevels[1] = managers
15       * employeeLevels[2] = directors
16       */
17      List<List<Employee>> employeeLevels;
18
19      /* queues for each call's rank */
20      List<List<Call>> callQueues;
21
```

```
22    protected  CallHandler() { ... }
23
24    /* Get instance of singleton class. */
25    public static CallHandler getInstance() {
26       if (instance == null) instance = new CallHandler();
27       return instance;
28    }
29
30    /* Gets the first available employee who can handle this call.
*/
31    public Employee getHandlerForCall(Call call) { ... }
32
33    /* Routes the call to an available employee, or saves in a queue
34     * if no employee available. */
35    public void dispatchCall(Caller caller) {
36       Call call = new Call(caller);
37       dispatchCall(call);
38    }
39
40    /* Routes the call to an available employee, or saves in a queue
41     * if no employee available. */
42    public void dispatchCall(Call call) {
43       /* Try to route the call to an employee with minimal rank. */
44       Employee emp = getHandlerForCall(call);
45       if (emp != null) {
46          emp.receiveCall(call);
47          call.setHandler(emp);
48       } else {
49          /* Place the call into corresponding call queue according
50           * to its rank. */
51          call.reply("Please wait for free employee to reply");
52          callQueues.get(call.getRank().getValue()).add(call);
53       }
54    }
55
56    /* An employee got free. Look for a waiting call that emp. can
57     * serve. Return true if we assigned a call, false otherwise. */
58    public boolean assignCall(Employee emp) { ... }
59 }
```

Call represents a call from a user. A call has a minimum rank and is assigned to the first employee who can handle it.

```
1   public class Call {
2      /* Minimal rank of employee who can handle this call. */
3      private Rank rank;
4
5      /* Person who is calling. */
6      private Caller caller;
7
8      /* Employee who is handling call. */
```

```
9       private Employee handler;
10
11      public Call(Caller c) {
12          rank = Rank.Responder;
13          caller = c;
14      }
15
16      /* Set employee who is handling call. */
17      public void setHandler(Employee e) { handler = e; }
18
19      public void reply(String message) { ... }
20      public Rank getRank() { return rank; }
21      public void setRank(Rank r) { rank = r; }
22      public Rank incrementRank() { ... }
23      public void disconnect() { ... }
24  }
```

Employee is a super class for the `Director`, `Manager`, and `Respondent` classes. It is implemented as an abstract class since there should be no reason to instantiate an Employee type directly.

```
1   abstract class Employee {
2       private Call currentCall = null;
3       protected Rank rank;
4
5       public Employee() { }
6
7       /* Start the conversation */
8       public void receiveCall(Call call) { ... }
9
10      /* the issue is resolved, finish the call */
11      public void callCompleted() { ... }
12
13      /* The issue has not been resolved. Escalate the call, and
14       * assign a new call to the employee. */
15      public void escalateAndReassign() { ... }
16      }
17
18      /* Assign a new call to an employee, if the employee is free. */
19      public boolean assignNewCall() { ... }
20
21      /* Returns whether or not the employee is free. */
22      public boolean isFree() { return currentCall == null; }
23
24      public Rank getRank() { return rank; }
25  }
26
```

The `Respondent`, `Director`, and `Manager` classes are now just simple extensions of the Employee class.

```
1   class Director extends Employee {
```

```
2      public Director() {
3          rank = Rank.Director;
4      }
5  }
6
7  class Manager extends Employee {
8      public Manager() {
9          rank = Rank.Manager;
10     }
11 }
12
13 class Respondent extends Employee {
14     public Respondent() {
15         rank = Rank.Responder;
16     }
17 }
```

This is just one way of designing this problem. Note that there are many other ways that are equally good.

This may seem like an awful lot of code to write in an interview, and it is. We've been much more thorough here than you would need. In a real interview, you would likely be much lighter on some of the details until you have time to fill them in.

8.3 *Design a musical jukebox using object-oriented principles.*

pg 106

SOLUTION

In any object-oriented design question, you first want to start off with asking your interviewer some questions to clarify design constraints. Is this jukebox playing CDs? Records? MP3s? Is it a simulation on a computer, or is it supposed to represent a physical jukebox? Does it take money, or is it free? And if it takes money, which currency? And does it deliver change?

Unfortunately, we don't have an interviewer here that we can have this dialogue with. Instead, we'll make some assumptions. We'll assume that the jukebox is a computer simulation that closely mirrors physical jukeboxes, and we'll assume that it's free.

Now that we have that out of the way, we'll outline the basic system components:

- Jukebox
- CD
- Song
- Artist
- Playlist

- Display (displays details on the screen)

Now, let's break this down further and think about the possible actions.

- Playlist creation (includes add, delete, and shuffle)

- CD selector

- Song selector

- Queuing up a song

- Get next song from playlist

A user also can be introduced:

- Adding

- Deleting

- Credit information

Each of the main system components translates roughly to an object, and each action translates to a method. Let's walk through one potential design.

The Jukebox class represents the body of the problem. Many of the interactions between the components of the system, or between the system and the user, are channeled through here.

```
1   public class Jukebox {
2      private CDPlayer cdPlayer;
3      private User user;
4      private Set<CD> cdCollection;
5      private SongSelector ts;
6
7      public Jukebox(CDPlayer cdPlayer, User user,
8                     Set<CD> cdCollection, SongSelector ts) {
9         ...
10     }
11
12     public Song getCurrentSong() {
13        return ts.getCurrentSong();
14     }
15
16     public void setUser(User u) {
17        this.user = u;
18     }
19  }
```

Like a real CD player, the CDPlayer class supports storing just one CD at a time. The CDs that are not in play are stored in the jukebox.

```
1   public class CDPlayer {
2      private Playlist p;
3      private CD c;
4
```

```
5    /* Constructors. */
6    public CDPlayer(CD c, Playlist p) { ... }
7    public CDPlayer(Playlist p) { this.p = p; }
8    public CDPlayer(CD c) { this.c = c; }
9
10   /* Play song */
11   public void playSong(Song s) { ... }
12
13   /* Getters and setters */
14   public Playlist getPlaylist() { return p; }
15   public void setPlaylist(Playlist p) { this.p = p; }
16
17   public CD getCD() { return c; }
18   public void setCD(CD c) { this.c = c; }
19 }
```

The Playlist manages the current and next songs to play. It is essentially a wrapper class for a queue and offers some additional methods for convenience.

```
1  public class Playlist {
2     private Song song;
3     private Queue<Song> queue;
4     public Playlist(Song song, Queue<Song> queue) {
5        ...
6     }
7     public Song getNextSToPlay() {
8        return queue.peek();
9     }
10    public void queueUpSong(Song s) {
11       queue.add(s);
12    }
13 }
```

The classes for CD, Song, and User are all fairly straightforward. They consist mainly of member variables and getters and setters.

```
1  public class CD {
2     /* data for id, artist, songs, etc */
3  }
4
5  public class Song {
6     /* data for id, CD (could be null), title, length, etc */
7  }
8
9  public class User {
10    private String name;
11    public String getName() { return name; }
12    public void setName(String name) {   this.name = name; }
13    public long getID() { return ID; }
14    public void setID(long iD) { ID = iD; }
15    private long ID;
16    public User(String name, long iD) { ... }
```

```
17    public User getUser() { return this; }
18    public static User addUser(String name, long iD) { ... }
19  }
```

This is by no means the only "correct" implementation. The interviewer's responses to initial questions, as well as other constraints, will shape the design of the jukebox classes.

8.4   *Design a parking lot using object-oriented principles.*

pg 106

SOLUTION

The wording of this question is vague, just as it would be in an actual interview. This requires you to have a conversation with your interviewer about what types of vehicles it can support, whether the parking lot has multiple levels, and so on.

For our purposes right now, we'll make the following assumptions. We made these specific assumptions to add a bit of complexity to the problem without adding too much. If you made different assumptions, that's totally fine.

- The parking lot has multiple levels. Each level has multiple rows of spots.

- The parking lot can park motorcycles, cars, and buses.

- The parking lot has motorcycle spots, compact spots, and large spots.

- A motorcycle can park in any spot.

- A car can park in either a single compact spot or a single large spot.

- A bus can park in five large spots that are consecutive and within the same row. It cannot park in small spots.

In the below implementation, we have created an abstract class Vehicle, from which Car, Bus, and Motorcycle inherit. To handle the different parking spot sizes, we have just one class ParkingSpot which has a member variable indicating the size.

```
1   public enum VehicleSize { Motorcycle, Compact, Large }
2
3   public abstract class Vehicle {
4       protected ArrayList<ParkingSpot> parkingSpots =
5           new ArrayList<ParkingSpot>();
6       protected String licensePlate;
7       protected int spotsNeeded;
8       protected VehicleSize size;
9
10      public int getSpotsNeeded() { return spotsNeeded; }
11      public VehicleSize getSize() { return size; }
12
13      /* Park vehicle in this spot (among others, potentially) */
```

```
14    public void parkInSpot(ParkingSpot s) { parkingSpots.add(s); }
15
16    /* Remove car from spot, and notify spot that it's gone */
17    public void clearSpots() { ... }
18
19    /* Checks if the spot is big enough for the vehicle (and is
20     * available). This compares the SIZE only. It does not check if it
21     * has enough spots. */
22    public abstract boolean canFitInSpot(ParkingSpot spot);
23 }
24
25 public class Bus extends Vehicle {
26    public Bus() {
27       spotsNeeded = 5;
28       size = VehicleSize.Large;
29    }
30
31    /* Checks if the spot is a Large. Doesn't check num of spots */
32    public boolean canFitInSpot(ParkingSpot spot) { ... }
33 }
34
35 public class Car extends Vehicle {
36    public Car() {
37       spotsNeeded = 1;
38       size = VehicleSize.Compact;
39    }
40
41    /* Checks if the spot is a Compact or a Large. */
42    public boolean canFitInSpot(ParkingSpot spot) { ... }
43 }
44
45 public class Motorcycle extends Vehicle {
46    public Motorcycle() {
47       spotsNeeded = 1;
48       size = VehicleSize.Motorcycle;
49    }
50
51    public boolean canFitInSpot(ParkingSpot spot) { ... }
52 }
```

The ParkingLot class is essentially a wrapper class for an array of Levels. By implementing it this way, we are able to separate out logic that deals with actually finding free spots and parking cars out from the broader actions of the ParkingLot. If we didn't do it this way, we would need to holding parking spots in some sort of double array (or hash table which maps from a level number to the list of spots). It's cleaner to just separate ParkingLot from Level.

```
1  public class ParkingLot {
2     private Level[] levels;
```

```
3      private final int NUM_LEVELS = 5;
4
5      public ParkingLot() { ... }
6
7      /* Park the vehicle in a spot (or multiple spots).
8       * Return false if failed. */
9      public boolean parkVehicle(Vehicle vehicle) { ... }
10 }
11
12 /* Represents a level in a parking garage */
13 public class Level {
14     private int floor;
15     private ParkingSpot[] spots;
16     private int availableSpots = 0; // number of free spots
17     private static final int SPOTS_PER_ROW = 10;
18
19     public Level(int flr, int numberSpots) { ... }
20
21     public int availableSpots() { return availableSpots; }
22
23     /* Find a place to park this vehicle. Return false if failed. */
24     public boolean parkVehicle(Vehicle vehicle) { ... }
25
26     /* Park a vehicle starting at the spot spotNumber, and
27      * continuing until vehicle.spotsNeeded. */
28     private boolean parkStartingAtSpot(int num, Vehicle v) { ... }
29
30     /* Find a spot to park this vehicle. Return index of spot, or -1
31      * on failure. */
32     private int findAvailableSpots(Vehicle vehicle) { ... }
33
34     /* When a car was removed from the spot, increment
35      * availableSpots */
36     public void spotFreed() { availableSpots++; }
37 }
```

The ParkingSpot is implemented by having just a variable which represents the size of the spot. We could have implemented this by having classes for LargeSpot, CompactSpot, and MotorcycleSpot which inherit from ParkingSpot, but this is probably overkill. The spots probably do not have different behaviors, other than their sizes.

```
1  public class ParkingSpot {
2      private Vehicle vehicle;
3      private VehicleSize spotSize;
4      private int row;
5      private int spotNumber;
6      private Level level;
7
8      public ParkingSpot(Level lvl, int r, int n, VehicleSize s) {...}
```

```
9
10     public boolean isAvailable() { return vehicle == null; }
11
12     /* Check if the spot is big enough and is available */
13     public boolean canFitVehicle(Vehicle vehicle) { ... }
14
15     /* Park vehicle in this spot. */
16     public boolean park(Vehicle v) { ... }
17
18     public int getRow() { return row; }
19     public int getSpotNumber() { return spotNumber; }
20
21     /* Remove vehicle from spot, and notify level that a new spot is
22      * available */
23     public void removeVehicle() { ... }
24  }
```

A full implementation of this code, including executable test code, is provided in the downloadable code attachment.

8.5   *Design the data structures for an online book reader system.*

pg 106

SOLUTION

Since the problem doesn't describe much about the functionality, let's assume we want to design a basic online reading system which provides the following functionality:

- User membership creation and extension.

- Searching the database of books.

- Reading a book.

- Only one active user at a time

- Only one active book by this user.

To implement these operations we may require many other functions, like get, set, update, and so on. The objects required would likely include User, Book, and Library.

The class OnlineReaderSystem represents the body of our program. We could implement the class such that it stores information about all the books, deals with user management, and refreshes the display, but that would make this class rather hefty. Instead, we've chosen to tear off these components into Library, UserManager, and Display classes.

```
1  public class OnlineReaderSystem {
2      private Library library;
3      private UserManager userManager;
4      private Display display;
```

```
5
6     private Book activeBook;
7     private User activeUser;
8
9     public OnlineReaderSystem() {
10       userManager = new UserManager();
11       library = new Library();
12       display = new Display();
13     }
14
15     public Library getLibrary() { return library;   }
16     public UserManager getUserManager() { return userManager; }
17     public Display getDisplay() { return display; }
18
19     public Book getActiveBook() { return activeBook; }
20     public void setActiveBook(Book book) {
21       activeBook = book;
22       display.displayBook(book);
23     }
24
25     public User getActiveUser() { return activeUser; }
26     public void setActiveUser(User user) {
27       activeUser = user;
28       display.displayUser(user);
29     }
30 }
```

We then implement separate classes to handle the user manager, the library, and the display components.

```
1   public class Library {
2     private Hashtable<Integer, Book> books;
3
4     public Book addBook(int id, String details) {
5       if (books.containsKey(id)) {
6         return null;
7       }
8       Book book = new Book(id, details);
9       books.put(id, book);
10      return book;
11    }
12
13    public boolean remove(Book b) { return remove(b.getID()); }
14    public boolean remove(int id) {
15      if (!books.containsKey(id)) {
16        return false;
17      }
18      books.remove(id);
19      return true;
20    }
21
```

```
22     public Book find(int id) {
23         return books.get(id);
24     }
25 }
26
27 public class UserManager {
28     private Hashtable<Integer, User> users;
29
30     public User addUser(int id, String details, int accountType) {
31         if (users.containsKey(id)) {
32             return null;
33         }
34         User user = new User(id, details, accountType);
35         users.put(id, user);
36         return user;
37     }
38
39     public boolean remove(User u) {
40         return remove(u.getID());
41     }
42
43     public boolean remove(int id) {
44         if (!users.containsKey(id)) {
45             return false;
46         }
47         users.remove(id);
48         return true;
49     }
50
51     public User find(int id) {
52         return users.get(id);
53     }
54 }
55
56 public class Display {
57     private Book activeBook;
58     private User activeUser;
59     private int pageNumber = 0;
60
61     public void displayUser(User user) {
62         activeUser = user;
63         refreshUsername();
64     }
65
66     public void displayBook(Book book) {
67         pageNumber = 0;
68         activeBook = book;
69
70         refreshTitle();
71         refreshDetails();
```

```
72        refreshPage();
73    }
74
75    public void turnPageForward() {
76        pageNumber++;
77        refreshPage();
78    }
79
80    public void turnPageBackward() {
81        pageNumber--;
82        refreshPage();
83    }
84
85    public void refreshUsername() { /* updates username display */ }
86    public void refreshTitle() { /* updates title display */ }
87    public void refreshDetails() { /* updates details display */   }
88    public void refreshPage() { /* updated page display */ }
89 }
```

The classes for User and Book simply hold data and provide little true functionality.

```
1   public class Book {
2       private int bookId;
3       private String details;
4
5       public Book(int id, String det) {
6           bookId = id;
7           details = det;
8       }
9
10      public int getID() { return bookId;  }
11      public void setID(int id) { bookId = id; }
12      public String getDetails() { return details; }
13      public void setDetails(String d) { details = d; }
14  }
15
16  public class User {
17      private int userId;
18      private String details;
19      private int accountType;
20
21      public void renewMembership() {  }
22
23      public User(int id, String details, int accountType) {
24          userId = id;
25          this.details = details;
26          this.accountType = accountType;
27      }
28
29      /* Getters and setters */
30      public int getID() { return userId; }
```

```
31    public void setID(int id) { userId = id; }
32    public String getDetails() {
33        return details;
34    }
35
36    public void setDetails(String details) {
37        this.details = details;
38    }
39    public int getAccountType() { return accountType; }
40    public void setAccountType(int t) { accountType = t; }
41 }
```

The decision to tear off user management, library, and display into their own classes, when this functionality could have been in the general OnlineReaderSystem class, is an interesting one. On a very small system, making this decision could make the system overly complex. However, as the system grows, and more and more functionality gets added to OnlineReaderSystem, breaking off such components prevents this main class from getting overwhelmingly lengthy.

8.6   *Implement a jigsaw puzzle. Design the data structures and explain an algorithm to solve the puzzle. You can assume that you have a fitsWith method which, when passed two puzzle pieces, returns true if the two pieces belong together.*

pg 106

SOLUTION

We will assume that we have a traditional, simple jigsaw puzzle. The puzzle is grid-like, with rows and columns. Each piece is located in a single row and column and has four edges. Each edge comes in one of three types: inner, outer, and flat. A corner piece, for example, will have two flat edges and two other edges, which could be inner or outer.

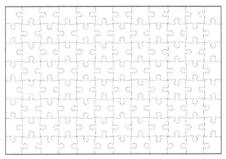

As we solve the jigsaw puzzle (manually or algorithmically), we'll need to store the position of each piece. We could think about the position as absolute or relative:

- *Absolute Position:* "This piece is located at position (12, 23)." Absolute position would belong to the Piece class itself and would include an orientation as well.

- *Relative Position:* "I don't know where this piece is actually located, but I know that it is next to this other piece." The relative position would belong to the Edge class.

For our solution, we will use only the relative position, by adjoining edges to neighboring edges.

A potential object-oriented design looks like the following:

```
1   class Edge {
2       enum Type { inner, outer, flat }
3       Piece parent;
4       Type type;
5       int index; // Index into Piece.edges
6       Edge attached_to; // Relative position.
7
8       /* See Algorithm section. Returns true if the two pieces
9        * should be attached to each other. */
10      boolean fitsWith(Edge edge) { ... };
11  }
12
13  class Piece {
14      Edge[] edges;
15      boolean isCorner() { ... }
16  }
17
18  class Puzzle {
19      Piece[] pieces; /* Remaining pieces left to put away. */
20      Piece[][] solution;
21
22      /* See algorithm section. */
23      Edge[] inners, outers, flats;
24      Piece[] corners;
25
26      /* See Algorithm section. */
27      void sort() { ... }
28      void solve() { ...}
29  }
```

Algorithm to Solve the Puzzle

We will sketch this algorithm using a mix of pseudocode and real code.

Just as a kid might in solving a puzzle, we'll start with the easiest pieces first: the corners and edges. We can easily search through all the pieces to find just the edges. While we're at it though, it probably makes sense to group all the pieces by their edge types.

```
1   void sort() {
2       for each Piece p in pieces {
3           if (p has two flat edges) then add p to corners
```

```
4          for each edge in p.edges {
5              if edge is inner then add to inners
6              if edge is outer then add to outers
7          }
8      }
9  }
```

We now have a quicker way to zero in on potential matches for any given edge. We then go through the puzzle, line by line, to match pieces.

The solve method, implemented below, operates by picking an arbitrary corner to start with. It then finds an open edge on the corner and tries to match it to an open piece. When it finds a match, it does the following:

1. Attaches the edge.

2. Removes the edge from the list of open edges.

3. Finds the next open edge.

The next open edge is defined to be the one directly opposite the current edge, if it is available. If it is not available, then the next edge can be any other edge. This will cause the puzzle to be solved in a spiral-like fashion, from the outside to the inside.

The spiral comes from the fact that the algorithm always moves in a straight line, whenever possible. When we reach the end of the first edge, the algorithm moves to the only available edge on that corner piece—a 90-degree turn. It continues to take 90-degree turns at the end of each side until the entire outer edge of the puzzle is completed. When that last edge piece is in place, that piece only has one exposed edge remaining, which is again a 90-degree turn. The algorithm repeats itself for subsequent rings around the puzzle, until finally all the pieces are in place.

This algorithm is implemented below with Java-like pseudocode.

```
1   public void solve() {
2       /* Pick any corner to start with */
3       Edge currentEdge = getExposedEdge(corner[0]);
4
5       /* Loop will iterate in a spiral like fashion until the puzzle
6        * is full. */
7       while (currentEdge != null) {
8           /* Match with opposite edges. Inners with outers, etc. */
9           Edge[] opposites = currentEdge.type == inner ?
10                              outers : inners;
11          for each Edge fittingEdge in opposites {
12              if (currentEdge.fitsWith(fittingEdge)) {
13                  attachEdges(currentEdge, fittingEdge); //attach edge
14                  removeFromList(currentEdge);
15                  removeFromList(fittingEdge);
16
17                  /* get next edge */
18                  currentEdge = nextExposedEdge(fittingEdge);
```

```
19                break; // Break out of inner loop. Continue in outer.
20        }
21      }
22    }
23 }
24
25 public void removeFromList(Edge edge) {
26    if (edge.type == flat) return;
27    Edge[] array = currentEdge.type == inner ? inners : outers;
28    array.remove(edge);
29 }
30
31 /* Return the opposite edge if possible. Else, return any exposed
32  * edge. */
33 public Edge nextExposedEdge(Edge edge) {
34    int next_index = (edge.index + 2) % 4; // Opposite edge
35    Edge next_edge = edge.parent.edges[next_index];
36    if isExposed(next_edge) {
37      return next_edge;
38    }
39    return getExposedEdge(edge.parent);
40 }
41
42 public Edge attachEdges(Edge e1, Edge e2) {
43    e1.attached_to = e2;
44    e2.attached_to = e1;
45 }
46
47 public Edge isExposed(Edge e1) {
48    return edge.type != flat && edge.attached_to == null;
49 }
50
51 public Edge getExposedEdge(Piece p) {
52    for each Edge edge in p.edges {
53      if (isExposed(edge)) {
54        return edge;
55      }
56    }
57    return null;
58 }
```

For simplicity, we've represented inners and outers as an Edge array. This is actually not a great choice, since we need to add and remove elements from it frequently. If we were writing real code, we would probably want to implement these variables as linked lists.

Writing the full code for this problem in an interview would be far, far too much work. More likely, you would be asked to just sketch out the code.

8.7 *Explain how you would design a chat server. In particular, provide details about the various backend components, classes, and methods. What would be the hardest problems to solve?*

pg 106

SOLUTION

Designing a chat server is a huge project, and it is certainly far beyond the scope of what could be completed in an interview. After all, teams of many people spend months or years creating a chat server. Part of your job, as a candidate, is to focus on an aspect of the problem that is reasonably broad, but focused enough that you could accomplish it during an interview. It need not match real life exactly, but it should be a fair representation of an actual implementation.

For our purposes, we'll focus on the core user management and conversation aspects: adding a user, creating a conversation, updating one's status, and so on. In the interest of time and space, we will not go into the networking aspects of the problem, or how the data actually gets pushed out to the clients.

We will assume that "friending" is mutual; I am only your contact if you are mine. Our chat system will support both group chat and one-on-one (private) chats. We will not worry about voice chat, video chat, or file transfer.

What specific actions does it need to support?

This is also something to discuss with your interviewer, but here are some ideas:

- Signing online and offline.
- Add requests (sending, accepting, and rejecting).
- Updating a status message.
- Creating private and group chats.
- Adding new messages to private and group chats.

This is just a partial list. If you have more time, you can add more actions.

What can we learn about these requirements?

We must have a concept of users, add request status, online status, and messages.

What are the core components of the system?

The system would likely consist of a database, a set of clients, and a set of servers. We won't include these parts in our object-oriented design, but we can discuss the overall view of the system.

The database will be used for more permanent storage, such as the user list or chat archives. A SQL database is a good bet, or, if we need more scalability, we could potentially use BigTable or a similar system.

For communication between the client and servers, using XML will work well. Although it's not the most compressed format (and you should point this out to your interviewer), it's nice because it's easy for both computers and humans to read. Using XML will make your debugging efforts easier—and that matters a lot.

The server will consist of a set of machines. Data will be divided up across machines, requiring us to potentially hop from machine to machine. When possible, we will try to replicate some data across machines to minimize the lookups. One major design constraint here is to prevent having a single point of failure. For instance, if one machine controlled all the user sign-ins, then we'd cut off millions of users potentially if a single machine lost network connectivity.

What are the key objects and methods?

The key objects of the system will be a concept of users, conversations, and status messages. We've implemented a `UserManagement` class. If we were looking more at the networking aspects of the problem, or a different component, we might have instead dived into those objects.

```
1   /* UserManager serves as a central place for core user actions. */
1   public class UserManager {
2       private static UserManager instance;
3       /* maps from a user id to a user */
4       private HashMap<Integer, User> usersById;
5
6       /* maps from an account name to a user */
7       private HashMap<String, User> usersByAccountName;
8
9       /* maps from the user id to an online user */
10      private HashMap<Integer, User> onlineUsers;
11
12      public static UserManager getInstance() {
13          if (instance == null) instance = new UserManager();
14          return instance;
15      }
16
17      public void addUser(User fromUser, String toAccountName) { ... }
18      public void approveAddRequest(AddRequest req) { ... }
19      public void rejectAddRequest(AddRequest req) { ... }
20      public void userSignedOn(String accountName) { ... }
21      public void userSignedOff(String accountName) { ... }
22  }
```

The method `receivedAddRequest`, in the `User` class, notifies User B that User A has requested to add him. User B approves or rejects the request (via `UserManager.approveAddRequest` or `rejectAddRequest`), and the `UserManager` takes care of adding the users to each other's contact lists.

The method `sentAddRequest` in the `User` class is called by `UserManager` to add an `AddRequest` to User A's list of requests. So the flow is:

1. User A clicks "add user" on the client, and it gets sent to the server.

2. User A calls `requestAddUser(User B)`.

3. This method calls `UserManager.addUser`.

4. `UserManager` calls both `User A.sentAddRequest` and `User B.receivedAddRequest`.

Again, this is just *one* way of designing these interactions. It is not the only way, or even the only "good" way.

```
1   public class User {
2       private int id;
3       private UserStatus status = null;
4
5       /* maps from the other participant's user id to the chat */
6       private HashMap<Integer, PrivateChat> privateChats;
7
8       /* maps from the group chat id to the group chat */
9       private ArrayList<GroupChat> groupChats;
10
11      /* maps from the other person's user id to the add request */
12      private HashMap<Integer, AddRequest> receivedAddRequests;
13
14      /* maps from the other person's user id to the add request */
15      private HashMap<Integer, AddRequest> sentAddRequests;
16
17      /* maps from the user id to the add request */
18      private HashMap<Integer, User> contacts;
19
20      private String accountName;
21      private String fullName;
22
23      public User(int id, String accountName, String fullName) { ... }
24      public boolean sendMessageToUser(User to, String content){ ... }
25      public boolean sendMessageToGroupChat(int id, String cnt){...}
26      public void setStatus(UserStatus status) { ... }
27      public UserStatus getStatus() { ... }
28      public boolean addContact(User user) { ... }
29      public void receivedAddRequest(AddRequest req) { ...}
30      public void sentAddRequest(AddRequest req) { ... }
31      public void removeAddRequest(AddRequest req) { ... }
32      public void requestAddUser(String accountName) { ... }
33      public void addConversation(PrivateChat conversation) { ... }
34      public void addConversation(GroupChat conversation) { ... }
35      public int getId() { ... }
```

```
36      public String getAccountName() { ... }
37      public String getFullName() { ... }
38  }
```

The Conversation class is implemented as an abstract class, since all Conversations must be either a GroupChat or a PrivateChat, and since these two classes each have their own functionality.

```
1   public abstract class Conversation {
2       protected ArrayList<User> participants;
3       protected int id;
4       protected ArrayList<Message> messages;
5
6       public ArrayList<Message> getMessages() { ... }
7       public boolean addMessage(Message m) { ... }
8       public int getId() { ... }
9   }
10
11  public class GroupChat extends Conversation {
12      public void removeParticipant(User user) { ... }
13      public void addParticipant(User user) { ... }
14  }
15
16  public class PrivateChat extends Conversation {
17      public PrivateChat(User user1, User user2) { ...
18      public User getOtherParticipant(User primary) { ... }
19  }
20
21  public class Message {
22      private String content;
23      private Date date;
24      public Message(String content, Date date) { ... }
25      public String getContent() { ... }
26      public Date getDate() { ... }
27  }
```

AddRequest and UserStatus are simple classes with little functionality. Their main purpose is to group data that other classes will act upon.

```
1   public class AddRequest {
2       private User fromUser;
3       private User toUser;
4       private Date date;
5       RequestStatus status;
6
7       public AddRequest(User from, User to, Date date) { ... }
8       public RequestStatus getStatus() { ... }
9       public User getFromUser() { ... }
10      public User getToUser() { ... }
11      public Date getDate() { ... }
12  }
13
```

```
14  public class UserStatus {
15      private String message;
16      private UserStatusType type;
17      public UserStatus(UserStatusType type, String message) { ... }
18      public UserStatusType getStatusType() { ... }
19      public String getMessage() { ... }
20  }
21
22  public enum UserStatusType {
23      Offline, Away, Idle, Available, Busy
24  }
25
26  public enum RequestStatus {
27      Unread, Read, Accepted, Rejected
28  }
```

The downloadable code attachment provides a more detailed look at these methods, including implementations for the methods shown above.

What problems would be the hardest to solve (or the most interesting)?

The following questions may be interesting to discuss with your interviewer further.

Q1: How do we know if someone is online—I mean, really, really know?

While we would like users to tell us when they sign off, we can't know for sure. A user's connection might have died, for example. To make sure that we know when a user has signed off, we might try regularly pinging the client to make sure it's still there.

Q2: How do we deal with conflicting information?

We have some information stored in the computer's memory and some in the database. What happens if they get out of sync? Which one is "right"?

Q3: How do we make our server scale?

While we designed out chat server without worrying—too much– about scalability, in real life this would be a concern. We'd need to split our data across many servers, which would increase our concern about out-of-sync data.

Q4: How we do prevent denial of service attacks?

Clients can push data to us—what if they try to DOS (denial of service) us? How do we prevent that?

8.8 *Othello is played as follows: Each Othello piece is white on one side and black on the other. When a piece is surrounded by its opponents on both the left and right sides, or both the top and bottom, it is said to be captured and its color is flipped. On your turn, you must capture at least one of your opponent's pieces. The game ends when either user has no more valid moves. The win is assigned to the person with the most pieces. Implement the object-oriented design for Othello.*

pg 106

SOLUTION

Let's start with an example. Suppose we have the following moves in an Othello game:

1. Initialize the board with two black and two white pieces in the center. The black pieces are placed at the upper left hand and lower right hand corners.

2. Play a black piece at (row 6, column 4). This flips the piece at (row 5, column 4) from white to black.

3. Play a white piece at (row 4, column 3). This flips the piece at (row 4, column 4) from black to white.

This sequence of moves leads to the board below.

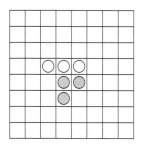

The core objects in Othello are probably the game, the board, the pieces (black or white), and the players. How do we represent these with elegant object-oriented design?

Should BlackPiece and WhitePiece be classes?

At first, we might think we want to have a `BlackPiece` class and a `WhitePiece` class, which inherit from an abstract `Piece`. However, this is probably not a great idea. Each piece may flip back and forth between colors frequently, so continuously destroying and creating what is really the same object is probably not wise. It may be better to just have a `Piece` class, with a flag in it representing the current color.

Do we need separate Board and Game classes?

Strictly speaking, it may not be necessary to have both a `Game` object and a `Board` object. Keeping the objects separate allows us to have a logical separation between the board (which contains just logic involving placing pieces) and the game (which involves times, game flow, etc.). However, the drawback is that we are adding extra layers to our program. A function may call out to a method in Game, only to have it immediately call Board. We have made the choice below to keep Game and Board separate, but you should discuss this with your interviewer.

Who keeps score?

We know we should probably have some sort of score keeping for the number of black and white pieces. But who should maintain this information? One could make a strong argument for either Game or Board maintaining this information, and possibly even for Piece (in static methods). We have implemented this with Board holding this information, since it can be logically grouped with the board. It is updated by Piece or Board calling colorChanged and colorAdded methods within Board.

Should Game be a Singleton class?

Implementing Game as a singleton class has the advantage of making it easy for anyone to call a method within Game, without having to pass around references to the Game object.

Making Game a singleton though means that it can only be instantiated once. Can we make this assumption? You should discuss this with your interviewer.

One possible design for Othello is below.

```
1   public enum Direction {
2       left, right, up, down
3   }
4
5   public enum Color {
6       White, Black
7   }
8
9   public class Game {
10      private Player[] players;
11      private static Game instance;
12      private Board board;
13      private final int ROWS = 10;
14      private final int COLUMNS = 10;
15
16      private Game() {
17          board = new Board(ROWS, COLUMNS);
18          players = new Player[2];
19          players[0] = new Player(Color.Black);
20          players[1] = new Player(Color.White);
21      }
22
23      public static Game getInstance() {
```

```
24        if (instance == null) instance = new Game();
25        return instance;
26     }
27
28     public Board getBoard() {
29        return board;
30     }
31  }
```

The Board class manages the actual pieces themselves. It does not handle much of the game play, leaving that up to the Game class.

```
1   public class Board {
2      private int blackCount = 0;
3      private int whiteCount = 0;
4      private Piece[][] board;
5
6      public Board(int rows, int columns) {
7         board = new Piece[rows][columns];
8      }
9
10     public void initialize() {
11        /* initialize center black and white pieces */
12     }
13
14     /* Attempt to place a piece of color color at (row, column).
15      * Return true if we were successful. */
16     public boolean placeColor(int row, int column, Color color) {
17        ...
18     }
19
20     /* flips pieces starting at (row, column) and proceeding in
21      * direction d. */
22     private int flipSection(int row, int column, Color color,
23                             Direction d) { ... }
24
25     public int getScoreForColor(Color c) {
26        if (c == Color.Black) return blackCount;
27        else return whiteCount;
28     }
29
30     /* Update board with additional newPieces pieces of color
31      * newColor. Decrease score of opposite color. */
32     public void updateScore(Color newColor, int newPieces) { ... }
33  }
```

As described earlier, we implement the black and white pieces with the Piece class, which has a simple Color variable representing whether it is a black or white piece.

```
1   public class Piece {
2      private Color color;
3      public Piece(Color c) { color = c; }
```

```
4
5    public void flip() {
6        if (color == Color.Black) color = Color.White;
7        else color = Color.Black;
8    }
9
10   public Color getColor() { return color; }
11 }
```

The Player holds only a very limited amount of information. It does not even hold its own score, but it does have a method one can call to get the score. Player. getScore() will call out to the GameManager to retrieve this value.

```
12 public class Player {
13     private Color color;
14     public Player(Color c) { color = c; }
15
16     public int getScore() { ... }
17
18     public boolean playPiece(int r, int c) {
19         return Game.getInstance().getBoard().placeColor(r, c, color);
20     }
21
22     public Color getColor() { return color; }
23 }
```

A fully functioning (automated) version of this code can be found in the downloadable code attachment.

Remember that in many problems, what you did is less important than *why* you did it. Your interviewer probably doesn't care much whether you chose implement Game as a singleton or not, but she probably does care that you took the time to think about it and discuss the trade-offs.

8.9   *Explain the data structures and algorithms that you would use to design an in-memory file system. Illustrate with an example in code where possible.*

pg 106

SOLUTION

Many candidates may see this problem and instantly panic. A file system seems so low level!

However, there's no need to panic. If we think through the components of a file system, we can tackle this problem just like any other object-oriented design question.

A file system, in its most simplistic version, consists of Files and Directories. Each Directory contains a set of Files and Directories. Since Files and Directories share so many characteristics, we've implemented them such that they inherit from the same class, Entry.

```
1   public abstract class Entry {
2       protected Directory parent;
3       protected long created;
4       protected long lastUpdated;
5       protected long lastAccessed;
6       protected String name;
7
8       public Entry(String n, Directory p) {
9           name = n;
10          parent = p;
11          created = System.currentTimeMillis();
12          lastUpdated = System.currentTimeMillis();
13          lastAccessed = System.currentTimeMillis();
14      }
15
16      public boolean delete() {
17          if (parent == null) return false;
18          return parent.deleteEntry(this);
19      }
20
21      public abstract int size();
22
23      public String getFullPath() {
24          if (parent == null) return name;
25          else return parent.getFullPath() + "/" + name;
26      }
27
28      /* Getters and setters. */
29      public long getCreationTime() { return created; }
30      public long getLastUpdatedTime() { return lastUpdated; }
31      public long getLastAccessedTime() { return lastAccessed; }
32      public void changeName(String n) { name = n; }
33      public String getName() { return name; }
34  }
35
36  public class File extends Entry {
37      private String content;
38      private int size;
39
40      public File(String n, Directory p, int sz) {
41          super(n, p);
42          size = sz;
43      }
44
45      public int size() { return size; }
46      public String getContents() { return content; }
47      public void setContents(String c) { content = c; }
48  }
```

```
49
50  public class Directory extends Entry {
51      protected ArrayList<Entry> contents;
52
53      public Directory(String n, Directory p) {
54          super(n, p);
55          contents = new ArrayList<Entry>();
56      }
57
58      public int size() {
59          int size = 0;
60          for (Entry e : contents) {
61              size += e.size();
62          }
63          return size;
64      }
65
66      public int numberOfFiles() {
67          int count = 0;
68          for (Entry e : contents) {
69              if (e instanceof Directory) {
70                  count++; // Directory counts as a file
71                  Directory d = (Directory) e;
72                  count += d.numberOfFiles();
73              } else if (e instanceof File) {
74                  count++;
75              }
76          }
77          return count;
78      }
79
80      public boolean deleteEntry(Entry entry) {
81          return contents.remove(entry);
82      }
83
84      public void addEntry(Entry entry) {
85          contents.add(entry);
86      }
87
88      protected ArrayList<Entry> getContents() { return contents; }
89  }
```

Alternatively, we could have implemented Directory such that it contains separate lists for files and subdirectories. This makes the numberOfFiles() method a bit cleaner, since it doesn't need to use the instanceof operator, but it does prohibit us from cleanly sorting files and directories by dates or names.

8.10   *Design and implement a hash table which uses chaining (linked lists) to handle collisions.*

pg 106

SOLUTION

Suppose we are implementing a hash table that looks like Hash<K, V>. That is, the hash table maps from objects of type K to objects of type V.

At first, we might think our data structure would look something like this:

```
1   public class Hash<K, V> {
2      LinkedList<V>[] items;
3      public void put(K key, V value) { ... }
4      public V get(K key) { ... }
5   }
```

Note that items is an array of linked lists, where items[i] is a linked list of all objects with keys that map to index i (that is, all the objects that collided at i).

This would seem to work until we think more deeply about collisions.

Suppose we have a very simple hash function that uses the string length.

```
1   public int hashCodeOfKey(K key) {
2      return key.toString().length() % items.length;
3   }
```

The keys jim and bob will map to the same index in the array, even though they are different keys. We need to search through the linked list to find the actual object that corresponds to these keys. But how would we do that? All we've stored in the linked list is the value, not the original key.

This is why we need to store both the value and the original key.

One way to do that is to create another object called Cell which pairs keys and values. With this implementation, our linked list is of type Cell.

The code below uses this implementation.

```
1   public class Hash<K, V> {
2      private final int MAX_SIZE = 10;
3      LinkedList<Cell<K, V>>[] items;
4
5      public Hash() {
6         items = (LinkedList<Cell<K, V>>[]) new LinkedList[MAX_SIZE];
7      }
8
9      /* Really, really stupid hash. */
10     public int hashCodeOfKey(K key) {
11        return key.toString().length() % items.length;
12     }
13
```

```
14    public void put(K key, V value) {
15       int x = hashCodeOfKey(key);
16       if (items[x] == null) {
17          items[x] = new LinkedList<Cell<K, V>>();
18       }
19
20       LinkedList<Cell<K, V>> collided = items[x];
21
22       /* Look for items with same key and replace if found */
23       for (Cell<K, V> c : collided) {
24          if (c.equivalent(key)) {
25             collided.remove(c);
26             break;
27          }
28       }
29
30       Cell<K, V> cell = new Cell<K, V>(key, value);
31       collided.add(cell);
32    }
33
34    public V get(K key) {
35       int x = hashCodeOfKey(key);
36       if (items[x] == null) {
37          return null;
38       }
39       LinkedList<Cell<K, V>> collided = items[x];
40       for (Cell<K, V> c : collided) {
41          if (c.equivalent(key)) {
42             return c.getValue();
43          }
44       }
45
46       return null;
47    }
48 }
```

The Cell class pairs the data value and its key. This will allow us to search through the linked list (created by "colliding," but different, keys) and find the object with the exact key value.

```
1  public class Cell<K, V> {
2     private K key;
3     private V value;
4     public Cell(K k, V v) {
5        key = k;
6        value = v;
7     }
8
9     public boolean equivalent(Cell<K, V> c) {
10        return equivalent(c.getKey());
11     }
```

```
12
13    public boolean equivalent(K k) {
14        return key.equals(k);
15    }
16
17    public K getKey() { return key; }
18    public V getValue() { return value; }
19  }
```

Another common implementation for a hash table is to use a binary search tree as the underlying data structure. Retrieving an element will no longer be O(1) (although, technically, it's not O(1) if there are many collisions), but it prevents us from creating an unnecessarily large array to hold items.

Recursion and Dynamic Programming

Concepts and Algorithms: Solutions | **Chapter 9**

9.1 *A child is running up a staircase with n steps, and can hop either 1 step, 2 steps, or 3 steps at a time. Implement a method to count how many possible ways the child can run up the stairs.*

pg 109

SOLUTION

We can approach this problem from the top down. On the very last hop, up to the nth step, the child could have done either a single, double, or triple step hop. That is, the last move might have been a single step hop from step n-1, a double step hop from step n-2, or a triple step hop from step n-3. The total number of ways of reaching the last step is therefore the sum of the number of ways of reaching each of the last three steps.

A simple implementation of this code is below.

```
1   public int countWays(int n) {
2       if (n < 0) {
3           return 0;
4       } else if (n == 0) {
5           return 1;
6       } else {
7           return countWays(n - 1) + countWays(n - 2) +
8                   countWays(n - 3);
9       }
10  }
```

Like the Fibonacci problem, the runtime of this algorithm is exponential (specifically, $O(3^N)$), since each call branches out to three more calls. This means that countWays is called many times for the same values, which is unnecessary. We can fix this through dynamic programming.

```
11  public static int countWaysDP(int n, int[] map) {
12      if (n < 0) {
13          return 0;
14      } else if (n == 0) {
15          return 1;
16      } else if (map[n] > -1) {
17          return map[n];
18      } else {
19          map[n] = countWaysDP(n - 1, map) +
20                   countWaysDP(n - 2, map) +
21                   countWaysDP(n - 3, map);
22          return map[n];
23      }
24  }
```

Regardless of whether or not you use dynamic programming, note that the number of ways will quickly overflow the bounds of an integer. By the time you get to just n = 37, the result has already overflowed. Using a long will delay, but not completely solve, this issue.

9.2 *Imagine a robot sitting on the upper left corner of an X by Y grid. The robot can only move in two directions: right and down. How many possible paths are there for the robot to go from (0, 0) to (X, Y)?*

FOLLOW UP

Imagine certain spots are "off limits," such that the robot cannot step on them. Design an algorithm to find a path for the robot from the top left to the bottom right.

pg 109

SOLUTION

We need to count the number of ways of making a path with X right steps and Y down steps. This path will have X+Y steps total.

To build a path, we are essentially selecting X times to move right out of a total of X+Y moves. Thus, the number of total paths must be the number of ways of selecting X items out of X+Y items. This is given by the binomial expression (a.k.a., "n choose r"):

$$\binom{n}{r} = \frac{n!}{r!\,(n-r)!}$$

In terms of this problem, the expression is:

$$\binom{X+Y}{X} = \frac{(X+Y)!}{X!\,Y!}$$

If you didn't know the binomial expression, you could still deduce how to solve this problem.

Think about each path as a string of length X+Y consisting X 'R's and Y 'D's. We know that the number of strings we can make with X+Y *unique* characters is (X+Y)!. However, in this case, X of the characters are 'R's and Y are 'D's. Since the 'R's can be rearranged in X! ways, each of which is identical, and we can do an equivalent thing with the 'D's, we need to divide out by X! and Y!. We then get the same expression as we had before:

$$\frac{(X+Y)!}{X!\,Y!}$$

Follow Up: Find a path (with off limit spots)

If we picture our grid, the only way to move to spot (X, Y) is by moving to one of the adjacent spots: (X-1, Y) or (X, Y-1). So, we need to find a path to either (X-1, Y) or (X, Y-1).

How do we find a path to those spots? To find a path to (X-1, Y) or (X, Y-1), we need to move to one of its adjacent cells. So, we need to find a path to a spot adjacent to (X-1, Y), which are coordinates (X-2, Y) and (X-1, Y-1), or a spot adjacent to

(X,Y-1), which are spots (X-1,Y-1) and (X,Y-2). Observe that we list the point (X-1,Y-1) twice; we'll discuss that issue later.

So then, to find a path from the origin, we just work backwards like this. Starting from the last cell, we try to find a path to each of its adjacent cells. The recursive code below implements this algorithm.

```
1   public boolean getPath(int x, int y, ArrayList<Point> path) {
2      Point p = new Point(x, y);
3      path.add(p);
4      if (x == 0 && y == 0) {
5         return true; // found a path
6      }
7      boolean success = false;
8      if (x >= 1 && isFree(x - 1, y)) { // Try left
9         success = getPath(x - 1, y, path); // Free! Go left
10     }
11     if (!success && y >= 1 && isFree(x, y - 1)) { // Try up
12        success = getPath(x, y - 1, path); // Free! Go up
13     }
14     if (!success) {
15        path.remove(p); // Wrong way! Better stop going this way
16     }
17     return success;
18  }
```

Earlier, we'd mentioned an issue with duplicate paths. To find a path to (X,Y), we look for a path to an adjacent coordinate: (X-1,Y) or (X,Y-1). Of course, if one of those squares is off limits, we ignore it. Then, we look at their adjacent coordinates: (X-2,Y), (X-1,Y-1), (X-1,Y-1), and (X,Y-2). The spot (X-1,Y-1) appears twice, which means that we're duplicating effort. Ideally, we should remember that we already visited (X-1,Y-1) so that we don't waste our time.

This is what the dynamic programming algorithm below does.

```
1   public boolean getPath(int x, int y, ArrayList<Point> path,
2                          Hashtable<Point, Boolean> cache) {
3      Point p = new Point(x, y);
4      if (cache.containsKey(p)) { // Already visited this cell
5         return cache.get(p);
6      }
7      path.add(p);
8      if (x == 0 && y == 0) {
9         return true; // found a path
10     }
11     boolean success = false;
12     if (x >= 1 && isFree(x - 1, y)) { // Try right
13        success = getPath(x - 1, y, path, cache); // Free!  Go right
14     }
15     if (!success && y >= 1 && isFree(x, y - 1)) { // Try down
16        success = getPath(x, y - 1, path, cache); // Free!  Go down
17     }
```

```
18    if (!success) {
19       path.remove(p); // Wrong way! Better stop going this way
20    }
21    cache.put(p, success); // Cache result
22    return success;
23 }
```

This simple change will make our code run substantially faster.

9.3   *A magic index in an array A[1...n-1] is defined to be an index such that A[i] = i. Given a sorted array of distinct integers, write a method to find a magic index, if one exists, in array A.*

FOLLOW UP

What if the values are not distinct?

pg 109

SOLUTION

Immediately, the brute force solution should jump to mind—and there's no shame in mentioning it. We simply iterate through the array, looking for an element which matches this condition.

```
1   public static int magicSlow(int[] array) {
2      for (int i = 0; i < array.length; i++) {
3         if (array[i] == i) {
4            return i;
5         }
6      }
7      return -1;
8   }
```

Given that the array is sorted though, it's very likely that we're supposed to use this condition.

We may recognize that this problem sounds a lot like the classic binary search problem. Leveraging the Pattern Matching approach for generating algorithms, how might we apply binary search here?

In binary search, we find an element k by comparing it to the middle element, x, and determining if k would land on the left or the right side of x.

Building off this approach, is there a way that we can look at the middle element to determine where a magic index might be? Let's look at a sample array:

-40	-20	-1	1	2	3	5	7	9	12	13
0	1	2	3	4	5	6	7	8	9	10

When we look at the middle element A[5] = 3, we know that the magic index must be on the right side, since A[mid] < mid.

Why couldn't the magic index be on the left side? Observe that when we move from i to i-1, the value at this index must decrease by at least 1, if not more (since the array is sorted and all the elements are distinct). So, if the middle element is already too small to be a magic index, then when we move to the left, subtracting k indexes and (at least) k values, all subsequent elements will also be too small.

We continue to apply this recursive algorithm, developing code that looks very much like binary search.

```
1   public static int magicFast(int[] array, int start, int end) {
2       if (end < start || start < 0 || end >= array.length) {
3           return -1;
4       }
5       int mid = (start + end) / 2;
6       if (array[mid] == mid) {
7           return mid;
8       } else if (array[mid] > mid){
9           return magicFast(array, start, mid - 1);
10      } else {
11          return magicFast(array, mid + 1, end);
12      }
13  }
14
15  public static int magicFast(int[] array) {
16      return magicFast(array, 0, array.length - 1);
17  }
```

Follow Up: What if the elements are not distinct?

If the elements are not distinct, then this algorithm fails. Consider the following array:

-10	-5	2	2	2	3	4	7	9	12	13
0	1	2	3	4	5	6	7	8	9	10

When we see that A[mid] < mid, we cannot conclude which side the magic index is on. It could be on the right side, as before. Or, it could be on the left side (as it, in fact, is).

Could it be *anywhere* on the left side? Not exactly. Since A[5] = 3, we know that A[4] couldn't be a magic index. A[4] would need to be 4 to be the magic index, but A[4] must be less than A[5].

In fact, when we see that A[5] = 3, we'll need to recursively search the right side as before. But, to search the left side, we can skip a bunch of elements and only recursively search elements A[0] through A[3]. A[3] is the first element that could be a magic index.

The general pattern is that we compare midIndex and midValue for equality first. Then, if they are not equal, we recursively search the left and right sides as follows:

- Left side: search indices start through Math.min(midIndex - 1, midValue).

- Right side: search indices Math.max(midIndex + 1, midValue) through end.

The code below implements this algorithm.

```
1   public static int magicFast(int[] array, int start, int end) {
2       if (end < start || start < 0 || end >= array.length) {
3           return -1;
4       }
5       int midIndex = (start + end) / 2;
6       int midValue = array[midIndex];
7       if (midValue == midIndex) {
8           return midIndex;
9       }
10
11      /* Search left */
12      int leftIndex = Math.min(midIndex - 1, midValue);
13      int left = magicFast(array, start, leftIndex);
14      if (left >= 0) {
15          return left;
16      }
17
18      /* Search right */
19      int rightIndex = Math.max(midIndex + 1, midValue);
20      int right = magicFast(array, rightIndex, end);
21
22      return right;
23  }
24
25  public static int magicFast(int[] array) {
26      return magicFast(array, 0, array.length - 1);
27  }
```

Note that in the above code, if the elements are all distinct, the method operates almost identically to the first solution.

9.4   *Write a method to return all subsets of a set.*

pg 109

SOLUTION

We should first have some reasonable expectations of our time and space complexity. How many subsets of a set are there? We can compute this by realizing that when we generate a subset, each element has the "choice" of either being in there or not. That is, for the first element, there are two choices: it is either in the set, or it is not. For the second, there are two, etc. So, doing {2 * 2 * ... } 2n times gives us 2^n subsets. We will therefore not be able to do better than $O(2^n)$ in time or space complexity.

The subsets of $\{a_1, a_2, \ldots, a_n\}$ are also called the powerset, $P(\{a_1, a_2, \ldots,$

Solutions to Chapter 9 | Recursion and Dynamic Programming

a_n}), or just P(n).

Solution #1: Recursion

This problem is a good candidate for the Base Case and Build approach. Imagine that we are trying to find all subsets of a set like S = {a_1, a_2, ..., a_n}. We can start with the Base Case.

Base Case: n = 0.

There is just one subset of the empty set: { }.

Case: n = 1.

There are two subsets of the set {a_1}: { }, {a_1}.

Case: n = 2.

There are four subsets of the set {a_1, a_2}: { }, {a_1}, {a_2}, {a_1, a_2}.

Case: n = 3.

Now here's where things get interesting. We want to find a way of generating the solution for n = 3 based on the prior solutions.

What is the difference between the solution for n = 3 and the solution for n = 2? Let's look at this more deeply:

```
P(2) = {}, {a₁}, {a₂}, {a₁, a₂}
P(3) = {}, {a₁}, {a₂}, {a₃}, {a₁, a₂}, {a₁, a₃}, {a₂, a₃},
       {a₁, a₂, a₃}
```

The difference between these solutions is that P(2) is missing all the subsets containing a_3.

```
P(3) - P(2) = {a₃}, {a₁, a₃}, {a₂, a₃}, {a₁, a₂, a₃}
```

How can we use P(2) to create P(3)? We can simply clone the subsets in P(2) and add a_3 to them:

```
P(2)      = {} , {a₁}, {a₂}, {a₁, a₂}
P(2) + a₃ = {a₃}, {a₁, a₃}, {a₂, a₃}, {a₁, a₂, a₃}
```

When merged together, the lines above make P(3).

Case: n > 0

Generating P(n) for the general case is just a simple generalization of the above steps. We compute P(n-1), clone the results, and then add a_n to each of these cloned sets.

The following code implements this algorithm:

```
1   ArrayList<ArrayList<Integer>> getSubsets(ArrayList<Integer> set,
2                                             int index) {
3       ArrayList<ArrayList<Integer>> allsubsets;
```

```
4     if (set.size() == index) { // Base case - add empty set
5        allsubsets = new ArrayList<ArrayList<Integer>>();
6        allsubsets.add(new ArrayList<Integer>()); // Empty set
7     } else {
8        allsubsets = getSubsets(set, index + 1);
9        int item = set.get(index);
10       ArrayList<ArrayList<Integer>> moresubsets =
11          new ArrayList<ArrayList<Integer>>();
12       for (ArrayList<Integer> subset : allsubsets) {
13          ArrayList<Integer> newsubset = new ArrayList<Integer>();
14          newsubset.addAll(subset); //
15          newsubset.add(item);
16          moresubsets.add(newsubset);
17       }
18       allsubsets.addAll(moresubsets);
19    }
20    return allsubsets;
21 }
```

This solution will be $O(2^n)$ in time and space, which is the best we can do. For a slight optimization, we could also implement this algorithm iteratively.

Solution #2: Combinatorics

While there's nothing wrong with the above solution, there's another way to approach it.

Recall that when we're generating a set, we have two choices for each element: (1) the element is in the set (the "yes" state) or (2) the element is not in the set (the "no" state). This means that each subset is a sequence of yeses / nos—e.g., "yes, yes, no, no, yes, no"

This gives us 2^n possible subsets. How can we iterate through all possible sequences of "yes" / "no" states for all elements? If each "yes" can be treated as a 1 and each "no" can be treated as a 0, then each subset can be represented as a binary string.

Generating all subsets, then, really just comes down to generating all binary numbers (that is, all integers). We iterate through all numbers from 1 to 2^n and translate the binary representation of the numbers into a set. Easy!

```
1   ArrayList<ArrayList<Integer>> getSubsets2(ArrayList<Integer> set) {
2      ArrayList<ArrayList<Integer>> allsubsets =
3         new ArrayList<ArrayList<Integer>>();
4      int max = 1 << set.size(); /* Compute 2^n */
5      for (int k = 0; k < max; k++) {
6         ArrayList<Integer> subset = convertIntToSet(k, set);
7         allsubsets.add(subset);
8      }
9      return allsubsets;
10  }
11
```

```
12  ArrayList<Integer> convertIntToSet(int x, ArrayList<Integer> set) {
13      ArrayList<Integer> subset = new ArrayList<Integer>();
14      int index = 0;
15      for (int k = x; k > 0; k >>= 1) {
16          if ((k & 1) == 1) {
17              subset.add(set.get(index));
18          }
19          index++;
20      }
21      return subset;
22  }
```

There's nothing substantially better or worse about this solution compared to the first one.

9.5   *Write a method to compute all permutations of a string*

pg 109

SOLUTION

Like in many recursive problems, the Base Case and Build approach will be useful. Assume we have a string S represented by the characters $a_1 a_2 \ldots a_n$.

Base Case: n = 1

The only permutation of S = a_1 is the string a_1.

Case: n = 2

The permutations of S = $a_1 a_2$ are the strings $a_1 a_2$ and $a_2 a_1$.

Case: n = 3

Here is where the cases get more interesting. How can we generate all permutations of $a_1 a_2 a_3$ given the permutations of $a_1 a_2$? That is, we need to generate

$$a_1 a_2 a_3, \ a_1 a_3 a_2, \ a_2 a_1 a_3, \ a_2 a_3 a_1, \ a_3 a_1 a_2, \ a_3 a_2 a_1$$

given

$$a_1 a_2, \ a_2 a_1.$$

The difference between these lists is that the first one contains a_3 while the second list does not. So, how can we generate $f(3)$ from $f(2)$? By pushing a_3 into every possible spot in the strings in $f(2)$.

Case: n > 0

For the general case, we just repeat this process. We solve for $f(n-1)$, and then push a_n into every spot in each of these strings.

The code below does just this.

```
1   public static ArrayList<String> getPerms(String str) {
2     if (str == null) {
3       return null;
4     }
5     ArrayList<String> permutations = new ArrayList<String>();
6     if (str.length() == 0) { // base case
7       permutations.add("");
8       return permutations;
9     }
10
11    char first = str.charAt(0); // get the first character
12    String remainder = str.substring(1); // remove the 1st character
13    ArrayList<String> words = getPerms(remainder);
14    for (String word : words) {
15      for (int j = 0; j <= word.length(); j++) {
16        String s = insertCharAt(word, first, j);
17        permutations.add(s);
18      }
19    }
20    return permutations;
21  }
22
23  public static String insertCharAt(String word, char c, int i) {
24    String start = word.substring(0, i);
25    String end = word.substring(i);
26    return start + c + end;
27  }
```

This solution takes O(n!) time, since there are n! permutations. We cannot do better than this.

9.6 *Implement an algorithm to print all valid (i.e., properly opened and closed) combinations of n-pairs of parentheses.*

pg 110

SOLUTION

Our first thought here might be to apply a recursive approach where we build the solution for f(n) by adding pairs of parentheses to f(n-1). That's certainly a good instinct.

Let's consider the solution for n = 3:

   (()())   ((()))   ()(())   (())()   ()()()

How might we build this from n = 2?

   (())   ()()

We can do this by inserting a pair of parentheses inside every existing pair of parentheses, as well as one at the beginning of the string. Any other places that we could insert parentheses, such as at the end of the string, would reduce to the earlier cases.

So, we have the following:

```
(()) -> (()()) /* inserted pair after 1st left paren */
     -> ((())) /* inserted pair after 2nd left paren */
     -> ()(()) /* inserted pair at beginning of string */
()() -> (())() /* inserted pair after 1st left paren */
     -> ()(()) /* inserted pair after 2nd left paren */
     -> ()()() /* inserted pair at beginning of string */
```

But wait—we have some duplicate pairs listed. The string ( ) (( )) is listed twice.

If we're going to apply this approach, we'll need to check for duplicate values before adding a string to our list.

```
1   public static Set<String> generateParens(int remaining) {
2       Set<String> set = new HashSet<String>();
3       if (remaining == 0) {
4           set.add("");
5       } else {
6           Set<String> prev = generateParens(remaining - 1);
7           for (String str : prev) {
8               for (int i = 0; i < str.length(); i++) {
9                   if (str.charAt(i) == '(') {
10                      String s = insertInside(str, i);
11                      /* Add s to set if it's not already in there. Note:
12                       * HashSet automatically checks for duplicates before
13                       * adding, so an explicit check is not necessary. */
14                      set.add(s);
15                  }
16              }
17              if (!set.contains("()" + str)) {
18                  set.add("()" + str);
19              }
20          }
21      }
22      return set;
23  }
24
25  public String insertInside(String str, int leftIndex) {
26      String left = str.substring(0, leftIndex + 1);
27      String right = str.substring(leftIndex + 1, str.length());
28      return left + "()" + right;
29  }
```

This works, but it's not very efficient. We waste a lot of time coming up with the duplicate strings.

We can avoid this duplicate string issue by building the string from scratch. Under this approach, we add left and right parens, as long as our expression stays valid.

On each recursive call, we have the index for a particular character in the string. We need to select either a left or a right paren. When can we use a left paren, and when can we use a right paren?

1. *Left Paren:* As long as we haven't used up all the left parentheses, we can always insert a left paren.

2. *Right Paren:* We can insert a right paren as long as it won't lead to a syntax error. When will we get a syntax error? We will get a syntax error if there are more right parentheses than left.

So, we simply keep track of the number of left and right parentheses allowed. If there are left parens remaining, we'll insert a left paren and recurse. If there are more right parens remaining than left (i.e., if there are more left parens in use than right parens), then we'll insert a right paren and recurse.

```
1   public void addParen(ArrayList<String> list, int leftRem,
2                          int rightRem, char[] str, int count) {
3     if (leftRem < 0 || rightRem < leftRem) return; // invalid state
4
5     if (leftRem == 0 && rightRem == 0) { /* no more parens left */
6       String s = String.copyValueOf(str);
7       list.add(s);
8     } else {
9       /* Add left paren, if there are any left parens remaining. */
10      if (leftRem > 0) {
11        str[count] = '(';
12        addParen(list, leftRem - 1, rightRem, str, count + 1);
13      }
14
15      /* Add right paren, if expression is valid */
16      if (rightRem > leftRem) {
17        str[count] = ')';
18        addParen(list, leftRem, rightRem - 1, str, count + 1);
19      }
20    }
21  }
22
23  public ArrayList<String> generateParens(int count) {
24    char[] str = new char[count*2];
25    ArrayList<String> list = new ArrayList<String>();
26    addParen(list, count, count, str, 0);
27    return list;
28  }
```

Because we insert left and right parentheses at each index in the string, and we never repeat an index, each string is guaranteed to be unique.

9.7 *Implement the "paint fill" function that one might see on many image editing programs. That is, given a screen (represented by a two-dimensional array of colors), a point, and a new color, fill in the surrounding area until the color changes from the original color.*

pg 110

SOLUTION

First, let's visualize how this method works. When we call `paintFill` (i.e., "click" paint fill in the image editing application) on, say, a green pixel, we want to "bleed" outwards. Pixel by pixel, we expand outwards by calling `paintFill` on the surrounding pixel. When we hit a pixel that is not green, we stop.

We can implement this algorithm recursively:

```
1   enum Color {
2      Black, White, Red, Yellow, Green
3   }
4
5   boolean paintFill(Color[][] screen, int x, int y, Color ocolor,
6                     Color ncolor) {
7      if (x < 0 || x >= screen[0].length ||
8          y < 0 || y >= screen.length) {
9         return false;
10     }
11     if (screen[y][x] == ocolor) {
12        screen[y][x] = ncolor;
13        paintFill(screen, x - 1, y, ocolor, ncolor); // left
14        paintFill(screen, x + 1, y, ocolor, ncolor); // right
15        paintFill(screen, x, y - 1, ocolor, ncolor); // top
16        paintFill(screen, x, y + 1, ocolor, ncolor); // bottom
17     }
18     return true;
19  }
20
21  boolean paintFill(Color[][] screen, int x, int y, Color ncolor){
22     return paintFill(screen, x, y, screen[y][x], ncolor);
23  }
```

Note the ordering of the x and y in `screen[y][x]`, and remember this when you hit graphical problem. Because x represents the *horizontal* axis (that is, it's left to right), it actually corresponds to the number of a column, not the number of rows. The value of y equals the number of rows. This is a very easy place to make a mistake in an interview, as well as in your daily coding.

9.8   *Given an infinite number of quarters (25 cents), dimes (10 cents), nickels (5 cents) and pennies (1 cent), write code to calculate the number of ways of representing n cents.*

pg 110

SOLUTION

This is a recursive problem, so let's figure out how to compute makeChange(n) using prior solutions (i.e., sub-problems).

Let's say n = 100. We want to compute the number of ways of making change for 100 cents. What is the relationship between this problem and its sub-problems?

We know that making change for 100 cents will involve either 0, 1, 2, 3, or 4 quarters. So:

makeChange(100) =
    makeChange(100 using 0 quarters) +
    makeChange(100 using 1 quarter) +
    makeChange(100 using 2 quarters) +
    makeChange(100 using 3 quarters) +
    makeChange(100 using 4 quarters)

Inspecting this further, we can see that some of these problems reduce. For example, makeChange(100 using 1 quarter) will equal makeChange(75 using 0 quarters). This is because, if we must use exactly one quarter to make change for 100 cents, then our only remaining choices involve making change for the remaining 75 cents.

We can apply the same logic to makeChange(100 using 2 quarters), makeChange(100 using 3 quarters) and makeChange(100 using 4 quarters). We have thus reduced the above statement to the following.

    makeChange(100) =
        makeChange(100 using 0 quarters) +
        makeChange(75 using 0 quarters) +
        makeChange(50 using 0 quarters) +
        makeChange(25 using 0 quarters) +
        1

Note that the final statement from above, makeChange(100 using 4 quarters), equals 1. We call this "fully reduced."

Now what? We've used up all our quarters, so now we can start applying our next biggest denomination: dimes.

Our approach for quarters applies to dimes as well, but we apply this for *each* of the four of five parts of the above statement. So, for the first part, we get the following statements:

    makeChange(100 using 0 quarters) =
        makeChange(100 using 0 quarters, 0 dimes) +

```
        makeChange(100 using 0 quarters, 1 dime)  +
        makeChange(100 using 0 quarters, 2 dimes) +
        ...
        makeChange(100 using 0 quarters, 10 dimes)

    makeChange(75 using 0 quarters) =
        makeChange(75 using 0 quarters, 0 dimes) +
        makeChange(75 using 0 quarters, 1 dime)  +
        makeChange(75 using 0 quarters, 2 dimes) +
        ...
        makeChange(75 using 0 quarters, 7 dimes)

    makeChange(50 using 0 quarters) =
        makeChange(50 using 0 quarters, 0 dimes) +
        makeChange(50 using 0 quarters, 1 dime)  +
        makeChange(50 using 0 quarters, 2 dimes) +
        ...
        makeChange(50 using 0 quarters, 5 dimes)

    makeChange(25 using 0 quarters) =
        makeChange(25 using 0 quarters, 0 dimes) +
        makeChange(25 using 0 quarters, 1 dime)  +
        makeChange(25 using 0 quarters, 2 dimes)
```

Each one of these, in turn, expands out once we start applying nickels. We end up with a tree-like recursive structure where each call expands out to four or more calls.

The base case of our recursion is the fully reduced statement. For example, make-Change(50 using 0 quarters, 5 dimes) is fully reduced to 1, since 5 dimes equals 50 cents.

This leads to a recursive algorithm that looks like this:

```
1   public int makeChange(int n, int denom) {
2     int next_denom = 0;
3     switch (denom) {
4     case 25:
5       next_denom = 10;
6       break;
7     case 10:
8       next_denom = 5;
9       break;
10    case 5:
11      next_denom = 1;
12      break;
13    case 1:
14      return 1;
15    }
16
17    int ways = 0;
18    for (int i = 0; i * denom <= n; i++) {
```

```
19        ways += makeChange(n - i * denom, next_denom);
20    }
21    return ways;
22 }
23
24 System.out.writeln(makeChange(100, 25));
```

Although we've implemented this to work for US currency, it can be easily extended to work for any other set of denominations.

9.9   *Write an algorithm to print all ways of arranging eight queens on an 8x8 chess board so that none of them share the same row, column or diagonal. In this case, "diagonal" means all diagonals, not just the two that bisect the board.*

pg 110

SOLUTION

We have eight queens which must be lined up on an 8x8 chess board such that none share the same row, column or diagonal. So, we know that each row and column (and diagonal) must be used exactly once.

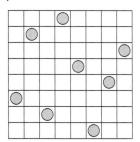

A "Solved" Board with 8 Queens

Picture the queen that is placed last, which we'll assume is on row 8. (This is an okay assumption to make since the ordering of placing the queens is irrelevant.) On which cell in row 8 is this queen? There are eight possibilities, one for each column.

So if we want to know all the valid ways of arranging 8 queens on an 8x8 chess board, it would be:

```
ways to arrange 8 queens on an 8x8 board =
    ways to arrange 8 queens on an 8x8 board with queen at (7, 0) +
    ways to arrange 8 queens on an 8x8 board with queen at (7, 1) +
    ways to arrange 8 queens on an 8x8 board with queen at (7, 2) +
    ways to arrange 8 queens on an 8x8 board with queen at (7, 3) +
    ways to arrange 8 queens on an 8x8 board with queen at (7, 4) +
    ways to arrange 8 queens on an 8x8 board with queen at (7, 5) +
    ways to arrange 8 queens on an 8x8 board with queen at (7, 6) +
    ways to arrange 8 queens on an 8x8 board with queen at (7, 7)
```

We can compute each one of these using a very similar approach:

```
ways to arrange 8 queens on an 8x8 board with queen at (7, 3) =
    ways to ... with queens at (7, 3) and (6, 0) +
    ways to ... with queens at (7, 3) and (6, 1) +
    ways to ... with queens at (7, 3) and (6, 2) +
    ways to ... with queens at (7, 3) and (6, 4) +
    ways to ... with queens at (7, 3) and (6, 5) +
    ways to ... with queens at (7, 3) and (6, 6) +
    ways to ... with queens at (7, 3) and (6, 7)
```

Note that we don't need to consider combinations with queens at (7, 3) and (6, 3), since this is a violation of the requirement that every queen is in its own row, column and diagonal.

Implementing this is now reasonably straightforward.

```
1   int GRID_SIZE = 8;
2
3   void placeQueens(int row, Integer[] columns,
4                         ArrayList<Integer[]> results) {
5       if (row == GRID_SIZE) { // Found valid placement
6           results.add(columns.clone());
7       } else {
8           for (int col = 0; col < GRID_SIZE; col++) {
9               if (checkValid(columns, row, col)) {
10                  columns[row] = col;  // Place queen
11                  placeQueens(row + 1, columns, results);
12              }
13          }
14      }
15  }
16
17  /* Check if (row1, column1) is a valid spot for a queen by checking
18   * if there is a queen in the same column or diagonal. We don't
19   * need to check it for queens in the same row because the calling
20   * placeQueen only attempts to place one queen at a time. We know
21   * this row is empty. */
22  boolean checkValid(Integer[] columns, int row1, int column1) {
23      for (int row2 = 0; row2 < row1; row2++) {
24          int column2 = columns[row2];
25          /* Check if (row2, column2) invalidates (row1, column1) as a
26           * queen spot. */
27
28          /* Check if rows have a queen in the same column */
29          if (column1 == column2) {
30              return false;
31          }
32
33          /* Check diagonals: if the distance between the columns
34           * equals the distance between the rows, then they're in the
35           * same diagonal. */
36          int columnDistance = Math.abs(column2 - column1);
```

```
37
38      /* row1 > row2, so no need for abs */
39      int rowDistance = row1 - row2;
40      if (columnDistance == rowDistance) {
41         return false;
42      }
43   }
44   return true;
45 }
```

Observe that since each row can only have one queen, we don't need to store our board as a full 8x8 matrix. We only need a single array where column[row] = c indicates that row r has a queen at column c.

9.10 *You have a stack of n boxes, with widths w_i, heights h_i, and depths d_i. The boxes cannot be rotated and can only be stacked on top of one another if each box in the stack is strictly larger than the box above it in width, height, and depth. Implement a method to build the tallest stack possible, where the height of a stack is the sum of the heights of each box.*

pg 110

SOLUTION

To tackle this problem, we need to recognize the relationship between the different sub-problems.

Imagine we had the following boxes: b_1, b_2, ..., b_n. The biggest stack that we can build with all the boxes equals the max of (biggest stack with bottom b_1, biggest stack with bottom b_2, ..., biggest stack with bottom b_n). That is, if we experimented with each box as a bottom and built the biggest stack possible with each, we would find the biggest stack possible.

But, how would we find the biggest stack with a particular bottom? Essentially the same way. We experiment with different boxes for the second level, and so on for each level

Of course, we only experiment with valid boxes. If b_5 is bigger than b_1, then there's no point in trying to build a stack that looks like {b_1, b_5 , ... }. We already know b_1 can't be below b_5.

The code below implements this algorithm recursively.

```
1   public ArrayList<Box> createStackR(Box[] boxes, Box bottom) {
2      int max_height = 0;
3      ArrayList<Box> max_stack = null;
4      for (int i = 0; i < boxes.length; i++) {
5         if (boxes[i].canBeAbove(bottom)) {
6            ArrayList<Box> new_stack = createStackR(boxes, boxes[i]);
7            int new_height = stackHeight(new_stack);
8            if (new_height > max_height) {
```

```
9                max_stack = new_stack;
10               max_height = new_height;
11           }
12       }
13   }
14
15   if (max_stack == null) {
16       max_stack = new ArrayList<Box>();
17   }
18   if (bottom != null) {
19       max_stack.add(0, bottom); // Insert in bottom of stack
20   }
21
22   return max_stack;
23 }
```

The problem in this code is that it gets very inefficient. We try to find the best solution that looks like $\{b_3, b_4, \dots\}$ even though we may have already found the best solution with b_4 at the bottom. Instead of generating these solutions from scratch, we can cache these results using dynamic programming.

```
1  public ArrayList<Box> createStackDP(Box[] boxes, Box bottom,
2          HashMap<Box, ArrayList<Box>> stack_map) {
3      if (bottom != null && stack_map.containsKey(bottom)) {
4          return stack_map.get(bottom);
5      }
6
7      int max_height = 0;
8      ArrayList<Box> max_stack = null;
9      for (int i = 0; i < boxes.length; i++) {
10         if (boxes[i].canBeAbove(bottom)) {
11             ArrayList<Box> new_stack =
12                 createStackDP(boxes, boxes[i], stack_map);
13             int new_height = stackHeight(new_stack);
14             if (new_height > max_height) {
15                 max_stack = new_stack;
16                 max_height = new_height;
17             }
18         }
19     }
20
21     if (max_stack == null) max_stack = new ArrayList<Box>();
22     if (bottom != null) max_stack.add(0, bottom);
23     stack_map.put(bottom, max_stack);
24
25     return (ArrayList<Box>)max_stack.clone();
26 }
```

You might ask why, in line 25, we have to cast `max_stack.clone()`. Isn't `max_stack` already of the correct data type? Yes, but we still need to cast.

The `clone()` method originally comes from the `Object` class and has the signature:

```
1   protected Object clone() { ... }
```

When we override a method, we can change the parameters, but we cannot change the return type. Therefore, if `Foo` were to inherit from `Object` and override `clone()`, its `clone()` method will still return an instance of type `Object`.

This is precisely what happens with the statement `(ArrayList<Box>)max_stack. clone()`. The stack class overrides `clone()`, but the method still must return an `Object`. So, we must cast its return value.

9.11   *Given a boolean expression consisting of the symbols 0, 1, &, |, and ^, and a desired boolean result value* `result`, *implement a function to count the number of ways of parenthesizing the expression such that it evaluates to* `result`.

pg 110

SOLUTION

As in other recursive problems, the key to this problem is to figure out the relationship between a problem and its sub-problems.

Suppose `int f(expression, result)` is a function which returns the count of all valid expressions which evaluate to result. We want to compute `f(1^0|0|1, true)` (that is, all ways of parenthesizing the expression `1^0|0|1` such that the expression evaluates to `true`). Each parenthesized expression must have an outermost pair of parentheses. So, we can say that:

```
f(1^0|0|1, true) = f(1 ^ (0|0|1), true) +
                   f((1^0) | (0|1), true) +
                   f((1^0|0) | 1, true)
```

That is, we can iterate through the expression, treating each operator as the first operator to be parenthesized.

Now, how do we compute one of these inner expressions, like `f((1^0) | (0|1), true)`? Well, in order for that expression to evaluate to `true`, either the left half or the right half must evaluate to `true`. So, the expression breaks down as:

```
f((1^0) | (0|1), true) =   f(1^0, true)  * f(0|1, true) +
                           f(1^0, false) * f(0|1, true) +
                           f(1^0, true)  * f(0|1, false)
```

We can implement a similar break down for each of the boolean operators:

```
f(exp1 | exp2, true)   =   f(exp1, true)  * f(exp2, true) +
                           f(exp1, true)  * f(exp2, false) +
                           f(exp1, false) * f(exp2, true)
f(exp1 & exp2, true)   =   f(exp1, true)  * f(exp2, true)
f(exp1 ^ exp2, true)   =   f(exp1, true)  * f(exp2, false) +
                           f(exp1, false) * f(exp2, true)
```

For the `false` results, we can perform a very similar operation:

```
f(exp1 | exp2, false)  =  f(exp1, false) * f(exp2, false)
f(exp1 & exp2, false)  =  f(exp1, false) * f(exp2, false) +
                          f(exp1, true)  * f(exp2, false) +
                          f(exp1, false) * f(exp2, true)
f(exp1 ^ exp2, false)  =  f(exp1, true)  * f(exp2, true) +
                          f(exp1, false) * f(exp2, false)
```

Implementing this is now just a matter of applying this recurrence relation. (Note: to keep the lines from wrapping unnecessarily and making the code very confusing, we've implemented this with extra short variable names.)

```java
1   public int f(String exp, boolean result, int s, int e) {
2     if (s == e) {
3       if (exp.charAt(s) == '1' && result) {
4         return 1;
5       } else if (exp.charAt(s) == '0' && !result) {
6         return 1;
7       }
8       return 0;
9     }
10    int c = 0;
11    if (result) {
12      for (int i = s + 1; i <= e; i += 2) {
13        char op = exp.charAt(i);
14        if (op == '&') {
15          c += f(exp, true, s, i - 1) * f(exp, true, i + 1, e);
16        } else if (op == '|') {
17          c += f(exp, true, s, i - 1) * f(exp, false, i + 1, e);
18          c += f(exp, false, s, i - 1) * f(exp, true, i + 1, e);
19          c += f(exp, true, s, i - 1) * f(exp, true, i + 1, e);
20        } else if (op == '^') {
21          c += f(exp, true, s, i - 1) * f(exp, false, i + 1, e);
22          c += f(exp, false, s, i - 1) * f(exp, true, i + 1, e);
23        }
24      }
25    } else {
26      for (int i = s + 1; i <= e; i += 2) {
27        char op = exp.charAt(i);
28        if (op == '&') {
29          c += f(exp, false, s, i - 1) * f(exp, true, i + 1, e);
30          c += f(exp, true, s, i - 1) * f(exp, false, i + 1, e);
31          c += f(exp, false, s, i - 1) * f(exp, false, i + 1,e);
32        } else if (op == '|') {
33          c += f(exp, false, s, i - 1) * f(exp, false, i + 1,e);
34        } else if (op == '^') {
35          c += f(exp, true, s, i - 1) * f(exp, true, i + 1, e);
36          c += f(exp, false, s, i - 1) * f(exp, false, i + 1,e);
37        }
38      }
```

```
39       }
40       return c;
41   }
```

Although this works, it's not very efficient. This method will recompute f(exp) many times, for the same value of exp.

To solve this issue, we can use dynamic programming and cache the results of the different expressions. Note that we need to cache based on the expression and the result.

```
1   public int f(String exp, boolean result, int s, int e,
2                   HashMap<String, Integer> q) {
3       String key = "" + result + s + e;
4       if (q.containsKey(key)) {
5           return q.get(key);
6       }
7
8       if (s == e) {
9           if (exp.charAt(s) == '1' && result == true) {
10              return 1;
11          } else if (exp.charAt(s) == '0' && result == false) {
12              return 1;
13          }
14          return 0;
15      }
16      int c = 0;
17      if (result) {
18          for (int i = s + 1; i <= e; i += 2) {
19              char op = exp.charAt(i);
20              if (op == '&') {
21                  c += f(exp,true,s,i-1,q) * f(exp,true,i+1,e,q);
22              } else if (op == '|') {
23                  c += f(exp,true,s,i-1,q) * f(exp,false,i+1,e,q);
24                  c += f(exp,false,s,i-1,q) * f(exp,true,i+1,e,q);
25                  c += f(exp,true,s,i-1,q) * f(exp,true,i+1,e,q);
26              } else if (op == '^') {
27                  c += f(exp,true,s,i-1,q) * f(exp,false,i+1,e,q);
28                  c += f(exp,false,s,i-1,q) * f(exp,true,i+1,e,q);
29              }
30          }
31      } else {
32          for (int i = s + 1; i <= e; i += 2) {
33              char op = exp.charAt(i);
34              if (op == '&') {
35                  c += f(exp,false,s,i-1,q) * f(exp,true,i+1,e,q);
36                  c += f(exp,true,s,i-1,q) * f(exp,false,i+1,e,q);
37                  c += f(exp,false,s,i-1,q) * f(exp,false,i+1,e,q);
38              } else if (op == '|') {
39                  c += f(exp,false,s,i-1,q) * f(exp,false,i+1,e,q);
40              } else if (op == '^') {
```

```
41              c += f(exp,true,s,i-1,q) * f(exp,true,i+1,e,q);
42              c += f(exp,false,s,i-1,q) * f(exp,false,i+1,e,q);
43          }
44      }
45  }
46  q.put(key, c);
47  return c;
48 }
```

While this is nicely optimized with dynamic programming, it's still not as optimized as it could be. If we knew how many ways there were of parenthesizing an expression, then we could compute f(exp = false) by doing total(exp) - f(exp = true).

There *is* a closed form expression for the number of ways of parenthesizing an expression, but you wouldn't be expected to know it. It is given by the Catalan numbers, where n is the number of operators:

$$C_n = \frac{(2n)!}{(n+1)!\,n!}$$

With this adjustment, the code looks like the following.

```
1   public int f(String exp, boolean result, int s, int e,
2           HashMap<String, Integer> q) {
3       String key = "" + s + e;
4       int c = 0;
5       if (!q.containsKey(key)) {
6           if (s == e) {
7               if (exp.charAt(s) == '1') c = 1;
8               else c = 0;
9           }
10
11          for (int i = s + 1; i <= e; i += 2) {
12              char op = exp.charAt(i);
13              if (op == '&') {
14                  c += f(exp,true,s,i-1,q) * f(exp,true,i+1,e,q);
15              } else if (op == '|') {
16                  int left_ops = (i-1-s)/2; // parens on left
17                  int right_ops = (e - i - 1) / 2;  // parens on right
18                  int total_ways = total(left_ops) * total(right_ops);
19                  int total_false = f(exp,false,s,i-1,q) *
20                                    f(exp,false,i+1,e,q);
21                  c += total_ways - total_false;
22              } else if (op == '^') {
23                  c += f(exp,true,s,i-1,q) * f(exp,false,i+1,e,q);
24                  c += f(exp,false,s,i-1,q) * f(exp,true,i+1,e,q);
25              }
26          }
27          q.put(key, c);
28      } else {
29          c = q.get(key);
30      }
```

```
31    if (result) {
32        return c;
33    } else {
34        int num_ops = (e - s) / 2;
35        return total(num_ops) - c;
36    }
37 }
```

Scalability and Memory Limits

Concepts and Algorithms: Solutions

Chapter 10

Solutions to Chapter 10 | Scalability and Memory Limits

10.1 *Imagine you are building some sort of service that will be called by up to 1000 client applications to get simple end-of-day stock price information (open, close, high, low). You may assume that you already have the data, and you can store it in any format you wish. How would you design the client-facing service which provides the information to client applications? You are responsible for the development, rollout, and ongoing monitoring and maintenance of the feed. Describe the different methods you considered and why you would recommend your approach. Your service can use any technologies you wish, and can distribute the information to the client applications in any mechanism you choose.*

pg 115

SOLUTION

From the statement of the problem, we want to focus on how we actually distribute the information to clients. We can assume that we have some scripts that magically collect the information.

We want to start off by thinking about what the different aspects we should consider in a given proposal are:

- *Client Ease of Use:* We want the service to be easy for the clients to implement and useful for them.

- *Ease for Ourselves:* This service should be as easy as possible for us to implement, as we shouldn't impose unnecessary work on us. We need to consider in this not only the cost of implementing, but also the cost of maintenance.

- *Flexibility for Future Demands:* This problem is stated in a "what would you do in the real world" way, so we should think like we would in a real-world problem. Ideally, we do not want to overly constrain ourselves in the implementation, such that we can't be flexible if the requirements or demands change.

- *Scalability and Efficiency:* We should be mindful of the efficiency of our solution, so as not to overly burden our service.

With this framework in mind, we can consider various proposals.

Proposal #1

One option is that we could keep the data in simple text files and let clients download the data through some sort of FTP server. This would be easy to maintain in some sense, since files can be easily viewed and backed up, but it would require more complex parsing to do any sort of query. And, if additional data were added to our text file, it might break the clients' parsing mechanism.

Proposal #2

We could use a standard SQL database, and let the clients plug directly into that. This would provide the following benefits:

- Facilitates an easy way for the clients to do query processing over the data, in case there are additional features we need to support. For example, we could easily and efficiently perform a query such as "return all stocks having an open price greater than N and a closing price less than M."

- Rolling back, backing up data, and security could be provided using standard database features. We don't have to "reinvent the wheel," so it's easy for us to implement.

- Reasonably easy for the clients to integrate into existing applications. SQL integration is a standard feature in software development environments.

What are the disadvantages of using a SQL database?

- It's much heavier weight than we really need. We don't necessarily need all the complexity of a SQL backend to support a feed of a few bits of information.

- It's difficult for humans to be able to read it, so we'll likely need to implement an additional layer to view and maintain the data. This increases our implementation costs.

- Security: While a SQL database offers pretty well-defined security levels, we would still need to be very careful to not give clients access that they shouldn't have. Additionally, even if clients aren't doing anything "malicious," they might perform expensive and inefficient queries, and our servers would bear the costs of that.

These disadvantages don't mean that we shouldn't provide SQL access. Rather, they mean that we should be aware of the disadvantages.

Proposal #3

XML is another great option for distributing the information. Our data has fixed format and fixed size: company_name, open, high, low, closing price. The XML could look like this:

```
1   <root>
2       <date value="2008-10-12">
3           <company name="foo">
4               <open>126.23</open>
5               <high>130.27</high>
6               <low>122.83</low>
7               <closingPrice>127.30</closingPrice>
8           </company>
9           <company name="bar">
10              <open>52.73</open>
11              <high>60.27</high>
12              <low>50.29</low>
13              <closingPrice>54.91</closingPrice>
14          </company>
15      </date>
```

```
16    <date value="2008-10-11">  . . .  </date>
17  </root>
```

The advantages of this approach include the following:

- It's very easy to distribute, and it can also be easily read by both machines and humans. This is one reason that XML is a standard data model to share and distribute data.

- Most languages have a library to perform XML parsing, so it's reasonably easy for clients to implement.

- We can add new data to the XML file by adding additional nodes. This would not break the client's parser (provided they have implemented their parser in a reasonable way).

- Since the data is being stored as XML files, we can use existing tools for backing up the data. We don't need to implement our own backup tool.

The disadvantages may include:

- This solution sends the clients all the information, even if they only want part of it. It is inefficient in that way.

- Performing any queries on the data requires parsing the entire file.

Regardless of which solution we use for data storage, we could provide a web service (e.g., SOAP) for client data access. This adds a layer to our work, but it can provide additional security, and it may even make it easier for clients to integrate the system.

However—and this is a pro and a con—clients will be limited to grabbing the data only how we expect or want them to. By contrast, in a pure SQL implementation, clients could query for the highest stock price, even if this wasn't a procedure we "expected" them to need.

So which one of these would we use? There's no clear answer. The pure text file solution is probably a bad choice, but you can make a compelling argument for the SQL or XML solution, with or without a web service.

The goal of a question like this is not to see if you get the "correct" answer (there is no single correct answer). Rather, it's to see how you design a system, and how you evaluate trade-offs.

10.2   *How would you design the data structures for a very large social network like Facebook or LinkedIn? Describe how you would design an algorithm to show the connection, or path, between two people (e.g., Me -> Bob -> Susan -> Jason -> You).*

pg 115

SOLUTION

A good way to approach this problem is to remove some of the constraints and solve it for that situation first.

Step 1: Simplify the Problem—Forget About the Millions of Users

First, let's forget that we're dealing with millions of users. Design this for the simple case.

We can construct a graph by treating each person as a node and letting an edge between two nodes indicate that the two users are friends.

```
1   class Person {
2       Person[] friends;
3       // Other info
4   }
```

If I wanted to find the connection between two people, I would start with one person and do a simple breadth first search.

Why wouldn't a depth first search work well? Because it would be very inefficient. Two users might be only one degree of separation apart, but I could search millions of nodes in their "subtrees" before finding this relatively immediate connection.

Step 2: Handle the Millions of Users

When we deal with a service the size of LinkedIn or Facebook, we cannot possibly keep all of our data on one machine. That means that our simple Person data structure from above doesn't quite work—our friends may not live on the same machine as we do. Instead, we can replace our list of friends with a list of their IDs, and traverse as follows:

1. For each friend ID: int machine_index = getMachineIDForUser(personID);

2. Go to machine #machine_index

3. On that machine, do: Person friend = getPersonWithID(person_id);

The code below outlines this process. We've defined a class Server, which holds a list of all the machines, and a class Machine which represents a single machine. Both classes have hash tables to efficiently lookup data.

```
1   public class Server {
2       HashMap<Integer, Machine> machines =
3           new HashMap<Integer, Machine>();
4       HashMap<Integer, Integer> personToMachineMap =
5           new HashMap<Integer, Integer>();
6
7       public Machine getMachineWithId(int machineID) {
8           return machines.get(machineID);
9       }
10
11      public int getMachineIDForUser(int personID) {
12          Integer machineID = personToMachineMap.get(personID);
13          return machineID == null ? -1 : machineID;
```

```
14    }
15
16    public Person getPersonWithID(int personID) {
17        Integer machineID = personToMachineMap.get(personID);
18        if (machineID == null) return null;
19
20        Machine machine = getMachineWithId(machineID);
21        if (machine == null) return null;
22
23        return machine.getPersonWithID(personID);
24    }
25 }
26
27 public class Person {
28    private ArrayList<Integer> friendIDs;
29    private int personID;
30
31    public Person(int id) { this.personID = id; }
32
33    public int getID() { return personID; }
34    public void addFriend(int id) { friends.add(id); }
35 }
36
37 public class Machine {
38    public HashMap<Integer, Person> persons =
39        new HashMap<Integer, Person>();
40    public int machineID;
41
42    public Person getPersonWithID(int personID) {
43        return persons.get(personID);
44    }
45 }
```

There are more optimizations and follow up questions here than we could possibly discuss, but here are just a few thoughts.

Optimization: Reduce Machine Jumps

Jumping from one machine to another is expensive. Instead of randomly jumping from machine to machine with each friend, try to batch these jumps—e.g., if five of my friends live on one machine, I should look them up all at once.

Optimization: Smart Division of People and Machines

People are much more likely to be friends with people who live in the same country as they do. Rather than randomly dividing people up across machines, try to divide them up by country, city, state, and so on. This will reduce the number of jumps.

Question: Breadth First Search usually requires "marking" a node as visited. How

do you do that in this case?

Usually, in BFS, we mark a node as visited by setting a flag visited in its node class. Here, we don't want to do that. There could be multiple searches going on at the same time, so it's bad to just edit our data.

Instead, we could mimic the marking of nodes with a hash table to look up a node id and whether or not it's been visited.

Other Follow-Up Questions:

- In the real world, servers fail. How does this affect you?

- How could you take advantage of caching?

- Do you search until the end of the graph (infinite)? How do you decide when to give up?

- In real life, some people have more friends of friends than others, and are therefore more likely to make a path between you and someone else. How could you use this data to pick where you start traversing?

These are just a few of the follow-up questions you or the interviewer could raise. There are many others.

10.3 *Given an input file with four billion non-negative integers, provide an algorithm to generate an integer which is not contained in the file. Assume you have 1 GB of memory available for this task.*

FOLLOW UP

What if you have only 10 MB of memory? Assume that all the values are distinct.

pg 115

SOLUTION

There are a total of 2^{32}, or 4 billion, distinct integers possible (and non-negative 2^{31} integers). We have 1 GB of memory, or 8 billion bits.

Thus, with 8 billion bits, we can map all possible integers to a distinct bit with the available memory. The logic is as follows:

1. Create a bit vector (BV) with 4 billion bits. Recall that a bit vector is an array that compactly stores boolean values by using an array of ints (or another data type). Each int stores a sequence of 32 bits, or boolean values.

2. Initialize BV with all 0's.

3. Scan all numbers (num) from the file and call BV.set(num, 1).

4. Now scan again BV from the 0th index.

5. Return the first index which has a value of 0.

The following code demonstrates our algorithm.

```
1   long numberOfInts = ((long) Integer.MAX_VALUE) + 1;
2   byte[] bitfield2 = new byte [(int) (numberOfInts / 8)];
3   void findOpenNumber2() throws FileNotFoundException {
4     Scanner in = new Scanner(new FileReader("file.txt"));
5     while (in.hasNextInt()) {
6       int n = in.nextInt ();
7       /* Finds the corresponding number in the bitfield by using
8        * the OR operator to set the nth bit of a byte
9        * (e.g., 10 would correspond to the 2nd bit of index 2 in
10       * the byte array). */
11      bitfield [n / 8] |= 1 << (n % 8);
12    }
13
14    for (int i = 0; i < bitfield.length; i++) {
15      for (int j = 0; j < 8; j++) {
16        /* Retrieves the individual bits of each byte. When 0 bit
17         * is found, finds the corresponding value. */
18        if ((bitfield[i] & (1 << j)) == 0) {
19          System.out.println (i * 8 + j);
20          return;
21        }
22      }
23    }
24  }
```

Follow Up: What if we have only 10 MB memory?

It's possible to find a missing integer with two passes of the data set. We can divide up the integers into blocks of some size (we'll discuss how to decide on a size later). Let's just assume that we divide up the integers into blocks of 1000. So, block 0 represents the numbers 0 through 999, block 1 represents numbers 1000 - 1999, and so on.

Since all the values are distinct, we know how many values we *should* find in each block. So, we search through the file and count how many values are between 0 and 999, how many are between 1000 and 1999, and so on. If we count only 998 values in a particular range, then we know that a missing int must be in that range.

In the second pass, we'll actually look for which number in that range is missing. We use the bit vector approach from the first part of this problem. We can ignore any number outside of this specific range.

The question, now, is what is the appropriate block size? Let's define some variables as follows:

- Let rangeSize be the size of the ranges that each block in the first pass represents.

- Let arraySize represent the number of blocks in the first pass. Note that array-

$\text{Size} = 2^{32}$ / rangeSize, since there are 2^{32} integers.

We need to select a value for rangeSize such that the memory from the first pass (the array) and the second pass (the bit vector) fit.

First Pass: The Array

The array in the first pass can fit in 10 megabytes, or roughly 2^{23} bytes, of memory. Since each element in the array is an int, and an int is 4 bytes, we can hold an array of at most about 2^{21} elements. So, we can deduce the following:

Second Pass: The Bit Vector
$$\text{arraySize} = \frac{2^{32}}{\text{rangeSize}} \leq 2^{21}$$
$$\text{rangeSize} \geq \frac{2^{32}}{2^{21}}$$
$$\text{rangeSize} \geq 2^{11}$$

We need to have enough space to store rangeSize bits. Since we can fit 2^{23} bytes in memory, we can fit 2^{26} bits in memory. Therefore, we can conclude the following:

$$2^{11} \leq \text{rangeSize} \leq 2^{26}$$

These conditions give us a good amount of "wiggle room," but the nearer to the middle that we pick, the less memory will be used at any given time.

The below code provides one implementation for this algorithm.

```
1   int bitsize = 1048576; // 2^20 bits (2^17 bytes)
2   int blockNum = 4096; // 2^12
3   byte[] bitfield = new byte[bitsize/8];
4   int[] blocks = new int[blockNum];
5
6   void findOpenNumber() throws FileNotFoundException {
7       int starting = -1;
8       Scanner in = new Scanner (new FileReader ("file.txt"));
9       while (in.hasNextInt()) {
10          int n = in.nextInt();
11          blocks[n / (bitfield.length * 8)]++;
12      }
13
14      for (int i = 0; i < blocks.length; i++) {
15          if (blocks[i] < bitfield.length * 8){
16              /* if value < 2^20, then at least 1 number is missing in
17               * that section. */
18              starting = i * bitfield.length * 8;
19              break;
20          }
21      }
22
23      in = new Scanner(new FileReader ("file.txt"));
24      while (in.hasNextInt()) {
```

```
25        int n = in.nextInt();
26        /* If the number is inside the block that's missing
27         * numbers, we record it */
28        if (n >= starting && n < starting + bitfield.length * 8) {
29            bitfield [(n-starting) / 8] |= 1 << ((n - starting) % 8);
30        }
31    }
32
33    for (int i = 0 ; i < bitfield.length; i++) {
34        for (int j = 0; j < 8; j++) {
35            /* Retrieves the individual bits of each byte. When 0 bit
36             * is found, finds the corresponding value. */
37            if ((bitfield[i] & (1 << j)) == 0) {
38                System.out.println(i * 8 + j + starting);
39                return;
40            }
41        }
42    }
43 }
```

What if, as a potential follow up question, the interviewer asked you to solve the problem with even less memory? In this case we would do repeated passes using the approach from the first step. We'd first check to see how many integers are found within each sequence of a million elements. Then, in the second pass, we'd check how many integers are found in each sequence of a thousand elements. Finally, in the third pass, we'd apply the bit vector.

10.4 *You have an array with all the numbers from 1 to N, where N is at most 32,000. The array may have duplicate entries and you do not know what N is. With only 4 kilobytes of memory available, how would you print all duplicate elements in the array?*

pg 116

SOLUTION

We have 4 kilobytes of memory which means we can address up to $8 * 4 * 2^{10}$ bits. Note that $32 * 2^{10}$ bits is greater than 32000. We can create a bit vector with 32000 bits, where each bit represents one integer.

Using this bit vector, we can then iterate through the array, flagging each element v by setting bit v to 1. When we come across a duplicate element, we print it.

```
1  public static void checkDuplicates(int[] array) {
2      BitSet bs = new BitSet(32000);
3      for (int i = 0; i < array.length; i++) {
4          int num = array[i];
5          int num0 = num - 1; // bitset starts at 0, numbers start at 1
6          if (bs.get(num0)) {
7              System.out.println(num);
8          } else {
```

```
9              bs.set(num0);
10       }
11   }
12 }
13
14 class BitSet {
15    int[] bitset;
16
17    public BitSet(int size) {
18       bitset = new int[size >> 5]; // divide by 32
19    }
20
21    boolean get(int pos) {
22       int wordNumber = (pos >> 5); // divide by 32
23       int bitNumber = (pos & 0x1F); // mod 32
24       return (bitset[wordNumber] & (1 << bitNumber)) != 0;
25    }
26
27    void set(int pos) {
28       int wordNumber = (pos >> 5); // divide by 32
29       int bitNumber = (pos & 0x1F); // mod 32
30       bitset[wordNumber] |= 1 << bitNumber;
31    }
32 }
```

Note that while this isn't an especially difficult problem, it's important to implement this cleanly. This is why we defined our own bit vector class to hold a large bit vector. If our interviewer lets us (she may or may not), we could have of course used Java's built in BitSet class.

10.5 *If you were designing a web crawler, how would you avoid getting into infinite loops?*

pg 116

SOLUTION

The first thing to ask ourselves in this problem is how an infinite loop might occur. The simplest answer is that, if we picture the web as a graph of links, an infinite loop will occur when a cycle occurs.

To prevent infinite loops, we just need to detect cycles. One way to do this is to create a hash table where we set hash[v] to true after we visit page v.

This solution would mean crawling the web using breadth first search. Each time we visit a page, we gather all its links and insert them at the end of a queue. If we've already visited a page, we ignore it.

This is great—but what does it mean to visit page v? Is page v defined based on its content or its URL?

If it's defined based on its URL, we must recognize that URL parameters might indicate a completely different page. For example, the page `www.careercup.com/page?id=microsoft-interview-questions` is totally different from the page `www.careercup.com/page?id=google-interview-questions`. But, we can also append URL parameters arbitrarily to any URL without truly changing the page, provided it's not a parameter that the web application recognizes and handles. The page `www.careercup.com?foobar=hello` is the same as `www.careercup.com`.

"Okay, then," you might say, "let's define it based on its content." That sounds good too, at first, but it also doesn't quite work. Suppose I have some randomly generated content on the careercup.com home page. Is it a different page each time you visit it? Not really.

The reality is that there is probably no perfect way to define a "different" page, and this is where this problem gets tricky.

One way to tackle this is to have some sort of estimation for degree of similarity. If, based on the content and the URL, a page is deemed to be sufficiently similar to other pages, we *deprioritize* crawling its children. For each page, we would come up with some sort of signature based on snippets of the content and the page's URL.

Let's see how this would work.

We have a database which stores a list of items we need to crawl. On each iteration, we select the highest priority page to crawl. We then do the following:

1. Open up the page and create a signature of the page based on specific subsections of the page and its URL.

2. Query the database to see whether anything with this signature has been crawled recently.

3. If something with this signature has been recently crawled, insert this page back into the database at a low priority.

4. If not, crawl the page and insert its links into the database.

Under the above implementation, we never "complete" crawling the web, but we will avoid getting stuck in a loop of pages. If we want to allow for the possibility of "finishing" crawling the web (which would clearly happen only if the "web" were actually a smaller system, like an intranet), then we can set a minimum priority that a page must have to be crawled.

This is just one, simplistic solution, and there are many others that are equally valid. A problem like this will more likely resemble a conversation with your interviewer which could take any number of paths. In fact, the discussion of this problem could have taken the path of the very next problem.

10.6 *You have 10 billion URLs. How do you detect the duplicate documents? In this case, assume that "duplicate" means that the URLs are identical.*

pg 116

SOLUTION

Just how much space do 10 billion URLs take up? If each URL is an average of 100 characters, and each character is 4 bytes, then this list of 10 billion URLs will take up about 4 terabytes. We are probably not going to hold that much data in memory.

But, let's just pretend for a moment that we were miraculously holding this data in memory, since it's useful to first construct a solution for the simple version. Under this version of the problem, we would just create a hash table where each URL maps to true if it's already been found elsewhere in the list. (As an alternative solution, we could sort the list and look for the duplicate values that way. That will take a bunch of extra time and offers few advantages.)

Now that we have a solution for the simple version, what happens when we have all 400 gigabytes of data and we can't store it all in memory? We could solve this either by storing some of the data on disk or by splitting up the data across machines.

Solution #1: Disk Storage

If we stored all the data on one machine, we would do two passes of the document. The first pass would split the list of URLs into 400 chunks of 1 GB each. An easy way to do that might be to store each URL u in a file named `<x>.txt` where x = `hash(u) % 400`. That is, we divide up the URLs based on their hash value (modulo the number of chunks). This way, all URLs with the same hash value would be in the same file.

In the second pass, we would essentially implement the simple solution we came up with earlier: load each file into memory, create a hash table of the URLs, and look for duplicates.

Solution #2: Multiple Machines

The other solution is to perform essentially the same procedure, but to use multiple machines. In this solution, rather than storing the data in file `<x>.txt`, we would send the URL to machine x.

Using multiple machines has pros and cons.

The main pro is that we can parallelize the operation, such that all 400 chunks are processed simultaneously. For large amounts of data, this might result in a faster solution.

The disadvantage though is that we are now relying on 400 different machines to operate perfectly. That may not be realistic (particularly with more data and more machines), and we'll need to start considering how to handle failure. Additionally, we have increased the complexity of the system simply by involving so many machines.

Both are good solutions though, and both should be discussed with your interviewer.

10.7 *Imagine a web server for a simplified search engine. This system has 100 machines to respond to search queries, which may then call out using processSearch(string query) to another cluster of machines to actually get the result. The machine which responds to a given query is chosen at random, so you can not guarantee that the same machine will always respond to the same request. The method process- Search is very expensive. Design a caching mechanism to cache the results of the most recent queries. Be sure to explain how you would update the cache when data changes.*

pg 116

SOLUTION

Before getting into the design of this system, we first have to understand what the question means. Many of the details are somewhat ambiguous, as is expected in questions like this. We will make reasonable assumptions for the purposes of this solution, but you should discuss these details—in depth—with your interviewer.

Assumptions

Here are a few of the assumptions we make for this solution. Depending on the design of your system and how you approach the problem, you may make other assumptions. Remember that while some approaches are better than others, there is no one "correct" approach.

- Other than calling out to processSearch as necessary, all query processing happens on the initial machine that was called.

- The number of queries we wish to cache is large (millions).

- Calling between machines is relatively quick.

- The result for a given queries is an ordered list of URLs, each of which has an associated 50 character title and 200 character summary.

- The most popular queries are extremely popular, such that they would always appear in the cache.

Again, these aren't the *only* valid assumptions. This is just one reasonable set of assumptions.

System Requirements

When designing the cache, we know we'll need to support two primary functions:

- Efficient lookups given a key.

- Expiration of old data so that it can be replaced with new data.

In addition, we must also handle updating or clearing the cache when the results for a query change. Because some queries are very common and may permanently reside in the cache, we cannot just wait for the cache to naturally expire.

Step 1: Design a Cache for a Single System

A good way to approach this problem is to start by designing it for a single machine. So, how would you create a data structure that enables you to easily purge old data and also efficiently look up a value based on a key?

- A linked list would allow easy purging of old data, by moving "fresh" items to the front. We could implement it to remove the last element of the linked list when the list exceeds a certain size.

- A hash table allows efficient lookups of data, but it wouldn't ordinarily allow easy data purging.

How can we get the best of both worlds? By merging the two data structures. Here's how this works:

Just as before, we create a linked list where a node is moved to the front every time it's accessed. This way, the end of the linked list will always contain the stalest information.

In addition, we have a hash table that maps from a query to the corresponding node in the linked list. This allows us to not only efficiently return the cached results, but also to move the appropriate node to the front of the list, thereby updating its "freshness."

For illustrative purposes, abbreviated code for the cache is below. The code attachment provides the full code for this part. Note that in your interview, it is unlikely that you would be asked to write the full code for this as well as perform the design for the larger system.

```
1   public class Cache {
2       public static int MAX_SIZE = 10;
3       public Node head, tail;
4       public HashMap<String, Node> map;
5       public int size = 0;
6
7       public Cache() {
8           map = new HashMap<String, Node>();
9       }
10
11      /* Moves node to front of linked list */
12      public void moveToFront(Node node) { ... }
13      public void moveToFront(String query) { ... }
14
15      /* Removes node from linked list */
```

```
16    public void removeFromLinkedList(Node node) { ... }
17
18    /* Gets results from cache, and updates linked list */
19    public String[] getResults(String query) {
20      if (!map.containsKey(query)) return null;
21
22      Node node = map.get(query);
23      moveToFront(node); // update freshness
24      return node.results;
25    }
26
27    /* Inserts results into linked list and hash */
28    public void insertResults(String query, String[] results) {
29      if (map.containsKey(query)) { // update values
30        Node node = map.get(query);
31        node.results = results;
32        moveToFront(node); // update freshness
33        return;
34      }
35
36      Node node = new Node(query, results);
37      moveToFront(node);
38      map.put(query, node);
39
40      if (size > MAX_SIZE) {
41        map.remove(tail.query);
42        removeFromLinkedList(tail);
43      }
44    }
45 }
```

Step 2: Expand to Many Machines

Now that we understand how to design this for a single machine, we need to understand how we would design this when queries could be sent to many different machines. Recall from the problem statement that there's no guarantee that a particular query will be consistently sent to the same machine.

The first thing we need to decide is to what extent the cache is shared across machines. We have several options to consider.

Option 1: Each machine has its own cache.

A simple option is to give each machine its own cache. This means that if "foo" is sent to machine 1 twice in a short amount of time, the result would be recalled from the cache on the second time. But, if "foo" is sent first to machine 1 and then to machine 2, it would be treated as a totally fresh query both times.

This has the advantage of being relatively quick, since no machine-to-machine calls are used. The cache, unfortunately, is somewhat less effective as an optimization tool as many repeat queries would be treated as fresh queries.

Option 2: Each machine has a copy of the cache.

On the other extreme, we could give each machine a complete copy of the cache. When new items are added to the cache, they are sent to all machines. The entire data structure—linked list and hash table—would be duplicated.

This design means that common queries would nearly always be in the cache, as the cache is the same everywhere. The major drawback however is that updating the cache means firing off data to N different machines, where N is the size of the response cluster. Additionally, because each item effectively takes up N times as much space, our cache would hold much less data.

Option 3: Each machine stores a segment of the cache.

A third option is to divide up the cache, such that each machine holds a different part of it. Then, when machine i needs to look up the results for a query, machine i would figure out which machine holds this value, and then ask this other machine (machine j) to look up the query in j's cache.

But how would machine i know which machine holds this part of the hash table?

One option is to assign queries based on the formula hash(query) % N. Then, machine i only needs to apply this formula to know that machine j should store the results for this query.

So, when a new query comes in to machine i, this machine would apply the formula and call out to machine j. Machine j would then return the value from its cache or call processSearch(query) to get the results. Machine j would update its cache and return the results back to i.

Alternatively, you could design the system such that machine j just returns null if it doesn't have the query in its current cache. This would require machine i to call processSearch and then forward the results to machine j for storage. This implementation actually increases the number of machine-to-machine calls, with few advantages.

Step 3: Updating results when contents change

Recall that some queries may be so popular that, with a sufficiently large cache, they would permanently be cached. We need some sort of mechanism to allow cached results to be refreshed, either periodically or "on-demand" when certain content changes.

To answer this question, we need to consider when results would change (and you need to discuss this with your interviewer). The primary times would be when:

1. The content at a URL changes (or the page at that URL is removed).

2. The ordering of results change in response to the rank of a page changing.

3. New pages appear related to a particular query.

To handle situations #1 and #2, we could create a separate hash table that would tell us which cached queries are tied to a specific URL. This could be handled completely separately from the other caches, and reside on different machines. However, this solution may require a lot of data.

Alternatively, if the data doesn't require instant refreshing (which it probably doesn't), we could periodically crawl through the cache stored on each machine to purge queries tied to the updated URLs.

Situation #3 is substantially more difficult to handle. We could update single word queries by parsing the content at the new URL and purging these one-word queries from the caches. But, this will only handle the one word queries.

A good way to handle Situation #3 (and likely something we'd want to do anyway) is to implement an "automatic time-out" on the cache. That is, we'd impose a time out where *no* query, regardless of how popular it is, can sit in the cache for more than x minutes. This will ensure that all data is periodically refreshed.

Step 4: Further Enhancements

There are a number of improvement and tweaks you could make to this design depending on the assumptions you make and the situations you optimize for.

One such optimization is to better support the situation where some queries are very popular. For example, suppose (as an extreme example) a particular string constitutes 1% of all queries. Rather than machine i forwarding the request to machine j every time, machine i could forward the request just once to j, and then i could store the results in its own cache as well.

Alternatively, there may also be some possibility of doing some sort of re-architecture of the system to assign queries to machines based on their hash value (and therefore the location of the cache), rather than randomly. However, this decision may come with its own set of trade-offs.

Another optimization we could make is to the "automatic time out" mechanism. As initially described, this mechanism purges any data after X minutes. However, we may want to update some data (like current news) much more frequently than other data (like historical stock prices). We could implement time outs based on topic or based on URLs. In the latter situation, each URL would have a time out value based on how frequently the page has been updated in the past. The time out for the query would be the minimum of the time outs for each URL.

These are just a few of the enhancements we can make. Remember that in questions like this, there is no single correct way to solve the problem. These questions are about having a discussion with your interviewer about design criteria and demonstrating your general approach and methodology.

Sorting and Searching

Concepts and Algorithms: Solutions

11.1 *You are given two sorted arrays, A and B, where A has a large enough buffer at the end to hold B. Write a method to merge B into A in sorted order.*

pg 121

SOLUTION

Since we know that A has enough buffer at the end, we won't need to allocate additional space. Our logic should involve simply comparing elements of A and B and inserting them in order, until we've exhausted all elements in A and in B.

The only issue with this is that if we insert an element into the front of A, then we'll have to shift the existing elements backwards to make room for it. It's better to insert elements into the back of the array, where there's empty space.

The code below does just that. It works from the back of A and B, moving the largest elements to the back of A.

```
1   public static void merge(int[] a, int[] b, int lastA, int lastB) {
2       int indexA = lastA - 1; /* Index of last element in array a */
3       int indexB = lastB - 1; /* Index of last element in array b */
4       int indexMerged = lastB + lastA - 1; /* end of merged array */
5
6       /* Merge a and b, starting from the last element in each */
7       while (indexA >= 0 && indexB >= 0) {
8           /* end of a is > than end of b */
9           if (a[indexA] > b[indexB]) {
10              a[indexMerged] = a[indexA]; // copy element
11              indexMerged--; // move indices
12              indexA--;
13          } else {
14              a[indexMerged] = b[indexB]; // copy element
15              indexMerged--; // move indices
16              indexB--;
17          }
18      }
19
20      /* Copy remaining elements from b into place */
21      while (indexB >= 0) {
22          a[indexMerged] = b[indexB];
23          indexMerged--;
24          indexB--;
25      }
26  }
```

Note that you don't need to copy the contents of A after running out of elements in B. They are already in place.

11.2 *Write a method to sort an array of strings so that all the anagrams are next to each other.*

pg 121

SOLUTION

This problem asks us to group the strings in an array such that the anagrams appear next to each other. Note that no specific ordering of the words is required, other than this.

One way to do this is to just apply any standard sorting algorithm, like merge sort or quick sort, and modify the comparator. This comparator will be used to indicate that two strings which are anagrams of each other are equivalent.

What's the easiest way of checking if two words are anagrams? We could count the occurrences of the distinct characters in each string and return true if they match. Or, we could just sort the string. After all, two words which are anagrams will look the same once they're sorted.

The code below implements the comparator.

```
1   public class AnagramComparator implements Comparator<String> {
2       public String sortChars(String s) {
3           char[] content = s.toCharArray();
4           Arrays.sort(content);
5           return new String(content);
6       }
7
8       public int compare(String s1, String s2) {
9           return sortChars(s1).compareTo(sortChars(s2));
10      }
11  }
```

Now, just sort the arrays using this compareTo method instead of the usual one.

```
12  Arrays.sort(array, new AnagramComparator());
```

This algorithm will take O(n log(n)) time.

This may be the best we can do for a general sorting algorithm, but we don't actually need to fully sort the array. We only need to *group* the strings in the array by anagram.

We can do this by using a hash table which maps from the sorted version of a word to a list of its anagrams. So, for example, acre will map to the list {acre, race, care}. Once we've grouped all the words into these lists by anagram, we can then put them back into the array.

The code below implements this algorithm.

```
1   public void sort(String[] array) {
2       Hashtable<String, LinkedList<String>> hash =
3           new Hashtable<String, LinkedList<String>>();
```

```
4
5      /* Group words by anagram */
6      for (String s : array) {
7        String key = sortChars(s);
8        if (!hash.containsKey(key)) {
9          hash.put(key, new LinkedList<String>());
10       }
11       LinkedList<String> anagrams = hash.get(key);
12       anagrams.push(s);
13     }
14
15     /* Convert hash table to array */
16     int index = 0;
17     for (String key : hash.keySet()) {
18       LinkedList<String> list = hash.get(key);
19       for (String t : list) {
20         array[index] = t;
21         index++;
22       }
23     }
24  }
```

You may notice that the algorithm above is a modification of bucket sort.

11.3 *Given a sorted array of n integers that has been rotated an unknown number of times, write code to find an element in the array. You may assume that the array was originally sorted in increasing order.*

pg 121

SOLUTION

If this problem smells like binary search to you, you're right!

In classic binary search, we compare x with the midpoint to figure out if x belongs on the left or the right side. The complication here is that the array is rotated and may have an inflection point. Consider, for example, the following two arrays:

```
Array1: {10, 15, 20,  0,  5}
Array2: {50,  5, 20, 30, 40}
```

Note that both arrays have a midpoint of 20, but 5 appears on the left side of one and on the right side of the other. Therefore, comparing x with the midpoint is insufficient.

However, if we look a bit deeper, we can see that one half of the array must be ordered normally (in increasing order). We can therefore look at the normally ordered half to determine whether we should search the left or right half.

For example, if we are searching for 5 in Array1, we can look at the left element (10) and middle element (20). Since 10 < 20, the left half must be ordered normally. And, since 5 is not between those, we know that we must search the right half.

In Array2, we can see that since 50 > 20, the right half must be ordered normally. We turn to the middle (20) and right (40) element to check if 5 would fall between them. The value 5 would not; therefore, we search the left half.

The tricky condition is if the left and the middle are identical, as in the example array {2, 2, 2, 3, 4, 2}. In this case, we can check if the rightmost element is different. If it is, we can search just the right side. Otherwise, we have no choice but to search both halves.

```
1   public int search(int a[], int left, int right, int x) {
2      int mid = (left + right) / 2;
3      if (x == a[mid]) { // Found element
4         return mid;
5      }
6      if (right < left) {
7         return -1;
8      }
9
10     /* Either the left or right half must be normally ordered. Find
11      * out which side is normally ordered, and then use the normally
12      * ordered half to figure out which side to search to find x. */
13     if (a[left] < a[mid]) { // Left is normally ordered.
14        if (x >= a[left] && x <= a[mid]) {
15           return search(a, left, mid - 1, x); // Search left
16        } else {
17           return search(a, mid + 1, right, x); // Search right
18        }
19     } else if (a[mid] < a[left]) { // Right is normally ordered.
20        if (x >= a[mid] && x <= a[right]) {
21           return search(a, mid + 1, right, x); // Search right
22        } else {
23           return search(a, left, mid - 1, x); // Search left
24        }
25     } else if (a[left] == a[mid]) { // Left half is all repeats
26        if (a[mid] != a[right]) { // If right is diff., search it
27           return search(a, mid + 1, right, x); // search right
28        } else { // Else, we have to search both halves
29           int result = search(a, left, mid - 1, x); // Search left
30           if (result == -1) {
31              return search(a, mid + 1, right, x); // Search right
32           } else {
33              return result;
34           }
35        }
36     }
37     return -1;
38  }
```

This code will run in O(log n) if all the elements are unique. However, with many duplicates, the algorithm is actually O(n). This is because with many duplicates, we will often have to search both the left and right sides of the array (or subarrays).

Note that while this problem is not conceptually very complex, it is actually very difficult to implement flawlessly. Don't feel bad if you had trouble implementing it without a few bugs. Because of the ease of making off-by-one and other minor errors, you should make sure to test your code very thoroughly.

11.4 *Imagine you have a 20 GB file with one string per line. Explain how you would sort the file.*

pg 121

SOLUTION

When an interviewer gives a size limit of 20 gigabytes, it should tell you something. In this case, it suggests that they don't want you to bring all the data into memory.

So what do we do? We only bring part of the data into memory.

We'll divide the file into chunks which are x megabytes each, where x is the amount of memory we have available. Each chunk is sorted separately and then saved back to the file system.

Once all the chunks are sorted, we then merge the chunks, one by one. At the end, we have a fully sorted file.

This algorithm is known as external sort.

11.5 *Given a sorted array of strings which is interspersed with empty strings, write a method to find the location of a given string.*

pg 121

SOLUTION

If it weren't for the empty strings, we could simply use binary search. We would compare the string to be found, str, with the midpoint of the array, and go from there.

With empty strings interspersed, we can implement a simple modification of binary search. All we need to do is fix the comparison against mid, in case mid is an empty string. We simply move mid to the closest non-empty string.

The recursive code below to solve this problem can easily be modified to be iterative. We provide such an implementation in the code attachment.

```
1   public int searchR(String[] strings, String str, int first,
2                      int last) {
3       if (first > last) return -1;
4       /* Move mid to the middle */
5       int mid = (last + first) / 2;
```

```
6
7       /* If mid is empty, find closest non-empty string. */
8       if (strings[mid].isEmpty()) {
9          int left = mid - 1;
10         int right = mid + 1;
11         while (true) {
12            if (left < first && right > last) {
13               return -1;
14            } else if (right <= last && !strings[right].isEmpty()) {
15               mid = right;
16               break;
17            } else if (left >= first && !strings[left].isEmpty()) {
18               mid = left;
19               break;
20            }
21            right++;
22            left--;
23         }
24      }
25
26      /* Check for string, and recurse if necessary */
27      if (str.equals(strings[mid])) { // Found it!
28         return mid;
29      } else if (strings[mid].compareTo(str) < 0) { // Search right
30         return searchR(strings, str, mid + 1, last);
31      } else { // Search left
32         return searchR(strings, str, first, mid - 1);
33      }
34 }
35
36 public int search(String[] strings, String str) {
37    if (strings == null || str == null || str == "") {
38       return -1;
39    }
40    return searchR(strings, str, 0, strings.length - 1);
41 }
```

Careful consideration should be given to the situation when someone searches for the empty string. Should we find the location (which is an O(n) operation)? Or should we handle this as an error?

There's no correct answer here. This is an issue you should raise with your interviewer. Simply asking this question will demonstrate that are you a careful coder.

11.6   *Given an M x N matrix in which each row and each column is sorted in ascending order, write a method to find an element.*

pg 122

SOLUTION

As a first approach, we can do binary search on every row to find the element. This algorithm will be O(M log(N)), since there are M rows and it takes O(log(N)) time to search each one. This is a good approach to mention to your interviewer before you proceed with generating a better algorithm.

To develop an algorithm, let's start with a simple example.

15	20	40	85
20	35	80	95
30	55	95	105
40	80	100	120

Suppose we are searching for the element 55. How can we identify where it is?

If we look at the start of a row or the start of a column, we can start to deduce the location. If the start of a column is greater than 55, we know that 55 can't be in that column, since the start of the column is always the minimum element. Additionally, we know that 55 can't be in any columns on the right, since the first element of each column must increase in size from left to right. Therefore, if the start of the column is greater than the element x that we are searching for, we know that we need to move further to the left.

For rows, we can follow identical logic. If the start of a row is bigger than x, then we know we need to move upwards.

Observe that we can also make a similar conclusion by looking at the ends of columns or rows. If the end of a column or row is less than x, then we know that we must move down (for rows) or to the right (for columns) to find x. This is because the end is always the maximum element.

We can bring these observations together into a solution. The observations are the following:

- If the start of a column is greater than x, then x is to the left of the column.
- If the end of a column is less than x, then x is to the right of the column.
- If the start of a row is greater than x, then x is above that row.
- If the end of a row is less than x, then x is below that row.

We can begin in any number of places, but let's begin with looking at the starts of columns.

We need to start with the greatest column and work our way to the left. This means that our first element for comparison is array[0][c-1], where c is the number of columns. By comparing the start of columns to x (which is 55), we'll find that x must be in columns 0, 1, or 2. We will have stopped at array[0][2].

This element may not be the end of a row in the full matrix, but it is an end of a row of a submatrix. The same conditions apply. The value at array[0][2], which is 40, is less than 55, so we know we can move downwards.

We now have a submatrix to consider that looks like the following (the gray squares have been eliminated).

15	20	40	85
20	35	80	95
30	55	95	105
40	80	100	120

We can repeatedly apply these conditions to search for 55. Note that the only conditions we actually use are conditions 1 and 4.

The code below implements this elimination algorithm.

```
1   public static boolean findElement(int[][] matrix, int elem) {
2       int row = 0;
3       int col = matrix[0].length - 1;
4       while (row < matrix.length && col >= 0) {
5           if (matrix[row][col] == elem) {
6               return true;
7           } else if (matrix[row][col] > elem) {
8               col--;
9           } else {
10              row++;
11          }
12      }
13      return false;
14  }
```

Alternatively, we can apply a solution that more directly looks like binary search. The code is considerably more complicated, but it applies many of the same learnings.

Solution #2: Binary Search

Let's again look at a simple example.

15	20	70	85
20	35	80	95
30	55	95	105
40	80	100	120

We want to be able to leverage the sorting property to more efficiently find an element. So, we might ask ourselves, what does the unique ordering property of this matrix imply about where an element might be located?

We are told that every row and column is sorted. This means that element a[i][j] will be greater than the elements in row i between columns 0 and j - 1 and the elements in column j between rows 0 and i - 1.

Or, in other words:

```
a[i][0] <= a[i][1] <= ... <= a[i][j-1] <= a[i][j]
a[0][j] <= a[1][j] <= ... <= a[i-1][j] <= a[i][j]
```

Looking at this visually, the dark gray element below is bigger than all the light gray elements.

15	20	70	85
20	35	80	95
30	55	95	105
40	80	100	120

The light gray elements also have an ordering to them: each is bigger than the elements to the left of it, as well as the elements above it. So, by transitivity, the dark gray element is bigger than the entire square.

15	20	70	85
20	35	80	95
30	55	95	105
40	80	100	120

This means that for any rectangle we draw in the matrix, the bottom right hand corner will always be the biggest.

Likewise, the top left hand corner will always be the smallest. The colors below indicate what we know about the ordering of elements (light gray < dark gray < black):

15	20	70	85
20	35	80	95
30	55	95	105
40	80	120	120

Let's return to the original problem: suppose we were searching for the value 85. If we look along the diagonal, we'll find the elements 35 and 95. What does this tell us about the location of 85?

15	20	70	85
25	35	80	95
30	55	95	105
40	80	120	120

85 can't be in the black area, since 95 is in the upper left hand corner and is therefore the smallest element in that square.

85 can't be in the light gray area either, since 35 is in the lower right hand corner of that square.

85 must be in one of the two white areas.

So, we partition our grid into four quadrants and recursively search the lower left quadrant and the upper right quadrant. These, too, will get divided into quadrants and searched.

Observe that since the diagonal is sorted, we can efficiently search it using binary search.

The code below implements this algorithm.

```
1   public Coordinate findElement(int[][] matrix, Coordinate origin,
2                                  Coordinate dest, int x) {
3       if (!origin.inbounds(matrix) || !dest.inbounds(matrix)) {
4           return null;
5       }
6       if (matrix[origin.row][origin.column] == x) {
7           return origin;
8       } else if (!origin.isBefore(dest)) {
9           return null;
10      }
11
12      /* Set start to start of diagonal and end to the end of the
13       * diagonal. Since the grid may not be square, the end of the
14       * diagonal may not equal dest. */
15      Coordinate start = (Coordinate) origin.clone();
16      int diagDist = Math.min(dest.row - origin.row,
17                              dest.column - origin.column);
18      Coordinate end = new Coordinate(start.row + diagDist,
19                                      start.column + diagDist);
20      Coordinate p = new Coordinate(0, 0);
21
22      /* Do binary search on the diagonal, looking for the first
23       * element greater than x */
24      while (start.isBefore(end)) {
25          p.setToAverage(start, end);
26          if (x > matrix[p.row][p.column]) {
27              start.row = p.row + 1;
28              start.column = p.column + 1;
29          } else {
30              end.row = p.row - 1;
31              end.column = p.column - 1;
32          }
33      }
34
35      /* Split the grid into quadrants. Search the bottom left and the
36       * top right. */
37      return partitionAndSearch(matrix, origin, dest, start, x);
38  }
```

```
39
40  public Coordinate partitionAndSearch(int[][] matrix,
41          Coordinate origin, Coordinate dest, Coordinate pivot,
42          int elem) {
43      Coordinate lowerLeftOrigin =
44          new Coordinate(pivot.row, origin.column);
45      Coordinate lowerLeftDest =
46          new Coordinate(dest.row, pivot.column - 1);
47      Coordinate upperRightOrigin =
48          new Coordinate(origin.row, pivot.column);
49      Coordinate upperRightDest =
50          new Coordinate(pivot.row - 1, dest.column);
51
52      Coordinate lowerLeft =
53          findElement(matrix, lowerLeftOrigin, lowerLeftDest, elem);
54      if (lowerLeft == null) {
55          return findElement(matrix, upperRightOrigin,
56                          upperRightDest, elem);
57      }
58      return lowerLeft;
59  }
60
61  public static Coordinate findElement(int[][] matrix, int x) {
62      Coordinate origin = new Coordinate(0, 0);
63      Coordinate dest = new Coordinate(matrix.length - 1,
64                          matrix[0].length - 1);
65      return findElement(matrix, origin, dest, x);
66  }
67
68  public class Coordinate implements Cloneable {
69      public int row;
70      public int column;
71      public Coordinate(int r, int c) {
72          row = r;
73          column = c;
74      }
75
76      public boolean inbounds(int[][] matrix) {
77          return  row >= 0 && column >= 0 &&
78                  row < matrix.length && column < matrix[0].length;
79      }
80
81      public boolean isBefore(Coordinate p) {
82          return row <= p.row && column <= p.column;
83      }
84
85      public Object clone() {
86          return new Coordinate(row, column);
87      }
88
```

```
89   public void setToAverage(Coordinate min, Coordinate max) {
90       row = (min.row + max.row) / 2;
91       column = (min.column + max.column) / 2;
92   }
93 }
```

If you read all this code and thought, "there's no way I could do all this in an interview!" you're probably right. You couldn't. But, your performance on any problem is evaluated compared to other candidates on the same problem. So while you couldn't implement all this, neither can they. You are at no disadvantage when you get a tricky problem like this.

You help yourself out a bit by separating code out into other methods. For example, by pulling partitionAndSearch out into its own method, you will have an easier time outlining key aspects of the code. You can then come back to fill in the body for partitionAndSearch if you have time.

11.7 *A circus is designing a tower routine consisting of people standing atop one another's shoulders. For practical and aesthetic reasons, each person must be both shorter and lighter than the person below him or her. Given the heights and weights of each person in the circus, write a method to compute the largest possible number of people in such a tower.*

pg 122

SOLUTION

When we cut out all the "fluff" to this problem, we can understand that the problem is really the following.

We have a list of pairs of items. Find the longest sequence such that both the first and second items are in non-decreasing order.

If we apply the Simplify and Generalize approach (or the Pattern Matching approach), we can relate this problem to finding the longest increasing sequence in an array.

Sub-Problem: Longest Increasing Subsequence

If the elements do not need to stay in the same (relative) order, then we would simply sort the array. This makes the problem too trivial, so let's assume that the elements need to stay in the same relative order.

We can attempt to derive a recursive algorithm by looking at the array, element by element. First, we need to observe that knowing the longest increasing subsequence for A[0] through A[i] will not give us the answer for A[i + 1] and A[i + 2]. We can see this through a simple example:

```
Array: 13, 14, 10, 11, 12
Longest(0 through 0): 13
```

```
Longest(0 through 1): 13, 14
Longest(0 through 2): 13, 14
Longest(0 through 3): 13, 14   OR   10, 11
Longest(0 through 4): 10, 11, 12
```

If we only tried to build Longest(0 through 4) and Longest(0 through 3) off of the most recent solutions, we would not find the optimal solution.

However, we can use a different recursive approach. Rather than trying to find the longest increasing subsequence across elements 0 through i, we can find the longest subsequence which *ends* with element i. Using the above example, we do the following:

```
Array: 13, 14, 10, 11, 12
Longest(ending with A[0]): 13
Longest(ending with A[1]): 13, 14
Longest(ending with A[2]): 10
Longest(ending with A[3]): 10, 11
Longest(ending with A[4]): 10, 11, 12
```

Note that the longest sequence ending with A[i] can be found by looking at all the prior solutions. We simply append A[i] to the longest "valid" one, where valid means any list where A[i] > list.tail.

The Real Problem: Longest Increasing Subsequence of Pairs

Now that we know how to find the longest increasing subsequence of an array of integers, we can solve the real problem fairly easily. We simply sort the list of people by their heights, and then apply the longestIncreasingSubsequence algorithm on just their weights.

The code below implements this algorithm.

```
1   ArrayList<HtWt> getIncreasingSequence(ArrayList<HtWt> items) {
2      Collections.sort(items);
3      return longestIncreasingSubsequence(items);
4   }
5
6   void longestIncreasingSubsequence(ArrayList<HtWt> array,
7         ArrayList<HtWt>[] solutions, int current_index) {
8      if (current_index >= array.size() || current_index < 0) return;
9      HtWt current_element = array.get(current_index);
10
11     /* Find longest sequence we can append current_element to */
12     ArrayList<HtWt> best_sequence = null;
13     for (int i = 0; i < current_index; i++) {
14        if (array.get(i).isBefore(current_element)) {
15           best_sequence = seqWithMaxLength(best_sequence,
16                                 solutions[i]);
17        }
18     }
19
```

```
20    /* Append current_element */
21    ArrayList<HtWt> new_solution = new ArrayList<HtWt>();
22    if (best_sequence != null) {
23       new_solution.addAll(best_sequence);
24    }
25    new_solution.add(current_element);
26
27    /* Add to list and recurse */
28    solutions[current_index] = new_solution;
29    longestIncreasingSubsequence(array, solutions, current_index+1);
30 }
31
32 ArrayList<HtWt> longestIncreasingSubsequence(
33       ArrayList<HtWt> array) {
34    ArrayList<HtWt>[] solutions = new ArrayList[array.size()];
35    longestIncreasingSubsequence(array, solutions, 0);
36
37    ArrayList<HtWt> best_sequence = null;
38    for (int i = 0; i < array.size(); i++) {
39       best_sequence = seqWithMaxLength(best_sequence, solutions[i]);
40    }
41
42    return best_sequence;
43 }
44
45 /* Returns longer sequence */
46 ArrayList<HtWt> seqWithMaxLength(ArrayList<HtWt> seq1,
47       ArrayList<HtWt> seq2) {
48    if (seq1 == null) return seq2;
49    if (seq2 == null) return seq1;
50    return seq1.size() > seq2.size() ? seq1 : seq2;
51 }
52
53 public class HtWt implements Comparable {
54    /* declarations, etc */
55
56    /* used for sort method */
57    public int compareTo( Object s ) {
58       HtWt second = (HtWt) s;
59       if (this.Ht != second.Ht) {
60          return ((Integer)this.Ht).compareTo(second.Ht);
61       } else {
62          return ((Integer)this.Wt).compareTo(second.Wt);
63       }
64    }
65
66    /* Returns true if "this" should be lined up before "other."
67     * Note that it's possible that this.isBefore(other) and
68     * other.isBefore(this) are both false. This is different from
69     * the compareTo method, where if a < b then b > a. */
```

```
70    public boolean isBefore(HtWt other) {
71        if (this.Ht < other.Ht && this.Wt < other.Wt) return true;
72        else return false;
73    }
74 }
```

This algorithm operates in O(n²) time. An O(n log(n)) algorithm does exist, but it is considerably more complicated and it is highly unlikely that you would derive this in an interview—even with some help. However, if you are interested in exploring this solution, a quick internet search will turn up a number of explanations of this solution.

11.8 *Imagine you are reading in a stream of integers. Periodically, you wish to be able to look up the rank of a number x (the number of values less than or equal to x). Implement the data structures and algorithms to support these operations. That is, implement the method* track(int x), *which is called when each number is generated, and the method* getRankOfNumber(int x), *which returns the number of values less than or equal to x (not including x itself).*

pg 122

SOLUTION

A relatively easy way to implement this would be to have an array that holds all the elements in sorted order. When a new element comes in, we would need to shift the other elements to make room. Implementing getRankOfNumber would be quite efficient though. We would simply perform a binary search for n, and return the index.

However, this is very inefficient for inserting elements (that is, the track(int x) function). We need a data structure which is good at keeping relative ordering, as well as updating when we insert new elements. A binary search tree can do just that.

Instead of inserting elements into an array, we insert elements into a binary search tree. The method track(int x) will run in O(log n) time, where n is the size of the tree (provided, of course, that the tree is balanced).

To find the rank of a number, we could do an in-order traversal, keeping a counter as we traverse. The goal is that, by the time we find x, counter will equal the number of elements less than x.

As long as we're moving left during searching for x, the counter won't change. Why? Because all the values we're skipping on the right side are greater than x. After all, the very smallest element (with rank of 1) is the leftmost node.

When we move to the right though, we skip over a bunch of elements on the left. All of these elements are less than x, so we'll need to increment counter by the number of elements in the left subtree.

Rather than counting the size of the left subtree (which would be inefficient), we can track this information as we add new elements to the tree.

Let's walk through an example on the following tree. In the below example, the value in parentheses indicates the number of nodes in the left subtree (or, in other words, the rank of the node *relative* to its subtree).

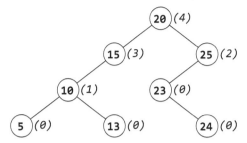

Suppose we want to find the rank of 24 in the tree above. We would compare 24 with the root, 20, and find that 24 must reside on the right. The root has 4 nodes in its left subtree, and when we include the root itself, this gives us five total nodes smaller than 24. We set `counter` to 5.

Then, we compare 24 with node 25 and find that 24 must be on the left. The value of `counter` does not update, since we're not "passing over" any smaller nodes. The value of `counter` is still 5.

Next, we compare 24 with node 23, and find that 24 must be on the right. `Counter` gets incremented by just 1 (to 6), since 23 has no left nodes.

Finally, we find 24 and we return `counter`: 6.

Recursively, the algorithm is the following:

```
1   int getRank(Node node, int x) {
2       if x is node.data
3           return node.leftSize()
4       if x is on left of node
5           return getRank(node.left, x)
6       if x is on right of node
7           return node.leftSize() + 1 + getRank(node.right, x)
8   }
```

The full code for this is below.

```
1   public class Question {
2       private static RankNode root = null;
3
4       public static void track(int number) {
5           if (root == null) {
6               root = new RankNode(number);
7           } else {
8               root.insert(number);
9           }
10      }
11
```

```
12    public static int getRankOfNumber(int number) {
13        return root.getRank(number);
14    }
15
16    ...
17 }
18
19 public class RankNode {
20    public int left_size = 0;
21    public RankNode left, right;
22    public int data = 0;
23    public RankNode(int d) {
24        data = d;
25    }
26
27    public void insert(int d) {
28        if (d <= data) {
29            if (left != null) left.insert(d);
30            else left = new RankNode(d);
31            left_size++;
32        } else {
33            if (right != null) right.insert(d);
34            else right = new RankNode(d);
35        }
36    }
37
38    public int getRank(int d) {
39        if (d == data) {
40            return left_size;
41        } else if (d < data) {
42            if (left == null) return -1;
43            else return left.getRank(d);
44        } else {
45            int right_rank = right == null ? -1 : right.getRank(d);
46            if (right_rank == -1) return -1;
47            else return left_size + 1 + right_rank;
48        }
49    }
50 }
```

Note how we've handled the case in which d is not found in the tree. We check for the -1 return value, and, when we find it, return -1 up the tree. It is important that you handle cases like this.

Testing

Concepts and Algorithms: Solutions

Chapter 12

Solutions to Chapter 12 | Testing

12.1 *Find the mistake(s) in the following code:*

```
1  unsigned int i;
2  for (i = 100; i >= 0; --i)
3     printf("%d\n", i);
```

pg 129

SOLUTION

There are two mistakes in this code.

First, note that an `unsigned int` is, by definition, always greater than or equal to zero. The for loop condition will therefore always be true, and it will loop infinitely.

The correct code to print all numbers from 100 to 1, is `i > 0`. If we truly wanted to print zero, we could add an additional `printf` statement after the for loop.

```
1  unsigned int i;
2  for (i = 100; i > 0; --i)
3     printf("%d\n", i);
```

One additional correction is to use %u in place of %d, as we are printing `unsigned int`.

```
1  unsigned int i;
2  for (i = 100; i > 0; --i)
3     printf("%u\n", i);
```

This code will now correctly print the list of all numbers from 100 to 1, in descending order.

12.2 *You are given the source to an application which crashes when it is run. After running it ten times in a debugger, you find it never crashes in the same place. The application is single threaded, and uses only the C standard library. What programming errors could be causing this crash? How would you test each one?*

pg 129

SOLUTION

The question largely depends on the type of application being diagnosed. However, we can give some general causes of random crashes.

1. *"Random Variable:"* The application may use some random number or variable component that may not be fixed for every execution of the program. Examples include user input, a random number generated by the program, or the time of day.

2. *Uninitialized Variable:* The application could have an uninitialized variable which, in some languages, may cause it to take on an arbitrary value. The values of this variable could result in the code taking a slightly different path each time.

3. *Memory Leak:* The program may have run out of memory. Other culprits are totally random for each run since it depends on the number of processes running at that

particular time. This also includes heap overflow or corruption of data on the stack.

4. *External Dependencies:* The program may depend on another application, machine, or resource. If there are multiple dependencies, the program could crash at any point.

To track down the issue, we should start with learning as much as possible about the application. Who is running it? What are they doing with it? What kind of application is it?

Additionally, although the application doesn't crash in exactly the same place, it's possible that it is linked to specific components or scenarios. For example, it could be that the application never crashes if it's simply launched and left untouched, and that crashes only appear at some point after loading a file. Or, it may be that all the crashes take place within the lower level components, such as file I/O.

It may be useful to approach this by elimination. Close down all other applications on the system. Track resource use very careful. If there are parts of the program we can disable, do so. Run it on a different machine and see if we experience the same issue. The more we can eliminate (or change), the easier we can track down the issue.

Additionally, we may be able to use tools to check for specific situations. For example, to investigate issue #2, we can utilize runtime tools which check for uninitialized variables.

These problems are as much about your brainstorming ability as they are about your approach. Do you jump all over the place, shouting out random suggestions? Or do you approach it in a logical, structured manner? Hopefully, it's the latter.

12.3 *We have the following method used in a chess game: boolean canMoveTo(int x, int y). This method is part of the Piece class and returns whether or not the piece can move to position (x, y). Explain how you would test this method.*

pg 129

SOLUTION

In this problem, there are two primary types of testing: extreme case validation (ensuring that the program doesn't crash on bad input), and general case testing. We'll start with the first type.

Testing Type #1: Extreme Case Validation

We need to ensure that the program handles bad or unusual input gracefully. This means checking the following conditions:

- Test with negative numbers for x and y
- Test with x larger than the width
- Test with y larger than the width

- Test with a completely full board
- Test with an empty or nearly empty board
- Test with far more white pieces than black
- Test with far more black pieces than white

For the error cases above, we should ask our interviewer whether we want to return false or throw an exception, and we should test accordingly.

Testing Type #2: General Testing:

General testing is much more expansive. Ideally, we would test every possible board, but there are far too many boards. We can, however, perform a reasonable coverage of different boards.

There are 6 pieces in chess, so we can test each piece against every other piece, in every possible direction. This would look something like the below code:

```
1   foreach piece a:
2      for each other type of piece b (6 types + empty space)
3         foreach direction d
4            Create a board with piece a.
5            Place piece b in direction d.
6            Try to move - check return value.
```

The key to this problem is recognizing that we can't test every possible scenario, even if we would like to. So, instead, we must focus on the essential areas.

12.4   *How would you load test a webpage without using any test tools?*

pg 129

SOLUTION

Load testing helps to identify a web application's maximum operating capacity, as well as any bottlenecks that may interfere with its performance. Similarly, it can check how an application responds to variations in load.

To perform load testing, we must first identify the performance critical scenarios and the metrics which fulfill our performance objectives. Typical criteria include:

- Response time
- Throughput
- Resource utilization
- Maximum load that the system can bear.

Then, we design tests to simulate the load, taking care to measure each of these criteria.

In the absence of formal testing tools, we can basically create our own. For example, we could simulate concurrent users by creating thousands of virtual users. We would write a multi-threaded program with thousands of threads, where each thread acts as a real-world user loading the page. For each user, we would programmatically measure response time, data I/O, etc.

We would then analyze the results based on the data gathered during the tests and compare it with the accepted values.

12.5 *How would you test a pen?*

pg 129

SOLUTION

This problem is largely about understanding the constraints and approaching the problem in a structured manner.

To understand the constraints, you should ask a lot of questions to understand the "who, what, where, when, how and why" of a problem (or as many of those as apply to the problem). Remember that a good tester understands exactly what he is testing before starting the work.

To illustrate the technique in this problem, let us guide you through a mock conversation.

Interviewer: How would you test a pen?

Candidate: Let me find out a bit about the pen. Who is going to use the pen?

Interviewer: Probably children.

Candidate: Okay, that's interesting. What will they be doing with it? Will they be writing, drawing, or doing something else with it?

Interviewer: Drawing.

Candidate: Ok, great. On what? Paper? Clothing? Walls?

Interviewer: On clothing.

Candidate: Great. What kind of tip does the pen have? Felt? Ball point? Is it intended to wash off, or is it intended to be permanent?

Interviewer: It's intended to wash off.

Many questions later, you may get to this:

Candidate: Okay, so as I understand it, we have a pen that is being targeted at 5 to 10 year olds. The pen has a felt tip and comes in red, green, blue and black. It's intended to wash off when clothing is washed. Is that correct?

The candidate now has a problem that is significantly different from what it initially seemed to be. This is not uncommon. In fact, many interviewers intentionally give a problem that seems clear (everyone knows what a pen is!), only to let you discover that it's quite a different problem from what it seemed. Their belief is that users do the same thing, though users do so accidentally.

Now that you understand what you're testing, it's time to come up with a plan of attack. The key here is *structure*.

Consider what the different components of the object or problem, and go from there. In this case, the components might be:

- *Fact check:* Verify that the pen is felt tip and that the ink is one of the allowed colors.
- *Intended use:* Drawing. Does the pen write properly on clothing?
- *Intended use:* Washing. Does it wash off of clothing (even if it's been there for an extended period of time)? Does it wash off in hot, warm and cold water?
- *Safety:* Is the pen safe (non-toxic) for children?
- *Unintended uses:* How else might children use the pen? They might write on other surfaces, so you need to check whether the behavior there is correct. They might also stomp on the pen, throw it, and so on. You'll need to make sure that the pen holds up under these conditions.

Remember that in any testing question, you need to test both the intended and unintended scenarios. People don't always use the product the way you want them to.

12.6 *How would you test an ATM in a distributed banking system?*

pg 129

SOLUTION

The first thing to do on this question is to clarify assumptions. Ask the following questions:

- Who is going to use the ATM? Answers might be "anyone," or it might be "blind people," or any number of other answers.
- What are they going to use it for? Answers might be "withdrawing money,""transferring money,""checking their balance," or many other answers.
- What tools do we have to test? Do we have access to the code, or just to the ATM?

Remember: a good tester makes sure she knows what she's testing!

Once we understand what the system looks like, we'll want to break down the problem into different testable components. These components include:

- Logging in
- Withdrawing money

- Depositing money
- Checking balance
- Transferring money

We would probably want to use a mix of manual and automated testing.

Manual testing would involve going through the steps above, making sure to check for all the error cases (low balance, new account, nonexistent account, and so on).

Automated testing is a bit more complex. We'll want to automate all the standard scenarios, as shown above, and we also want to look for some very specific issues, such as race conditions. Ideally, we would be able to set up a closed system with fake accounts and ensure that, even if someone withdraws and deposits money rapidly from different locations, he never gets money or loses money that he shouldn't.

Above all, we need to prioritize security and reliability. People's accounts must always be protected, and we must make sure that money is always properly accounted for. No one wants to unexpectedly lose money! A good tester understands the system priorities.

C and C++

Knowledge Based: Solutions

13.1 *Write a method to print the last K lines of an input file using C++.*

pg 139

SOLUTION

One brute force way could be to count the number of lines (N) and then print from N-K to Nth line. But, this requires two reads of the file, which is unnecessarily costly. We need a solution which allows us to read just once and be able to print the last K lines.

We can allocate an array for all K lines and the last K lines we've read in the array. So, initially, our array has lines 0 through K, then 1 through K+1, then 2 through K+2, and so on. Each time that we read a new line, we purge the oldest line from the array.

But, you might ask, wouldn't this require shifting elements in the array, which is also very expensive? No, not if we do it correctly. Instead of shifting the array each time, we will use a circular array.

With a circular array, we always replace the oldest item when we read a new line. The oldest item is tracked in a separate variable, which adjusts as we add new items.

The following is an example of a circular array:

```
step 1 (initially): array = {a, b, c, d, e, f}. p = 0
step 2 (insert g):  array = {g, b, c, d, e, f}. p = 1
step 3 (insert h):  array = {g, h, c, d, e, f}. p = 2
step 4 (insert i):  array = {g, h, i, d, e, f}. p = 3
```

The code below implements this algorithm.

```
1   void printLast10Lines(char* fileName) {
2       const int K = 10;
3       ifstream file (fileName);
4       string L[K];
5       int size = 0;
6
7       /* read file line by line into circular array */
8       while (file.good()) {
9           getline(file, L[size % K]);
10          size++;
11      }
12
13      /* compute start of circular array, and the size of it */
14      int start = size > K ? (size % K) : 0;
15      int count = min(K, size);
16
17      /* print elements in the order they were read */
18      for (int i = 0; i < count; i++) {
19          cout << L[(start + i) % K] << endl;
20      }
21  }
```

This solution will require reading in the whole file, but only ten lines will be in memory at any given point.

13.2 *Compare and contrast a hash table and an STL map. How is a hash table implemented? If the number of inputs is small, which data structure options can be used instead of a hash table?*

pg 139

SOLUTION

In a hash table, a value is stored by calling a hash function on a key. Values are not stored in sorted order. Additionally, since hash tables use the key to find the index that will store the value, an insert or lookup can be done in amortized O(1) time (assuming few collisions in the hash table). In a hash table, one must also handle potential collisions. This is often done by chaining, which means to create a linked list of all the values whose keys map to a particular index.

An STL map inserts the key/value pairs into a binary search tree based on the keys. There is no need to handle collisions, and, since the tree is balanced, the insert and lookup time is guaranteed to be O(log N).

How is a hash table implemented?

A hash table is traditionally implemented with an array of linked lists. When we want to insert a key/value pair, we map the key to an index in the array using a hash function. The value is then inserted into the linked list at that position.

Note that the elements in a linked list at a particular index of the array do not have the same key. Rather, hashFunction(key) is the same for these values. Therefore, in order to retrieve the value for a specific key, we need to store in each node both the exact key and the value.

To summarize, the hash table will be implemented with an array of linked lists, where each node in the linked list holds two pieces of data: the value and the original key. In addition, we will want to note the following design criteria:

1. We want to use a good hash function to ensure that the keys are well distributed. If they are not well distributed, then we would get a lot of collisions and the speed to find an element would decline.

2. No matter how good our hash function is, we will still have collisions, so we need a method for handling them. This often means chaining via a linked list, but it's not the only way.

3. We may also wish to implement methods to dynamically increase or decrease the hash table size depending on capacity. For example, when the ratio of the number of elements to the table size exceeds a certain threshold, we may wish to increase the hash table size. This would mean creating a new hash table and transferring the

Solutions to Chapter 13 | C and C++

entries from the old table to the new table. Because this is an expensive operation, we want to be careful to not do it too often.

What can be used instead of a hash table, if the number of inputs is small?

You can use an STL map or a binary tree. Although this takes $O(\log(n))$ time, the number of inputs may be small enough to make this time negligible.

13.3 *How do virtual functions work in C++?*

pg 139

SOLUTION

A virtual function depends on a "vtable" or "Virtual Table." If any function of a class is declared to be virtual, a vtable is constructed which stores addresses of the virtual functions of this class. The compiler also adds a hidden vptr variable in all such classes which points to the vtable of that class. If a virtual function is not overridden in the derived class, the vtable of the derived class stores the address of the function in its parent class. The vtable is used to resolve the address of the function when the virtual function is called. Dynamic binding in C++ is performed through the vtable mechanism.

Thus, when we assign the derived class object to the base class pointer, the vptr variable points to the vtable of the derived class. This assignment ensures that the most derived virtual function gets called.

Consider the following code.

```
1   class Shape {
2     public:
3       int edge_length;
4       virtual int circumference () {
5         cout << "Circumference of Base Class\n";
6         return 0;
7       }
8   };
9   class Triangle: public Shape {
10    public:
11      int circumference () {
12        cout<< "Circumference of Triangle Class\n";
13        return 3 * edge_length;
14      }
15  };
16  void main() {
17    Shape * x = new Shape();
18    x->circumference(); // "Circumference of Base Class"
19    Shape *y = new Triangle();
20    y->circumference(); // "Circumference of Triangle Class"
21  }
```

388 | Cracking the Coding Interview | Solutions to C and C++

In the previous example, circumference is a virtual function in the Shape class, so it becomes virtual in each of the derived classes (Triangle, etc). C++ non-virtual function calls are resolved at compile time with static binding, while virtual function calls are resolved at runtime with dynamic binding.

13.4 *What is the difference between deep copy and shallow copy? Explain how you would use each.*

pg 139

SOLUTION

A shallow copy copies all the member values from one object to another. A deep copy does all this and also deep copies any pointer objects.

An example of shallow and deep copy is below.

```
1   struct Test {
2      char * ptr;
3   };
4
5   void shallow_copy(Test & src, Test & dest) {
6      dest.ptr = src.ptr;
7   }
8
9   void deep_copy(Test & src, Test & dest) {
10     dest.ptr = (char*)malloc(strlen(src.ptr) + 1);
11     strcpy(dest.ptr, src.ptr);
12  }
```

Note that shallow_copy may cause a lot of programming runtime errors, especially with the creation and deletion of objects. Shallow copy should be used very carefully and only when a programmer really understands what he wants to do. In most cases, shallow copy is used when there is a need to pass information about a complex structure without actual duplication of data. One must also be careful with destruction of objects in a shallow copy.

In real life, shallow copy is rarely used. Deep copy should be used in most cases, especially when the size of the copied structure is small.

13.5 *What is the significance of the keyword "volatile" in C?*

pg 140

SOLUTION

The keyword volatile informs the compiler that the value of variable it is applied to can change from the outside, without any update done by the code. This may be done by the operating system, the hardware, or another thread. Because the value can change unexpectedly, the compiler will therefore reload the value each time from memory.

A volatile integer can be declared by either of the following statements:

```
int volatile x;
volatile int x;
```

To declare a pointer to a volatile integer, we do the following:

```
volatile int * x;
int volatile * x;
```

A volatile pointer to non-volatile data is rare, but can be done.

```
int * volatile x;
```

If you wanted to declare a volatile variable pointer for volatile memory (both pointer address and memory contained are volatile), you would do the following:

```
int volatile * volatile x;
```

Volatile variables are not optimized, which can be very useful. Imagine this function:

```
1  int opt = 1;
2  void Fn(void) {
3    start:
4      if (opt == 1) goto start;
5      else break;
6  }
```

At first glance, our code appears to loop infinitely. The compiler may try to optimize it to:

```
1  void Fn(void) {
2    start:
3      int opt = 1;
4      if (true)
5        goto start;
6  }
```

This becomes an infinite loop. However, an external operation might write '0' to the location of variable opt, thus breaking the loop.

To prevent the compiler from performing such optimization, we want to signal that another element of the system could change the variable. We do this using the volatile keyword, as shown below.

```
1  volatile int opt = 1;
2  void Fn(void) {
3    start:
4      if (opt == 1) goto start;
5      else break;
6  }
```

Volatile variables are also useful when multi-threaded programs have global variables and any thread can modify these shared variables. We may not want optimization on these variables.

13.6 *Why does a destructor in base class need to be declared virtual?*

pg 140

SOLUTION

Let's think about why we have virtual methods to start with. Suppose we have the following code:

```
1   class Foo {
2     public:
3       void f();
4   };
5
6   class Bar : public Foo {
7     public:
8       void f();
9   }
10
11  Foo * p = new Bar();
12  p->f();
```

Calling p->f() will result in a call to Foo::f(). This is because p is a pointer to Foo, and f() is not virtual.

To ensure that p->f() will invoke the most derived implementation of f(), we need to declare f() to be a virtual function.

Now, let's go back to our destructor. Destructors are used to clean up memory and resources. If Foo's destructor were not virtual, then Foo's destructor would be called, even when p is *really* of type Bar.

This is why we declare destructors to be virtual; we want to ensure that the destructor for the most derived class is called.

13.7 *Write a method that takes a pointer to a Node structure as a parameter and returns a complete copy of the passed in data structure. The Node data structure contains two pointers to other Nodes.*

pg 140

SOLUTION

The algorithm will maintain a mapping from a node address in the original structure to the corresponding node in the new structure. This mapping will allow us to discover previously copied nodes during a traditional depth first traversal of the structure. Traversals often mark visited nodes—the mark can take many forms and does not necessarily need to be stored in the node.

Thus, we have a simple recursive algorithm:

```
1  typedef map<Node*, Node*> NodeMap;
2
3  Node * copy_recursive(Node * cur, NodeMap & nodeMap) {
4      if(cur == NULL) {
5          return NULL;
6      }
7
8      NodeMap::iterator i = nodeMap.find(cur);
9      if (i != nodeMap.end()) {
10         // we've been here before, return the copy
11         return i->second;
12     }
13
14     Node * node = new Node;
15     nodeMap[cur] = node; // map current before traversing links
16     node->ptr1 = copy_recursive(cur->ptr1, nodeMap);
17     node->ptr2 = copy_recursive(cur->ptr2, nodeMap);
18     return node;
19 }
20
21 Node * copy_structure(Node * root) {
22     NodeMap nodeMap; // we will need an empty map
23     return copy_recursive(root, nodeMap);
24 }
```

13.8 *Write a smart pointer class. A smart pointer is a data type, usually implemented with templates, that simulates a pointer while also providing automatic garbage collection. It automatically counts the number of references to a SmartPointer<T*> object and frees the object of type T when the reference count hits zero.*

pg 140

SOLUTION

A smart pointer is the same as a normal pointer, but it provides safety via automatic memory management. It avoids issues like dangling pointers, memory leaks and allocation failures. The smart pointer must maintain a single reference count for all references to a given object.

This is one of those problems that seems, at first glance, pretty overwhelming, especially if you're not a C++ expert. One useful way to approach the problem is to divide the problem into two parts: (1) outline the pseudocode and approach and then (2) implement the detailed code.

In terms of the approach, we need a reference count variable that is incremented when we add a new reference to the object and decremented when we remove a reference. The code should look something like the below pseudocode:

```
1   template <class T> class SmartPointer {
2     /* The smart pointer class needs pointers to both the object
3      * itself and to the ref count. These must be pointers, rather
4      * than the actual object or ref count value, since the goal of
5      * a smart pointer is that the reference count is tracked across
6      * multiple smart pointers to one object. */
7     T * obj;
8     unsigned * ref_count;
9   }
```

We know we need constructors and a single destructor for this class, so let's add those first.

```
1   SmartPointer(T * object) {
2     /* We want to set the value of T * obj, and set the reference
3      * counter to 1. */
4   }
5
6   SmartPointer(SmarterPointer<T>& sptr) {
7     /* This constructor creates a new smart pointer that points to
8      * an existing object. We will need to first set obj and
9      * ref_count to pointer to sptr's obj and ref_count. Then,
10     * because we created a new reference to obj, we need to
11     * increment ref_count. */
12  }
13
14  ~SmartPointer(SmarterPointer<T> sptr) {
15    /* We are destroying a reference to the object. Decrement
16     * ref_count. If ref_count is 0, then free the memory created by
17     * the integer and destroy the object. */
18  }
```

There's one additional way that references can be created: by setting one SmartPointer equal to another. We'll want to override the equal operator to handle this, but for now, let's sketch the code like this.

```
19  onSetEquals(SmartPointer<T> ptr1, SmartPointer<T> ptr2) {
20    /* If ptr1 has an existing value, decrement its reference count.
21     * Then, copy the pointers to obj and ref_count over. Finally,
22     * since we created a new reference, we need to increment
23     * ref_count. */
24  }
```

Getting just the approach, even without filling in the complicated C++ syntax, would count for a lot. Finishing out the code is now just a matter of filling the details.

```
1   template <class T> class SmartPointer {
2     public:
3       SmartPointer(T * ptr) {
4         ref = ptr;
5         ref_count = (unsigned*)malloc(sizeof(unsigned));
6         *ref_count = 1;
7       }
```

```
8
9      SmartPointer(SmartPointer<T> & sptr) {
10         ref = sptr.ref;
11         ref_count = sptr.ref_count;
12         ++(*ref_count);
13     }
14
15     /* Override the equal operator, so that when you set one smart
16      * pointer equal to another the old smart pointer has its
17      * reference count decremented and the new smart pointer has its
18      * reference count incrememented. */
19     SmartPointer<T> & operator=(SmartPointer<T> & sptr) {
20         if (this == &sptr) return *this;
21
22         /* If already assigned to an object, remove one reference. */
23         if (*ref_count > 0) {
24            remove();
25         }
26
27         ref = sptr.ref;
28         ref_count = sptr.ref_count;
29         ++(*ref_count);
30         return *this;
31     }
32
33     ~SmartPointer() {
34         remove(); // Remove one reference to object.
35     }
36
37     T getValue() {
38         return *ref;
39     }
40
41   protected:
42     void remove() {
43         --(*ref_count);
44         if (*ref_count == 0) {
45            delete ref;
46            free(ref_count);
47            ref = NULL;
48            ref_count = NULL;
49         }
50     }
51
52     T * ref;
53     unsigned * ref_count;
54 };
```

The code for this problem is complicated, and you probably wouldn't be expected to
complete it flawlessly.

13.9 *Write an aligned malloc and free function that supports allocating memory such that the memory address returned is divisible by a specific power of two.*

pg 140

SOLUTION

Typically, with `malloc`, we do not have control over where the memory is allocated within the heap. We just get a pointer to a block of memory which could start at any memory address within the heap.

We need to work with these constraints by requesting enough memory that we can return a memory address which is divisible by the desired value.

Suppose we are requesting a 100-byte chunk of memory, and we want it to start at a memory address that is a multiple of 16. How much extra memory would we need to allocate to ensure that we can do so? We would need to allocate an extra 15 bytes. With these 15 bytes, plus another 100 bytes right after that sequence, we know that we would have a memory address divisible by 16 with space for 100 bytes.

We could then do something like:

```
1   void* aligned_malloc(size_t required_bytes, size_t alignment) {
2       int offset = alignment - 1;
3       void* p = (void*) malloc(required_bytes + offset);
4       void* q = (void*) (((size_t)(p) + offset) & ~(alignment - 1));
5       return q;
6   }
```

Line 4 is a bit tricky, so let's discuss it. Suppose `alignment` is 16. We know that somewhere in the first 16 bytes there is a memory address divisible by 16. By doing (p1 + 16) & 11..10000, we are moving q back to a memory address divisible by 16. Doing an AND of the last three bits of the memory address with 0000 guarantees us that this new value will be divisible by 16.

This solution is *almost* perfect, except for one big issue: how do we free the memory?

We've allocated an extra 15 bytes, in the above example, and we need to free them when we free the "real" memory.

We can do this by storing, in this "extra" memory, the address of where the full memory block begins. We will store this immediately before the aligned memory block. Of course, this means that we now need to allocate even *more* extra memory to ensure that we have enough space to store this pointer.

Specifically, to bytes aligned with `alignment`, we will need to allocate an additional `alignment - 1 + sizeof(void*)` bytes.

The code below implements this approach.

```
1   void* aligned_malloc(size_t required_bytes, size_t alignment) {
2       void* p1;   // original block
3       void** p2;  // aligned block
```

```
4      int offset = alignment - 1 + sizeof(void*);
5      if ((p1 = (void*)malloc(required_bytes + offset)) == NULL) {
6         return NULL;
7      }
8      p2 = (void**)(((size_t)(p1) + offset) & ~(alignment - 1));
9      p2[-1] = p1;
10     return p2;
11  }
12
13  void aligned_free(void *p2) {
14     /* for consistency, we use the same names as aligned_malloc*/.
15     void* p1 = ((void**)p2)[-1];
16     free(p1);
17  }
```

Let's look at how aligned_free works. The aligned_free method is passed in p2 (the same p2 as we had in aligned_malloc). We know, however, that the value of p1 (which points to the beginning of the full memory block) was stored just before p2.

If we treat p2 as a void** (or an array of void*'s), we can just look at the index - 1 to retrieve p1. Then, by freeing p1, we have deallocated the whole memory block.

13.10 *Write a function in C called my2DAlloc which allocates a two-dimensional array. Minimize the number of calls to malloc and make sure that the memory is accessible by the notation arr[i][j].*

pg 140

SOLUTION

As you may know, a two-dimensional array is essentially an array of arrays. Since we use pointers with arrays, we can use double pointers to create a double array.

The basic idea is to create a one-dimensional array of pointers. Then, for each array index, we create a new one-dimensional array. This gives us a two-dimensional array that can be accessed via array indices.

The code below implements this.

```
1   int** my2DAlloc(int rows, int cols) {
2      int** rowptr;
3      int i;
4      rowptr = (int**) malloc(rows * sizeof(int*));
5      for (i = 0; i < rows; i++) {
6         rowptr[i] = (int*) malloc(cols * sizeof(int));
7      }
8      return rowptr;
9   }
```

Observe how, in the above code, we've told rowptr where exactly each index should point. The below diagram represents how this memory is allocated.

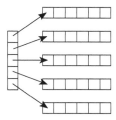

To free this memory, we cannot simply call free on rowptr. We need to make sure to free not only the memory from the first malloc call, but also each subsequent call.

```
1   void my2DDealloc(int** rowptr, int rows) {
2       for (i = 0; i < rows; i++) {
3           free(rowptr[i]);
4       }
5       free(rowptr);
6   }
```

Rather than allocating the memory in many different blocks (one block for each row, plus one block to specify *where* each row is located), we can allocate this in a consecutive block of memory. Conceptually, for a two dimensional array with five rows and six columns, this would look like the following.

If it seems strange to view the 2D array like this (and it probably does), remember that this is fundamentally no different than the first diagram. The only difference is that the memory is in a contiguous block, so our first five (in this example) elements point elsewhere in the same block of memory.

To implement this solution, we do the following.

```
1   int** my2DAlloc(int rows, int cols) {
2       int i;
3       int header = rows * sizeof(int*);
4       int data = rows * cols * sizeof(int);
5       int** rowptr = (int**)malloc(header + data);
6       if (rowptr == NULL) {
7           return NULL;
8       }
9
10      int* buf = (int*) (rowptr + rows);
11      for (i = 0; i < rows; i++) {
12          rowptr[i] = buf + i * cols;
13      }
14      return rowptr;
15  }
```

You should carefully observe what is happening on lines 11 through 13. If there are five rows of six columns each, `array[0]` will point to `array[5]`, `array[1]` will point to `array[11]`, and so on.

Then, when we actually call `array[1][3]`, the computer looks up `array[1]`, which is a pointer to another spot in memory—specifically, a pointer to `array[5]`. This element is treated as its own array, and we then get the third (zero-indexed) element from it.

Constructing the array in a single call to `malloc` has the added benefit of allowing disposal of the array with a single `free` call rather than using a special function to free the remaining data blocks.

Java

Knowledge Based: Solutions

Chapter 14

Solutions to Chapter 14 | Java

14.1 *In terms of inheritance, what is the effect of keeping a constructor private?*

pg 145

SOLUTION

Declaring the constructor private will ensure that no one outside of the class can directly instantiate the class. In this case, the only way to create an instance of the class is to provide a static public method, as is done when using the Factory Method Pattern.

Additionally, because the constructor is private, the class also cannot be inherited.

14.2 *In Java, does the finally block get executed if we insert a return statement inside the try block of a try-catch-finally?*

pg 145

SOLUTION

Yes, it will get executed. The `finally` block gets executed when the `try` block exits. Even when we attempt to exit within the `try` block (via a `return` statement, a `continue` statement, a `break` statement or any exception), the `finally` block will still be executed.

Note that there are some cases in which the `finally` block will not get executed, such as the following:

- If the virtual machine exits during `try/catch` block execution.
- If the thread which is executing the `try/catch` block gets killed.

14.3 *What is the difference between final, finally, and finalize?*

pg 145

SOLUTIONS

Despite their similar sounding names, `final`, `finally` and `finalize` have very different purposes. To speak in very general terms, `final` is used to control whether a variable, method, or class is "changeable." The `finally` keyword is used in a `try/catch` block to ensure that a segment of code is always executed. The `finalize()` method is called by the garbage collector once it determines that no more references exist.

Further detail on these keywords and methods is provided below.

final

The final statement has a different meaning depending on its context.

- When applied to a variable (primitive): The value of the variable cannot change.
- When applied to a variable (reference): The reference variable cannot point to any other object on the heap.
- When applied to a method: The method cannot be overridden.
- When applied to a class: The class cannot be subclassed.

finally

There is an optional finally block after the try block or after the catch block. Statements in the finally block will always be executed (except if Java Virtual Machine exits from the try block). The finally block is used to write the clean-up code.

finalize()

The finalize() method is called by the garbage collector when it determines that no more references exist. It is typically used to clean up resources, such as closing a file.

14.4 *Explain the difference between templates in C++ and generics in Java.*

pg 145

SOLUTION

Many programmers consider the concepts of templates and generics to be equivalent simply because both allow you to do something along the lines of List<String>. But, *how* each language does this, and *why*, varies significantly.

The implementation of Java generics is rooted in an idea of "type erasure." This technique eliminates the parameterized types when source code is translated to the Java Virtual Machine (JVM) byte code.

For example, suppose you have the Java code below:

```
1   Vector<String>  vector = new Vector<String>();
2   vector.add(new String("hello"));
3   String  str = vector.get(0);
```

During compilation, this code is re-written into:

```
1   Vector vector = new Vector();
2   vector.add(new String("hello"));
3   String  str = (String) vector.get(0);
```

The use of Java generics didn't really change much about our capabilities; it just made things a bit prettier. For this reason, Java generics are sometimes called "syntactic sugar."

This is quite different from C++. In C++, templates are essentially a glorified macro set, with the compiler creating a new copy of the template code for each type. Proof of this is in the fact that an instance of MyClass<Foo> will not share a static variable with

MyClass<Bar>. Two instances of MyClass<Foo>, however, will share a static variable.

To illustrate this, consider the code below:

```
1   /*** MyClass.h ***/
2   template<class T> class MyClass {
3     public:
4       static int val;
5       MyClass(int v) { val = v; }
6   };
7
8   /*** MyClass.cpp ***/
9   template<typename T>
10  int MyClass<T>::bar;
11
12  template class MyClass<Foo>;
13  template class MyClass<Bar>;
14
15  /*** main.cpp ***/
16  MyClass<Foo> * foo1 = new MyClass<Foo>(10);
17  MyClass<Foo> * foo2 = new MyClass<Foo>(15);
18  MyClass<Bar> * bar1 = new MyClass<Bar>(20);
19  MyClass<Bar> * bar2 = new MyClass<Bar>(35);
20
21  int f1 = foo1->val; // will equal 15
22  int f2 = foo2->val; // will equal 15
23  int b1 = bar1->val; // will equal 35
24  int b2 = bar2->val; // will equal 35
```

In Java, static variables would be shared across instances of MyClass, regardless of the different type parameters.

Because of their architectural differences, Java generics and C++ templates have a number of other differences. These include:

- C++ templates can use primitive types, like int. Java cannot and must instead use Integer.

- In Java, you can restrict the template's type parameters to be of a certain type. For instance, you might use generics to implement a CardDeck and specify that the type parameter must extend from CardGame.

- In C++, the type parameter can be instantiated, whereas Java does not support this.

- In Java, the type parameter (i.e., the Foo in MyClass<Foo>) cannot be used for static methods and variables, since these would be shared between MyClass<Foo> and MyClass<Bar>. In C++, these classes are different, so the type parameter can be used for static methods and variables.

- In Java, all instances of MyClass, regardless of their type parameters, are the same type. The type parameters are erased at runtime. In C++, instances with different type parameters are different types.

Remember that although Java generics and C++ templates look the same in many ways, they are very different.

14.5 *Explain what object reflection is in Java and why it is useful.*

pg 145

SOLUTION

Object Reflection is a feature in Java which provides a way to get reflective information about Java classes and objects, and perform operations such as:

1. Getting information about the methods and fields present inside the class at runtime.

2. Creating a new instance of a class.

3. Getting and setting the object fields directly by getting field reference, regardless of what the access modifier is.

The code below offers an example of object reflection.

```
1   /* Parameters */
2   Object[] doubleArgs = new Object[] { 4.2, 3.9 };
3
4   /* Get class */
5   Class rectangleDefinition = Class.forName("MyProj.Rectangle");
6
7   /* Equivalent: Rectangle rectangle = new Rectangle(4.2, 3.9); */
8   Class[] doubleArgsClass = new Class[] {double.class, double.class};
9   Constructor doubleArgsConstructor =
10      rectangleDefinition.getConstructor(doubleArgsClass);
11  Rectangle rectangle =
12      (Rectangle) doubleArgsConstructor.newInstance(doubleArgs);
13
14  /* Equivalent: Double area = rectangle.area(); */
15  Method m = rectangleDefinition.getDeclaredMethod("area");
16  Double area = (Double) m.invoke(rectangle);
```

This code does the equivalent of:

```
1   Rectangle rectangle = new Rectangle(4.2, 3.9);
2   Double area = rectangle.area();
```

Why Is Object Reflection Useful?

Of course, it doesn't seem very useful in the above example, but reflection can be very useful in particular cases.

Object reflection is useful for three main reasons:

Solutions to Chapter 14 | Java

1. It helps in observing or manipulating the runtime behavior of applications.

2. It can help in debugging or testing programs, as we have direct access to methods, constructors, and fields.

3. We can call methods by name when we don't know the method in advance. For example, we may let the user pass in a class name, parameters for the constructor, and a method name. We can then use this information to create an object and call a method. Doing these operations without reflection would require a complex series of if-statements, if it's possible at all.

14.6 *Implement a CircularArray class that supports an array-like data structure which can be efficiently rotated. The class should use a generic type, and should support iteration via the standard for (Obj o : circularArray) notation.*

pg 145

SOLUTION

This problem really has two parts to it. First, we need to implement the CircularArray class. Second, we need to support iteration. We will address these parts separately.

Implementing the CircularArray class

One way to implement the CircularArray class is to actually shift the elements each time we call rotate(int shiftRight). Doing this is, of course, not very efficient.

Instead, we can just create a member variable head which points to what should be conceptually viewed as the start of the circular array. Rather than shifting around the elements in the array, we just increment head by shiftRight.

The code below implements this approach.

```
1   public class CircularArray<T> {
2       private T[] items;
3       private int head = 0;
4
5       public CircularArray(int size) {
6           items = (T[]) new Object[size];
7       }
8
9       private int convert(int index) {
10          if (index < 0) {
11              index += items.length;
12          }
13          return (head + index) % items.length;
14      }
15
16      public void rotate(int shiftRight) {
17          head = convert(shiftRight);
```

```
18    }
19
20    public T get(int i) {
21       if (i < 0 || i >= items.length) {
22          throw new java.lang.IndexOutOfBoundsException("...");
23       }
24       return items[convert(i)];
25    }
26
27    public void set(int i, T item) {
28       items[convert(i)] = item;
29    }
30 }
```

There are a number of things here which are easy to make mistakes on, such as:

- We cannot create an array of the generic type. Instead, we must either cast the array or define items to be of type List<T>. For simplicity, we have done the former.

- The % operator will return a negative value when we do negValue % posVal. For example, -8 % 3 is -2. This is different from how mathematicians would define the modulus function. We must add items.length to a negative index to get the correct positive result.

- We need to be sure to consistently convert the raw index to the rotated index. For this reason, we have implemented a convert function that is used by other methods. Even the rotate function uses convert. This is a good example of code reuse.

Now that we have the basic code for CircularArray out of the way, we can focus on implementing an iterator.

Implementing the Iterator Interface

The second part of this question asks us to implement the CircularArray class such that we can do the following:

```
1  CircularArray<String> array = ...
2  for (String s : array) { ... }
```

Implementing this requires implementing the Iterator interface.

To implement the Iterator interface, we need to do the following:

- Modify the CircularArray<T> definition to add implements Iterable<T>. This will also require us to add an iterator() method to CircularArray<T>.

- Create a CircularArrayIterator<T> which implements Iterator<T>. This will also require us to implement, in the CircularArrayIterator, the methods hasNext(), next(), and remove().

Once we've done the above items, the for loop will "magically" work.

In the code below, we have removed the aspects of CircularArray which were iden-

Solutions to Chapter 14 | Java

tical to the earlier implementation.

```
1   public class CircularArray<T> implements Iterable<T> {
2       ...
3       public Iterator<T> iterator() {
4           return new CircularArrayIterator<T>(this);
5       }
6
7       private class CircularArrayIterator<TI> implements Iterator<TI>{
8           /* current reflects the offset from the rotated head, not
9            * from the actual start of the raw array. */
10          private int _current = -1;
11          private TI[] _items;
12
13          public CircularArrayIterator(CircularArray<TI> array){
14              _items = array.items;
15          }
16
17          @Override
18          public boolean hasNext() {
19              return _current < items.length - 1;
20          }
21
22          @Override
23          public TI next() {
24              _current++;
25              TI item = (TI) _items[convert(_current)];
26              return item;
27          }
28
29          @Override
30          public void remove() {
31              throw new UnsupportedOperationException("...");
32          }
33      }
34  }
```

In the above code, note that the first iteration of the for loop will call hasNext() and then next(). Be very sure that your implementation will return the correct values here.

When you get a problem like this one in an interview, there's a good chance you don't remember exactly what the various methods and interfaces are called. In this case, work through the problem as well as you can. If you can reason out what sorts of methods one might need, that alone will show a good degree of competency.

Databases

Knowledge Based: Solutions   **Chapter 15**

Solutions to Chapter 15 | Databases

Questions 1 through 3 refer to the below database schema:

Apartments		Buildings		Tenants	
AptID	int	BuildingID	int	TenantID	int
UnitNumber	varchar	ComplexID	int	TenantName	varchar
BuildingID	int	BuildingName	varchar		
		Address	varchar		

Complexes		AptTenants		Requests	
ComplexID	int	TenantID	int	RequestID	int
ComplexName	varchar	AptID	int	Status	varchar
				AptID	int
				Description	varchar

Note that each apartment can have multiple tenants, and each tenant can have multiple apartments. Each apartment belongs to one building, and each building belongs to one complex.

15.1 *Write a SQL query to get a list of tenants who are renting more than one apartment.*

pg 152

SOLUTION

To implement this, we can use the HAVING and GROUP BY clauses and then perform an INNER JOIN with Tenants.

```
1   SELECT TenantName
2   FROM Tenants
3   INNER JOIN
4     (SELECT TenantID
5      FROM AptTenants
6      GROUP BY TenantID
7      HAVING count(*) > 1) C
8   ON Tenants.TenantID = C.TenantID
```

Whenever you write a GROUP BY clause in an interview (or in real life), make sure that anything in the SELECT clause is either an aggregate function or contained within the GROUP BY clause.

15.2 *Write a SQL query to get a list of all buildings and the number of open requests (Requests in which status equals 'Open').*

pg 152

SOLUTION

This problem uses a straightforward join of Requests and Apartments to get a list of building IDs and the number of open requests. Once we have this list, we join it again with the Buildings table.

```
1   SELECT BuildingName, ISNULL(Count, 0) as 'Count'
2   FROM Buildings
3   LEFT JOIN
4     (SELECT Apartments.BuildingID, count(*) as 'Count'
5     FROM Requests INNER JOIN Apartments
6     ON Requests.AptID = Apartments.AptID
7     WHERE Requests.Status = 'Open'
8     GROUP BY Apartments.BuildingID) ReqCounts
9   ON ReqCounts.BuildingID = Buildings.BuildingID
```

Queries like this that utilize sub-queries should be thoroughly tested, even when coding by hand. It may be useful to test the inner part of the query first, and then test the outer part.

15.3 *Building #11 is undergoing a major renovation. Implement a query to close all requests from apartments in this building.*

pg 152

SOLUTION

UPDATE queries, like SELECT queries, can have WHERE clauses. To implement this query, we get a list of all apartment IDs within building #11 and the list of update requests from those apartments.

```
1   UPDATE Requests
2   SET Status = 'Closed'
3   WHERE AptID IN
4     (SELECT AptID
5     FROM Apartments
6     WHERE BuildingID = 11)
```

15.4 *What are the different types of joins? Please explain how they differ and why certain types are better in certain situations.*

pg 152

SOLUTION

JOIN is used to combine the results of two tables. To perform a JOIN, each of the tables must have at least one field that will be used to find matching records from the other table. The join type defines which records will go into the result set.

Let's take for example two tables: one table lists the "regular" beverages, and another lists the calorie-free beverages. Each table has two fields: the beverage name and its product code. The "code" field will be used to perform the record matching.

Regular Beverages:

Name	Code
Budweiser	BUDWEISER
Coca-Cola	COCACOLA
Pepsi	PEPSI

Calorie-Free Beverages:

Name	Code
Diet Coca-Cola	COCACOLA
Fresca	FRESCA
Diet Pepsi	PEPSI
Pepsi Light	PEPSI
Purified Water	Water

If we wanted to join Beverage with Calorie-Free Beverages, we would have many options. These are discussed below.

- INNER JOIN: The result set would contain only the data where the criteria match. In our example, we would get three records: one with a COCACOLA code and two with PEPSI codes.

- OUTER JOIN: An OUTER JOIN will always contain the results of INNER JOIN, but it may also contain some records that have no matching record in the other table. OUTER JOINs are divided into the following subtypes:

  » LEFT OUTER JOIN, or simply LEFT JOIN: The result will contain all records from the left table. If no matching records were found in the right table, then its fields will contain the NULL values. In our example, we would get four records. In addition to INNER JOIN results, BUDWEISER would be listed, because it was in the left table.

  » RIGHT OUTER JOIN, or simply RIGHT JOIN: This type of join is the opposite of LEFT JOIN. It will contain every record from the right table; the missing fields from the left table will be NULL. Note that if we have two tables, A and B, then we can say that the statement A LEFT JOIN B is equivalent to the statement B RIGHT JOIN A. In our example above, we will get five records. In addition to INNER JOIN results, FRESCA and WATER records will be listed.

  » FULL OUTER JOIN: This type of join combines the results of the LEFT and RIGHT JOINS. All records from both tables will be included in the result set, regardless of whether or not a matching record exists in the other table. If no matching record was found, then the corresponding result fields will have a NULL value. In our example, we will get six records.

15.5 *What is denormalization? Explain the pros and cons.*

pg 152

SOLUTION

Denormalization is a database optimization technique in which we add redundant data to one or more tables. This can help us avoid costly joins in a relational database.

By contrast, in a traditional normalized database, we store data in separate logical tables and attempt to minimize redundant data. We may strive to have only one copy of each piece of data in the database.

For example, in a normalized database, we might have a Courses table and a Teachers table. Each entry in Courses would store the teacherID for a Course but not the teacherName. When we need to retrieve a list of all Courses with the Teacher name, we would do a join between these two tables.

In some ways, this is great; if a teacher changes his or her name, we only have to update the name in one place.

The drawback, however, is that if the tables are large, we may spend an unnecessarily long time doing joins on tables.

Denormalization, then, strikes a different compromise. Under denormalization, we decide that we're okay with some redundancy and some extra effort to update the database in order to get the efficiency advantages of fewer joins.

Cons of Denormalization	Pros of Denormalization
Updates and inserts are more expensive.	Retrieving data is faster since we do fewer joins.
Denormalization can make update and insert code harder to write.	Queries to retrieve can be simpler (and therefore less likely to have bugs), since we need to look at fewer tables.
Data may be inconsistent. Which is the "correct" value for a piece of data?	
Data redundancy necessitates more storage.	

In a system that demands scalability, like that of any major tech companies, we almost always use elements of both normalized and denormalized databases.

15.6 *Draw an entity-relationship diagram for a database with companies, people, and professionals (people who work for companies).*

pg 152

SOLUTION

People who work for Companies are Professionals. So, there is an ISA ("is a") relationship between People and Professionals (or we could say that a Professional is derived from People).

Each Professional has additional information such as degree and work experiences in addition to the properties derived from People.

A Professional works for one company at a time, but Companies can hire many Professionals. So, there is a many-to-one relationship between Professionals and Companies. This "Works For" relationship can store attributes such as an employee's start date and salary. These attributes are defined only when we relate a Professional with a Company.

A Person can have multiple phone numbers, which is why Phone is a multi-valued attribute.

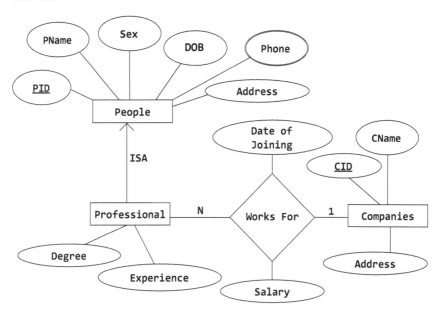

15.7 *Imagine a simple database storing information for students' grades. Design what this database might look like and provide a SQL query to return a list of the honor roll students (top 10%), sorted by their grade point average.*

pg 152

SOLUTION

In a simplistic database, we'll have at least three objects: `Students`, `Courses`, and `CourseEnrollment`. `Students` will have at least a student name and ID and will likely have other personal information. `Courses` will contain the course name and ID and will likely contain the course description, professor, and other information. `CourseEnrollment` will pair `Students` and `Courses` and will also contain a field for `CourseGrade`.

Students	
StudentID	int
StudentName	varchar(100)
Address	varchar(500)

Courses	
CourseID	int
CourseName	varchar(100)
ProfessorID	int

CourseEnrollment	
CourseID	int
StudentID	int
Grade	float
Term	int

This database could get arbitrarily more complicated if we wanted to add in professor information, billing information, and other data.

Using the Microsoft SQL Server TOP ... PERCENT function, we might (incorrectly) first try a query like this:

```
1   /* Incorrect Code */
2   SELECT  TOP 10 PERCENT AVG(CourseEnrollment.Grade) AS GPA,
3       CourseEnrollment.StudentID
4   FROM CourseEnrollment
5   GROUP BY CourseEnrollment.StudentID
6   ORDER BY AVG(CourseEnrollment.Grade)
```

The problem with the above code is that it will return literally the top 10% of rows, when sorted by GPA. Imagine a scenario in which there are 100 students, and the top 15 students all have 4.0 GPAs. The above function will only return 10 of those students, which is not really what we want. In case of a tie, we want to include the students who tied for the top 10% -- even if this means that our honor roll includes more than 10% of the class.

To correct this issue, we can build something similar to this query, but instead first get the GPA cut off.

```
1   DECLARE @GPACutOff float;
2   SET @GPACutOff = (SELECT min(GPA) as 'GPAMin'
3       FROM (
4           SELECT TOP 10 PERCENT AVG(CourseEnrollment.Grade) AS GPA
5           FROM CourseEnrollment
6           GROUP BY CourseEnrollment.StudentID
7           ORDER BY GPA desc)
8       Grades);
```

Then, once we have @GPACutOff defined, selecting the students with at least this GPA is reasonably straightforward.

```
1   SELECT StudentName, GPA
2   FROM (
3       SELECT AVG(CourseEnrollment.Grade) AS GPA,
4               CourseEnrollment.StudentID
5       FROM CourseEnrollment
6       GROUP BY CourseEnrollment.StudentID
7       HAVING AVG(CourseEnrollment.Grade) >= @GPACutOff) Honors
8   INNER JOIN Students ON Honors.StudentID = Student.StudentID
```

Be very careful about what implicit assumptions you make. If you look at the above database description, what potentially incorrect assumption do you see? One is that each course can only be taught by one professor. At some schools, courses may be taught by multiple professors.

However, you *will* need to make some assumptions, or you'd drive yourself crazy. Which assumptions you make is less important than just recognizing *that* you made assumptions. Incorrect assumptions, both in the real world and in an interview, can be dealt with *as long as they are acknowledged*.

Remember, additionally, that there's a trade-off between flexibility and complexity. Creating a system in which a course can have multiple professors does increase the database's flexibility, but it also increases its complexity. If we tried to make our database flexible to every possible situation, we'd wind up with something hopelessly complex.

Make your design reasonably flexible, and state any other assumptions or constraints. This goes for not just database design, but object-oriented design and programming in general.

Threads and Locks

Knowledge Based: Solutions

Chapter 16

Solutions to Chapter 16 | Threads and Locks

16.1 *What's the difference between a thread and a process?*

pg 159

SOLUTION

Processes and threads are related to each other but are fundamentally different.

A process can be thought of as an instance of a program in execution. A process is an independent entity to which system resources (e.g., CPU time and memory) are allocated. Each process is executed in a separate address space, and one process cannot access the variables and data structures of another process. If a process wishes to access another process' resources, inter-process communications have to be used. These include pipes, files, sockets, and other forms.

A thread exists within a process and shares the process' resources (including its heap space). Multiple threads within the same process will share the same heap space. This is very different from processes, which cannot directly access the memory of another process. Each thread still has its own registers and its own stack, but other threads can read and write the heap memory.

A thread is a particular execution path of a process. When one thread modifies a process resource, the change is immediately visible to sibling threads.

16.2 *How would you measure the time spent in a context switch?*

pg 159

SOLUTION

This is a tricky question, but let's start with a possible solution.

A context switch is the time spent switching between two processes (i.e., bringing a waiting process into execution and sending an executing process into waiting/terminated state). This happens in multitasking. The operating system must bring the state information of waiting processes into memory and save the state information of the currently running process.

In order to solve this problem, we would like to record the timestamps of the last and first instruction of the swapping processes. The context switch time is the difference in the timestamps between the two processes.

Let's take an easy example: Assume there are only two processes, P_1 and P_2.

P_1 is executing and P_2 is waiting for execution. At some point, the operating system must swap P_1 and P_2—let's assume it happens at the Nth instruction of P_1. If $t_{x,k}$ indicates the timestamp in microseconds of the kth instruction of process x, then the context switch would take $t_{2,1}$ - $t_{1,n}$ microseconds.

The tricky part is this: how do we know when this swapping occurs? We cannot, of course, record the timestamp of every instruction in the process.

Another issue is that swapping is governed by the scheduling algorithm of the operating system and there may be many kernel level threads which are also doing context switches. Other processes could be contending for the CPU or the kernel handling interrupts. The user does not have any control over these extraneous context switches. For instance, if at time $t_{1,n}$ the kernel decides to handle an interrupt, then the context switch time would be overstated.

In order to overcome these obstacles, we must first construct an environment such that after P_1 executes, the task scheduler immediately selects P_2 to run. This may be accomplished by constructing a data channel, such as a pipe, between P_1 and P_2 and having the two processes play a game of ping-pong with a data token.

That is, let's allow P_1 to be the initial sender and P_2 to be the receiver. Initially, P_2 is blocked (sleeping) as it awaits the data token. When P_1 executes, it delivers the token over the data channel to P_2 and immediately attempts to read a response token. However, since P_2 has not yet had a chance to run, no such token is available for P_1 and the process is blocked. This relinquishes the CPU.

A context switch results and the task scheduler must select another process to run. Since P_2 is now in a ready-to-run state, it is a desirable candidate to be selected by the task scheduler for execution. When P_2 runs, the roles of P_1 and P_2 are swapped. P_2 is now acting as the sender and P_1 as the blocked receiver. The game ends when P_2 returns the token to P_1.

To summarize, an iteration of the game is played with the following steps:

1. P_2 blocks awaiting data from P_1.

2. P_1 marks the start time.

3. P_1 sends token to P_2.

4. P_1 attempts to read a response token from P_2. This induces a context switch.

5. P_2 is scheduled and receives the token.

6. P_2 sends a response token to P_1.

7. P_2 attempts read a response token from P_1. This induces a context switch.

8. P_1 is scheduled and receives the token.

9. P_1 marks the end time.

The key is that the delivery of a data token induces a context switch. Let T_d and T_r be the time it takes to deliver and receive a data token, respectively, and let T_c be the amount of time spent in a context switch. At step 2, P_1 records the timestamp of the delivery of the token, and at step 9, it records the timestamp of the response. The amount of time elapsed, T, between these events may be expressed by:

$$T = 2 * (T_d + T_c + T_r)$$

This formula arises because of the following events: P_1 sends a token (3), the CPU context switches (4), P_2 receives it (5). P_2 then sends the response token (6), the CPU context switches (7), and finally P_1 receives it (8).

P_1 will be able to easily compute T, since this is just the time between events 3 and 8. So, to solve for T_c, we must first determine the value of $T_d + T_r$.

How can we do this? We can do this by measuring the length of time it takes P_1 to send and receive a token to itself. This will not induce a context switch since P_1 is running on the CPU at the time it sent the token and will not block to receive it.

The game is played a number of iterations to average out any variability in the elapsed time between steps 2 and 9 that may result from unexpected kernel interrupts and additional kernel threads contending for the CPU. We select the smallest observed context switch time as our final answer.

However, all we can ultimately say that this is an approximation which depends on the underlying system. For example, we make the assumption that P_2 is selected to run once a data token becomes available. However, this is dependent on the implementation of the task scheduler and we cannot make any guarantees.

That's okay; it's important in an interview to recognize when your solution might not be perfect.

16.3 *In the famous dining philosophers problem, a bunch of philosophers are sitting around a circular table with one chopstick between each of them. A philosopher needs both chopsticks to eat, and always picks up the left chopstick before the right one. A deadlock could potentially occur if all the philosophers reached for the left chopstick at the same time. Using threads and locks, implement a simulation of the dining philosophers problem that prevents deadlocks.*

pg 160

SOLUTION

First, let's implement a simple simulation of the dining philosophers problem in which we don't concern ourselves with deadlocks. We can implement this solution by having Philosopher extend Thread, and Chopstick call lock.lock() when it is picked up and lock.unlock() when it is put down.

```
1   public class Chopstick {
2       private Lock lock;
3
4       public Chopstick() {
5           lock = new ReentrantLock();
6       }
7
8       public void pickUp() {
9           void lock.lock();
```

```
10      }
11
12      public void putDown() {
13          lock.unlock();
14      }
15  }
16
17  public class Philosopher extends Thread {
18      private int bites = 10;
19      private Chopstick left;
20      private Chopstick right;
21
22      public Philosopher(Chopstick left, Chopstick right) {
23          this.left = left;
24          this.right = right;
25      }
26
27      public void eat() {
28          pickUp();
29          chew();
30          putDown();
31      }
32
33      public void pickUp() {
34          left.pickUp();
35          right.pickUp();
36      }
37
38      public void chew() { }
39
40      public void putDown() {
41          left.putDown();
42          right.putDown();
43      }
44
45      public void run() {
46          for (int i = 0; i < bites; i++) {
47              eat();
48          }
49      }
50  }
```

Running the above code may lead to a deadlock if all the philosophers have a left chopstick and are waiting for the right one.

To prevent deadlocks, we can implement a strategy where a philosopher will put down his left chopstick if he is unable to obtain the right one.

```
1   public class Chopstick {
2       /* same as before */
3
```

```
4      public boolean pickUp() {
5          return lock.tryLock();
6      }
7  }
8
9  public class Philosopher extends Thread {
10     /* same as before */
11
12     public void eat() {
13         if (pickUp()) {
14             chew();
15             putDown();
16         }
17     }
18
19     public boolean pickUp() {
20         /* attempt to pick up */
21         if (!left.pickUp()) {
22             return false;
23         }
24         if (!right.pickUp()) {
25             left.putDown();
26             return false;
27         }
28         return true;
29     }
30 }
```

In the above code, we need to be sure to release the left chopstick if we can't pick up the right one—and to not call putDown() on the chopsticks if we never had them in the first place.

16.4   *Design a class which provides a lock only if there are no possible deadlocks.*

pg 160

SOLUTION

There are several common ways to prevent deadlocks. One of the popular ways is to require a process to declare upfront what locks it will need. We can then verify if a deadlock would be created by issuing these locks, and we can fail if so.

With these constraints in mind, let's investigate how we can detect deadlocks. Suppose this was the order of locks requested:

```
A = {1, 2, 3, 4}
B = {1, 3, 5}
C = {7, 5, 9, 2}
```

This may create a deadlock because we could have the following scenario:

```
A locks 2, waits on 3
B locks 3, waits on 5
C locks 5, waits on 2
```

We can think about this as a graph, where 2 is connected to 3, 3 is connected to 5, and 5 is connected to 2. A deadlock is represented by a cycle. An edge (w, v) exists in the graph if a process declares that it will request lock v immediately after lock w. For the earlier example, the following edges would exist in the graph: (1, 2), (2, 3), (3, 4), (1, 3), (3, 5), (7, 5), (5, 9), (9, 2). The "owner" of the edge does not matter.

This class will need a declare method, which threads and processes will use to declare what order they will request resources in. This declare method will iterate through the declare order, adding each contiguous pair of elements (v, w) to the graph. Afterwards, it will check to see if any cycles have been created. If any cycles have been created, it will backtrack, removing these edges from the graph, and then exit.

We just have one final component to discuss: how do we detect a cycle? We can detect a cycle by doing a depth first search through each connected component (i.e., each connected part of the graph). Complex algorithms exist to select all the connected components of a graph, but our work in this problem does not require this degree of complexity.

We know that if a cycle was created, one of our new edges must be to blame. Thus, as long as our depth first search touches all of these edges at some point, then we know that we have fully searched for a cycle.

The pseudocode for this special case cycle detection looks like this:

```
1  boolean checkForCycle(locks[] locks) {
2     touchedNodes = hash table(lock -> boolean)
3     initialize touchedNodes to false for each lock in locks
4     for each (lock x in process.locks) {
5        if (touchedNodes[x] == false) {
6           if (hasCycle(x, touchedNodes)) {
7              return true;
8           }
9        }
10    }
11    return false;
12 }
13
14 boolean hasCycle(node x, touchedNodes) {
15    touchedNodes[r] = true;
16    if (x.state == VISITING) {
17       return true;
18    } else if (x.state == FRESH) {
19       ... (see full code below)
20    }
21 }
```

In the above code, note that we may do several depth first searches, but touchedNodes is only initialized once. We iterate until all the values in touchedNodes are false.

The code below provides further details. For simplicity, we assume that all locks and processes (owners) are ordered sequentially.

```
1   public class LockFactory {
2       private static LockFactory instance;
3
4       private int numberOfLocks = 5; /* default */
5       private LockNode[] locks;
6
7       /* Maps from a process or owner to the order that the owner
8        * claimed it would call the locks in */
9       private Hashtable<Integer, LinkedList<LockNode>> lockOrder;
10
11      private LockFactory(int count) { ... }
12      public static LockFactory getInstance() { return instance; }
13
14      public static synchronized LockFactory initialize(int count) {
15          if (instance == null) instance = new LockFactory(count);
16          return instance;
17      }
18
19      public boolean hasCycle(
20              Hashtable<Integer, Boolean> touchedNodes,
21              int[] resourcesInOrder) {
22          /* check for a cycle */
23          for (int resource : resourcesInOrder) {
24              if (touchedNodes.get(resource) == false) {
25                  LockNode n = locks[resource];
26                  if (n.hasCycle(touchedNodes)) {
27                      return true;
28                  }
29              }
30          }
31          return false;
32      }
33
34      /* To prevent deadlocks, force the processes to declare upfront
35       * what order they will need the locks in. Verify that this
36       * order does not create a deadlock (a cycle in a directed
37       * graph) */
38      public boolean declare(int ownerId, int[] resourcesInOrder) {
39          Hashtable<Integer, Boolean> touchedNodes =
40              new Hashtable<Integer, Boolean>();
41
42          /* add nodes to graph */
43          int index = 1;
44          touchedNodes.put(resourcesInOrder[0], false);
```

```
45      for (index = 1; index < resourcesInOrder.length; index++) {
46         LockNode prev = locks[resourcesInOrder[index - 1]];
47         LockNode curr = locks[resourcesInOrder[index]];
48         prev.joinTo(curr);
49         touchedNodes.put(resourcesInOrder[index], false);
50      }
51
52      /* if we created a cycle, destroy this resource list and
53       * return false */
54      if (hasCycle(touchedNodes, resourcesInOrder)) {
55         for (int j = 1; j < resourcesInOrder.length; j++) {
56            LockNode p = locks[resourcesInOrder[j - 1]];
57            LockNode c = locks[resourcesInOrder[j]];
58            p.remove(c);
59         }
60         return false;
61      }
62
63      /* No cycles detected. Save the order that was declared, so
64       * that we can verify that the process is really calling the
65       * locks in the order it said it would. */
66      LinkedList<LockNode> list = new LinkedList<LockNode>();
67      for (int i = 0; i < resourcesInOrder.length; i++) {
68         LockNode resource = locks[resourcesInOrder[i]];
69         list.add(resource);
70      }
71      lockOrder.put(ownerId, list);
72
73      return true;
74   }
75
76   /* Get the lock, verifying first that the process is really
77    * calling the locks in the order it said it would. */
78   public Lock getLock(int ownerId, int resourceID) {
79      LinkedList<LockNode> list = lockOrder.get(ownerId);
80      if (list == null) return null;
81
82      LockNode head = list.getFirst();
83      if (head.getId() == resourceID) {
84         list.removeFirst();
85         return head.getLock();
86      }
87      return null;
88   }
89 }
90
91 public class LockNode {
92    public enum VisitState { FRESH, VISITING, VISITED };
93
94    private ArrayList<LockNode> children;
```

```
95     private int lockId;
96     private Lock lock;
97     private int maxLocks;
98
99     public LockNode(int id, int max) { ... }
100
101    /* Join "this" to "node", checking to make sure that it doesn't
102     * create a cycle */
103    public void joinTo(LockNode node) { children.add(node); }
104    public void remove(LockNode node) { children.remove(node); }
105
106    /* Check for a cycle by doing a depth-first-search. */
107    public boolean hasCycle(
108        Hashtable<Integer, Boolean> touchedNodes) {
109      VisitState[] visited = new VisitState[maxLocks];
110      for (int i = 0; i < maxLocks; i++) {
111        visited[i] = VisitState.FRESH;
112      }
113      return hasCycle(visited, touchedNodes);
114    }
115
116    private boolean hasCycle(VisitState[] visited,
117        Hashtable<Integer, Boolean> touchedNodes) {
118      if (touchedNodes.containsKey(lockId)) {
119        touchedNodes.put(lockId, true);
120      }
121
122      if (visited[lockId] == VisitState.VISITING) {
123        /* We looped back to this node while still visiting it, so
124         * we know there's a cycle. */
125        return true;
126      } else if (visited[lockId] == VisitState.FRESH) {
127        visited[lockId] = VisitState.VISITING;
128        for (LockNode n : children) {
129          if (n.hasCycle(visited, touchedNodes)) {
130            return true;
131          }
132        }
133        visited[lockId] = VisitState.VISITED;
134      }
135      return false;
136    }
137
138    public Lock getLock() {
139      if (lock == null) lock = new ReentrantLock();
140      return lock;
141    }
142
143    public int getId() { return lockId; }
144 }
```

As always, when you see code this complicated and lengthy, you wouldn't be expected to write all of it. More likely, you would be asked to sketch out pseudocode and possibly implement one of these methods.

16.5 *Suppose we have the following code:*

```
public class Foo {
    public Foo() { ... }
    public void first() { ... }
    public void second() { ... }
    public void third() { ... }
}
```

The same instance of Foo will be passed to three different threads. ThreadA will call first, threadB will call second, and threadC will call third. Design a mechanism to ensure that first is called before second and second is called before third.

pg 160

SOLUTION

The general logic is to check if first() has completed before executing second(), and if second() has completed before calling third(). Because we need to be very careful about thread safety, simple boolean flags won't do the job.

What about using a lock to do something like the below code?

```
1  public class FooBad {
2      public int pauseTime = 1000;
3      public ReentrantLock lock1;
4      public ReentrantLock lock2;
5
6      public FooBad() {
7          try {
8              lock1 = new ReentrantLock();
9              lock2 = new ReentrantLock();
10             lock3 = new ReentrantLock();
11
12             lock1.lock();
13             lock2.lock();
14             lock3.lock();
15         } catch (...) { ... }
16     }
17
18     public void first() {
19         try {
20             ...
21             lock1.unlock(); // mark finished with first()
```

```
22       } catch (...) { ... }
23   }
24
25   public void second() {
26       try {
27           lock1.lock(); // wait until finished with first()
28           lock1.unlock();
29           ...
30
31           lock2.unlock(); // mark finished with second()
32       } catch (...) { ... }
33   }
34
35   public void third() {
36       try {
37           lock2.lock(); // wait until finished with third()
38           lock2.unlock();
39           ...
40       } catch (...) { ... }
41   }
42 }
```

This code won't actually quite work due to the concept of *lock ownership*. One thread is actually performing the lock (in the FooBad constructor), but different threads attempt to unlock the locks. This is not allowed, and your code will raise an exception. A lock in Java is owned by the same thread which locked it.

Instead, we can replicate this behavior with semaphores. The logic is identical.

```
1  public class Foo {
2      public Semaphore sem1;
3      public Semaphore sem2;
4
5      public Foo() {
6          try {
7              sem1 = new Semaphore(1);
8              sem2 = new Semaphore(1);
9              sem3 = new Semaphore(1);
10
11             sem1.acquire();
12             sem2.acquire();
13             sem3.acquire();
14         } catch (...) { ... }
15     }
16
17     public void first() {
18         try {
19             ...
20             sem1.release();
21         } catch (...) { ... }
22     }
```

```
23
24    public void second() {
25      try {
26        sem1.acquire();
27        sem1.release();
28        ...
29        sem2.release();
30      } catch (...) { ... }
31    }
32
33    public void third() {
34      try {
35        sem2.acquire();
36        sem2.release();
37        ...
38      } catch (...) { ... }
39    }
40  }
```

16.6 *You are given a class with synchronized method A and a normal method C. If you have two threads in one instance of a program, can they both execute A at the same time? Can they execute A and C at the same time?*

pg 160

SOLUTION

By applying the word `synchronized` to a method, we ensure that two threads cannot execute the method *on the same object* at the same time.

So, the answer to the first part really depends. If the two threads have the same instance of the object, then no, they cannot simultaneously execute method A. However, if they have different instances of the object, then they can.

Conceptually, you can see this by considering locks. A synchronized method applies a lock on that method in that specific instance of the object, thereby blocking any other threads from executing the method on the same object.

The two threads would, however, be able to execute different methods on the object, since the lock is applied at the "method + object level."

Although the question doesn't specifically ask about this, note that if both methods were synchronized and static, `thread1` would not be able to execute method A while `thread2` is executing method B. This is only if *both* methods are static (and synchronized).

Moderate

Additional Review Problems: Solutions | **Chapter 17**

Solutions to Chapter 17 | Moderate

17.1   *Write a function to swap a number in place (that is, without temporary variables).*

pg 163

SOLUTION

This is a classic interview problem, and it's a reasonably straightforward one. We'll walk through this using a_0 to indicate the original value of a and b_0 to indicate the original value of b. We'll also use diff to indicate the value of a_0 - b_0.

Let's picture these on a number line for the case where a > b.

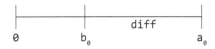

First, we briefly set a to diff, which is the right side of the above number line. Then, when we add b and diff (and store that value in b), we get a_0. We now have b = a_0 and a = diff. All that's left to do is to set a equal to a_0 - diff, which is just b - a.

The code below implements this.

```
1   public static void swap(int a, int b) {
2       // Example for a = 9, b = 4
3       a = a - b; // a = 9 - 4 = 5
4       b = a + b; // b = 5 + 4 = 9
5       a = b - a; // a = 9 - 5
6
7       System.out.println("a: " + a);
8       System.out.println("b: " + b);
9   }
```

We can implement a similar solution with bit manipulation. The benefit of this solution is that it works for more data types than just integers.

```
1   public static void swap_opt(int a, int b) {
2       // Example for a = 101 (in binary) and b = 110
3       a = a^b; // a = 101^110 = 011
4       b = a^b; // b = 011^110 = 101
5       a = a^b; // a = 011^101 = 110
6
7       System.out.println("a: " + a);
8       System.out.println("b: " + b);
9   }
```

This code works by using XORs. The easiest way to see how this works is by looking at it for a two bits p and q. We will again use the notation p_0 and q_0 to indicate the original values.

If we can correctly swap two bits, then we know the entire operation works correctly. Let's walk through this line-by-line.

```
1   p = p₀^q₀   /* 0 if p₀ = q₀, 1 if p₀ != q₀ */
2   q = p^q₀    /* equals value of p₀ */
3   p = p^q     /* equals value of q₀ */
```

In line 1, doing the operation $p = p_0 \wedge q_0$ will result in a 0 if $p_0 = q_0$ and a 1 if $p_0 \: != \: q_0$.

In line 2, we do $q = p \wedge q_0$. We can examine this for the two possible values of p. Since we are trying to eventually swap the original values of p and q, we want this operation to return the value of p_0.

- Case p = 0: In this case, $p_0 = q_0$, so we need this operation to return either p_0 or q_0. XORing any value with 0 will always return the original value, so we know that this operation will correctly return q_0 (or p_0).

- Case p = 1: In this case, $p_0 \: != \: q_0$. We need this operation to return a 1 if q_0 is 0 and a 0 if p_0 is 1. This is exactly what an XOR with 1 will do.

In line 3, we do $p = p \wedge q$. Let's again examine this for the two possible values of p. Our goal is to return q_0. Observe that q now equals p_0, so we are really doing $p \wedge p_0$.

- Case p = 0: Since $p_0 = q_0$, we want to return either p_0 or q_0—either will do. By doing $0 \wedge p_0$, we return p_0, which equals q_0.

- Case p = 1: Here, we are doing $1 \wedge p_0$. This will flip the value of p_0, which is exactly what we want, since $p_0 \: != \: q_0$.

We have now set p equal to q_0 and q equal to p_0. Thus, since our operation correctly swaps each bit, we know it will correctly swap the entire int.

17.2   *Design an algorithm to figure out if someone has won a game of tic-tac-toe.*

pg 164

SOLUTION

At first glance, this problem seems really straightforward. We're just checking a tic-tac-toe board; how hard could it be? It turns out that the problem is a bit more complex, and there is no single "perfect" answer. The optimal solution very much depends on your preferences.

There are a few major design decisions to consider:

1. Will hasWon be called just once, or many times (for instance, as part of a tic-tac-toe website)? If the latter is the case, we may want to add pre-processing time in order to optimize the runtime of hasWon.

2. Tic-tac-toe is usually on a 3x3 board. Do we want to design for just that, or do we want to implement it as an NxN solution?

3. In general, how much do we prioritize compactness of code vs. speed of execution vs. clarity of code? Remember that the most efficient code may not always be the best. Your ability to understand and maintain the code matters too.

Solution #1: If hasWon is called many times

There are only 3^9, or about 20,000 tic-tac-toe boards (assuming a 3x3 board). We can therefore represent our tic-tac-toe board as an int, with each digit representing a piece (0 means Empty, 1 means Red, 2 means Blue). We set up a hash table or array in advance with all possible boards as keys and the value indicating who has won. Our function then is simply this:

```
1   public int hasWon(int board) {
2       return winnerHashtable[board];
3   }
```

To convert a board (represented by a char array) to an int, we can use what is essentially a "base 3" representation. Each board is represented as $3^0 v_0 + 3^1 v_1 + 3^2 v_2 + \ldots + 3^8 v_8$, where v_i is a 0 if the space is empty, a 1 if it's a "blue spot" and a 2 if it's a "red spot."

```
1   public static int convertBoardToInt(char[][] board) {
2       int factor = 1;
3       int sum = 0;
4       for (int i = 0; i < board.length; i++) {
5           for (int j = 0; j < board[i].length; j++) {
6               int v = 0;
7               if (board[i][j] == 'x') {
8                   v = 1;
9               } else if (board[i][j] == 'o') {
10                  v = 2;
11              }
12              sum += v * factor;
13              factor *= 3;
14          }
15      }
16      return sum;
17  }
```

Now, looking up the winner of a board is just a matter of looking it up in a hash table.

Of course, if we need to convert a board into this format every time we want to check for a winner, we haven't saved ourselves any time compared with the other solutions. But, if we can store the board this way from the very beginning, then the lookup process will be very efficient.

Solution #2: Designing for just a 3x3 board

If we really only want to implement a solution for a 3x3 board, the code is relatively short and simple. The only complex part is trying to be clean and organized, without writing too much duplicated code.

```
1   Piece hasWon1(Piece[][] board) {
2       for (int i = 0; i < board.length; i++) {
3           /* Check Rows */
4           if (board[i][0] != Piece.Empty &&
5               board[i][0] == board[i][1] &&
```

```
6              board[i][0] == board[i][2]) {
7          return board[i][0];
8        }
9
10       /* Check Columns */
11       if (board[0][i] != Piece.Empty &&
12           board[0][i] == board[1][i] &&
13           board[0][i] == board[2][i]) {
14         return board[0][i];
15       }
16     }
17
18     /* Check Diagonal */
19     if (board[0][0] != Piece.Empty &&
20         board[0][0] == board[1][1] &&
21         board[0][0] == board[2][2]) {
22       return board[0][0];
23     }
24
25     /* Check Reverse Diagonal */
26     if (board[2][0] != Piece.Empty &&
27         board[2][0] == board[1][1] &&
28         board[2][0] == board[0][2]) {
29       return board[2][0];
30     }
31     return Piece.Empty;
32   }
```

Solution #3: Designing for an NxN board

This is a straightforward extension of the code for a 3x3 board. The code attachment provides several other ways, but we have listed one below.

```
1    Piece hasWon3(Piece[][] board) {
2      int N = board.length;
3      int row = 0;
4      int col = 0;
5
6      /* Check rows */
7      for (row = 0; row < N; row++) {
8        if (board[row][0] != Piece.Empty) {
9          for (col = 1; col < N; col++) {
10           if (board[row][col] != board[row][col-1]) break;
11         }
12         if (col == N) return board[row][0];
13       }
14     }
15
16     /* Check columns */
17     for (col = 0; col < N; col++) {
```

```
18       if (board[0][col] != Piece.Empty) {
19          for (row = 1; row < N; row++) {
20             if (board[row][col] != board[row-1][col]) break;
21          }
22          if (row == N) return board[0][col];
23       }
24    }
25
26    /* Check diagonal (top left to bottom right) */
27    if (board[0][0] != Piece.Empty) {
28       for (row = 1; row < N; row++) {
29          if (board[row][row] != board[row-1][row-1]) break;
30       }
31       if (row == N) return board[0][0];
32    }
33
34    /* Check diagonal (bottom left to top right) */
35    if (board[N-1][0] != Piece.Empty) {
36       for (row = 1; row < N; row++) {
37          if (board[N-row-1][row] != board[N-row][row-1]) break;
38       }
39       if (row == N) return board[N-1][0];
40    }
41
42    return Piece.Empty;
43 }
```

Regardless of how you solve the problem, the algorithms for the problem are not especially challenging. The tricky part is understanding how to code in a clean and maintainable way, and this is exactly what your interviewer is attempting to assess.

17.3   *Write an algorithm which computes the number of trailing zeros in n factorial.*

pg 163

SOLUTION

A simple approach is to compute the factorial, and then count the number of trailing zeros by continuously dividing by ten. The problem with this though is that the bounds of an int would be exceeded very quickly. To avoid this issue, we can look at this problem mathematically.

Consider a factorial like 19!:

19! = 1*2*3*4*5*6*7*8*9*10*11*12*13*14*15*16*17*18*19

A trailing zero is created with multiples of 10, and multiples of 10 are created with pairs of 5-multiples and 2-multiples.

For example, in 19!, the following terms create the trailing zeros:

19! = 2 * ... * 5 * ... * 10 * ... * 15 * 16 * ...

To count the number of zeros, therefore, we only need to count the pairs of multiples of 5 and 2. There will always be more multiples of 2 than 5 though, so simply counting the number of multiples of 5 is sufficient.

One "gotcha" here is 15 contributes a multiple of 5 (and therefore one trailing zero), while 25 contributes two (because 25 = 5 * 5).

There are two different ways of writing this code.

The first way is to iterate through all the numbers from 2 through n, counting the number of times that 5 goes into each number.

```
1   /* If the number is a 5 of five, return which power of 5.
2    *      5 -> 1,
3    *      25-> 2, etc.
4    */
5   public int factorsOf5(int i) {
6       int count = 0;
7       while (i % 5 == 0) {
8           count++;
9           i /= 5;
10      }
11      return count;
12  }
13
14  public int countFactZeros(int num) {
15      int count = 0;
16      for (int i = 2; i <= num; i++) {
17          count += factorsOf5(i);
18      }
19      return count;
20  }
```

This isn't bad, but we can make it a little more efficient by directly counting the factors of 5. Under this approach, we would first count the number of multiples of 5 that are between 1 and n (which is n/5), then the number of multiples of 25 (n/25), then 125, and so on.

To count how many multiples of m are in n, we can just divide n by m.

```
1   public int countFactZeros(int num) {
2       int count = 0;
3       if (num < 0) {
4           return -1;
5       }
6       for (int i = 5; num / i > 0; i *= 5) {
7           count += num / i;
8       }
9       return count;
10  }
```

Solutions to Chapter 17 | Moderate

This problem is a bit of a brain teaser, but it can be approached logically (as shown above). By thinking through what exactly will contribute a zero, you can come up with a solution. You should be very clear in your rules upfront so that you can implement this correctly.

17.4 *Write a method which finds the maximum of two numbers. You should not use if-else or any other comparison operator.*

pg 163

SOLUTION

A common way of implementing a max function is to look at the sign of a - b. In this case, we can't use a comparison operator on this sign, but we *can* use multiplication.

Let k equal the sign of a - b such that if a - b >= 0, then k is 1. Else, k = 0. Let q be the inverse of k.

We can then implement the code as follows:

```
1   /* Flips a 1 to a 0 and a 0 to a 1 */
2   public static int flip(int bit) {
3       return 1^bit;
4   }
5
6   /* Returns 1 if a is positive, and 0 if a is negative */
7   public static int sign(int a) {
8       return flip((a >> 31) & 0x1);
9   }
10
11  public static int getMaxNaive(int a, int b) {
12      int k = sign(a - b);
13      int q = flip(k);
14      return a * k + b * q;
15  }
```

This code almost works. It fails, unfortunately, when a - b overflows. Suppose, for example, that a is INT_MAX - 2 and b is -15. In this case, a - b will be greater than INT_MAX and will overflow, resulting in a negative value.

We can implement a solution to this problem by using the same approach. Our goal is to maintain the condition where k is 1 when a > b. We will need to use more complex logic to accomplish this.

When does a - b overflow? It will overflow only when a is positive and b is negative, or the other way around. It may be difficult to specially detect the overflow condition, but we *can* detect when a and b have different signs. Note that if a and b have different signs, then we want k to equal sign(a).

The logic looks like:

```
1   if a and b have different signs:
2       // if a > 0, then b < 0, and k = 1.
3       // if a < 0, then b > 0, and k = 0.
4       // so either way, k = sign(a)
5       let k = sign(a)
6   else
7       let k = sign(a - b) // overflow is impossible
```

The code below implements this, using multiplication instead of if-statements.

```
1   public static int getMax(int a, int b) {
2       int c = a - b;
3
4       int sa = sign(a); // if a >= 0, then 1 else 0
5       int sb = sign(b); // if b >= 1, then 1 else 0
6       int sc = sign(c); // depends on whether or not a - b overflows
7
8       /* Goal: define a value k which is 1 if a > b and 0 if a < b.
9        * (if a = b, it doesn't matter what value k is) */
10
11      // If a and b have different signs, then k = sign(a)
12      int use_sign_of_a = sa ^ sb;
13
14      // If a and b have the same sign, then k = sign(a - b)
15      int use_sign_of_c = flip(sa ^ sb);
16
17      int k = use_sign_of_a * sa + use_sign_of_c * sc;
18      int q = flip(k); // opposite of k
19
20      return a * k + b * q;
21  }
```

Note that for clarity, we split up the code into many different methods and variables. This is certainly not the most compact or efficient way to write it, but it does make what we're doing much cleaner.

Solutions to Chapter 17 | Moderate

17.5 *The Game of Master Mind is played as follows:*

The computer has four slots, and each slot will contain a ball that is red (R), yellow (Y), green (G) or blue (B). For example, the computer might have RGGB (Slot #1 is red, Slots #2 and #3 are green, Slot #4 is blue).

You, the user, are trying to guess the solution. You might, for example, guess YRGB.

When you guess the correct color for the correct slot, you get a "hit." If you guess a color that exists but is in the wrong slot, you get a "pseudo-hit." Note that a slot that is a hit can never count as a pseudo-hit.

For example, if the actual solution is RGBY and you guess GGRR, you have one hit and one pseudo-hit.

Write a method that, given a guess and a solution, returns the number of hits and pseudo-hits.

SOLUTION

This problem is straightforward, but it's surprisingly easy to make little mistakes. You should check your code *extremely* thoroughly, on a variety of test cases.

We'll implement this code by first creating a frequency array which stores how many times each character occurs in `solution`, excluding times when the slot is a "hit." Then, we iterate through `guess` to count the number of pseudo-hits.

The code below implements this algorithm.

```
1   public class Result {
2       public int hits = 0;
3       public int pseudoHits = 0;
4
5       public String toString() {
6           return "(" + hits + ", " + pseudoHits + ")";
7       }
8   }
9
10  public int code(char c) {
11      switch (c) {
12      case 'B':
13          return 0;
14      case 'G':
15          return 1;
16      case 'R':
17          return 2;
18      case 'Y':
19          return 3;
20      default:
21          return -1;
```

Cracking the Coding Interview | Solutions to Moderate

```
22    }
23  }
24
25  public static int MAX_COLORS = 4;
26
27  public Result estimate(String guess, String solution) {
28      if (guess.length() != solution.length()) return null;
29
30      Result res = new Result();
31      int[] frequencies = new int[MAX_COLORS];
32
33      /* Compute hits and build frequency table */
34      for (int i = 0; i < guess.length(); i++) {
35          if (guess.charAt(i) == solution.charAt(i)) {
36              res.hits++;
37          } else {
38              /* Only increment the frequency table (which will be used
39               * for pseudo-hits) if it's not a hit. If it's a hit, the
40               * slot has already been "used." */
41              int code = code(solution.charAt(i));
42              frequencies[code]++;
43          }
44      }
45
46      /* Compute pseudo-hits */
47      for (int i = 0; i < guess.length(); i++) {
48          int code = code(guess.charAt(i));
49          if (code >= 0 && frequencies[code] > 0 &&
50              guess.charAt(i) != solution.charAt(i)) {
51              res.pseudoHits++;
52              frequencies[code]--;
53          }
54      }
55      return res;
56  }
```

Note that the easier the algorithm for a problem is, the more important it is to write clean and correct code. In this case, we've pulled code(char c) into its own method, and we've created a Result class to hold the result, rather than just printing it.

17.6 *Given an array of integers, write a method to find indices m and n such that if you sorted elements m through n, the entire array would be sorted. Minimize n - m (that is, find the smallest such sequence).*

pg 164

SOLUTION

Before we begin, let's make sure we understand what our answer will look like. If we're looking for just two indices, this indicates that some middle section of the array will be sorted, with the start and end of the array already being in order.

Now, let's approach this problem by looking at an example.

```
1, 2, 4, 7, 10, 11, 7, 12, 6, 7, 16, 18, 19
```

Our first thought might be to just find the longest increasing subsequence at the beginning and the longest increasing subsequence at the end.

```
left:    1, 2, 4, 7, 10, 11
middle: 7, 12
right:   6, 7, 16, 18, 19
```

These subsequences are easy to generate. We just start from the left and the right sides, and work our way inward. When an element is out of order, then we have found the end of our increasing / decreasing subsequence.

In order to solve our problem though, we would need to be able to sort the middle part of the array and, by doing just that, get all the elements in the array in order. Specifically, the following would have to be true:

```
/* all items on left are smaller than all items in middle */
min(middle) > end(left)

/* all items in middle are smaller than all items in right */
max(middle) < start(right)
```

Or, in other words, for all elements:

```
left < middle < right
```

In fact, this condition will *never* be met. The middle section is, by definition, the elements that were out of order. That is, it is *always* the case that `left.end > middle.start` and `middle.end > right.start`. Thus, you cannot sort the middle to make the entire array sorted.

But, what we can do is *shrink* the left and right subsequences until the earlier conditions are met.

Let min equal `min(middle)` and max equal `max(middle)`.

On the left side, we start with the end of the subsequence (value 11, at element 5) and move to the left. Once we find an element i such that `array[i] < min`, we know that we could sort the middle and have that part of the array appear in order.

Then, we do a similar thing on the right side. The value max equals 12. So, we begin with the start of the right subsequence (value 6) and move to the right. We compare the max of 12 to 6, then 7, then 16. When reach 16, we know that no elements smaller than 12 could be after it (since it's an increasing subsequence). Thus, the middle of the array could now be sorted to make the entire array sorted.

The following code implements this algorithm.

```
1   int findEndOfLeftSubsequence(int[] array) {
2       for (int i = 1; i < array.length; i++) {
3           if (array[i] < array[i - 1]) return i - 1;
4       }
5       return array.length - 1;
6   }
7
8   int findStartOfRightSubsequence(int[] array) {
9       for (int i = array.length - 2; i >= 0; i--) {
10          if (array[i] > array[i + 1]) return i + 1;
11      }
12      return 0;
13  }
14
15  int shrinkLeft(int[] array, int min_index, int start) {
16      int comp = array[min_index];
17      for (int i = start - 1; i >= 0; i--) {
18          if (array[i] <= comp) return i + 1;
19      }
20      return 0;
21  }
22
23  int shrinkRight(int[] array, int max_index, int start) {
24      int comp = array[max_index];
25      for (int i = start; i < array.length; i++) {
26          if (array[i] >= comp) return i - 1;
27      }
28      return array.length - 1;
29  }
30
31  void findUnsortedSequence(int[] array) {
32      /* find left subsequence */
33      int end_left = findEndOfLeftSubsequence(array);
34
35      /* find right subsequence */
36      int start_right = findStartOfRightSubsequence(array);
37
38      /* find min and max element of middle */
39      int min_index = end_left + 1;
40      if (min_index >= array.length) return; // Already sorted
41
42      int max_index = start_right - 1;
43      for (int i = end_left; i <= start_right; i++) {
44          if (array[i] < array[min_index]) min_index = i;
45          if (array[i] > array[max_index]) max_index = i;
46      }
47
48      /* slide left until less than array[min_index] */
49      int left_index = shrinkLeft(array, min_index, end_left);
50
```

```
51    /* slide right until greater than array[max_index] */
52    int right_index = shrinkRight(array, max_index, start_right);
53
54    System.out.println(left_index + " " + right_index);
55  }
```

Note the use of other methods in this solution. Although we could have jammed it all into one method, it would have made the code a lot harder to understand, maintain, and test. In your interview coding, you should prioritize these aspects.

17.7 *Given any integer, print an English phrase that describes the integer (e.g., "One Thousand, Two Hundred Thirty Four").*

pg 164

SOLUTION

This is not an especially challenging problem, but it is a somewhat tedious one. The key is to be organized in how you approach the problem—and to make sure you have good test cases.

We can think about converting a number like 19,323,984 as converting each of three 3-digit segments of the number, and inserting "thousands" and "millions" in between as appropriate. That is,

```
convert(19,323,984) =   convert(19) + " million " +
                        convert(323) + " thousand " +
                        convert(984)
```

The code below implements this algorithm.

```
1   public String[] digits = {"One", "Two", "Three", "Four", "Five",
2       "Six", "Seven", "Eight", "Nine"};
3   public String[] teens = {"Eleven", "Twelve", "Thirteen",
4       "Fourteen", "Fifteen", "Sixteen", "Seventeen", "Eighteen",
5       "Nineteen"};
6   public static String[] tens = {"Ten", "Twenty", "Thirty", "Forty",
7       "Fifty", "Sixty", "Seventy", "Eighty", "Ninety"};
8   public static String[] bigs = {"", "Thousand", "Million"};
9
10  public static String numToString(int number) {
11      if (number == 0) {
12          return "Zero";
13      } else if (number < 0) {
14          return "Negative " + numToString(-1 * number);
15      }
16
17      int count = 0;
18      String str = "";
19
20      while (number > 0) {
```

```
21      if (number % 1000 != 0) {
22          str = numToString100(number % 1000) + bigs[count] +
23              " " + str;
24      }
25      number /= 1000;
26      count++;
27  }
28
29  return str;
30 }
31
32 public static String numToString100(int number) {
33     String str = "";
34
35     /* Convert hundreds place */
36     if (number >= 100) {
37         str += digits[number / 100 - 1] + " Hundred ";
38         number %= 100;
39     }
40
41     /* Convert tens place */
42     if (number >= 11 && number <= 19) {
43         return str + teens[number - 11] + " ";
44     } else if (number == 10 || number >= 20) {
45         str += tens[number / 10 - 1] + " ";
46         number %= 10;
47     }
48
49     /* Convert ones place */
50     if (number >= 1 && number <= 9) {
51         str += digits[number - 1] + " ";
52     }
53
54     return str;
55 }
```

The key in a problem like this is to make sure you consider all the special cases. There are a lot of them.

17.8 *You are given an array of integers (both positive and negative). Find the contiguous sequence with the largest sum. Return the sum.*

pg 164

SOLUTION

This is a challenging problem, but an extremely common one. Let's approach this by looking at an example:

2   3   -8   -1   2   4   -2   3

If we think about our array as having alternating sequences of positive and negative numbers, we can observe that we would never include only part of a negative subsequence or part of a positive sequence. Why would we? Including part of a negative subsequence would make things unnecessarily negative, and we should just instead not include that negative sequence at all. Likewise, including only part of a positive subsequence would be strange, since the sum would be even bigger if we included the whole thing.

For the purposes of coming up with our algorithm, we can think about our array as being a sequence of alternating negative and positive *numbers*. Each number corresponds to the sum of a subsequence of positive numbers of a subsequence of negative numbers. For the array above, our new reduced array would be:

$$5 \quad -9 \quad 6 \quad -2 \quad 3$$

This doesn't give away a great algorithm immediately, but it does help us to better understand what we're working with.

Consider the array above. Would it ever make sense to have {5, -9} in a subsequence? No. These numbers sum to -4, so we're better off not including either number, or possibly just having the sequence be just {5}).

When would we want negative numbers included in a subsequence? Only if it allows us to join two positive subsequences, each of which have a sum greater than the negative value.

We can approach this in a step-wise manner, starting with the first element in the array.

When we look at 5, this is the biggest sum we've seen so far. We set maxSum to 5, and sum to 5. Then, we consider -9. If we added it to sum, we'd get a negative value. There's no sense in extending the subsequence from 5 to -9 (which "reduces" to a sequence of just -4), so we just reset the value of sum.

Now, we consider 6. This subsequence is greater than 5, so we update both maxSum and sum.

Next, we look at -2. Adding this to 6 will set sum to 4. Since this is still a "value add" (when adjoined to another, bigger sequence), we *might* want {6, -2} in our max subsequence. We'll update sum, but not maxSum.

Finally, we look at 3. Adding 3 to sum (4) gives us 7, so we update maxSum. The max subsequence is therefore the sequence {6, -2, 3}.

When we look at this in the full expanded array, our logic is identical. The code below implements this algorithm.

```
1   public static int getMaxSum(int[] a) {
2       int maxsum = 0;
3       int sum = 0;
4       for (int i = 0; i < a.length; i++) {
5           sum += a[i];
```

```
6      if (maxsum < sum) {
7        maxsum = sum;
8      } else if (sum < 0) {
9        sum = 0;
10     }
11   }
12   return maxsum;
13 }
```

If the array is all negative numbers, what is the correct behavior? Consider this simple array {-3, -10, -5}. You could make a good argument that the maximum sum is either:

1. -3 (if you assume the subsequence can't be empty)

2. 0 (the subsequence has length 0)

3. MINIMUM_INT (essentially the error case).

We went with option #2 (maxSum = 0), but there's no "correct" answer. This is a great thing to discuss with your interviewer; it will show how detail oriented you are.

17.9 *Design a method to find the frequency of occurrences of any given word in a book.*

pg 164

SOLUTION

The first question that you should ask your interviewer is if you'll be doing this operation once or repeatedly. That is, are you simply asking for the frequency of "dog," or might you ask for "dog," and then "cat," "mouse," and so on?

Solution: Single Query

In this case, we simply go through the book, word by word, and count the number of times that a word appears. This will take O(n) time. We know we can't do better than that since we must look at every word in the book.

Solution: Repetitive Queries

If we're doing the operation repeatedly, then we can probably afford to take some time and extra memory to do pre-processing on the book. We can create a hash table which maps from a word to its frequency. The frequency of any word can be easily looked up in O(1) time. The code for this is below.

```
1  Hashtable<String, Integer> setupDictionary(String[] book) {
2    Hashtable<String, Integer> table =
3      new Hashtable<String, Integer>();
4    for (String word : book) {
5      word = word.toLowerCase();
```

```
6      if (word.trim() != "") {
7         if (!table.containsKey(word)) {
8            table.put(word, 0);
9         }
10        table.put(word, table.get(word) + 1);
11     }
12   }
13   return table;
14 }
15
16 int getFrequency(Hashtable<String, Integer> table, String word) {
17   if (table == null || word == null) return -1;
18   word = word.toLowerCase();
19   if (table.containsKey(word)) {
20      return table.get(word);
21   }
22   return 0;
23 }
```

Note that a problem like this is actually relatively easy. Thus, the interviewer is going to be looking heavily at how careful you are. Did you check for error conditions?

17.10 *Since XML is very verbose, you are given a way of encoding it where each tag gets mapped to a pre-defined integer value. The language/grammar is as follows:*

```
Element     --> Tag Attributes END Children END
Attribute   --> Tag Value
END         --> 0
Tag         --> some predefined mapping to int
Value       --> string value END
```

For example, the following XML might be converted into the compressed string below (assuming a mapping of family -> 1, person ->2, firstName -> 3, lastName -> 4, state -> 5).

```
<family lastName="McDowell" state="CA">
    <person firstName="Gayle">Some Message</person>
</family>
```

Becomes:

```
1 4 McDowell 5 CA 0 2 3 Gayle 0 Some Message 0 0
```

Write code to print the encoded version of an XML element (passed in Element and Attribute objects).

pg 164

SOLUTION

Since we know the element will be passed in as an Element and Attribute, our code is reasonably simple. We can implement this by applying a tree-like approach.

We repeatedly call `encode()` on parts of the XML structure, handling the code in slightly different ways depending on the type of the XML element.

```
1   public static void encode(Element root, StringBuffer sb) {
2       encode(root.getNameCode(), sb);
3       for (Attribute a : root.attributes) {
4           encode(a, sb);
5       }
6       encode("0", sb);
7       if (root.value != null && root.value != "") {
8           encode(root.value, sb);
9       } else {
10          for (Element e : root.children) {
11              encode(e, sb);
12          }
13      }
14      encode("0", sb);
15  }
16
17  public static void encode(String v, StringBuffer sb) {
18      sb.append(v);
19      sb.append(" ");
20  }
21
22  public static void encode(Attribute attr, StringBuffer sb) {
23      encode(attr.getTagCode(), sb);
24      encode(attr.value, sb);
25  }
26
27  public static String encodeToString(Element root) {
28      StringBuffer sb = new StringBuffer();
29      encode(root, sb);
30      return sb.toString();
31  }
```

Observe in line 17, the use of the very simple encode method for a string. This is somewhat unnecessary; all it does is insert the string and a space following it. However, using this method is a nice touch as it ensures that every element will be inserted with a space surrounding it. Otherwise, it might be easy to break the encoding by forgetting to append the empty string.

17.11 *Implement a method rand7() given rand5(). That is, given a method that generates a random number between 0 and 4 (inclusive), write a method that generates a random number between 0 and 6 (inclusive).*

pg 165

SOLUTION

To implement this function correctly, we must have each of the values between 0 and 6 returned with 1/7th probability.

First Attempt (Fixed Number of Calls)

As a first attempt, we might try to generate all numbers between 0 and 9, and then mod the resulting value by 7. Our code for it might look something like this:

```
1   int rand7() {
2       int v = rand5() + rand5();
3       return v % 7;
4   }
```

Unfortunately, the above code will not generate the values with equal probability. We can see this by looking at how the results of each call to rand5() will correspond to the return result of the rand7() function.

1st Call	2nd Call	Result		1st Call	2nd Call	Result
0	0	0		2	3	5
0	1	1		2	4	6
0	2	2		3	0	3
0	3	3		3	1	4
0	4	4		3	2	5
1	0	1		3	3	6
1	1	2		3	4	0
1	2	3		4	0	4
1	3	4		4	1	5
1	4	5		4	2	6
2	0	2		4	3	0
2	1	3		4	4	1
2	2	4				

Each individual row has a 1 in 25 chance of occurring, since there are two calls to rand5() and each distributes its results with 1/5th probability. If you count up the number of times each number occurs, you'll note that this rand7() function will return 4 with 5/25th probability but return 0 with just 3/25th probability. This means that our function has failed; the results do not have probability 1/7th.

Now, imagine we modify our function to add an if-statement, to change the constant multiplier, or to insert a new call to rand5(). We will still wind up with a similar looking table, and the probability of getting any one of those rows will be $1/5^k$, where k is the number of calls to rand5() in that row. Different rows may have different number of calls.

The probability of winding up with the result of the rand7() function being, say, 6 would be the sum of the probabilities of all rows that result in 6. That is:

$$P(\text{rand7}() = 6) = 1/5^i + 1/5^j + \ldots + 1/5^m$$

We know that, in order for our function to be correct, this probability must equal 1/7.

This is impossible though. Because 5 and 7 are relatively prime, no series of reciprocal powers of 5 will result in 1/7.

Does this mean the problem is impossible? Not exactly. Strictly speaking, it means that, as long as we can list out the combinations of rand5() results that will result in a particular value of rand7(), the function will not give well distributed results.

We can still solve this problem. We just have to use a while loop, and realize that there's no telling just how many turns will be required to return a result.

Second Attempt (Nondeterministic Number of Calls)

As soon as we've allowed for a while loop, our work gets much easier. We just need to generate a range of values where each value is equally likely (and where the range has at least seven elements). If we can do this, then we can discard the elements greater than the previous multiple of 7, and mod the rest of them by 7. This will get us a value within the range of 0 to 6, with each value being equally likely.

In the below code, we generate the range 0 through 24 by doing 5 * rand5() + rand5(). Then, we discard the values between 21 and 24, since they would otherwise make rand7() unfairly weighted towards 0 through 3. Finally, we mod by 7 to give us the values in the range 0 to 6 with equal probability.

Note that because we discard values in this approach, we have no guarantee on the number of rand5() calls it may take to return a value. This is what is meant by a *nondeterministic* number of calls.

```
1   public static int rand7() {
2       while (true) {
3           int num = 5 * rand5() + rand5();
4           if (num < 21) {
5               return num % 7;
6           }
7       }
8   }
```

Observe that doing 5 * rand5() + rand5() gives us exactly one way of getting each number in its range (0 to 24). This ensures that each value is equally probable.

Could we instead do 2 * rand5() + rand5()? No, because the values wouldn't be equally distributed. For example, there would be two ways of getting a 6 (6=2*1+4 and 6 = 2*2+2) but only one way of getting a 0 (0=2*0+0). The values in the range are not equally probable.

There *is* a way that we can use 2 * rand5() and still get an identically distributed

Chapter 17 | Moderate

range, but it's much more complicated. See below.

```
1   public int rand7() {
2       while (true) {
3           int r1 = 2 * rand5(); /* evens between 0 and 9 */
4           int r2 = rand5(); /* used later to generate a 0 or 1 */
5           if (r2 != 4) { /* r2 has extra even num-discard the extra */
6               int rand1 = r2 % 2; /* Generate 0 or 1 */
7               int num = r1 + rand1; /* will be in the range 0 to 9 */
8               if (num < 7) {
9                   return num;
10              }
11          }
12      }
13  }
```

In fact, there is an infinite number of ranges we can use. The key is to make sure that the range is big enough and that all values are equally likely.

17.12 *Design an algorithm to find all pairs of integers within an array which sum to a specified value.*

pg 165

SOLUTION

We can approach this problem in two ways. The "preferred" solution depends on your preferences between time efficiency, space efficiency, and code complexity.

Simple Solution

One easy and (time) efficient solution involves a hash map from integers to integers. This algorithm works by iterating through the array. On each element x, look up sum - x in the hash table and, if it exists, print (x, sum - x). Add x to the hash table, and go to the next element.

Alternate Solution

First, let's start with a definition. If we're trying to find a pair of numbers that sums to z, the *complement* of x will be z - x (that is, the number that can be added to x to make z). For example, if we're trying to find a pair of numbers that sums to 12, the complement of –5 would be 17.

Now, imagine we have the following sorted array: {-2 -1 0 3 5 6 7 9 13 14}. Let first point to the head of the array and last point to the end of the array. To find the complement of first, we just move last backwards until we find it. If first + last < sum, then there is no complement for first. We can therefore move first forward. We stop when first is greater than last.

Why must this find all complements for `first`? Because the array is sorted and we're trying progressively smaller numbers. When the sum of `first` and `last` is less than the sum, we know that trying even smaller numbers (as `last`) won't help us find a complement.

Why must this find all complements for `last`? Because all pairs must be made up of a `first` and a `last`. We've found all complements for `first`, therefore we've found all complements of `last`.

```
1   void printPairSums(int[] array, int sum) {
2       Arrays.sort(array);
3       int first = 0;
4       int last = array.length - 1;
5       while (first < last) {
6           int s = array[first] + array[last];
7           if (s == sum) {
8               System.out.println(array[first] + " " + array[last]);
9               first++;
10              last--;
11          } else {
12              if (s < sum) first++;
13              else last--;
14          }
15      }
16  }
```

17.13 *Consider a simple node-like data structure called BiNode, which has pointers to two other nodes. The data structure BiNode could be used to represent both a binary tree (where node1 is the left node and node2 is the right node) or a doubly linked list (where node1 is the previous node and node2 is the next node). Implement a method to convert a binary search tree (implemented with BiNode) into a doubly linked list. The values should be kept in order and the operation should be performed in place (that is, on the original data structure).*

pg 165

SOLUTION

This seemingly complex problem can be implemented quite elegantly using recursion. You will need to understand recursion very well to solve it.

Picture a simple binary search tree:

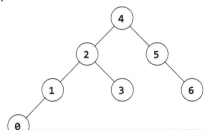

The convert method should transform it into the below doubly linked list:

0 <-> 1 <-> 2 <-> 3 <-> 4 <-> 5 <-> 6

Let's approach this recursively, starting with the root (node 4).

We know that the left and right halves of the tree form their own "sub-parts" of the linked list (that is, they appear consecutively in the linked list). So, if we recursively converted the left and right subtrees to a doubly linked list, could we build the final linked list from those parts?

Yes! We would simply merge the different parts.

The pseudocode looks something like:

```
1   BiNode convert(BiNode node) {
2       BiNode left = convert(node.left);
3       BiNode right = convert(node.right);
4       mergeLists(left, node, right);
5       return left; // front of left
6   }
```

To actually implement the nitty-gritty details of this, we'll need to get the head and tail of each linked list. We can do this several different ways.

Solution #1: Additional Data Structure

The first, and easier, approach is to create a new data structure called NodePair which holds just the head and tail of a linked list. The convert method can then return something of type NodePair.

The code below implements this approach.

```
1   private class NodePair {
2       BiNode head;
3       BiNode tail;
4
5       public NodePair(BiNode head, BiNode tail)  {
6           this.head = head;
7           this.tail = tail;
8       }
9   }
10
11  public NodePair convert(BiNode root) {
12      if (root == null) {
13          return null;
14      }
15
16      NodePair part1 = convert(root.node1);
17      NodePair part2 = convert(root.node2);
18
19      if (part1 != null) {
```

```
20        concat(part1.tail, root);
21     }
22
23     if (part2 != null) {
24        concat(root, part2.head);
25     }
26
27     return new NodePair(part1 == null ? root : part1.head,
28                         part2 == null ? root : part2.tail);
29  }
30
31  public static void concat(BiNode x, BiNode y) {
32     x.node2 = y;
33     y.node1 = x;
34  }
```

The above code still converts the BiNode data structure in place. We're just using Node-Pair as a way to return additional data. We could have alternatively used a two-element BiNode array to fulfill the same purposes, but it looks a bit messier (and we like clean code, especially in an interview).

It'd be nice, though, if we could do this without these extra data structures—and we can.

Solution #2: Retrieving the Tail

Instead of returning the head and tail of the linked list with NodePair, we can return just the head, and then we can use the head to find the tail of the linked list.

```
1   public static BiNode convert(BiNode root) {
2      if (root == null) {
3         return null;
4      }
5
6      BiNode part1 = convert(root.node1);
7      BiNode part2 = convert(root.node2);
8
9      if (part1 != null) {
10        concat(getTail(part1), root);
11     }
12
13     if (part2 != null) {
14        concat(root, part2);
15     }
16
17     return part1 == null ? root : part1;
18  }
19
20  public static BiNode getTail(BiNode node) {
21     if (node == null) return null;
```

```
22    while (node.node2 != null) {
23        node = node.node2;
24    }
25    return node;
26 }
```

Other than a call to getTail, this code is almost identical to the first solution. It is not, however, very efficient. A leaf node at depth d will be "touched" by the getTail method d times (one for each node above it), leading to an $O(N^2)$ overall runtime, where N is the number of nodes in the tree.

Solution #3: Building a Circular Linked List

We can build our third and final approach off of the second one.

This approach requires returning the head and tail of the linked list with BiNode. We can do this by returning each list as the head of a *circular* linked list. To get the tail, then, we simply call head.node1.

```
1    public static BiNode convertToCircular(BiNode root) {
2        if (root == null) {
3            return null;
4        }
5
6        BiNode part1 = convertToCircular(root.node1);
7        BiNode part3 = convertToCircular(root.node2);
8
9        if (part1 == null && part3 == null) {
10           root.node1 = root;
11           root.node2 = root;
12           return root;
13       }
14       BiNode tail3 = (part3 == null) ? null : part3.node1;
15
16       /* join left to root */
17       if (part1 == null) {
18           concat(part3.node1, root);
19       } else {
20           concat(part1.node1, root);
21       }
22
23       /* join right to root */
24       if (part3 == null) {
25           concat(root, part1);
26       } else {
27           concat(root, part3);
28       }
29
30       /* join right to left */
31       if (part1 != null && part3 != null) {
```

```
32        concat(tail3, part1);
33    }
34
35    return part1 == null ? root : part1;
36 }
37
38 /* Convert list to a circular linked list, and then break the
39  * circular connection. */
40 public static BiNode convert(BiNode root) {
41    BiNode head = convertToCircular(root);
42    head.node1.node2 = null;
43    head.node1 = null;
44    return head;
45 }
```

Observe that we have moved the main parts of the code into `convertToCircular`. The `convert` method calls this method to get the head of the circular linked list, and then breaks the circular connection.

The approach takes O(N) time, since each node is only touched an average of once (or, more accurately, O(1) times).

17.14 *Oh, no! You have just completed a lengthy document when you have an unfortunate Find/Replace mishap. You have accidentally removed all spaces, punctuation, and capitalization in the document. A sentence like "I reset the computer. It still didn't boot!" would become "iresetthecomputeritstilldidntboot". You figure that you can add back in the punctuation and capitalization later, once you get the individual words properly separated. Most of the words will be in a dictionary, but some strings, like proper names, will not.*

Given a dictionary (a list of words), design an algorithm to find the optimal way of "unconcatenating" a sequence of words. In this case, "optimal" is defined to be the parsing which minimizes the number of unrecognized sequences of characters.

For example, the string "jesslookedjustliketimherbrother" would be optimally parsed as "JESS looked just like TIM her brother". This parsing has seven unrecognized characters, which we have capitalized for clarity.

pg 165

SOLUTION

Some interviewers like to cut to the chase and give you the specific problems. Others, though, like to give you a lot of unnecessary context, like this problem has. It's useful in such cases to boil down the problem to what it's really all about.

In this case, the problem is really about finding a way to break up a string into separate words such that as few characters as possible are "left out" of the parsing.

Note that we do not attempt to "understand" the string. We could just as well parse "thisisawesome" to be "this is a we some" as we could "this is awesome."

The key to this problem is to find a way to define the solution (that is, parsed string) in terms of its subproblems. One way to do this is to recurse through the string. At each point, the optimal parsing is the better of two possible decisions:

1. Inserting a space after this character.

2. Not inserting a space after this character.

We'll walk through this problem for the string thit as shown below. For clarity, we will use the following notation:

*   CAPITALIZE the invalid (non-dictionary) words

*   Underline valid words

*   **Bold** characters that are adjoined to each other (since they have no space between them).

These **bold** characters are within strings that are still being "processed," and we have therefore not yet made a decision as to whether they are valid or invalid (in the dictionary or not).

```
1    p(thit)
2       = min(T + p(hit), p(thit)) --> 1 inv.
3          T + p(hit) = min(T + H + p(it), T + p(hit)) --> 1 inv.
4             T + H + p(it) = min(T + H + i + p(t), T + H + p(it)) --> 2
5                T + H + i + p(t) = T + H + i + T = 3 invalid
6                T + H + p(it) = T + H + it = 2 invalid
7             T + p(hit) = min(T + hi + p(t), T + p(hit)) --> 1 inv.
8                T + hi + p(t) = T + hi + T = 2 invalid
9                T + p(hit) = T + hit = 1 invalid
10         p(thit) = min(TH + p(it), p(thit)) --> 2 inv.
11            TH + p(it) = min(TH + i + p(t), TH + p(it)) --> 2 inv.
12               TH + i + p(t) = TH + i + T = 3 invalid
13               TH + p(it) = TH + it = 2 invalid
14         p(thit) = min(THI + p(t), p(thit)) --> 4 inv.
15            THI + p(t) = THI + T = 4 invalid
16         p(thit) = THIT = 4 invalid
```

In the above steps, observe that each level divides into two parts. The first splits the string and the second adjoins it.

For example, when we first call p(thit), the current character being processed is just the first t. We recurse in two different directions. The first one (line 3) inserts a space after t and tries to find the most optimal way of parsing hit. The second one (line 10) tries to find the most optimal way of parsing such that there is no space between t and h. As we do this repeatedly, we will eventually look at every possible way of parsing the string.

The code below implements this solution. For simplicity, we have implemented this algorithm to return only the number of invalid characters.

```
1   public int parseSimple(int wordStart, int wordEnd) {
2       if (wordEnd >= sentence.length()) {
3           return wordEnd - wordStart;
4       }
5
6       String word = sentence.substring(wordStart, wordEnd + 1);
7
8       /* break current word */
9       int bestExact = parseSimple(wordEnd + 1, wordEnd + 1);
10      if (!dictionary.contains(word)) {
11          bestExact += word.length();
12      }
13
14      /* extend current word */
15      int bestExtend = parseSimple(wordStart, wordEnd + 1);
16
17      /* find best */
18      return Math.min(bestExact, bestExtend);
19  }
```

There are two major optimizations we can make to this code:

- Some of the recursive cases overlap. For example, in the earlier walkthrough, we repeatedly compute the optimal parsing for it. Instead, we should just cache this result the first time we compute it, and reuse it later. We can use dynamic programming to do this.

- In some cases, we may be able to predict that a particular parsing will produce invalid strings. For example, if we were trying to parse the string xten, there are no words that begin with xt. Our current solution, however, will attempt to parse the string as xt + p(en), xte + p(n), and xten. Each time we will find that such words do not exist in the dictionary. Instead, we should just put a space after the x and do the best parsing we can from there. How can we quickly know that there are no strings beginning with xt? By using a trie.

The code below implements both of these optimizations.

```
1   public int parseOptimized(int wordStart, int wordEnd,
2                             Hashtable<Integer, Integer> cache) {
3       if (wordEnd >= sentence.length()) {
4           return wordEnd - wordStart;
5       }
6       if (cache.containsKey(wordStart)) {
7           return cache.get(wordStart);
8       }
9
10      String currentWord = sentence.substring(wordStart, wordEnd + 1);
11
12      /* check if prefix is in dictionary (false --> partial match) */
```

```
13      boolean validPartial = dictionary.contains(currentWord, false);
14
15      /* break current word */
16      int bestExact = parseOptimized(wordEnd + 1, wordEnd + 1, cache);
17
18      /* if full string is not in dictionary, add to invalid count. */
19      if (!validPartial || !dictionary.contains(currentWord, true)) {
20         bestExact += currentWord.length();
21      }
22
23      /* extend current word */
24      int bestExtend = Integer.MAX_VALUE;
25      if (validPartial) {
26         bestExtend = parseOptimized(wordStart, wordEnd + 1, cache);
27      }
28
29      /* find best */
30      int min = Math.min(bestExact, bestExtend);
31      cache.put(wordStart, min); // Cache result
32      return min;
33 }
```

Observe that we use a hash table to cache results. The key is the index of the *start* of the word. That is, we're caching the best way to parse the rest of the string.

We can make this code return the fully parsed string, but it's a bit more tedious. We will need to use a wrapper class called Result so that we can return both the number of invalid characters and the optimal string. Had we been implementing this with C++, we could have instead just passed a value by reference.

```
1   public class Result {
2       public int invalid = Integer.MAX_VALUE;
3       public String parsed = "";
4       public Result(int inv, String p) {
5          invalid = inv;
6          parsed = p;
7       }
8
9       public Result clone() {
10          return new Result(this.invalid, this.parsed);
11       }
12
13      public static Result min(Result r1, Result r2) {
14          if (r1 == null) {
15             return r2;
16          } else if (r2 == null) {
17             return r1;
18          }
19          return r2.invalid < r1.invalid ? r2 : r1;
20       }
21 }
```

```
22
23 public Result parse(int wordStart, int wordEnd,
24                     Hashtable<Integer, Result> cache) {
25   if (wordEnd >= sentence.length()) {
26     return new Result(wordEnd - wordStart,
27       sentence.substring(wordStart).toUpperCase());
28   }
29   if (cache.containsKey(wordStart)) {
30     return cache.get(wordStart).clone();
31   }
32   String currentWord = sentence.substring(wordStart, wordEnd + 1);
33   boolean validPartial = dictionary.contains(currentWord, false);
34   boolean validExact = validPartial &&
35                     dictionary.contains(currentWord, true);
36
37   /* break current word */
38   Result bestExact = parse(wordEnd + 1, wordEnd + 1, cache);
39   if (validExact) {
40     bestExact.parsed = currentWord + " " + bestExact.parsed;
41   } else {
42     bestExact.invalid += currentWord.length();
43     bestExact.parsed = currentWord.toUpperCase() + " " +
44                     bestExact.parsed;
45   }
46
47   /* extend current word */
48   Result bestExtend = null;
49   if (validPartial) {
50     bestExtend = parse(wordStart, wordEnd + 1, cache);
51   }
52
53   /* find best */
54   Result best = Result.min(bestExact, bestExtend);
55   cache.put(wordStart, best.clone());
56   return best;
57 }
```

Be very careful in dynamic programming problems of how you cache objects. If the value you are caching is an object and not a primitive data type, it is very likely that you need to clone the object. You will see this in lines 30 and 55 above. If we don't clone it, future calls to parse will unintentionally modify the values in the cache.

Hard

Additional Review Problems: Solutions

Chapter 18

Solutions to Chapter 18 | Hard

18.1   *Write a function that adds two numbers. You should not use + or any arithmetic operators.*

pg 167

SOLUTION

Our first instinct in problems like these should be that we're going to have to work with bits. Why? Because when you take away the + sign, what other choice do we have? Plus, that's how computers do it!

Our next thought should be to really, really understand how addition works. We can walk through an addition problem to see if we can understand something new—some pattern—and then see if we can replicate that with code.

So let's do just that—let's walk through an addition problem. We'll work in base 10 so that it's easier to see.

To add 759 + 674, I would usually add `digit[0]` from each number, carry the one, add `digit[1]` from each number, carry the one, and so on. You could take the same approach in binary: add each digit, and carry the one as necessary.

Can we make this a little easier? Yes! Imagine I decided to split apart the "addition" and "carry" steps. That is, I do the following:

1. Add 759 + 674, but "forget" to carry. I then get 323.

2. Add 759 + 674 but only do the carrying, rather than the addition of each digit. I then get 1110.

3. Add the result of the first two operations (recursively, using the same process described in step 1 and 2): 1110 + 323 = 1433.

Now, how would we do this in binary?

1. If I add two binary numbers together, but forget to carry, the ith bit in the sum will be 0 only if a and b have the same ith bit (both 0 or both 1). This is essentially an XOR.

2. If I add two numbers together but *only* carry, I will have a 1 in the ith bit of the sum only if bits i - 1 of a and b are both 1s. This is an AND, shifted.

3. Now, recurse until there's nothing to carry.

The following code implements this algorithm.

```
1   public static int add(int a, int b) {
2       if (b == 0) return a;
3       int sum = a ^ b; // add without carrying
4       int carry = (a & b) << 1; // carry, but don't add
5       return add(sum, carry); // recurse
6   }
```

Problems requiring us to implement core operations like addition and subtraction are relatively common. The key in all of these problems is to dig into how these operations

---

are usually implemented, so that we can re-implement them with the constraints of the given problem.

18.2 *Write a method to shuffle a deck of cards. It must be a perfect shuffle—in other words, each of the 52! permutations of the deck has to be equally likely. Assume that you are given a random number generator which is perfect.*

pg 167

SOLUTION

This is a very well-known interview question, and a well-known algorithm. If you aren't one of the lucky few to already know this algorithm, read on.

Let's start with a brute force approach. We could randomly select cards and put them into a new deck. Of course, we know that we'll actually implement the deck as an array, so we need some way of marking the spot as "dead."

```
Original Deck (Before Picking 4):  [1] [2] [3] [4] [5]
```

```
/* Pick a random element to move into the front of the shuffled
 * deck. Mark element in original array as "dead," so that we
 * don't select it again. */
Shuffled Deck (After Picking 4):   [4] [?] [?] [?] [?]
Original Deck (After Picking 4):   [1] [2] [3] [X] [5]
```

The tricky part is, how do we mark [4] as dead such that we prevent that element from being picked again? One way to do it is to swap the now-dead [4] with the first card in the deck:

```
Original Deck (Before Picking 4):  [1] [2] [3] [4] [5]
```

```
/* Pick a random element to move into the front of the shuffled
 * deck. Have element 1 replace the just-selected element. */
Shuffled Deck (After Picking 4):   [4] [?] [?] [?] [?]
Original Deck (After Picking 4):   [X] [2] [3] [1] [5]
```

```
/* Pick a random element to move into the next spot in the
 * shuffled deck. Have element 2 replace the just-selected
 * element. */
Shuffled Deck (After Picking 3):   [4] [3] [?] [?] [?]
Original Deck (After Picking 3):   [X] [X] [2] [1] [5]
```

By doing it this way, it's much easier for the algorithm to "know" that the first k cards are dead than that, for example, the third, fourth, and ninth cards are dead.

We can also optimize this by merging the shuffled deck and the original deck into one.

```
Original Deck (Before Picking 4):  [1] [2] [3] [4] [5]
```

```
/* Select a random element between 1 and 5 to swap with element 1.
 * For this example, we'll assume we selected element 4.
```

```
* Afterwards, element 1 is "dead." */
Original Deck (After Picking 4):    [4] [2] [3] [1] [5]


/* Element 1 is now dead. Select a random element to swap with
 * element 2. For this example, we'll assume we selected element
 * 3.*/
Original Deck (After Picking 3):    [4] [3] [2] [1] [5]


/* Repeat. For all i between 0 and n-1, swap a random element j
 * (j >= i, j < n) with element i. */
```

This is an easy algorithm to implement iteratively:

```
1   public void shuffleArray(int[] cards) {
2       int temp, index;
3       for (int i = 0; i < cards.length; i++) {
4           /* Cards with indices 0 through i-1 have already been chosen
5            * (they have been moved to the front), so we are now
6            * selecting a random card with an index greater than or
7            * equal to i. */
8           index = (int) (Math.random() * (cards.length - i)) + i;
9           temp = cards[i];
10          cards[i] = cards[index];
11          cards[index] = temp;
12      }
13  }
```

This algorithm is challenging to come up with on your own, but very commonly asked. It's worth your time to make sure you truly understand how it works before your interview.

18.3 *Write a method to randomly generate a set of m integers from an array of size n. Each element must have equal probability of being chosen.*

pg 167

SOLUTION

Our first instinct on this problem might be to randomly pick elements from the array and put them into our new subset array. But then, what if we pick the same element twice? Ideally, we'd want to somehow "shrink" the array to no longer contain that element. Shrinking is expensive though because of all the shifting required.

Instead of shrinking / shifting, we can swap the element with one at the beginning of the array and then "remember" that the array now only includes elements j and greater. That is, when we pick subset[0] to be array[k], we replace array[k] with the first element in the array. When we pick subset[1], we consider array[0] to be "dead" and we pick a random element y between 1 and array.size(). We then set subset[1] equal to array[y], and set array[y] equal to array[1]. Elements 0 and 1 are now "dead." Subset[2] is now chosen from array[2] through array[array.

size()], and so on.

```
1   /* Random number between lower and higher, inclusive */
2   public static int rand(int lower, int higher) {
3       return lower + (int)(Math.random() * (higher - lower + 1));
4   }
5
6   /* Pick M elements from original array. Clone original array so
7    * that we don't destroy the input. */
8   public static int[] pickMRandomly(int[] original, int m) {
9       int[] subset = new int[m];
10      int[] array = original.clone();
11      for (int j = 0; j < m; j++) {
12          int index = rand(j, array.length - 1);
13          subset[j] = array[index];
14          array[index] = array[j]; // array[j] is now "dead"
15      }
16      return subset;
17  }
```

18.4 *Write a method to count the number of 2s between 0 and n.*

pg 167

SOLUTION

Our first approach to this problem can be—and probably should be—a brute force solution. Remember that interviewers want to see how you're approaching a problem. Offering a brute force solution is a great way to start.

```
1   /* Counts the number of '2' digits between 0 and n */
2   int numberOf2sInRange(int n) {
3       int count = 0;
4       for (int i = 2; i <= n; i++) { // Might as well start at 2
5           count += numberOf2s(i);
6       }
7       return count;
8   }
9
10  /* Counts the number of '2' digits in a single number */
11  int numberOf2s(int n) {
12      int count = 0;
13      while (n > 0) {
14          if (n % 10 == 2) {
15              count++;
16          }
17          n = n / 10;
18      }
19      return count;
20  }
```

The only interesting part is that it's probably cleaner to separate out numberOf2s into a separate method. This demonstrates an eye for code cleanliness.

Improved Solution

Rather than looking at the problem by ranges of numbers, we can look at the problem digit by digit. Picture a sequence of numbers:

```
0    1    2    3    4    5    6    7    8    9
10   11   12   13   14   15   16   17   18   19
20   21   22   23   24   25   26   27   28   29
...
110  111  112  113  114  115  116  117  118  119
```

We know that roughly one tenth of the time, the last digit wil be a 2 since it happens once in any sequence of ten numbers. In fact, any digit is a 2 roughly one tenth of the time.

We say "roughly" because there are (very common) boundary conditions. For example, between 1 and 100, the 10s digit is a 2 exactly $1/10^{th}$ of the time. However, between 1 and 37, the 10s digit is a 2 much more than $1/10^{th}$ of the time.

We can work out what exactly the ratio is by looking at the three cases individually: digit < 2, digit = 2, and digit > 2.

Case digit < 2

Consider the value x = 61523 and d = 3, and observe that x[d] = 1 (that is, the dth digit of x is 1). There are 2s at the 3rd digit in the ranges 2000 - 2999, 12000 - 12999, 22000 - 22999, 32000 - 32999, 42000 - 42999, and 52000 - 52999. We will not yet have hit the range 62000 - 62999, so there are 6000 2s total in the 3rd digit. This is the same amount as if we were just counting all the 2s in the 3rd digit between 1 and 60000.

In other words, we can round *down* to the nearest 10^{d+1}, and then divide by 10, to compute the number of 2s in the dth digit.

```
if x[d] < 2: count2sInRangeAtDigit(x, d) =
    let y = round down to nearest 10^(d+1)
    return y / 10
```

Case digit > 2

Now, let's look at the case where dth digit of x is greater than 2 (x[d] > 2). We can apply almost the exact same logic to see that there are the same number of 2s in the 3rd digit in the range 0 - 63525 as there as in the range 0 - 70000. So, rather than rounding down, we round up.

```
if x[d] > 2: count2sInRangeAtDigit(x, d) =
    let y = round up to nearest 10^(d+1)
    return y / 10
```

Case digit = 2

The final case may be the trickiest, but it follows from the earlier logic. Consider x = 62523 and d = 3. We know that there are the same ranges of 2s from before (that is, the ranges 2000 - 2999, 12000 - 12999, ..., 52000 - 52999). How many appear in the 3rd digit in the final, partial range from 62000 - 62523? Well, that should be pretty easy. It's just 524 (62000, 62001, ..., 62523).

```
if x[d] = 2: count2sInRangeAtDigit(x, d) =
    let y = round down to nearest 10^{d+1}
    let z = right side of x (i.e., x % 10^d)
    return y / 10 + z + 1
```

Now, all you need is to iterate through each digit in the number. Implementing this code is reasonably straightforward.

```
1   public static int count2sInRangeAtDigit(int number, int d) {
2       int powerOf10 = (int) Math.pow(10, d);
3       int nextPowerOf10 = powerOf10 * 10;
4       int right = number % powerOf10;
5
6       int roundDown = number - number % nextPowerOf10;
7       int roundUp = roundDown + nextPowerOf10;
8
9       int digit = (number / powerOf10) % 10;
10      if (digit < 2) { // if the digit in spot digit is
11          return roundDown / 10;
12      } else if (digit == 2) {
13          return roundDown / 10 + right + 1;
14      } else {
15          return roundUp / 10;
16      }
17  }
18
19  public static int count2sInRange(int number) {
20      int count = 0;
21      int len = String.valueOf(number).length();
22      for (int digit = 0; digit < len; digit++) {
23          count += count2sInRangeAtDigit(number, digit);
24      }
25      return count;
26  }
```

This question requires very careful testing. Make sure to generate a list of test cases, and to work through each of them.

18.5 *You have a large text file containing words. Given any two words, find the shortest distance (in terms of number of words) between them in the file. Can you make the searching operation in O(1) time? What about the space complexity for your solution?*

pg 167

SOLUTION

We will assume for this question that it doesn't matter whether word1 or word2 appears first. This is a question you should ask your interviewer. If the word order does matter, we can make the small modification shown in the code below.

To solve this problem, we can traverse the file just once. We remember throughout our traversal where we've last seen word1 and word2, storing the locations in `lastPosWord1` and `lastPosWord2`. When we come across word1, we compare it to `lastPosWord2` and update `min` as necessary, and then update `lastPosWord1`. We do the equivalent operation on word2. At the end of the traversal, we will have the minimum distance.

The code below implements this algorithm.

```
1   public int shortest(String[] words, String word1, String word2) {
2       int min = Integer.MAX_VALUE;
3       int lastPosWord1 = -1;
4       int lastPosWord2 = -1;
5       for (int i = 0; i < words.length; i++) {
6           String currentWord = words[i];
7           if (currentWord.equals(word1)) {
8               lastPosWord1 = i;
9               // Comment following 3 lines if word order matters
10              int distance = lastPosWord1 - lastPosWord2;
11              if (lastPosWord2 >= 0 && min > distance) {
12                  min = distance;
13              }
14          } else if (currentWord.equals(word2)) {
15              lastPosWord2 = i;
16              int distance = lastPosWord2 - lastPosWord1;
17              if (lastPosWord1 >= 0 && min > distance) {
18                  min = distance;
19              }
20          }
21      }
22      return min;
23  }
```

If we need to repeat the operation for other pairs of words, we can create a hash table with each word and the locations where it occurs. We then just need to find the minimum (arithmetic) difference between a value in `listA` and a value in `listB`.

There are several ways to compute the minimum difference between a value in `listA` and a value in `listB`. Consider the following lists:

```
listA: {1, 2, 9, 15, 25}
listB: {4, 10, 19}
```

We can merge these lists into one sorted list, but "tag" each number with the original list. Tagging can be done by wrapping each value in a class that has two member variables: `data` (to store the actual value) and `listNumber`.

```
list: {1a, 2a, 4b, 9a, 10b, 15a, 19b, 25a}
```

Finding the minimum distance is now just a matter of traversing this merged list to find the minimum distance between two consecutive numbers which have different list tags. In this case, the solution would be a distance of 1 (between 9a and 10b).

18.6 *Describe an algorithm to find the smallest one million numbers in one billion numbers. Assume that the computer memory can hold all one billion numbers.*

pg 167

SOLUTION

There are a number of ways to approach this problem. We will go through three of them: sorting, min heap, and selection rank.

Solution 1: Sorting

We can sort the elements in ascending order and then take the first million numbers from that. The time complexity is $O(n \log(n))$.

Solution 2: Min Heap

We can use a min heap to solve this problem. We first create a max heap (largest element at the top) for the first million numbers.

Then, we traverse through the list. On each element, we insert it into the list and delete the largest element.

At the end of the traversal, we will have a heap containing the smallest one million numbers. This algorithm is $O(n \log(m))$, where m is the number of values we are looking for.

Approach 3: Selection Rank Algorithm (if you can modify the original array)

Selection Rank is a well-known algorithm in computer science to find the ith smallest (or largest) element in an array in linear time.

If the elements are unique, you can find the ith smallest element in expected $O(n)$ time. The basic algorithm operates works like this:

1. Pick a random element in the array and use it as a "pivot." Partition elements around the pivot, keeping track of the number of elements on the left side of the partition.

2. If there are exactly i elements on the left, then you just return the biggest element on the left.

3. If the left side is bigger than i, repeat the algorithm on just the left part of the array.

4. If the left side is smaller than i, repeat the algorithm on the right, but look for the element with rank i - leftSize.

The code below implements this algorithm.

```
1   public int partition(int[] array, int left, int right, int pivot) {
2       while (true) {
3           while (left <= right && array[left] <= pivot) {
4               left++;
5           }
6
7           while (left <= right && array[right] > pivot) {
8               right--;
9           }
10
11          if (left > right) {
12              return left - 1;
13          }
14          swap(array, left, right);
15      }
16  }
17
18  public int rank(int[] array, int left, int right, int rank) {
19      int pivot = array[randomIntInRange(left, right)];
20
21      /* Partition and return end of left partition */
22      int leftEnd = partition(array, left, right, pivot);
23
24      int leftSize = leftEnd - left + 1;
25      if (leftSize == rank + 1) {
26          return max(array, left, leftEnd);
27      } else if (rank < leftSize) {
28          return rank(array, left, leftEnd, rank);
29      } else {
30          return rank(array, leftEnd + 1, right, rank - leftSize);
31      }
32  }
```

Once you have found the ith smallest element, you can run through the array to find all values less than or equal to this element.

If the elements are not unique (which they are unlikely to be), we can tweak this algorithm slightly to accomodate this change. However, we no longer have as tight of a guarantee on the runtime.

There is an algorithm that can *guarantee* that we can find the ith smallest element in linear time, regardless of the uniqueness of the elements. However, the complexity of this algorithm is far beyond the scope of this interview. If you are interested though, you can look up the algorithm in CLRS' Introduction to Algorithms textbook.

18.7 *Given a list of words, write a program to find the longest word made of other words in the list.*

pg 168

SOLUTION

This problem seems complex, so let's simplify it. What if we just wanted to know the longest word made of *two* other words in the list?

We could solve this by iterating through the list, from the longest word to the shortest word. For each word, we would split it into all possible pairs and check if both the left and right side are contained in the list.

The pseudocode for this would look like the following:

```
1   String getLongestWord(String[] list) {
2       String[] array = list.SortByLength();
3       /* Create map for easy lookup */
4       HashMap<String, Boolean> map = new HashMap<String, Boolean>;
5
6       for (String str : array) {
7           map.put(str, true);
8       }
9
10      for (String s : array) {
11          // Divide into every possible pair
12          for (int i = 1; i < s.length(); i++) {
13              String left = s.substring(0, i);
14              String right = s.substring(i);
15              // Check if both sides are in the array
16              if (map[left] == true && map[right] == true) {
17                  return s;
18              }
19          }
20      }
21      return str;
22  }
```

This works greater for when we just want to know composites of two words. But what if a word could be formed by any number of other words?

In this case, we could apply a very similar approach, with one modification: rather than simply looking up if the right side is in the array, we would recursively see if we can build the right side from the other elements in the array.

The code below implements this algorithm:

```
1   String printLongestWord(String arr[]) {
2       HashMap<String, Boolean> map = new HashMap<String, Boolean>();
3       for (String str : arr) {
4           map.put(str, true);
5       }
6       Arrays.sort(arr, new LengthComparator()); // Sort by length
7       for (String s : arr) {
8           if (canBuildWord(s, true, map)) {
9               System.out.println(s);
10              return s;
11          }
12      }
13      return "";
14  }
15
16  boolean canBuildWord(String str, boolean isOriginalWord,
17                       HashMap<String, Boolean> map) {
18      if (map.containsKey(str) && !isOriginalWord) {
19          return map.get(str);
20      }
21      for (int i = 1; i < str.length(); i++) {
22          String left = str.substring(0, i);
23          String right = str.substring(i);
24          if (map.containsKey(left) && map.get(left) == true &&
25              canBuildWord(right, false, map)) {
26              return true;
27          }
28      }
29      map.put(str, false);
30      return false;
31  }
```

Note that in this solution we have performed a small optimization. We use a dynamic programming approach to cache the results between calls. This way, if we repeatedly need to check if there's any way to build "testingtester," we'll only have to compute it once.

A boolean flag isOriginalWord is used to complete the above optimization. The method canBuildWord is called for the original word and for each substring, and its first step is to check the cache for a previously calculated result. However, for the original words, we have a problem: map is initialized to true for them, but we don't want to return true (since a word cannot be composed solely of itself). Therefore, for the original word, we simply bypass this check using the isOriginalWord flag.

18.8 *Given a string s and an array of smaller strings T, design a method to search s for each small string in T.*

pg 168

SOLUTION

First, create a suffix tree for s. For example, if your word were bibs, you would create the following tree:

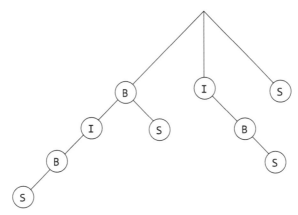

Then, all you need to do is search in the suffix tree for each string in T. Note that if "B" were a word, you would come up with two locations.

```
1   public class SuffixTree {
2     SuffixTreeNode root = new SuffixTreeNode();
3     public SuffixTree(String s) {
4       for (int i = 0; i < s.length(); i++) {
5         String suffix = s.substring(i);
6         root.insertString(suffix, i);
7       }
8     }
9
10    public ArrayList<Integer> search(String s) {
11      return root.search(s);
12    }
13  }
14
15  public class SuffixTreeNode {
16    HashMap<Character, SuffixTreeNode> children = new
17                     HashMap<Character, SuffixTreeNode>();
18    char value;
19    ArrayList<Integer> indexes = new ArrayList<Integer>();
20    public SuffixTreeNode() { }
21
22    public void insertString(String s, int index) {
```

```
23        indexes.add(index);
24        if (s != null && s.length() > 0) {
25            value = s.charAt(0);
26            SuffixTreeNode child = null;
27            if (children.containsKey(value)) {
28                child = children.get(value);
29            } else {
30                child = new SuffixTreeNode();
31                children.put(value, child);
32            }
33            String remainder = s.substring(1);
34            child.insertString(remainder, index);
35        }
36    }
37
38    public ArrayList<Integer> search(String s) {
39        if (s == null || s.length() == 0) {
40            return indexes;
41        } else {
42            char first = s.charAt(0);
43            if (children.containsKey(first)) {
44                String remainder = s.substring(1);
45                return children.get(first).search(remainder);
46            }
47        }
48        return null;
49    }
50 }
```

18.9   Numbers are randomly generated and passed to a method. Write a program to find
and maintain the median value as new values are generated.

pg 168

SOLUTIONS

One solution is to use two priority heaps: a max heap for the values below the median,
and a min heap for the values above the median. This will divide the elements roughly
in half, with the middle two elements as the top of the two heaps. This makes it trivial
to find the median.

What do we mean by "roughly in half," though? "Roughly" means that, if we have an odd
number of values, one heap will have an extra value. Observe that the following is true:

- If maxHeap.size() > minHeap.size(), then heap1.top() will be the median.

- If maxHeap.size() == minHeap.size(), then the average of maxHeap.top()
  and minHeap.top() will be the median.

By the way in which we rebalance the heaps, we will ensure that it is always maxHeap with extra element.

The algorithm works as follows. When a new value arrives, it is placed in the maxHeap if the value is less than or equal to the median, otherwise it is placed into the minHeap. The heap sizes can be equal, or the maxHeap may have one extra element. This constraint can easily be restored by shifting an element from one heap to the other. The median is available in constant time, by looking at the top element(s). Updates take $O(\log(n))$ time.

```
1   private Comparator<Integer> maxHeapComparator;
2   private Comparator<Integer> minHeapComparator;
3   private PriorityQueue<Integer> maxHeap, minHeap;
4
5   public void addNewNumber(int randomNumber) {
6      /* Note: addNewNumber maintains a condition that
7       * maxHeap.size() >= minHeap.size() */
8      if (maxHeap.size() == minHeap.size()) {
9         if ((minHeap.peek() != null) &&
10           randomNumber > minHeap.peek()) {
11           maxHeap.offer(minHeap.poll());
12           minHeap.offer(randomNumber);
13        } else {
14           maxHeap.offer(randomNumber);
15        }
16     } else {
17        if(randomNumber < maxHeap.peek()) {
18           minHeap.offer(maxHeap.poll());
19           maxHeap.offer(randomNumber);
20        }
21        else {
22           minHeap.offer(randomNumber);
23        }
24     }
25  }
26
27  public static double getMedian() {
28     /* maxHeap is always at least as big as minHeap. So if maxHeap
29      * is empty, then minHeap is also. */
30     if (maxHeap.isEmpty()) {
31        return 0;
32     }
33     if (maxHeap.size() == minHeap.size()) {
34        return ((double)minHeap.peek()+(double)maxHeap.peek()) / 2;
35     } else {
36        /* If maxHeap and minHeap are of different sizes, then
37         * maxHeap must have one extra element. Return maxHeap's
38         * top element.*/
39        return maxHeap.peek();
40     }
41  }
```

18.10 *Given two words of equal length that are in a dictionary, write a method to trans-form one word into another word by changing only one letter at a time. The new word you get in each step must be in the dictionary.*

pg 168

SOLUTION

Although this problem seems tough, it's actually a straightforward modification of breadth first search. Each word in our "graph" branches to all words in the dictionary that are one edit away. The interesting part is the implementation. Specifically, should we build a graph as we go?

We could, but there's an easier way. We can instead use a "backtrack map." In this back-track map, if B[v] = w, then you know that you edited v to get w. When we reach our end word, we can use this backtrack map repeatedly to reverse our path. See the code below:

```
1   LinkedList<String> transform(String startWord, String stopWord,
2       Set<String> dictionary) {
3       startWord = startWord.toUpperCase();
4       stopWord = stopWord.toUpperCase();
5       Queue<String> actionQueue = new LinkedList<String>();
6       Set<String> visitedSet = new HashSet<String>();
7       Map<String, String> backtrackMap =
8           new TreeMap<String, String>();
9
10      actionQueue.add(startWord);
11      visitedSet.add(startWord);
12
13      while (!actionQueue.isEmpty()) {
14          String w = actionQueue.poll();
15          /* For each possible word v from w with one edit operation */
16          for (String v : getOneEditWords(w)) {
17              if (v.equals(stopWord)) {
18                  // Found our word! Now, back track.
19                  LinkedList<String> list = new LinkedList<String>();
20                  // Append v to list
21                  list.add(v);
22                  while (w != null) {
23                      list.add(0, w);
24                      w = backtrackMap.get(w);
25                  }
26                  return list;
27              }
28              /* If v is a dictionary word */
29              if (dictionary.contains(v)) {
30                  if (!visitedSet.contains(v)) {
31                      actionQueue.add(v);
32                      visitedSet.add(v); // mark visited
```

```
33                    backtrackMap.put(v, w);
34                }
35            }
36        }
37    }
38    return null;
39 }
40
41 Set<String> getOneEditWords(String word) {
42    Set<String> words = new TreeSet<String>();
43    for (int i = 0; i < word.length(); i++) {
44        char[] wordArray = word.toCharArray();
45        // change that letter to something else
46        for (char c = 'A'; c <= 'Z'; c++) {
47            if (c != word.charAt(i)) {
48                wordArray[i] = c;
49                words.add(new String(wordArray));
50            }
51        }
52    }
53    return words;
54 }
```

Let n be the length of the start word and m be the number of like-sized words in the dictionary. The runtime of this algorithm is O(nm) since the while loop will dequeue at most m unique words. The for loop is O(n) since it walks down the string applying a fixed number of replacements for each character.

18.11 *Imagine you have a square matrix, where each cell (pixel) is either black or white. Design an algorithm to find the maximum subsquare such that all four borders are filled with black pixels.*

pg 168

SOLUTION

Like many problems, there's an easy way and a hard way to solve this. We'll go through both solutions.

The "Simple" Solution: O(N⁴)

We know that the biggest possible square has a length of size N, and there is only one possible square of size NxN. We can easily check for that square and return if we find it.

If we do not find a square of size NxN, we can try the next best thing: (N-1) x (N-1). We iterate through all squares of this size and return the first one we find. We then do the same for N-2, N-3, and so on. Since we are searching progressively smaller squares, we know that the first square we find is the biggest.

Our code works as follows:

```
1   Subsquare findSquare(int[][] matrix) {
2     for (int i = matrix.length; i >= 1; i--) {
3       Subsquare square = findSquareWithSize(matrix, i);
4       if (square != null) return square;
5     }
6     return null;
7   }
8
9   Subsquare findSquareWithSize(int[][] matrix, int squareSize) {
10    /* On an edge of length N, there are (N - sz + 1) squares of
11     * length sz. */
12    int count = matrix.length - squareSize + 1;
13
14    /* Iterate through all squares with side length squareSize. */
15    for (int row = 0; row < count; row++) {
16      for (int col = 0; col < count; col++) {
17        if (isSquare(matrix, row, col, squareSize)) {
18          return new Subsquare(row, col, squareSize);
19        }
20      }
21    }
22    return null;
23  }
24
25  boolean isSquare(int[][] matrix, int row, int col, int size) {
26    // Check top and bottom border.
27    for (int j = 0; j < size; j++){
28      if (matrix[row][col+j] == 1) {
29        return false;
30      }
31      if (matrix[row+size-1][col+j] == 1){
32        return false;
33      }
34    }
35
36    // Check left and right border.
37    for (int i = 1; i < size - 1; i++){
38      if (matrix[row+i][col] == 1){
39        return false;
40      }
41      if (matrix[row+i][col+size-1] == 1){
42        return false;
43      }
44    }
45    return true;
46  }
```

Pre-Processing Solution: O(N³)

A large part of the slowness of the "simple" solution above is due to the fact we have to do O(N) work each time we want to check a potential square. By doing some pre-processing, we can cut down the time of isSquare to O(1). The time of the whole algorithm is reduced to O(N³).

If we analyze what isSquare does, we realize that all it ever needs to know is if the next squareSize items, on the right of as well as below particular cells, are zeros. We can pre-compute this data in a straightforward, iterative fashion.

We iterate from right to left, bottom to top. At each cell, we do the following computation:

```
if A[r][c] is white, zeros right and zeros below are 0
else A[r][c].zerosRight = A[r][c + 1].zerosRight + 1
     A[r][c].zerosBelow = A[r + 1][c].zerosBelow + 1
```

Below is an example of these values for a potential matrix.

(0s right, 0s below)

0,0	1,3	0,0
2,2	1,2	0,0
2,1	1,1	0,0

Original Matrix

W	B	W
B	B	W
B	B	W

Now, instead of iterating through O(N) elements, the isSquare method just needs to check zerosRight and zerosBelow for the corners.

Our code for this algorithm is below. Note that findSquare and findSquareWithSize is equivalent, other than a call to processMatrix and working with a new data type thereafter.

```
1   public class SquareCell {
2       public int zerosRight = 0;
3       public int zerosBelow = 0;
4       /* declaration, getters, setters */
5   }
6
7   Subsquare findSquare(int[][] matrix) {
8       SquareCell[][] processed = processSquare(matrix);
9       for (int i = matrix.length; i >= 1; i--) {
10          Subsquare square = findSquareWithSize(processed, i);
11          if (square != null) return square;
12      }
13      return null;
14  }
15
```

```
16  Subsquare findSquareWithSize(SquareCell[][] processed,
17                              int squareSize) {
18    /* equivalent to first algorithm */
19  }
20
21
22  boolean isSquare(SquareCell[][] matrix, int row, int col,
23                   int size) {
24    SquareCell topLeft = matrix[row][col];
25    SquareCell topRight = matrix[row][col + size - 1];
26    SquareCell bottomLeft = matrix[row + size - 1][col];
27    if (topLeft.zerosRight < size) { // Check top edge
28      return false;
29    }
30    if (topLeft.zerosBelow < size) { // Check left edge
31      return false;
32    }
33    if (topRight.zerosBelow < size) { // Check right edge
34      return false;
35    }
36    if (bottomLeft.zerosRight < size) { // Check bottom edge
37      return false;
38    }
39    return true;
40  }
41
42  SquareCell[][] processSquare(int[][] matrix) {
43    SquareCell[][] processed =
44      new SquareCell[matrix.length][matrix.length];
45
46    for (int r = matrix.length - 1; r >= 0; r--) {
47      for (int c = matrix.length - 1; c >= 0; c--) {
48        int rightZeros = 0;
49        int belowZeros = 0;
50        // only need to process if it's a black cell
51        if (matrix[r][c] == 0) {
52          rightZeros++;
53          belowZeros++;
54          // next column over is on same row
55          if (c + 1 < matrix.length) {
56            SquareCell previous = processed[r][c + 1];
57            rightZeros += previous.zerosRight;
58          }
59          if (r + 1 < matrix.length) {
60            SquareCell previous = processed[r + 1][c];
61            belowZeros += previous.zerosBelow;
62          }
63        }
64        processed[r][c] = new SquareCell(rightZeros, belowZeros);
65      }
```

```
66     }
67     return processed;
68 }
```

18.12 *Given an NxN matrix of positive and negative integers, write code to find the subma-*
trix with the largest possible sum.

pg 168

SOLUTION

This problem can be approached in a variety of ways. We'll start with the brute force
solution and then optimize the solution from there.

Brute Force Solution: O(N⁶)

Like many "maximizing" problems, this problem has a straightforward brute force solution. This solution simply iterates through all possible submatrices, computes the sum,
and finds the biggest.

To iterate through all possible submatrices (with no duplicates), we simply need to
iterate through all order pairs of rows, and then all ordered pairs of columns.

This solution is $O(N^6)$, since we iterate through $O(N^4)$ submatrices and it takes $O(N^2)$
time to compute the area of each.

Dynamic Programming Solution: O(N⁴)

Notice that the earlier solution is made slower by a factor of $O(N^2)$ simply because
computing the sum of a matrix is so slow. Can we reduce the time to compute the area?
Yes! In fact, we can reduce the time of computeSum to $O(1)$.

Consider the following rectangle:

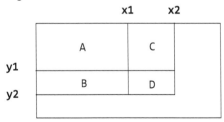

Suppose we knew the following values:

```
ValD = area(point(0, 0) -> point(x2, y2))
ValC = area(point(0, 0) -> point(x2, y1))
ValB = area(point(0, 0) -> point(x1, y2))
ValA = area(point(0, 0) -> point(x1, y1))
```

Each Val* starts at the origin and ends at the bottom right corner of a subrectangle.

With these values, we know the following:

    area(D) = ValD - area(A union C) - area(A union B) + area(A).

Or, written another way:

    area(D) = ValD - ValB - ValC + ValA

We can efficiently compute these values for all points in the matrix by using similar logic:

    Val(x, y) = Val(x - 1, y) + Val(y - 1, x) - Val(x - 1, y - 1) +
                M[x][y]

We can precompute all such values, and then efficiently find the maximum submatrix.

The following code implements this algorithm.

```
1   int getMaxMatrix(int[][] original) {
2       int maxArea = Integer.MIN_VALUE; // Important! Max may be < 0
3       int rowCount = original.length;
4       int columnCount = original[0].length;
5       int[][] matrix = precomputeMatrix(original);
6       for (int row1 = 0; row1 < rowCount; row1++) {
7           for (int row2 = row1; row2 < rowCount; row2++) {
8               for (int col1 = 0; col1 < columnCount; col1++) {
9                   for (int col2 = col1; col2 < columnCount; col2++) {
10                      maxArea = Math.max(maxArea, computeSum(matrix,
11                          row1, row2, col1, col2));
12                  }
13              }
14          }
15      }
16      return maxArea;
17  }
18
19  int[][] precomputeMatrix(int[][] matrix) {
20      int[][] sumMatrix = new int[matrix.length][matrix[0].length];
21      for (int i = 0; i < matrix.length; i++) {
22          for (int j = 0; j < matrix.length; j++) {
23              if (i == 0 && j == 0) { // first cell
24                  sumMatrix[i][j] = matrix[i][j];
25              } else if (j == 0) { // cell in first column
26                  sumMatrix[i][j] = sumMatrix[i - 1][j] + matrix[i][j];
27              } else if (i == 0) { // cell in first row
28                  sumMatrix[i][j] = sumMatrix[i][j - 1] + matrix[i][j];
29              } else {
30                  sumMatrix[i][j] = sumMatrix[i - 1][j] +
31                      sumMatrix[i][j - 1] - sumMatrix[i - 1][j - 1] +
32                      matrix[i][j];
33              }
34          }
35      }
36      return sumMatrix;
37  }
```

```
38
39  int computeSum(int[][] summatrix, int i1, int i2, int j1, int j2) {
40      if (i1 == 0 && j1 == 0) { // starts at row 0, column 0
41          return summatrix[i2][j2];
42      } else if (i1 == 0) { // start at row 0
43          return summatrix[i2][j2] - summatrix[i2][j1 - 1];
44      } else if (j1 == 0) { // start at column 0
45          return summatrix[i2][j2] - summatrix[i1 - 1][j2];
46      } else {
47          return summatrix[i2][j2] - summatrix[i2][j1 - 1]
48              - summatrix[i1 - 1][j2] + summatrix[i1 - 1][j1 - 1];
49      }
50  }
```

Optimized Solution: O(N³)

Believe it or not, an even more optimal solution exists. If we have R rows and C columns, we can solve it in $O(R^2C)$ time.

Recall the solution to the maximum subarray problem: Given an array of integers, find the subarray with the largest sum." We can find the maximum subarray in $O(N)$ time. We will leverage this solution for this problem.

Every submatrix can be represented by a contiguous sequence of rows and a contiguous sequence of columns. If we were to iterate through every contiguous sequence of rows, we would then just need to find, for each of those, the set of columns that give us the highest sum. That is:

```
1  maxSum = 0
2  foreach rowStart in rows
3      foreach rowEnd in rows
4          /* We have a number of possible submatrices with rowStart
5           * and rowEnd as the top and bottom edge of the matrix.
6           * Find the colStart and colEnd edges that give the
7           * highest sum. */
8          maxSum = max(runningMaxSum, maxSum)
9  return maxSum
```

Now, the question is, how do we efficiently find the "best" colStart and colEnd? Here's where things get really fun.

Picture a submatrix:

rowStart

9	-8	1	3	-2
-3	7	6	-2	4
6	-4	-4	8	-7
12	-5	3	9	-5

rowEnd

We want to find the colStart and colEnd that give us the highest possible sum of all submatrices with rowStart as their top edge and rowEnd as their bottom edge. To do this, we can sum up each column and then apply the maximumSubArray function explained at the beginning of this problem.

For the earlier example, the maximum subarray is the first through fourth column. This means that the maximum submatrix is (rowStart, first column) through (rowEnd, fourth column).

We now have pseudocode that looks like the following.

```
1   maxSum = 0
2   foreach rowStart in rows
3      foreach rowEnd in rows
4         foreach col in columns
5            partialSum[col] = sum of matrix[rowStart, col] through
6                              matrix[rowEnd, col]
7         runningMaxSum = maxSubArray(partialSum)
8      maxSum = max(runningMaxSum, maxSum)
9   return maxSum
```

The sum in lines 5 and 6 takes R*C time to compute (since it iterates through rowStart through rowEnd), so this gives us a runtime of $O(R^3C)$. We're not quite done yet.

In lines 5 and 6, we're basically adding up a[0]...a[i] from scratch, even though in the previous iteration of the outer for loop, we already added up a[0]...a[i-1]. Let's cut out this duplicated effort.

```
1   maxSum = 0
2   foreach rowStart in rows
3      clear array partialSum
4      foreach rowEnd in rows
5         foreach col in columns
6            partialSum[col] += matrix[rowEnd, col]
7         runningMaxSum = maxSubArray(partialSum)
8      maxSum = max(runningMaxSum, maxSum)
9   return maxSum
```

Our full code looks like this:

```
1   public void clearArray(int[] array) {
2      for (int i = 0; i < array.length; i++) {
3         array[i] = 0;
4      }
5   }
6
7   public static int maxSubMatrix(int[][] matrix) {
8      int rowCount = matrix.length;
9      int colCount = matrix[0].length;
10
11     int[] partialSum = new int[colCount];
12     int maxSum = 0; // Max sum is an empty matrix
13
```

```
14   for (int rowStart = 0; rowStart < rowCount; rowStart++) {
15     clearArray(partialSum);
16
17     for (int rowEnd = rowStart; rowEnd < rowCount; rowEnd++) {
18       for (int i = 0; i < colCount; i++) {
19         partialSum[i] += matrix[rowEnd][i];
20       }
21
22       int tempMaxSum = maxSubArray(partialSum, colCount);
23
24       /* If you want to track the coordinates, add code here to
25        * do that. */
26       maxSum = Math.max(maxSum, tempMaxSum);
27     }
28   }
29   return maxSum;
30 }
31
32 public static int maxSubArray(int array[], int N) {
33   int maxSum = 0;
34   int runningSum = 0;
35
36   for (int i = 0; i < N; i++) {
37     runningSum += array[i];
38     maxSum = Math.max(maxSum, runningSum);
39
40     /* If runningSum is < 0, no point in trying to continue the
41      * series. Reset. */
42     if (runningSum < 0) {
43       runningSum = 0;
44     }
45   }
46   return maxSum;
47 }
```

This was an extremely complex problem. You would not be expected to figure out this entire problem in an interview without a lot of help from your interviewer.

18.13 *Given a list of millions of words, design an algorithm to create the largest possible rectangle of letters such that every row forms a word (reading left to right) and every column forms a word (reading top to bottom). The words need not be chosen consecutively from the list, but all rows must be the same length and all columns must be the same height.*

pg 168

SOLUTION

Many problems involving a dictionary can be solved by doing some pre-processing.

Solutions to Chapter 18 | Hard

Where can we do pre-processing?

Well, if we're going to create a rectangle of words, we know that each row must be the same length and each column must be the same length. So, let's group the words of the dictionary based on their sizes. Let's call this grouping D, where D[i] contains the list of words of length i.

Next, observe that we're looking for the largest rectangle. What is the absolute largest rectangle that could be formed? It's length(largest word)².

```
1   int maxRectangle = longestWord * longestWord;
2   for z = maxRectangle to 1 {
3     for each pair of numbers (i, j) where i*j = z {
4       /* attempt to make rectangle. return if successful. */
5     }
6   }
```

By iterating from the biggest possible rectangle to the smallest, we ensure that the first valid rectangle we find will be the largest possible one.

Now, for the hard part: makeRectangle(int l, int h). This method attempts to build a rectangle of words which has length l and height h.

One way to do this is to iterate through all (ordered) sets of h words and then check if the columns are also valid words. This will work, but it's rather inefficient.

Imagine that we are trying to build a 6x5 rectangle and the first couple rows are:

    there
    queen
    pizza
    .....

At this point, we know that the first column starts with tqp. We know—or *should* know—that no dictionary word starts with tqp. Why do we bother continuing to build a rectangle when we know we'll fail to create a valid one in the end?

This leads us to a more optimal solution. We can build a trie to easily look up if a substring is a prefix of a word in the dictionary. Then, when we build our rectangle, row by row, we check to see if the columns are all valid prefixes. If not, we fail immediately, rather than continue to try to build this rectangle.

The code below implements this algorithm. It is long and complex, so we will go through it step-by-step.

First, we do some pre-processing to group words by their lengths. We create an array of tries (one for each word length), but hold off on building the tries until we need them.

```
1   WordGroup[] groupList = WordGroup.createWordGroups(list);
2   int maxWordLength = groupList.length;
3   Trie trieList[] = new Trie[maxWordLength];
```

The maxRectangle method is the "main" part of our code. It starts with the biggest possible rectangle area (which is maxWordLength^2) and tries to build a rectangle of that size. If it fails, it subtracts one from the area and attempts this new, smaller size. The first rectangle that can be successfully built is guaranteed to be the biggest.

```
1   Rectangle maxRectangle() {
2       int maxSize = maxWordLength * maxWordLength;
3       for (int z = maxSize; z > 0; z--) { // start from biggest area
4           for (int i = 1; i <= maxWordLength; i ++ ) {
5               if (z % i == 0) {
6                   int j = z / i;
7                   if (j <= maxWordLength) {
8                       /* Create a rectangle of length i and height j. Note
9                        * that i * j = z. */
10                      Rectangle rectangle = makeRectangle(i, j);
11                      if (rectangle != null) {
12                          return rectangle;
13                      }
14                  }
15              }
16          }
17      }
18      return null;
19  }
```

The makeRectangle method is called by maxRectangle and tries to build a rectangle of a specific length and height.

```
1   Rectangle makeRectangle(int length, int height) {
2       if (groupList[length-1] == null ||
3           groupList[height-1] == null) {
4           return null;
5       }
6
7       /* Create trie for word length if we haven't yet */
8       if (trieList[height - 1] == null) {
9           LinkedList<String> words = groupList[height - 1].getWords();
10          trieList[height - 1] = new Trie(words);
11      }
12
13      return makePartialRectangle(length, height,
14                          new Rectangle(length));
15  }
```

The makePartialRectangle method is where the action happens. It is passed in the intended, final length and height, and a partially formed rectangle. If the rectangle is already of the final height, then we just check to see if the columns form valid, complete words, and return.

Otherwise, we check to see if the columns form valid prefixes. If they do not, then we immediately break since there is no way to build a valid rectangle off of this partial one.

But, if everything is okay so far, and all the columns are valid prefixes of words, then we search through all the words of the right length, append each to the current rectangle, and recursively try to build a rectangle off of {current rectangle with new word appended}.

```
1   Rectangle makePartialRectangle(int l, int h, Rectangle rectangle) {
2       if (rectangle.height == h) { // Check if complete rectangle
3           if (rectangle.isComplete(l, h, groupList[h - 1])) {
4               return rectangle;
5           } else {
6               return null;
7           }
8       }
9
10      /* Compare columns to trie to see if potentially valid rect */
11      if (!rectangle.isPartialOK(l, trieList[h - 1])) {
12          return null;
13      }
14
15      /* Go through all words of the right length. Add each one to the
16       * current partial rectangle, and attempt to build a rectangle
17       * recursively. */
18      for (int i = 0; i < groupList[l-1].length(); i++) {
19          /* Create a new rectangle which is this rect + new word. */
20          Rectangle orgPlus =
21              rectangle.append(groupList[l-1].getWord(i));
22
23          /* Try to build a rectangle with this new, partial rect */
24          Rectangle rect = makePartialRectangle(l, h, orgPlus);
25          if (rect != null) {
26              return rect;
27          }
28      }
29      return null;
30  }
```

The Rectangle class represents a partially or fully formed rectangle of words. The method isPartialOk can be called to check if the rectangle is, thus far, a valid one (that is, all the columns are prefixes of words). The method isComplete serves a similar function, but checks if each of the columns makes a full word.

```
1   public class Rectangle {
2       public int height, length;
3       public char [][] matrix;
4
5       /* Construct an "empty" rectangular. Length is fixed, but height
6        * vary as we add words. */
7       public Rectangle(int l) {
8           height = 0;
9           length = l;
10      }
11
```

```
12    /* Construct a rectangular array of letters of the specified
13     * length and height, and backed by the specified matrix of
14     * letters. (It is assumed that the length and height specified
15     * as arguments are consistent with the array argument's
16     * dimensions.) */
17    public Rectangle(int length, int height, char[][] letters) {
18      this.height = letters.length;
19      this.length = letters[0].length;
20      matrix = letters;
21    }
22
23    public char getLetter (int i, int j) { return matrix[i][j]; }
24    public String getColumn(int i) { ... }
25
26    /* Check if all columns are valid. All rows are already known to
27     * be valid since they were added directly from dictionary. */
28    public boolean isComplete(int l, int h, WordGroup groupList) {
29      if (height == h) {
30        /* Check if each column is a word in the dictionary. */
31        for (int i = 0; i < l; i++) {
32          String col = getColumn(i);
33          if (!groupList.containsWord(col)) {
34            return false;
35          }
36        }
37        return true;
38      }
39      return false;
40    }
41
42    public boolean isPartialOK(int l, Trie trie) {
43      if (height == 0) return true;
44      for (int i = 0; i < l; i++ ) {
45        String col = getColumn(i);
46        if (!trie.contains(col)) {
47          return false;
48        }
49      }
50      return true;
51    }
52
53    /* Create a new Rectangle by taking the rows of the current
54     * rectangle and appending s. */
55    public Rectangle append(String s) { ... }
56  }
```

The WordGroup class is a simple container for all words of a specific length. For easy lookup, we store the words in a hash table as well as in an ArrayList.

The lists in WordGroup are created through a static method called createWordGroups.

```
1   public class WordGroup {
2      private Hashtable<String, Boolean> lookup =
3         new Hashtable<String, Boolean>();
4      private ArrayList<String> group = new ArrayList<String>();
5
6      public boolean containsWord(String s) {
7         return lookup.containsKey(s);
8      }
9
10     public void addWord (String s) {
11        group.add(s);
12        lookup.put(s, true);
13     }
14
15     public int length() { return group.size(); }
16     public String getWord(int i) { return group.get(i); }
17     public ArrayList<String> getWords() { return group; }
18
19     public static WordGroup[] createWordGroups(String[] list) {
20        WordGroup[] groupList;
21        int maxWordLength = 0;
22        /* Find the length of the longest word */
23        for (int i = 0; i < list.length; i++) {
24           if (list[i].length() > maxWordLength) {
25              maxWordLength = list[i].length();
26           }
27        }
28
29        /* Group the words in the dictionary into lists of words of
30         * same length.groupList[i] will contain a list of words,
31         * each of length (i+1). */
32        groupList = new WordGroup[maxWordLength];
33        for (int i = 0; i < list.length; i++) {
34           /* We do wordLength - 1 instead of just wordLength since
35            * this is used as an index and no words are of length 0 */
36           int wordLength = list[i].length() - 1;
37           if (groupList[wordLength] == null) {
38              groupList[wordLength] = new WordGroup();
39           }
40           groupList[wordLength].addWord(list[i]);
41        }
42        return groupList;
43     }
44  }
```

The full code for this problem, including the code for Trie and TrieNode, can be found in the code attachment. Note that in a problem as complex as this, you'd most likely only need to write the pseudocode. Writing the entire code would be nearly impossible in such a short amount of time.

Acknowledgements

Everything in life is about teamwork, and this book is no exception. There are many people who have helped me along the way, and while I can in no way repay them, I would like to at least show my sincere gratitude.

First, to my husband John, for supporting me in everything, and for challenging me to take this book to the next level. I quite literally could not have done this without him.

Second, to my mother, who taught me that writing code is important, but being able to write English is even more important. She is truly an exceptional engineer, entrepreneur and, most importantly, mother.

Third, to all my friends for their encouragement, but especially Carleton English. Whether it's lending me a helping hand or a friendly ear, she's always been there for me.

Last but not least, to all of my readers who have sent in their feedback and suggestions: thank you. I would especially like to acknowledge Vinit Shah and Pranay Varma for their diligent review of the questions in the book. You went far, far beyond the call of duty. Your teammates and managers should count themselves incredibly fortunate.

Once again, thank you all.

Index

Index

Index

Index

About the Author

Gayle Laakmann McDowell has worked for Microsoft, Apple, and Google as a software engineer.

Most recently, McDowell spent three years at Google as a Software Engineer, where she was one of the company's lead interviewers and served on Google's hiring committee. She interviewed over 150 candidates in the U.S. and abroad, assessed over 1000 candidate interview packets for the hiring committee, and reviewed hundreds more resumes.

In addition to her experience as an interviewer, she has interviewed with—and received offers from—twelve tech companies, including Microsoft, Google, Amazon, IBM, and Apple.

In 2005, McDowell founded CareerCup.com to bring her wealth of experience on both sides of the interview table to candidates. CareerCup.com offers a database of thousands of interview questions from major companies and a forum for interview advice.

McDowell's second book, *The Google Resume: How to Prepare for a Career and Land a Job at Apple, Microsoft, Google or Any Top Tech Company*, provides a broader look at the interview process for major tech companies. It offers insight on how anyone, from college freshmen to marketing professionals, can position themselves for a career at one of these companies.

McDowell holds a bachelor's and master's degree in Computer Science from the University of Pennsylvania and an MBA from the Wharton School.

She lives in Palo Alto, California.

Made in the USA
Lexington, KY
20 September 2012